CAGNEY

CAGNEY

The Actor as Auteur

by

Patrick McGilligan

A. S. BARNES & COMPANY, INC.

SAN DIEGO

Published by A. S. Barnes & Co.
Copyright © 1975, 1982 by Patrick McGilligan

Distributed in the United States by
Oak Tree Publications, Inc.
San Diego, California

Library of Congress Cataloging in Publication Data

McGilligan, Patrick.
  Cagney.
  Filmography: p.
  Bibliography: p.
  Includes index.
  1. Cagney, James, 1899–   .   I. Title.
PN2287.C23M3   1982   791.43′028′0924 [B]   81-19152
ISBN 0-498-02586-1   AACR2

Revised Edition
1 2 3 4 5 6 7 8 9 85 84 83 82
Printed and bound in the United States of America

To Beanie of Wauwatosa.

Contents

Acknowledgments

When A. S. Barnes suggested bringing out a new edition of *Cagney: The Actor as Auteur* to coincide with the actor's "comeback" in *Ragtime*, I volunteered to go one step further and revise the entire manuscript. Ten years ago, when I first began to research and write about James Cagney, I was at a distinct disadvantage. This was before Cagney's public reappearance at the American Film Institute's Life Achievement Award banquet, before the publication of his autobiography, well before *Ragtime*. Indeed, in 1972, there was not yet a single book on the market devoted to Cagney's life. What I could make of his rich and problematic career was left to my imagination and to the geography of my resources at the archives of the University of Wisconsin in Madison.

This new edition allows me to correct errors of fact and to incorporate my further research and interviews conducted with his principal writers and directors over the last decade. The first edition, it is fair to say, has been almost completely restructured and rewritten. My earlier themes have not been much altered, but some pertinent details — some surprising details — have. Writers, for example, were undeservedly neglected in the first edition, and I hope that is somewhat remedied here. Movies such as *Kiss Tomorrow Goodbye* received an academic importance in the first edition that cannot help but be diminished when they are understood in the proper context of Cagney's career.

My over-all feeling about Cagney has not changed, not since I first began viewing Cagney and Humphrey Bogart movies as an independent study project in college, comparing the two stars, and finding myself drawn to the mystery of Cagney, and curious about the lack of recognition accorded such a magnificent performer. The recognition, for Cagney, was still to come. The mystery, for me, has not abated.

Portions of this book originally appeared in issues of *The Velvet Light Trap, Take One*, and as film notes for the Cagney retrospective at the New York Cultural Center in Spring 1973.

Photos courtesy of The Memory Shop (New York); Collectors Bookstore, Eddie Brandt's Saturday Matinee, and Larry Edmunds' Bookshop (Los Angeles); The Museum of Modern Art (MOMA); the Academy of Motion Picture Arts and Sciences (AMPAS); the British Film Institute (BFI); United Press International; Wide World Photos; Alen MacWeeney and *Rolling Stone* magazine; the Homer Dickens Still Collection; University of California at Los Angeles Film Archives; Howard Hawks Collection, Brigham Young University; Wisconsin Center for Film and Theatre Research (WCTR) Marc Wanamaker/Bison Archives; John Bright, Ivan Goff, Allen Eyles, and Jeanne Cagney.

The author would like to acknowledge the following persons for aiding and abetting this book in its present form:

Tino Balio, Diana Balio, Susan Dalton, Maxine Fleckner, and the helpful folks at the Wisconsin Center for Film and Theatre Research at the University of Wisconsin in Madison.

Russell Campbell and John Davis, for the sanctuary of *The Velvet Light Trap*.

Joseph McBride, Andrew Sarris and David Thomson, for their encouragement and example.

Especially, John Bright—a man with promise—and William Cagney, the *other* Cagney.

Jeanne Frissell, who read the manuscript and made refinements.

And Larry Platt and JoAnn Fisher, my editors at A. S. Barnes, who went above and beyond the call of duty.

Publicity still of James Cagney, 1932. (WCTR)

Introductory

If you've never been poor, you're automatically a stranger to more than half the men and women in the world. You're cut off from them. You have no idea why they're hard as nails where they're hard and soft as fools where they're soft.
                                                        JAMES CAGNEY
                                                     Interview, 1930s

In the 1930s James Cagney used to read some of the scripts submitted to him by the Warner Brothers' management—stories that he had no choice but to star in according to the rigors of his contract—and rush inside the bathroom of his house to vomit. Literally. That is how graphic was the measure of his sensibility and of his integrity as an artist.

Not that the word "art" or "artist" ever applied to Cagney in his own mind. To himself, he was just a kid who revered his mother and her Irish–Catholic outlook and who struggled to escape the gutter and its dark, uncertain future. He taught himself to be an expert song-and-dance man because it paid more than wrapping bundles at Wanamaker's, and because it was a better outlet for his musculature and grace than what otherwise might have been a life of crime.

He was just a mug—"all India-rubber muscle, steel-faced," in Pat O'Brien's words—who got lucky in Hollywood and stayed lucky for half a century. Hollywood appealed to him not half as much as a good buck and wing. His art was just a job, and one that he fretted was somewhat less important than being a doctor—which he almost became—like his brothers, Harry and Ed.

Of course his story is more complicated than that, for Cagney, growing up in the shadow of Broadway, knew art, believed in art, and aspired to art. But he saw himself as a late-starter, someone never fulfilled by his possibilities—save maybe once, in *Yankee Doodle Dandy*. Being a Cagney, he did his best to earn his salary. But he was never satisfied. He bucked the studios at a time when the studios were holy writ—fought for better stories, casting, directors; walked out on his contract three times; went to court against Warner Bros.; broke ground for other actors while damaging his own faith and prospects.

Cagney viewed *The Public Enemy* as an opportunity for leverage and for the actor to spread his wings. It became the studio's—and public's—image of him. It became his straitjacket. Small wonder that, years later, Cagney had little but deprecating memories of the many tough-guy portrayals that, for movie buffs, constituted his legacy and enduring persona.

The real Cagney was never the cocky alley cat of so many motion pictures—except, briefly, as a youth; the chip on his shoulder he had rested in the past and in his heart. Fans who were chumps would stop Bogie on Hollywood Boulevard and challenge him to a stand-off, winding up in a bloody scrape. Cagney was probably the toughest, physically, of the male Hollywood stars—a street-fighter, a nut for his physical regimen, someone who would hesitate to butter his potatoes for fear of being slowed down by the added poundage. When people would stop Cagney on Hollywood Boulevard outside Musso and Frank's Grill, blocking his path with a mocking dare, he would step aside with a sweet, disarming smile and a patient deferral to their obvious superiority.

In more ways than one Cagney debunked his glamour with fans—in his films and in his life. He thought of himself as one of them, albeit with an Horatio Alger blessing. In the 1930s he was more than just their symbol, he was active in all of the politically left-of-center causes of the era, a proponent of progress for mankind. His politics provide an intriguing wrinkle to the life of someone who was perhaps the least egocentric, the least swashbuckling, the least bacchanalian in his private behavior of all the major stars. Cagney's disenchantment with the Left coincided with his disillusionment with Hollywood, and he eventually abandoned both, swinging to the Right and retiring from motion pictures when he grew more and more removed, more doubtful about his place in the world.

Volatile and animated as a youth, Cagney was serene and civilized as an adult, withdrawn, all of his tensions, all of his secrets, curled up tightly inside of himself. Few were privileged to know him well. To most he was "private, slightly aloof," remembered Elia Kazan, "so intense that you felt you were breaking a silence when you talked to him."

Despite the surface calm, he was nervous on stage, nervous among crowds, ironically more composed in front of the camera. His stomach churned when he watched his own performances in movies—which he rarely did—and when he first heard the rat-a-tat speed of his own voice on the soundtrack, he wondered in alarm whether anyone would understand the words. Sometimes he had to be pushed on stage—or in front of the camera—from the wings; and history is fortunate that there were always believers, especially his brother William—who kept pushing.

Perfectly controlled off screen, his curled-up mystery would flash like lightning into rage or tears at the single word "action!" when the camera rolled. He could not be categorized as a single-take man or as a premature method actor; Cagney had no method, per se. Whatever it was that worked, it was inside of him. He simply trusted in himself when he was acting. And when the scripts failed him, as they often did, he would add something of his own, dropping in a touch of Cagney so that even the numerous tough guys are not all quite the same.

From slums to riches. From left-wing to right-wing. From star to recluse. From sociopathic tough guy (on camera) to amateur poet and artist, gentleman farmer, dutiful citizen, sterling husband and father.

Walt Whitman wrote, "Do I contradict myself?/Very well then I contradict myself,/I am large, I contain multitudes."

Cagney contained multitudes: "Contradictions" is not simply a word convenient to the symmetry of this introduction, it is a word used by members of the Cagney family to describe one of their own. The contradictions in Cagney's personality kept kith and kin as ceaselessly fascinated over the decades as it did critics and audiences. And no one has ever fully reconciled those contradictions between the off-screen and on-screen Cagney—not even, one suspects, Cagney himself.

The Cagney who smashed Mae Clarke in the face with a grapefruit is only one Cagney, one extreme of the legacy. His George M. Cohan is another. Thankfully, there are plenty others, including the Cagneys in movies that made him nauseous to make, lo, these many years ago. Sincerely, it was always a marvel to him that the Cagney of those years past seems destined to delight and captivate future audiences forever.

Patrick McGilligan
April 22, 1982

Early glamour still, pre-PUBLIC ENEMY.

1
True-Life Story

With Babe Ruth, Jack Dempsey, F. Scott Fitzgerald, the early Stutz Bearcat car, the last of the beaded speakeasy hostesses, he was an image in the American scheme of things; of the Roaring Twenties and the Tepid Thirties, of the dust bowls and the bread lines and the gang wars. He is the saga maker of the hard kid who couldn't be pushed too far. In real life, Jimmy is a gentle man, who draws and paints, reads, raises prize cattle, farms, is happily married, has much family. He still grins that crooked mick grin that made him famous. He'll even lift his fists at you for a mock blow, but he was never the Jimmy Cagney he imprinted on so much film stock—just a dancer gone wrong.

PAT O'BRIEN
The Wind at My Back

James Francis Cagney, Jr. was born above his father's saloon near the corner of Avenue D and 8th Street in New York City on July 17, 1899. His father, James Francis Cagney, Sr., was a stout bartender who traced his Irish ancestry back to the O'Caignes of County Leitrim—and was, from all accounts, a gentlehearted alcoholic. His mother, Carolyn Nelson Cagney, was half Irish and half Norwegian and plagued by a gallbladder condition that kept her in and out of hospitals. James was the second of five surviving children in the Cagney brood. Two others died in infancy. Harry, the eldest, was two years older than James, and grew up to become a physician. Edward (born in 1902) also became a physician; William (born in 1904) became an actor, a businessman, and his brother James' intimate advisor; and Jeanne (born in 1919), the doted-upon "baby" of the family and the only girl, became an actress.

Though he would be formally billed as James during his career, everyone—family and friends as well as the fans who cried out his name in moviehouses—called him Jimmy. Studio publicists were to revise the date of his birth to 1904, hoping to shave five years off his relatively late start in motion pictures, but the truth is otherwise. Indeed, the publicity material, which appeared with increasing regularity in fan magazines and other periodicals after his first film appearance in 1930, could be misleading. Many of the articles were planted by studio press agents; others were sham accounts by well-intentioned but misguided

James Francis Cagney, Jr. at age one.
(Homer Dickens Still Collection)

journalists. And Cagney himself was known to be inconsistent about the details of his life. Often it was left to the imagination of publicists to fill in the gaps. Unlike many movie stars, Cagney was stubbornly private and did not cultivate or encourage a cult of his personality.

One magazine of the 1930s that purported to tell Cagney's "True-Life Story" dished up a typically glowing rendition of his boyhood. "He was quiet and well behaved," the magazine reported. "He seemed to be born with gentle manners. He learned his lessons well and earned good marks. He never played hookey nor 'sassed' the teacher. He was never told to 'see the principal.' He was never a problem child." According to another fan-magazine version of his childhood, Cagney was nicknamed "Cellar Door Cagney" by companions because of his knack for tap dancing on slanting cellar doors. According to yet another ersatz biographical account, the youthful Cagney was a budding artist who whiled away the hours sketching on sidewalks.

As Cagney was to recollect in his autobiography, *Cagney By Cagney* (Double-day, 1976), it was actually a childhood "surrounded by trouble, illness and my dad's alcoholism." His father's tavern bordered on the vice-ridden area of New York known as Hell's Kitchen. When Cagney was eight, the family settled in the brownstone neighborhood between Third Avenue and Lexington near 96th Street in the Yorkville district. It was, he remembered, "a street of stark tragedy," punctuated by the comings and goings of police sirens and ambulances, a melting-pot cityscape not unlike the one depicted in the opening panorama of *Angels With Dirty Faces*. Cagney learned to speak Yiddish from Eastern European immigrant Jews, and he learned to use his fists to defend himself from neighborhood toughs. His "rep" was as one of the better street fighters on the Upper East Side—in fact, he boxed as an amateur, and was runner-up for the New York State lightweight crown; he even made tentative preparations for turning professional before his mother forbade a career in the ring. But fighting, it seems, was something he did only out of necessity—not relish. "Jimmy was a contradiction in many respects," his brother William recalled, "because he whipped just about everybody on the East Side and yet almost all of his fights were because some pal of his had been hurt." Cagney's own nature was more like his father's, whimsical and reflective—soulful, with the mask of toughness.

In the summer of 1905, when Cagney was five years old, an incident occurred that made a lasting impression on him. His father rented a horse-drawn carriage, and the Cagneys went for a two-week trip to visit a great aunt at the corner of Chestnut Street and Bay Avenue in Green Field (now Flatbush), a location that was then in the open country. The contrast between the serenity of the countryside and the dog-eat-dog metropolis was striking to the young boy. He never forgot the rich stable smell of the carriage seat—"pure manure." Morning glories—which he remembered blooming in his great aunt's front yard—became his favorite flowers. In his heart he became a country boy. "It is enough to say," he wrote in his autobiography, "that I have loved the country ever since, totally."

Many of the neighborhood toughs grew up to become hardened criminals and met their fates in the electric chair. When as a teenager Cagney played exhibition baseball games at prisons and reformatories—he was catcher for the Original Nut Club of Yorkville—the shout of "Hello, Red!" rang out again and again from old acquaintances in convict stripes. But the Cagney boys never embraced crime: their mother instilled them with old-fashioned values, a work ethic, and goals of high achievement. Life was severe and all earnings went into a family kitty. As soon as he was old enough to qualify for a work permit, at age 14, Cagney became a copy boy for *The New York Sun*. The jobs that followed included stints as a bouncer, a switchboard operator, book custodian for The New York Public Library, bellhop at the Friar's Club, junior architect at a waterworks, and ticket taker on a Hudson River excursion line. He worked days when not in school, and nights and weekends. "It was good for me," he later recalled. "I feel sorry for the kid who has too cushy a time of it. Suddenly he has to come face-to-face with the realities of life without any papa or mama to do his thinking for him."

An earnest student, Cagney graduated from Stuyvesant High School in 1917 and enrolled at Columbia University, joining the camouflage unit of the Student Army Training Corps (the precursor of ROTC) to help pay expenses. He was an avid reader (one youthful favorite—Romaine Rolland's *Jean Christophe*) and had ambitions of becoming a commercial artist. He took German from Professor Frank Mankiewicz, the father of film-director-to-be Joseph L. Mankiewicz. He played in the school band as a drummer. Then, in the fall of 1918 after barely six months at Columbia, his dreams and hard work were cut short. A Spanish influenza epidemic swept the Eastern seaboard, and Cagney's father, his health weakened by heavy drinking, died at 41.

It was a devastating episode for the family but, characteristically, they pulled together. Cagney himself became a teetotaler and rarely touched liquor for the rest of his life. The tragedy forced him to drop out of Columbia and to odd-job full-time to help support the family. Mother Carrie Cagney, a flaming-red, curlyhaired beauty with an indomitable spirit, was their guiding force, "a mother 24 hours a day." As Cagney later recalled,

> That was her job and she did it full time, over time. She pitted herself firmly against the forces of our environment—the streets, the schools, the boys we met, the things we were bound to hear, the influences we couldn't wholly escape. She talked with us, not at us. She told us that what you give in life you also get back in kind. She taught us that what you do is done again, to you. She showed us clearly that ugliness, crime and vulgarity pay their own dividends in ugliness, crime and vulgarity.

That tightly knit family code was to become one of the abiding influences of Cagney's life—shaping not only his Irish (lapsed) Catholic outlook, but also creeping into the details and thematic viewpoints of his movies (sometimes, as in the case of *White Heat*, perversely). "Our motto was united we stand, divided we fall," Cagney once explained.

> I can't remember a time when, if any one of us had three bucks, he didn't throw it immediately into the kitty. We never thought of doing anything else. Boys who worked for their own pocket money were beyond our understanding. And doing things together, as Mother drummed into our heads, sharing everything, working for the common end, instead of each going off in separate directions, gave us the feeling we were strong. The trouble with most poor families is that they don't have that community feeling and alone they're helpless in a tough world.

It was in his late teens that Cagney first detected a change within himself—the rowdy, show-off adolescent was becoming shy and self-conscious. Even at that age, he was "a contradiction in many respects," to be sure. The turbulence of his upbringing nurtured, in his character, warring sensibilities that were to play themselves out in his life and in his work. A gut fighter, ironically he had no appetite for the fray. A city boy, he was enamored of the country. Later, in movies, he came to epitomize the modern urban Everyman, whereas he actually feared automobiles and the latest jet-age conveniences—and identified, nostalgically, with the simpler life he remembered from his earliest childhood at the turn of the century.

Cagney, pugnacious at age 14. (United Press International Photo)

As a teenager; at the beach with brother Bill. (Homer Dickens Still Collection)

Cagney as a "chorus girl," second from left, in a vaudeville act. (Homer Dickens Still Collection)

From Vaudeville to Broadway

As a boy, Cagney delved into the world of amateur theatricals. He painted scenery for a Chinese pantomime at the Lenox Hill Settlement House, and one night when his older brother Harry was ill, he substituted for him, playing a role in one of the productions. As he later explained, "I had leanings toward art and Mom thought I could learn to paint by working on the scenery used by the theatrical group, while I earned bring-home pay by racking up pool balls and acting as a doorman." Intrigued by his initial acting foray, he joined the acting society of the Settlement House and began picking up other parts. He played an Oriental in a Japanese musical comedy called *What for Why?* He performed as Pagliaccio in an Italian harlequinade. He executed a leading role in Lord Dunsany's one-act play, *The Lost Silk Hat*. He essayed the role of Picard in *The Two Orphans*, a period costume melodrama produced by the Dramatic Society of Hunter College, then all-girl, which borrowed Settlement House boys for the male parts.

One of his more distinctive roles was in a two-act play called *The Faun*, also produced by the Settlement House. "I was the faun," he told *The Saturday Evening Post* years later. "I had my hair in ringlets and a goatskin around my middle, and I pranced around the stage speaking lines like this: 'Nay, sweet, give it to me' and 'Spring is running through the fields chased by the wynd.' 'The wayward wynd ran its fingers through the pine tree's hair.'" Elsewhere Cagney recalled: "It was a touchy project in our East Side neighborhood and I expected to be attacked on my way home and have my ears chewed by characters of my own age who were outraged by my own riot curls."

In the autumn of 1919, subsequent to his father's death, Cagney was working a six-day week as a package wrapper at Wanamaker's department store when he learned from another clerk (an ex-vaudevillian) that a chorus role was opening up in a revue at Keith's 86th Street Theatre. The pay was $25 weekly—double what Cagney was earning at Wanamaker's. The revue was *Every Sailor*, based on *Every Woman*, a wartime diversion that had featured a chorus of servicemen dolled up as women. *Every Woman* had been presented before President Woodrow Wilson in France during the peace conference talks, and producer Phil Dunning had engaged the troupe and converted it into a vaudeville attraction upon its return to the states. Though he had no training as a dancer, Cagney auditioned for the available role—that of a "chorus girl." As he recalled later, "There was nothing to the audition. The stage manager showed me the steps and said, 'Do this.' I watched his feet and, being a good mimic, I did what he did. But I quit that act after two months. The high heels I wore on stage gave me a quick jerky walk—a kind of occupational sea legs—and I got tired of my pals saying to me, 'Lengthen it out, Red,' to remind me how to walk properly."

So the first professional job of the actor who later became the cinema's quintessential tough guy was as a female impersonator. "It was a knockabout act, purely burlesque," Cagney later remembered.

> We had a lot of fun and it never occurred to any of us to be ashamed of it. It might seem strange and unbelievable, taking into account my habitual desire to go unnoticed. But again, this illustrates what I mean when I say that I am not shy or self-conscious when I am on the stage or screen. For there I am not myself. I am not that fellow, Jim Cagney, at all. I certainly lost all consciousness of him when I put on skirts, wig, paint, powder, feathers and spangles. Besides, that was the time, right after the war, when service acts were still fresh in mind, when female impersonators were the vogue.

Cagney's mother was skeptical about his future in show business and urged him to abandon his fledgling footlights career. "To her," he recalled, "it was no way to use what education I had." So he took work for a spell at a brokerage firm on Broad Street as a runner; then he answered another "open call" audition for the chorus of *Pitter Patter*, a musical comedy adapted from the farce *Caught in the Rain* by William Collier and Grant Stuart. "I didn't know the highland fling from a sailor's hornpipe," Cagney said, "and I couldn't even sing 'Sweet Adeline' but I needed that job. Fifty applicants assembled. I watched the fellow's feet next to me and did what he did." He got the part—and thus launched a decade-long period of work in vaudeville and on Broadway. When *Pitter Patter* opened at the Longacre Theatre in New York City on September 29, 1920, the reviews were lukewarm—but *Variety*, for one, praised the efforts of the chorus (which included, besides Cagney, future Warner Brothers' stock company crony Allen Jenkins). And after a decent run of 110 performances in New York, the show, with Cagney, went on the road for another 32 weeks.

Also in the chorus—Frances Willard Vernon, whose nickname was "Bill" or "Billie," a small-town Iowan who had run away from home to break into show business. Like Cagney, she was also a dancer with an "instinctive gift of rhythm," in his words. They fell in love. At the time, she remembered later, he seemed driven and "couldn't let go and have fun." Indeed, Cagney's extra duties for *Pitter Patter* included laying out clothes for the leading man (Ernest Truex) and keeping track of luggage during the road tour, for which he received a sum of $50 weekly, twice his *Every Sailor* salary. He also understudied the leading man. In 1922, after saving a little money, he and Billie were married, and they stayed happily married thereafter—with never so much as a hint of scandal or acrimony, rare among Hollywood couples.

After *Pitter Patter* closed in 1921, the newlyweds joined the vaudeville network—criss-crossing paths on the tank-town circuit, or "Cagney circuit" as they called it, performing in a variety of acts. Cagney worked in *Dot's My Boy*, a piece about a Jewish actor with an Irish pseudonym, which was written, directed, produced, and originally had starred Hugh Herbert (another eventual member of the Warners' stock company). Cagney toured for a stretch with the Jaffe troupe, headed by Ada Jaffe, the mother of actor Sam Jaffe. Meanwhile, Billie was partnered in a "sister" act with Wynne Gibson, later a Paramount contract ingenue. In early 1922, the Jaffe troupe and the "sister" act were conveniently brought under the same umbrella in a Shubert revue called *Lew Fields' Ritz Girls*.

When *Lew Fields' Ritz Girls* ran out of money in St. Louis in 1922, Cagney and Billie set out for California to visit her mother and to explore opportunities in motion pictures. Cagney tried opening up a dance studio in Los Angeles, but the few students who applied were as experienced as he. With a new partner, Harry Gribbon, he introduced a vaudeville routine in San Pedro, but it flopped. Cagney also made the rounds of Hollywood casting departments but found no takers. "For thirty-five dollars a month, we rented a tiny house in Los Angeles, and Billie cooked on a next-to-nothing budget," he later recalled.

> I don't know how she did it, but we gained weight. We hit all the movie studios but we found nothing. We couldn't even get past the front gate. Then we began to get hints from some of Billie's 'well-wishers' that she'd made a mistake in marrying a hoofer who couldn't even earn a thin dime, and gradually I became aware of a question hanging above me in the air: 'Why don't you go back East where you came from? You're not doing yourself or anybody else any good here in California.'

After borrowing emergency funds from friends, Cagney and Billie wended their way back to New York City and the familiarity of the vaudeville network. For the next three years, Cagney worked primarily in vaudeville—growing seasoned and confident, improving steadily as a hoofer, studying and imitating the great dance-masters who commanded the circuit (and adding his own twists to their routines). He and Billie teamed up as Vernon and Nye, the Nye being a rearrangement of the second syllable of his last name. ("My wife was much better known than I was," Cagney later explained. "Her name meant some-

Rare publicity photo of Charles Bickford and Cagney appearing as hoboes in Maxwell Anderson's OUTSIDE LOOKING IN on Broadway in 1925, with Brigadier Wallace Winchell at Salvation Army headquarters in New York City. (WCTR)

thing, mine didn't.'') One of the Vernon and Nye routines, called ''Out of Town Papers,'' featured Cagney as a supposed city slicker and Billie as a small-town type who meet on a street corner where the sophisticate hawks newspapers. But as the skit evolves, it is revealed that the city slicker is also from a small town, the same one—a place called Kokomo. The skit ends with a song in duet, Billie singing a joyous rendition of ''Home Sweet Home'' and Cagney belting out a New York lyric: ''Well, there's no doubt about it/I cannot live without it/I surely want to shout about it night and day/There's just one place I want to be/And that's the place that's haunting me/And that's Broadway.'' ''We toured the South with this act and we laid a seven-tier cake,'' Cagney said. ''With my thick New York accent and my fast talk, nobody south of Washington, D.C. could understand what I said. Thank goodness they understood it when we danced.''

At times the vaudeville life must have seemed like a never-ending sequence of dingy rooms and one-burner hot plates. Now and then Cagney grew discouraged migrating from act to act, but Billie was staunch in her encouragement and in her belief in him. One of his stints deserves a footnote in any vaudeville history. In 1925, Cagney replaced an actor named Archie Leach in a skit called Parker, Rand and Leach. When *Variety* deigned to review the newly constituted trio, the paper commented, "Two boys and a girl with a skit idea that gets nowhere. It is a turn without the semblance of a punch. There are no laughs and the songs mean little. One of the boys [Cagney] can dance." Students of film trivia know that Archie Leach changed his name and went on to Hollywood and his own fulfilling career in motion pictures as Cary Grant.

One of Cagney's more noteworthy vaudeville bits was playing a dramatic scene with Victor Kilian, who later received Broadway acclaim in Eugene O'Neill's *Desire Under the Elms*. When a part in *Elms* opened up, Kilian remembered Cagney and arranged an audition for him. Cagney lost the part, but the producer remembered him later when he was casting the part of the young roughneck in *Outside Looking In*, a three-act play written by Maxwell Anderson and based on Jim Tully's hobo story, *Beggars of Life*. Charles Bickford was cast as Oklahoma Red, and Cagney played Little Red, his first significant departure from his background as a hoofer. His key scene occurred in the second act when he was tried by his fellow hoboes in a kangaroo court. When *Outside Looking In* opened in September of 1925 at the Village Theatre, an experimental house, Cagney's performance was favorably received by the New York critics.

Robert Benchley, then drama critic for *Life* magazine, wrote,

> Wherever Mr. MacGowan [the director] found two redheads like Charles Bickford and James Cagney, who were evidently born to play Oklahoma Red and Little Red, he was guided by the hand of the casting God. Mr. Bickford's characterization is the first important one of the year and is likely to remain at the top for some time, while Mr. Cagney, in a less spectacular role, makes a few minutes silence during his mock-trial scene something that many a more established actor might watch with profit.

Critic Percy Hammond rhapsodized: "John Barrymore's Hamlet would be a mere feat of elocution compared to Cagney's characterization." Burns Mantle wrote that overall the play contained "the most honest acting now to be seen in New York."

When *Outside Looking In* folded after 113 performances, Cagney was invited to join the London company of *Broadway*, a popular gangster melodrama. Written by Philip Dunning (producer of *Every Sailor*) and George Abbott, *Broadway* is about a dancer who gets embroiled with the underworld. Cagney was offered the lead role of Roy Lane; Billie was given a slot as a dancer. But Cagney irked producer Jed Harris during rehearsals by refusing to imitate the much-acclaimed

With Sophia Delza in
THE GRAND STREET FOLLIES OF 1928.
(Homer Dickens Still Collection)

performance of Lee Tracy, his predecessor in the role, and shortly before the cast was due to sail, Cagney was abruptly fired. Ironically, the Cagneys already had their trunks aboard ship, and a farewell party had been thrown by the New York cast for the London replacements. Instead, Lee Tracy took the London assignment, and Cagney was given the sop of understudying the Roy Lane character in New York; later, in mid-1927, he replaced Roy R. Lloyd in the lesser role of Mike. "We had Equity run-of-the-mill contracts," Cagney later recalled, "so they had to keep paying us and they put us in as understudies in the New York company of *Broadway*, but all the actors in town knew of my being fired and my confidence drained out of my toes."

Yet Cagney rebounded. In 1927 he secured a respectable part in Daniel N. Rubin's *Women Go On Forever*, a melodrama directed by John Cromwell (who eventually became a Hollywood film director). Though the show garnered decidedly mixed reviews after opening at the Forrest Theatre on September 7, 1927, it ran for 117 performances, largely on the drawing strength of its star, Mary Boland. But it was also Boland, a noted farceur, who hampered popular acceptance of this somber boarding-house drama. Cagney said that "On opening night, Mary's first word was 'hummph!' and the audience broke up. That was the end of the play. We ran for eighteen weeks but it wasn't the play we started with."

To make ends meet, the Cagneys opened the Cagné School of Dance in nearby Elizabeth, New Jersey—with Billie, now retired from active performing, doing most of the instruction, while Cagney kept busy on Broadway. Two productions enhanced his slowly growing reputation: *The Grand Street Follies of 1928* and *The Grand Street Follies of 1929* (both played at the Booth Theatre). The 1928 version was the greater triumph in the opinion of critics, who appreciated the topical merriment—the take-offs on *Dracula*, *Romeo and Juliet*, and *Porgy and Bess* and the imitations of Helen Hayes, Mae West, Charles Lindbergh, and others. Cagney (with Michel Fokine) staged many of the clever dance numbers and received plaudits for his own dancing, notably a tango tap finale. After a summer stock respite in Cleveland and Stockbridge, Massachusetts, Cagney returned to star in the 1929 variation of the *Follies*. But the freshness of the *Follies* format had diminished, and the topical element had been expanded to include historical parodies that were disliked by many reviewers. One critic complained: "It has all the sophistication and verve of an 1884 almanac of a rainy afternoon in the Louvre." Cagney performed in all eight skits. In one, "A.B.C. of Traffic," he played a dancing cop.

At least Cagney's own notices were good—bringing him to the attention of successful playwright George (*The Torchbearers*; *The Show-Off*) Kelly, who was looking for a "fresh mutt" (Cagney's words) for his new play, *Maggie the Magnificent*. Cagney was cast as Elwood, "the scapegrace son," in what was yet another dreary boarding-house melodrama. Though the play ran only 32 performances and generally received mediocre reviews, it was, as Cagney himself later termed it, the "turning point" of his career. Kelly (who wrote and directed) was one of the leading dramatists of the era, so critics diligently scrutinized the production, and though they found fault with the play's construction, they liked Cagney. And they also liked another vaudevillian in the cast—a born-in-a-trunk hoofer named Joan Blondell who, like Cagney, was as versatile as she was ambitious. In a match-up that was to prove classic, Blondell played a wise-cracking floozie, and Cagney played her boyfriend.

"She (Blondell) chews gum with a menacing virtuosity, struts up and down before the mirror and wriggles across to the drug store for a 'pineapple tempta-tion,'" wrote Brooks Atkinson in *The New York Times*, commenting on Blondell's performance. "If she were given her head, she might alter the design of the play completely." Added Robert Littell, critic of *The New York World*: "Except for the tantalizingly brief appearance of Joan Blondell, a sympathetic young lover by Frank Rowand, and the perfect gashouse lingo of James Cagney, the acting was, to say the least, hard and graceless."

On the strength of their reviews, the nascent team of Cagney and Blondell was reunited some months later as the second leads in Marie Baumer's *Penny Arcade*, a humorless tale about bootlegging and murder in a carnival setting. Cagney

Early snapshot of Cagney on the Warner Brothers lot in Burbank. (WCTR)

played Harry Delano, the bad-seed son of Ma Delano, proprietor of a Coney Island "penny arcade." Blondell played Myrtle, his gal-friend, who provides Harry with an alibi after he kills his bootlegging boss in a burst of anger. Directed and co-produced by William Keighley (later Cagney's frequent director at Warner Brothers), *Penny Arcade* ran for only 24 performances, and was reviewed harshly by many critics for its florid melodramatics. Yet Cagney and Blondell were invariably singled out for flattery. *Theatre* magazine wrote: "Mr. Cagney is giving an excellent performance as the weak, amoral son, and his confession of the crime to his mother stands out as the high-point of the play." Brooks Atkinson concurred: "The play contains an excellent performance by James Cagney as the weakling." Blondell was adjudged "better than acceptable."

What is more, entertainer Al Jolson purchased the play for $20,000 and resold the motion picture rights to Warner Brothers, stipulating that stars Cagney and

Blondell go along with the sale. Warners was reluctant to guarantee their stage roles to Cagney and Blondell until after a screen test, and indeed they were tested for the lead parts in the film version before being assigned to re-create the characters they had originated on Broadway. Cagney was contracted at $500 weekly for three weeks only (the projected shooting schedule), with round-trip train fare between New York and California guaranteed. Billie stayed in New York, mindful of the frustrations and disappointments of the last Hollywood go-round. When, in April of 1930, Cagney stepped off the train at La Grande Station in Los Angeles to begin filming *Penny Arcade*, he was three months shy of his thirty-first birthday.

Sinner's Holiday

To say the least, Cagney had mixed emotions about returning to California and the prospect of work in motion pictures. On the one hand, he was short of being firmly established as a stage name. His anxiety at appearing before theater audiences was legendary among his fellow thespians—he kept a bucket in the wings for ritual nausea and vomiting before each performance; and he never projected his personality as keenly on the stage as he did, subsequently, on the screen. But the East Coast was his home territory and vaudeville and Broadway a tradition, to him, that was grand and honorable. His cohorts—among them, struggling actors, Pat O'Brien and Spencer Tracy—were still in New York. And so were the headliners he admired: People like Lowell Sherman—whose strategy of dropping "goodies,"—moments of vulnerability or humor—into his villainous portrayals stuck with Cagney. ("Anything they can laugh at, they can't hate," Cagney was fond of saying.) He missed the theater gossip and his favorite nighttime haunts. Hollywood he regarded as (in the words of his autobiography) "the big league for con men and frauds." He never came to admire the directors "out there" the way he cherished the memory of working on the stage with Cromwell, Kelly, and Keighley. Consequently, he never really settled in—never mixed really, never fraternized, never became part of the nightclubbing and glamorous social whirl. His replies to the questionnaire the Warner Brothers publicity department gave him upon his arrival in 1930 were characteristically concise and unenthusiastic. Under the heading "ambition" he scrawled: "To retire to the backwoods permanently." How did you come to take up stage or screen work? "Needed a job."

Yet times were obviously different in Hollywood in 1930 than they were in 1922. Talking pictures were all the vogue, and the welcome mat was out for stage actors, who commanded a mystique by their very ability to utter dialogue convincingly. Suddenly, stage-trained New Yorkers enticed by steady employment were flocking to the film capital. Among them was an actress named Evalyn Knapp, who was making her motion picture debut as the female lead of *Penny Arcade*, and before the year was out Cagney would be joined by pals

With Joan Blondell in their debut picture, SINNER'S HOLIDAY. (WCTR)

O'Brien, Tracy, and others. Apart from being just plain mesmerizing, Cagney's high-pitched, staccato delivery was historically propitious to the advent of sound, and according to Joan Blondell, the reaction to him after the first day's dailies was instantaneous. "Late the following morning," Blondell recalled,

> the scuttlebutt on the set was that the biggies, en masse, were on the way down there. Nonsense, unheard of—but there they were—Jack Warner, Darryl Zanuck, Lew Schreiber, and Hal Wallis—all smiling, surrounding Jimmy, signing him to a five-year contract. They had just seen the rushes of the day before and were taking no chances that Cagney would disappear into thin air before lunch.

His immediate future seemed secure—and shortly, Billie arrived from New York.

After a title change to the more lurid *Sinner's Holiday*, Cagney's first motion picture opened in New York City in October of 1930. It was an auspicious debut,

Mother complex in SINNER'S HOLIDAY; With Lucille LaVerne.

even if the picture itself, as directed by John G. Adolfi, is dull and hackneyed in many respects, clocking in at under sixty minutes. Cagney was younger than he would ever be in films again, his features given a stark purity by Ira Morgan's high-contrast photography. However theatricalized, his portrayal of overgrown juvenile delinquency was startling for its deeply felt identification. Mordaunt Hall of *The New York Times* wrote that "the most impressive acting is done by

James Cagney in the role of Harry Delano. His fretful tenseness during the closing scenes is conveyed with sincerity." *The Exhibitor's Herald World* commented that "Cagney has by no means an easy role in his portrayal of a highly nervous youth who by nature cannot go straight. It is the type of part which can be spoiled by the slightest shade of overacting, but Cagney carries his characterization in each sequence just far enough."

Seen today, *Sinner's Holiday* is badly dated, but Cagney's performance is still arresting, and the role itself, the Harry Delano character, establishes a fascinating and logical cornerstone to Cagney's career. His first movie role was that of a criminal, yet Harry Delano is not the professional sort. Instead, he is a young punk, a happy-go-lucky bootlegger who cannot see the disadvantages of illegality, who lacks education in the school of hard knocks. When he murders, he is duly punished by imprisonment. Yet he deserves the compassion of the audience, according to a contrivance of the story, because his dead father was an irresponsible alcoholic whose diseased condition somehow infected the no-good son. In this fashion Harry Delano trades on the sympathy of moviegoers—and that audience sympathy was to remain a calculated element of Cagney's persona throughout the course of his career.

Only Delano's Ma (Lucille Laverne), in the first of several memorable Cagney–mother relationships, is unswervingly faithful to her weak-willed son. A sour, hardbitten character, a forerunner of the Ma Jarrett character in *White Heat*, Ma Delano attempts without success to pin the unsolved murder on her daughter's patently innocent ex-con fiancé (Grant Withers). At first, Delano bluffs his Ma and will not confess his involvement in the crime. "If you're in a jam, let me help you," she pleads with him. "Ain't I always been your pal?" Delano replies, evasively. The bond between them is intense, even though she suspects he is lying. Then, when she finally fathoms his deed, he collapses at her feet, sobs in her lap, and is reduced to infantilism in a terrifyingly credible scene, before she forgives him. In the end, jaunty and brave, he is handcuffed and led away by a cop. He pauses briefly to hug his Ma. "Forget it, sweetheart," he says in his tossed-off manner. "Don't cry. You know I love you."

Cagney's Ma was to crop up frequently after *Sinner's Holiday*—it may be that no other American actor has been shadowed so closely on screen by his nearest and dearest of kin. For example, Cagney's successor "tough guy" of the 1940s, Humphrey Bogart, was rarely seen in movies with his "mother." Only two instances readily spring to mind—a bitter, wretched reunion in William Wyler's *Dead End* and a comic set-up in *All Through the Night*. The Bogart persona emphatically denied the existence of a supportive family member; Bogart was rootless, independent, a loner. Bogart relied on the distance he kept from his audience as a factor of his appeal. But Cagney's appeal, conversely, depended on the innately sympathetic qualities he projected and on the implicit notion that he was an ordinary Joe, with instincts, feelings, and problems shared by the population at large.

Drawing on the tender associations of motherhood, the omnipresence of his Ma was one of the bonds between star and audience that exonerated the more antisocial actions of the Cagney character. In *Public Enemy*, producer Darryl F. Zanuck was to brag, "I gave Cagney one redeeming trait. He was a no-good bastard but he loved his mother, and somehow or other you felt a certain affection and rooting interest for him, even though he is despicable." Zanuck's point (if not his usurpation of the screenwriters' creativity) is well taken—Cagney's "mother" gave audiences someone to root for when she materialized—notably in such later movies as *The Public Enemy, The Irish in Us, Each Dawn I Die, Yankee Doodle Dandy,* and *White Heat.* In each, Cagney's attachment to his "mother" is a pivotal aspect of the plot. And if his "mother" was absent from the plotline of a given film, he could often rely on the attentions of a "surrogate mother," a representative older woman at whom he directed the rapt devotion of a boyish son. This occurs in *He Was Her Man, Devil Dogs of the Air,* or *Johnny Come Lately*—the latter a particularly good example, since the surrogate mother figure becomes the film's entire focus when the Cagney character sidesteps the advances of a female ingenue and instead plays separate, exquisite "romantic" scenes with Grace George, Hattie McDaniel, and Marjorie Main, three middle-aged actresses.

The natural culmination of this "mother" proclivity was such films as *The Irish in Us* or *Yankee Doodle Dandy,* in which Cagney's family ethic is given full, unabashed celebration; or, in a vastly different context, *White Heat*—for if Cagney's relationship with his Ma was usually simple and wholesome enough to warrant incessant hugs and kisses before the camera, it could also border on the obsessive and fanatical. In that sense, all the traces of the more neurotic "mother complex" of *White Heat* can be detected in the earlier *Sinner's Holiday.* Like Ma Jarrett, Ma Delano exerts a bizarre, psychotic control over Harry Delano. Helpless, he follows her instructions every whit, even when she maliciously plots the false arrest of her daughter's lover. And, child-like, he sits in her lap—just as he sits in the lap of his Ma in *White Heat* some 20 years later in a more famous scene that harks back to *Sinner's Holiday.* In writing about *White Heat,* critics have commented on the audacity of Cody Jarrett's mother complex, and suggested that few actors could carry off such a highly charged subtext. For Cagney, who made a career of the mother complex, and to whom his own family ethic and mother-love was so fierce, it was quite natural.

Doorway to Hell, Other Men's Women, and *The Millionaire*

After *Sinner's Holiday,* Cagney became a full-fledged member of the Warners' stock company and shifted into high gear. Within his first six months in Hollywood he was to appear in four films. At the time, Warners (and its affiliate, First National) was a factory churning out an average of one picture per week for the millions of avid moviegoers in the United States. Actors and technicians

With wife Billie and pet dog in early 1930s. (WCTR)

worked six, sometimes seven, days a week, as well as nights and weekends, to meet high-pressure deadlines—conditions that eventually resulted in industry-wide unionization demands. Players at Warners were groggily shuttled from the set of one picture to another on the same afternoon. In the interests of economy, printing more than one "take" had to be personally okayed by the head of production. "The films of the 1930s were just programmers," Cagney liked to say later on, self-deprecatingly, "and if anyone was practicing Art, I never saw it." In the midst of the Depression, Hollywood had the trappings of a boomtown—but no one thought it would last. Cagney himself always enjoyed quoting a conversation that took place at the time between Ralph Bellamy and Clark Gable in a coffee shop on Hollywood Boulevard, during which Gable, the future King of Hollywood averred, "I'm so sure that it *won't* go on that I'm not going to buy anything—*anything*—that I can't take back with me on the train."

For Cagney, *Sinner's Holiday* was followed in 1930 by *Doorway to Hell*, directed by a droll, affable, ex-film extra of Falstaffian girth named Archie Mayo whose

The confessional scene, Cagney's high point in DOORWAY TO HELL. (WCTR)

adroitness at any genre made him useful on the Warners' lot. It provided Cagney with his second "criminal" role and moved him further along that path of typecasting. Lew Ayres, fresh from his impressive starring role in Lewis Milestone's Academy Award-winning version of Erich Maria Remarque's *All Quiet on The Western Front*, released earlier in 1930, was borrowed from Universal for the part of a big-shot hoodlum named Louis Ricarno, whose character was vaguely modelled after Al Capone (in the story by Rowland Brown). Cagney played the second lead, Mileway, Ricarno's pal and top lieutenant. When Ricarno quits the rackets and departs for an extended vacation in the South (a la Capone's own trips from Chicago to his Florida retreat), Mileway succeeds him in the crime world. Yet their friendship is revealed as hollow when Mileway cheats on the sly with Ricarno's girlfriend (Dorothy Matthews). At the conclusion, Mileway is jailed, and Ricarno is killed, setting the stage for a cautionary final crawl: "The doorway to hell is a one-way door."

Though *Doorway* is largely forgotten today, it was a critical and financial hit, and it helped to solidify Cagney's popularity at the box office. The two lead performances are a contrast: Ayres, stolid, low-key and rather boyish; Cagney, jittery with energy and charm. Two scenes are particularly noteworthy. One, virulent in its social criticism, has Ricarno visiting the slums of his childhood in New York City and pointing to the hovel where neighborhood milk was sold. His brother and sister, he says bitterly, died of typhus-infected milk. The other scene was Cagney's moment in the limelight. It occurs late in the story when

Cagney (right) with Grant Withers (center) and others in climactic scene from William Wellman's OTHER MEN'S WOMEN. (BFI)

Mileway is given the third degree by a roomful of police. In an outburst of fear, the young gangster confesses. Like the confession scene in *Sinner's Holiday*—already the "confession" was part of the scheme of Cagney's movies, a dramatic device that gave audiences an excuse to "forgive" the tough guy his sundry indiscretions—it is a sharply acted and graphically drawn moment, a high point of the film.

Next on the agenda for Cagney was William Wellman's *Other Men's Women*, also released in 1930; a less coherent film (albeit with some unwonted twists) in which Cagney played a comparatively minor role. The story, written by a well-known ex-actress named Maude Fulton, is somewhat weak and muddled, dealing with a love triangle among friends who work side-by-side on a railroad. Much of the plot is belabored; the only excitement is saved for a momentary thrill at the elaborate climax when Jack (Regis Toomey), who has been blinded, rides a speeding locomotive to his death, plunging over a faulty bridge into a river. Cagney plays one of the acquaintances of fellow railroad worker Bill

With George Arliss, selling life insurance in THE MILLIONAIRE. (BFI)

(Grant Withers, again). In his fleeting spin before the cameras he is loud and noticeable. During a dance-hall scene, Cagney tosses off a few flashy dance steps before the camera cuts away.

For *The Millionaire*, made in 1930 but released in 1931, it seemed at first as if Cagney had won another bit part of no consequence—for he was to be on the screen for less than five minutes. George Arliss, who played the title character, was the undisputed monarch of the studio, having won the Best Actor Oscar for 1929/1930's *Disraeli*. Hence, he had casting authority, unusual for an actor on the Warners' payroll. In his autobiography, *My Ten Years in the Studio* (New York: Little, Brown and Co., 1940), he described how Cagney swayed him at their first meeting.

> Just now and then I feel sure of my man by one brief interview, in the casting office. There was a small but important part in *The Millionaire*—the part of an insurance agent. The scene was entirely with me, and [it] was the turning point in the story. I knew it depended largely on the actor of this small part whether my change of mental attitude would appear convinc-

ing. I saw several promising young men without being much impressed, one way or the other, but there was one more waiting to be seen; he was a lithe, smallish man. I knew at once he was right; as I talked to him, I was sure he could give me everything I wanted. He wasn't acting to me now, he wasn't trying to impress me; he was just being natural and, I thought, a trifle independent for a bit actor; there was a suggestion of "Here I am; take me or leave me and hurry up." As I came to my decision, I remember saying, "Let him come just as he is—those clothes—and no make-up stuff. Just as he is." The man was James Cagney. I was lucky!

Despite the brevity of his role, the film was not without impact for Cagney. Arliss, wedded to the idiom of the silent film, went through his retired millionaire's act at a snail's pace. His style as an actor was leisurely and measured. At the point at which Cagney enters the storyline, playing an insurance salesman who urges the millionaire to forego retirement and resume activity, it is as if adrenaline has been momentarily pumped into the picture. Cagney is brusque and extroverted, clamorous and speedy. Smoking a pipe, moving it to whistle between his teeth, clinching his eyes incredulously, the insurance salesman offers a torrent of friendly advice to the millionaire on how to stop loafing. "If I was a man like you, you know what I would do?" he asks, adopting a mock confidential tone. Then he adjusts the shawl around Arliss's shoulder—a simple gesture but one that added a shading to the character; it was Cagney's suggestion on the set and an example of his predilection for dropping his own "goodies" into a script to flesh out his characters. When Cagney exits, Arliss sits as though stunned. It is the comparison of two disparate acting styles: the one, more traditional and dignified, representing a quieter age past; the other, vibrant and unchecked, representing the future.

"Just as he is"—there is little indication that Cagney was very different in those early days from what he was to become. It is as if he arrived in Hollywood full-blown, very much himself, without having to undergo the build-up or long period of searching for his niche that so many other stars endured. Already more than a trifle independent, he was alert to his own potential. He roamed the corridors of the studio asking the writers to beef up his parts and checking on stories in development. Around town he was acquiring a stable of enthusiasts who took notice of this upstart who could steal a scene from the likes of veteran George Arliss even in so brief a sequence. Director Lewis Milestone wanted him for the Hildy Johnson part in the movie version of *The Front Page*. (Producer Howard Hughes said no, complaining that he was "a little runt.") Cagney had other admirers as well—among them, two Chicago writers under contract at Warners named Kubec Glasmon and John Bright. They were preparing a novel for filming called *Beer and Blood*, and they had Cagney in mind for the leading role.

Screenwriters: (l to r) Robert Lord, John Bright, Wilson Mizner, and Kubec Glasmon in the early 1930s. (Courtesy of John Bright)

2
Glasmon and Bright

Cagney, in spite of the coincidence of his character with the American tough guy, whether it's a racketeer or a taxi driver, is an independent actor in his own right and as finished and flexible an artist as there is in the talkies today. He has resisted every attempt to have himself exhausted by being made to act the same character in every play. Few new actors ever can survive the prestige of their first success. Cagney has an inspired sense of timing, an arrogant style, a pride in the control of his body, and a conviction and lack of self-consciousness that are unique in the deserts of the American screen.

No one expresses more clearly in terms of pictorial action the delights of violence, the overtones of a semiconscious sadism, the tendency toward destruction, toward anarchy which is the basis of American sex appeal.

LINCOLN KIRSTEIN
The Hound and Horn, 1932

Kubec Glasmon was an ex-druggist from Chicago. John Bright—his protégé, writing partner and friend—was ten years his junior. In high school Bright had worked as a soda jerk and delivery boy in Glasmon's drugstore on the north side of Chicago and later in another Glasmon-owned pharmacy in the "badlands" of the south side. An aspiring writer, Bright had also worked as a copy boy one summer on *The Chicago Daily News* where he apprenticed in the shadow of one Ben Hecht. Glasmon took young Bright under his wing and financed his first book, an H. L. Menckenish biography of Chicago's notorious underworld-linked mayor, "Big Bill" Thompson. With insurance money from a drugstore fire, the two of them traveled to New York in 1930 to find a publisher for Bright's book, and from there they continued to California via the Panama Canal, half in pursuit of a young woman fancied by Bright. Once in Hollywood, they rented a cottage and began their first collaboration—a novel called *Beer and Blood* that drew on their familiarity with gangsters (some of whom had trafficked in liquor in Glasmon's drugstore) and Chicago life during Prohibition. Glasmon, who never actually sat down at the typewriter, had a knack for dialogue and characterizations; Bright structured the telling and in the writing tried to give the story social scope. It was a dialectic that worked.

The original draft of *Beer and Blood* (subtitled *The Story of a Couple O'Wrong Guys*) was 300 single-spaced pages long and drew on many historical characters

25

and incidents. It was only natural that the two would-be screenwriters would take their unpublished novel to Warner Brothers—since Warners, under newly appointed head of production Darryl F. Zanuck, was beginning to specialize in stories shaped from the headlines, particularly gangster tales. Warners purchased *Beer and Blood* for $1800 on December 1, 1930, and Glasmon and Bright were offered studio contracts. At their first story conference, Zanuck told the two writers that *Beer and Blood* related too many interweaving stories where it ought to focus on one. The story it should tell, Zanuck explained, was that of Tom Powers, the "public enemy" character, an ordinary slum kid whose environment thrust him into a life of bootlegging and a downward spiral of crime. Because of Glasmon and Bright's relative inexperience, the technical continuity was being assigned to a contract writer, Harvey Thew. And Zanuck already had the casting in mind—young, smoothly handsome Eddie Woods, who had given such an impressive performance as the stool pigeon in Helen Grace Carlysle's novel *Mother's Cry*, would play Tom Powers. The lesser part of his pal would be played by a studio contract player, James Cagney.

Babes in the business, Glasmon and Bright looked at each other blankly and said nothing. Later, Zanuck, director William Wellman, and everybody on the lot but the night watchman would claim credit for casting Cagney as the lead in *The Public Enemy*, but the truth is the screenwriters were rooting for him from the outset. They had seen his earlier pictures, and Cagney had dropped by their office at the Burbank studio, cheerfully urging them to pad his dialogue; they had been struck by his presence and vitality. Bright and he became friends. The screenwriters tried out a couple of Tom Powers' scenes on Cagney and were convinced. Zanuck's casting was often impulsive and dubious—though he was a dynamic producer, it was one of his weak points in those early days—and Glasmon and Bright were sick at heart about it. Zanuck was imperious and refused to be crossed, especially on the subject of casting. And it didn't help matters that Eddie Woods was engaged to marry the daughter of Louella O. Parsons, a powerful figure in Hollywood at the time by virtue of her position as gossip columnist of the Hearst newspaper chain.

As it happened, director Archie Mayo had been slated to do *The Public Enemy* picture, but he wanted to get away from the gangster niche after *Doorway to Hell*, and he persuaded Zanuck to let him direct a Constance Bennett vehicle instead. Hence, the screenwriters began to woo "Wild Bill" Wellman—a carousing, two-fisted, bigger-than-life, ex-Lafayette Escadrille flyer turned Hollywood director, whose macho flair was balanced, in his work on the screen, by unusual sensitivity. Wellman was a sports and hunting buddy of Zanuck's, which was one of the reasons why he was presently employed by Warners; idle between projects, he was assigned an office across the corridor from Glasmon and Bright's. After the two of them cornered Wellman in the studio cafeteria and told him the story of *Beer and Blood*, Wellman grew excited and went to Zanuck and demanded the assignment, vowing to make the "toughest" gangster picture ever filmed. Zanuck turned the reins over to his sporting companion.

Preparing to shoot real bullets; director William Wellman (with tousled hair) and Cagney on set of THE PUBLIC ENEMY. (MOMA)

Now the screenwriters went to work on Wellman and had Cagney read the Tom Powers part for the director. At this point, in January of 1931, a few days of shooting had already elapsed—so quickly had the studio moved on *Beer and Blood*. But the footage consisted mainly of establishing shots, and Wellman was fully swayed. Again he went to Zanuck and this time made a forceful argument on behalf of Cagney as Tom Powers. When Zanuck broached the possible reaction of Louella O. Parsons, Wellman taunted him, "Are you going to let some newspaperwoman run your business?" After Zanuck viewed the existing dailies, the casting was switched. The writers were called into Zanuck's office where he grandly announced the switch as his idea, ordering them to embroider the lead part. Cagney became Tom Powers. Eddie Woods never recovered from the disappointment or the setback to his career, and shortly thereafter he quit acting and returned to New York and a career in real estate.

"Born to play the part"—a cliché to be sure but one that has to be reckoned with in the casting of Cagney as Tom Powers. Unlike his previous parts, it was a full-bodied character—not unlike the youths he had observed and known so well growing up in New York's "guerrilla jungle"; not unlike aspects of himself. Wellman was an action director, not an actor's director—part of his legend came from using real bullets for authenticity during the filming of certain scenes in *Public Enemy*; yet he did not have to tell Cagney how to play Tom Powers, nor did anyone. The actor was primed for it. Though he was a soft-spoken, serene gentleman on the surface—"very private, always a great distance from everybody," in the words of John Bright—the despondency and violence of his boyhood were like depth charges in his personality. Beneath the surface lurked Tom Powers. "He could turn it on for the camera," explained William Cagney. "That was his gift."

The Public Enemy

Beer and Blood was never published. Instead it was revised and filmed as *The Public Enemy*: a parable, as it were, of a nervy slum delinquent named Tom Powers (Cagney) and his descent into hell. Together with easygoing partner–pal Matt Doyle (Eddie Woods), Powers graduates from juvenile pranks to gangland rum-running. Romantically, he is torn between two women, both moll types, Kitty (Mae Clarke) and Gwen (Jean Harlow). His mother (Beryl Mercer) implores him to give up his life of crime, and his brother Mike (Donald Cook), a strait-laced war veteran, openly quarrels with Tom during a strained family scene given a bite of comedy by a keg of illegal beer in the middle of the family dinner table. (In his pictures, Cagney's family feuds were invariably with the men of the clan.)

When rival gangsters murder Matt, a vengeful Tom invades the headquarters of the competing mob and is himself mortally injured during a wild shootout. That scene concludes with a spectacular ballet of death, whereby the wounded Tom trips and stumbles into the gutter while rain pours down. Hospitalized, Tom is reconciled with his family. But it is too late for contrition (or resurrection). Ma Powers is humming gaily as she tidies up her son's bedroom, anticipating his return home from the hospital ward. Mike is anxious, however, having been unnerved by rumors that a faction of gangsters plans to kill Tom in retaliation. A knock on the door signals the famous denouement. Stiff and bandaged like a mummy, the figure of Tom Powers falls face forward into the camera.

A recognized classic nowadays, *The Public Enemy* remains eminently watchable as a grim slice of naturalistic fiction. If it is occasionally melodramatic in its family segments, it has a moral potency and social sweep that other gangster pictures of the early sound era lack. Movies such as *Little Caesar* or *Scarface* were notorious for patterning their title characters after such real-life criminals as Al Capone, but *The Public Enemy* was deliberately anonymous, the story of a common man, an Everyman. Even the name, Tom Powers, that awfully simple, forgettable monicker, implied that much. When Tom sneeringly informs his brother that only suckers live within the law, he is expressing a code widespread among people in the age of bread lines and Hoovervilles, the 1930s. As a sop to the Hays Office (the morality unit of the Motion Picture Producers and Dis-

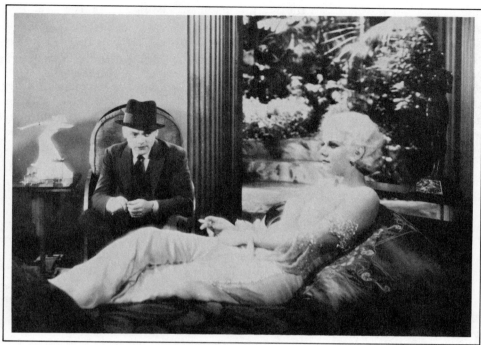

With Jean Harlow, playing his moll, in PUBLIC ENEMY.

tributors of America under the stewardship of Will Hays), Warners added a narrated postscript, warning of the fatal consequences of a life of crime. But audiences saw themselves, not some glamorous page-one figure of crime, in luckless Tom Powers.

Director Wellman brought to the story a feeling for the Prohibition era as well as a marked empathy for the character of Tom Powers (like the "public enemy," Wellman was a delinquent and hell-raiser in his youth). *Public Enemy* is one of the most satisfying of his early sound works over a long career that sputtered at intervals. It is also one of his more cinematic in pulse and composition—thanks partly to cameraman Devereaux Jennings, a leading Warners technician of the 1930s, whose lens work is effulgent. The cast, meanwhile, proves a mixed bag: Donald Cook seems overwrought and Beryl Mercer, saccharine; Mae Clarke is reliable if bland; Eddie Woods is mildly engaging; and Jean Harlow (on loan from Howard Hughes), though she was lambasted by contemporary critics for a clumsy characterization, gave a performance that over time looks earnest and classy.

It was Cagney who made the difference. His Tom Powers was "the most ruthless, unsentimental appraisal of the meanness of a petty killer that the cinema has yet devised," in the words of Richard Watts, Jr. of *The New York Herald Tribune*. Ruthless, unsentimental—and strangely appealing. As critic Robert Warshow has argued in his well-known essay, "The Gangster as Tragic Hero," all gangster figures in motion pictures and literature can be construed as being mysteriously alluring. But Cagney's Tom Powers had a playfulness and resiliency that belied—and deepened—tragedy. The burst of dancing on a city street curb after Tom Powers is first smitten with Gwen was just such a Cagney goodie. His omnipresent smile was another. Whatever the horror, Cagney would be grinning like a jack-o-lantern. Always the smile. It was to become one of his trademarks.

As critic Kenneth Tynan was to write later, "In *Public Enemy*, he [Cagney] presented for the first time, a hero who was callous and evil, while being simultaneously equipped with charm, courage and a sense of fun. The result was that in one stroke Cagney abolished both the convention of the pure hero and that of approximate equipoise between vice and virtue." According to Tynan's astute appraisal, Cagney "invented a new screen character" that "morally and psychologically" would dominate the entire 1930s.

Two scenes are crucial for understanding the evolving Cagney persona. In one, Gwen maternally cradles the head of Tom Powers in her arms, and enunciates a flawless interpretation of the "public enemy's" fascination. "You are different, Tommy," she tells him,

> very different. And I've discovered it isn't only a difference in manner and outward appearances, it's a difference in basic character. The men I know . . . and I've known dozens of them . . . oh, they're so nice, so polished, so considerate. Most women like that, Tommy, I guess they're afraid of the other kind. I thought I was, too. But you're so strong. You don't give, you take. Oh Tommy, I could love you to death.

The other scene, one of the most famous in film history, is really just a momentary gesture, captured in the enduring still photograph of Tom Powers slapping Kitty (Clarke) in the face with half a grapefruit. More has been written about this single moment in *Public Enemy* than perhaps any other scene in Hollywood annals, analyzing it from this or that convenient perspective. Consequently, there is a welter of conflicting claims as to its origin. "It was my idea, the grapefruit," boasted producer Zanuck years later, "I think I thought of it in a script conference. When I made *Public Enemy* I was way ahead in thinking. No love story, but loaded with sex and violence." Actress Mae Clarke remembered, "It wasn't even written into the script." Director Wellman maintained, "We needed something big right there in the picture. Well, that grapefruit on the table looked inviting and I didn't like the dame [Clarke] much anyhow. So I told Jimmy to try socking her with it—but hard. He did." Wellman asserted that the impulse for the grapefruit-bashing sprang from a deep-seated urge on his part to punch his own wife, aviatrix Marjorie Crawford, in the face over breakfast.

The grapefruit heard 'round the world; with Mae Clarke in PUBLIC ENEMY.

Actually, the grapefruit scene *was* in the script. Indeed, it was in the original novel draft, *Beer and Blood* (to quote: "Tom glared at her for a full minute, then picked up his grapefruit, and threw it viciously in her face"). Glasmon and Bright had modelled the idea after an incident reported in Chicago circles in which a petty hoodlum named Hymie Weiss smacked his girlfriend in the face with an omelette. If Zanuck and Wellman did anything to improve the idea, it was to enforce the degree of scripted violence. According to screenwriter Bright, however, it was Cagney who provided the telling detail—by twisting the grapefruit so that its edges cut into the flesh. But that is getting ahead of the story, for what happened on the set makes for a good footnote to the lore.

As the grapefruit scene was one of his favorites, screenwriter Bright was present on the set that day. It was one of the last scenes to be filmed—the movie was being shot out of continuity—and it was one of the last days of work for Mae Clarke. She arrived with a head cold and a sore nose and pulled Cagney aside, asking him to simulate his grapefruit socko because of her illness. Cagney approached the cameraman and asked Jennings to "fix the angle so I can fake it." Wellman overheard the two of them talking and collared Cagney while the scene was being lit. Bright was nearby and overheard the exchange. "Look, Jimmy," said Wellman, his temper aflare, "this is the best scene in the picture. This scene will be talked about for a century. And it will make you into one of the biggest stars in the business. Now, I understand you have some arrangement with that broad to fake it—true or not?" Cagney replied, "Yeah—but she's got a sore nose!" Wellman countered, "Fuck her nose! I don't care. You give it to her hard—but really give it to her. Don't fuck it up. Make it real. And *I'll* take care of Jennings!"

Cagney paced back and forth outside the sound stage, unsure of what to do. Finally he decided Wellman was right and he had to go through with the scene as written. So when the cameras rolled and Cagney hit Mae Clarke in the face with the grapefruit, the look on her face was *real*, not only because Cagney's thrust was real—but he added that painful twist. And not only was it a look of agony, but of genuine betrayal. In the script the ending was supposed to be Kitty dousing Tom Powers with ice water (to quote *Beer and Blood*: "Choking and stunned, blinded by the acrid juice, Kitty leaped to her feet, seized her glass of water and doused him with it"). The off-camera ending on the set was even better. The moment Wellman yelled "cut!" Clarke leaped up and slugged Cagney and began cursing like a longshoreman through her tears. "You s.o.b.! You double-crossing Irish!" she shouted at Cagney. "You too, you bastard!" to Wellman. "You too, you goddam writer!" to Bright. Livid with anger, she stormed off the set and off the lot. Only a single take had been filmed. That night, the cameraman, the director, the writers, and Cagney stayed up all night waiting for the footage to come back from the lab, worrying. No matter—the shot was perfect.

The scene galvanized audiences of the day. "It was just about the first time, if not the very first," Cagney later wrote, "that a woman had been treated like a broad on the screen, instead of like a delicate flower." As Bosley Crowther put it, "This was and remains one of the cruellest, most startling acts ever committed on film—not because it is especially painful (except to the woman's smidge of pride), but because it shows such a hideous debasement of regard for another human being." The key to the scene seems to be Wellman's frank admission that "I didn't like the dame much anyhow." In conception and effect, the grapefruit scene was brazenly misogynistic, and that misogyny was to fester at the core of the Cagney persona. Not only did his treatment of Clarke in *Public Enemy* define Cagney to a generation of moviegoers, but it swelled a tradition of male-dominated filmdom that still thrives.

In his silvery years, Cagney liked to blame another actor, Clark Gable, for instigating the trend in Hollywood movies of violence toward women, citing the example of *Night Nurse*, another Wellman film, released some six months before *Public Enemy*, in which Gable had slapped Barbara Stanwyck in the face. But *Night Nurse* did not have the same effect among critics and moviegoers. The grapefruit scene was to exert a distant but tangible influence on movies for years to come, reverberating far into the future of American "hardboiled" cinema. When Lee Marvin tosses scalding hot coffee into the face of Gloria Grahame in Fritz Lang's *The Big Heat* 20 years later, his actions are derived from Tom Powers' in *The Public Enemy*. When Richard Widmark shoves an old lady in a wheelchair down a flight of stairs in Henry Hathaway's *Kiss of Death* in 1947, his abnormal cruelty can be traced to the subversive inspiration of Tom Powers. Though the brief, harsh grapefruit incident merely dramatized the less conspicuous misogynistic elements of the *Public Enemy* story (including, for example, the vague resentment nursed by Tom Powers as a boy for young Molly Doyle in the opening scenes), it struck a chord of shock and honesty, and helped to taint the future relationship of men and women in the world of Hollywood make-believe.

Smart Money with Edward G. Robinson

It would be another four months before the release of *Public Enemy* in the summer of 1931 and the immediate fame that followed it. In the interim Cagney made another picture as a supporting player—the last movie he would make in that capacity for another quarter-century. The lead was a formidable actor—Edward G. Robinson, who had made a considerable reputation on the stage before cementing his screen immortality in 1931 with *Little Caesar*, released the month *Public Enemy* was being filmed. Now Robinson was one of the kingpins of the lot, a favorite of Jack Warner. Under producer Hal Wallis at the First National unit, Robinson never worked as prolifically as Cagney did in the 1930s, and he was permitted to be more picky about his vehicles. (For example, Robinson made three films in 1931; Cagney made five.) After *Little Caesar* Robinson's next picture was supposed to be a newspaper yarn, *Five Star Final*, but Zanuck had the idea of pairing "Little Rico" with budding "tough guy" Cagney, and Glasmon and Bright were handed the assignment of scripting the original story devised by Lucien Hubbard and Joseph Jackson. At first, they called it *Larceny Lane*, after Peacock Alley, a hangout for con men and grifters in Chicago's Congress Hotel.

A little background here: Robinson was a "method" actor before the word became vogue. A veteran of the Yiddish Theatre, he had to assume a role as if donning a costume, piece by piece, methodically, to feel the characterization completely. Cagney was the opposite—he projected facets of his own personality on the screen and was not very introspective about his roles. For *Little Caesar*, Robinson had demanded expensive, custom-made, pearl-button shoes as part of his costume, believing that Al Capone wore identical footwear. (The joke around the Warners lot was that in the scene where Robinson chose to exhibit the prized shoes, he was filmed by director Mervyn LeRoy from the waist up.) Cagney, on the other hand, wore dancing taps on the bottoms of his shoes regardless of the role, so he could get some hoofing exercise in during filming gaps. Their teaming in *Smart Money* (as *Larceny Lane* was eventually retitled) is not only the single opportunity to see the two of them together in a movie, but it is also a study in performance contrasts.

When Glasmon and Bright finished the story, Robinson was called in by Zanuck, who knew it would be a problem to inveigle the prideful star into

Filming SMART MONEY with Edward G. Robinson (center) and director Alfred E. Green (far right) in 1930. (MOMA)

appearing in a non-First National picture. With Glasmon and Bright listening, Zanuck launched into a flavorful account of the story—about a hick country barber who triumphs as a big-city gambler (with the part of his pal to be played by Cagney). Zanuck was animated, and even got down on his hands and knees to talk to the dice during an imaginary crap game, but Robinson held back, prepared to say no. Finally, exasperated by Robinson's lack of visible response, Zanuck said, "And Eddie, I want you to design your own costume!" At this, Robinson perked up and began to murmur: "I can see it—checkered vest, houndstooth jacket," and so on. Zanuck tried to continue, but Robinson cut him off, "Love it, Darryl! Great story!" He went away and designed his own costume and showed up filled with enthusiasm, on the sound stages for *Smart Money*, without ever having heard the final two-thirds of the story.

In *Smart Money* Robinson played Nick Venizelos, a countryfied barber with a penchant for gambling who travels to the metropolis with grandiose dreams of fortune making. By a combination of stealth and genius, Nick becomes a famed and successful games player apprehensively kept under surveillance by police. Cagney plays Jack, Nick's assistant barber and erstwhile friend from back home, who joins him in New York City. Jack is suspicious of Irene (Evalyn Knapp) who has been rescued by Nick from suicide—and who, covertly, is an informant for the police. When Nick is ultimately betrayed, Jack flares violently, and slaps the "dirty little stool pigeon." Unable to accept Irene's treachery, Nick strikes back, knocking Jack to the floor of his suite and accidentally killing his buddy. The police arrive and Nick is bound for prison—but not before wagering two to one, with his customary good humor, that he will be freed in five years instead of the allotted ten.

A ploddingly paced film, unimaginatively directed by Alfred E. Green, *Smart Money* is nevertheless distinguished by the acting of its two principals. Robinson, so ferocious as Little Rico, could be a performer of great warmth and placidity, and his Nick is instilled with an almost-saintly beneficence. Cagney is the reverse: sharp, edgy, challenging, and lurking in the background like a tomcat ready to pounce. Robinson dominates the film, but Cagney appears fleetingly in the beginning, joins the story in earnest in the middle, and departs as a corpse before the finis. Yet *Smart Money* was an important transitional film in Cagney's career. By costarring the young, relatively unknown with Robinson so soon after the reception accorded *Little Caesar*, Warners bolstered Cagney's box-office standing and—especially in that brief moment of violence in the final passages of the movie—reinforced his emergence as a "tough guy." When Jack smacks Irene at the climax of *Smart Money*, it was already the second time that Cagney had manhandled a woman on the screen, a sign from Warners that he was being settled in a groove.

Ironically, by the time *Smart Money* was released it already seemed anachronistic in Cagney's unequal billing. Indeed, *Public Enemy* had bested the box-office receipts of *Little Caesar* at Warners' showcase theater, the Strand in New York—winning a bet for Darryl Zanuck from Colonel "Billy" Wilkerson, publisher of *The Hollywood Reporter*, on that score. Though both Cagney and Robinson were to play other gangsters, Cagney's type would always be more universal, and in time Robinson would be haunted by the specific identification of Little Rico. Cagney and Robinson never became close—they were too unalike—though they were polite acquaintances and found themselves on the same political committees in the "united front" atmosphere of the 1930s. Yet if there was some coldness, there was also mutual admiration. In interviews before his death Robinson was to admit ruefully that the one regret of his long and prestigious career was that he had never had the range to do a musical like James Cagney.

Blondell Crazy

Joan Blondell was easily Cagney's toughest female costar, a female Cagney as it were—the most temperamentally and professionally suited to his disposition. As critic Kenneth Tynan put it, she was "a perfect punch bag for his clenched,

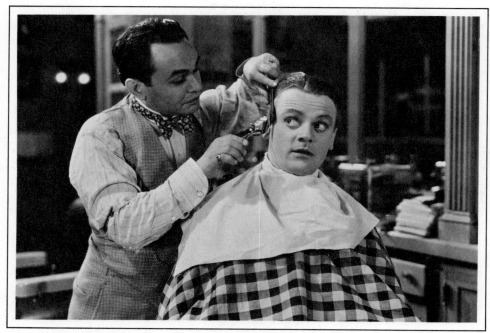

A study in contrasts; with Edward G. Robinson in SMART MONEY. (WCTR)

explosive talent.'' Her parents were vaudevillians, and she had toured with the family act not only in the United States but in Europe, China, and Australia before meeting Cagney at a crowded audition for a George Kelly play in the Bond Building in New York City in 1929. ''Suddenly, a few feet from where I was standing, squashed,'' she later wrote, ''I became aware of a young man's unforgettable face grinning at me. His hair was a Van Gogh Renoir Titian red, with blobs of gold waving through. His eyes were delft blue, fringed with the longest, thickest lashes I had ever seen. He blinked his eyes at me, and since I had never seen a blink like that before, I instantaneously fell in love. The jolt was so horrendous, I kept my eyes floorward.'' They were to become costars in the play (*Maggie the Magnificent*) and dear, lifelong friends.

Blondell specialized in playing hard-shelled but winsome characters with the proverbial heart of gold. Often typecast as a golddigger early in her professional life, she proved infinitely versatile and reliable in every performance over an extensive career—a tried-and-true, hard-working pro. She came into her own in the early 1930s as Cagney's costar. They made seven films in tandem; in three of them—*Other Men's Women*, *The Public Enemy*, and *The Crowd Roars*—Blondell played secondary parts that barely intersected with Cagney's own. Their scenes together in *Sinner's Holiday* have the recognizable give-and-take of their later,

Paired in his first comedy with Joan Blondell in BLONDE CRAZY.

more shrewdly calculated vehicles—with Cagney trying to bluff his way into her good graces; with Blondell, gum-chewing and wisecracking, wickedly out for her own best interests. But the picture itself was too hidebound to count for much. It was *Blonde Crazy*, Cagney's follow-up to *Smart Money*, that was to establish them as the premiere romantic screen duo of the early 1930s. Again, the story (again tentatively called *Larceny Lane*) was written by Glasmon and Bright—their only Warners' script without tag-along collaborators. The writers were as admiring of Blondell as of Cagney and wrote expressly with her in mind.

A tight, breezy little story about two con artists on a cross-country spree, *Blonde Crazy* represents Cagney's first comedy outing. He plays Bert Harris, an enterprising bellhop who forms a partnership with a cynical hotel chambermaid named Ann Roberts (Blondell) and embarks on an escalating whirlwind of big-shot swindles (including a hilarious "fleece" scene with Warners' regular Guy Kibbee). Roy Del Ruth directed the richly episodic script written by the *Public Enemy* dependables, which had as its unifying thread the relationship between bellhop Cagney and chambermaid Blondell. Their lovemaking is only implied, of course (partly because of cinematic convention); indeed, there is a running gag whereby Bert is slapped by Ann every time his flirtations exceed her notions of common decency. But the repartee is sexy, and they are at their best—Cagney, slippery; Blondell, nonchalant—in the cleverly muted love scenes. The whole elaborate conceit works because Blondell is never at a disadvantage—sustaining the balance, standing up indomitably to Cagney's roughneck manliness. When, for example, Ann slaps Bert after he lures her into a hotel room, Bert says mockingly, "I'd like to have you slap me like that every day." Unimpressed by his cockiness, she slaps him again and with a pert smile stalks off. In this way the seriousness of their romance is belittled throughout the *Blonde Crazy* story until, finally, Bert loses Ann to a socially respectable businessman type (Ray Milland). But their mutual attraction for one another is resolved by an ending in which they are reunited and vow to marry, albeit under the cloud of Bert's going to prison for one cheating scheme too many.

Today this lively comedy is being gratefully rediscovered by feminists who appreciate the equilibrium established between the two stars. "The film's casual and continuous triumph," wrote Molly Haskell in *The Village Voice*, on the occasion of a New York City revival of *Blonde Crazy* in the 1970s,

> is the rapport between Cagney and Blondell—buddies, would-be lovers, he calling her "honey," going up ironically on the second syllable, she self-reliant and soft, giving as much as she gets and more. Blondell's beauty as a "broad" is that she can outsmart the man without unsexing him. Cagney's beauty as a man is that he can be made a fool of without becoming a fool. They flesh out the spare Warners script with intimations of love, life, confidence and sexual equality that only reinforce all one's suspicions that they don't make movie stars—or men—like they used to.

Evidently, the sexual intimations of *Blonde Crazy* were *too* pronounced for its day. With the erotic and violent *Public Enemy* already in release, censors and moral guardians took up a Cagney watch as *Blonde Crazy* was being filmed in June and July of 1931. Along with such stars as Mae West and Jean Harlow, Cagney—particularly when paired with Blondell—became a favorite target of the Hays Office. *Public Enemy* was filmed before script submission to the Hays Office became mandatory in Hollywood in late 1931, but *Blonde Crazy* was not so fortunate. Production records show that Cagney and Blondell returned to a revised *Blonde Crazy* script in late September and, with John G. Adolfi directing retakes, worked past midnight for a couple of days on a revamped Hays-prescribed ending. The new dialogue did little real damage, but emphasized a conventional morality: Bert's contrition about his criminal misdeeds, Ann's reflections on her failed marriage (to the businessman), and her misgivings about her impending divorce. Even so, *Blonde Crazy* was—and is—a risqué lark.

Taxi!

While the reaction to *The Public Enemy* mounted, Cagney was back East for an extended summer vacation—unpaid—with Warners caught unawares and lack-

With Loretta Young in Glasmon and Bright's TAXI! (AMPAS)

ing a property for him ready to go before the cameras. There, he had ample time to assess the response—the lines of moviegoers forming on Times Square, the critical raves, the strangers who stopped him on the street for autographs, the first fan-magazine notices. Though Glasmon and Bright were frantically preparing another script for him, Bright was privately encouraging Cagney to demand a higher salary and better working conditions. The actor was particularly incensed by the minor clauses of the standard Warners' contract, which typically required stars to make personal appearances on behalf of other performers' movies, sometimes traveling in grandiose publicity caravans with every available member of the stock company.*

*In her autobiography, *The Lonely Life* (New York: G. P. Putnam, 1962), actress Bette Davis described one such galling experience, the Roosevelt Victory Caravan in 1932, dispatched cross-country by the Warners' brass to honor FDR at his inauguration. The "special, gold-leafed Pullman train" stopped in major U.S. cities, publicizing Warners' films. Cagney was along for the ride. "The whole affair was fabulous," wrote Davis with manifest resentment, "traveling in such luxury during the Depression. We were afraid we might incite a revolution; but unlike the eighteenth century Frenchmen, Americans love their royalty and we were welcomed everywhere with open arms, although a few did stick their tongues out at us."

Cagney was making $550 weekly. In mid August the studio asked him to return to work and Cagney refused to report, demanding a higher salary and certain perks (like, say, vacation *with* pay). Amid much speculation in the press, he was immediately put on suspension for three weeks. Then, with his agent striving in good faith to negotiate a new deal, Cagney returned to Hollywood in September to film a story called "The Blind Spot," based on an unproduced play by renowned playwright (and Columbia University professor) Kenyon Nicholson, whose play *The Barker* was the hit of the 1926–1927 Broadway season and who was held in great esteem by Warners' executives. It was not until the last day of filming, October 13, 1931, however, that the imbroglio was settled—with all increases (Cagney was to receive $1400 per week, with escalating clauses and benefits) made retroactive.

The behind-the-scenes conflicts of "The Blind Spot" were possibly more dramatic, therefore, than the movie itself. Cagney's precipitous walkout had astonished Warners' higher-ups, not to mention the industry as a whole, and memos flew back and forth between Jack Warner and Zanuck arguing that Cagney be "disciplined" for his rebellious attitude. But he didn't back down after he arrived in Hollywood for filming. Conveniently, he "forgot" his dialogue whenever word of stalled negotiations hit the set. In his autobiography, *My First Hundred Years in Hollywood* (Random House, 1964), Warner was to recall a confrontation on the set that arose when Cagney delayed filming by refusing to shut a door properly. And there were other, non-Cagney tensions brewing besides—political disagreements between screenwriters Glasmon and Bright over the story (Hollywood's first explicitly prounion tract) and arguments about the casting. Glasmon and Bright preferred Blondell again, thinking her perfect for the role of the Brooklynese girlfriend of the rebel cabbie hero of "The Blind Spot." But Zanuck, concerned about possible Hays Office interference and stuck with a commitment for Loretta Young, decided on Young.

As it happened, little of the Nicholson play survived in the rewriting of Glasmon and Bright, who retitled the story *Taxi!* and turned it into an actionful, prolabor melodrama that was unfortunately diverted, halfway, into a clichéd gangsterish subplot. The story: A small band of independent taxi drivers, led by Matt Nolan (Cagney), resists the hoodlum tactics of a massive taxi trust. The taxi wars and Nolan's flickering romance with Sue Reilly (Young) consume the first half of the picture; the second half is given over to an almost manic depiction of Nolan's urge to revenge the murder of his brother (Ray Cooke). The union politics are left behind. The focus on Nolan's explosive temper, an aspect of Cagney's persona accented by writers and directors over the years, pulls the movie off center. Nonetheless, *Taxi!* is fast moving, realistic, and larded with smart urban vignettes. Directed (again) by Roy Del Ruth, it has an excellent Warners' ensemble in George E. Stone, Guy Kibbee, Matt McHugh, Polly Walters, and George Raft as a dancer in a public contest (who wins, incidentally, over Cagney and partner Loretta Young). Cagney not only dances briefly for the first time in movies but has an amusing taxi-driver's flare-up in Yiddish (a language he still spoke fluently from his melting-pot childhood). And though Young *is* less believably Brooklynese than Blondell, she is also unpretentious and endearing—the interaction between cool-headed Sue Reilly and fiery Matt Nolan is a delight to watch. She is so determined to make a gentleman out of the hothead that she good-naturedly corrects his shortcomings while en route to the marriage license bureau.

The Crowd Roars

Without much ado Cagney segued into work on his next picture—to be directed by Howard Hawks. Even in those days, Hawks was held in high regard in Hollywood as a superior, literate director who appreciated good story material and knew what to do with people and the camera. Hawks maintained his independence by flitting from studio to studio with personal projects. As such, his projects usually reflected some Hawksian passion, and he could bargain for an unusual degree of freedom in his modus operandi, often filming at a more relaxed pace than other contemporary directors and (as was the case at Warners with *The Crowd Roars*) filming on-location, away from studio interference. *The Crowd Roars* was a story he worked up with Seton I. Miller, a favorite Hawks scenarist who had written the Oscar-nominated *The Criminal Code* for Hawks the previous year. The plot, Hawks admitted in later years, was lifted from Kenyon Nicholson's play *The Barker*, with the racetrack milieu substituted for carnival life. Hawks requested Glasmon and Bright as screenwriters, and he asked for Cagney in the leading role.

The movie's gimmick was to include footage of famous race-car drivers of the era (such as Billy Arnold, the winner of the Indianapolis 500 of 1930, who can be glimpsed with Cagney in the pit during one of the many races in the movie). So Glasmon and Bright and Hawks traveled to Indianapolis to mingle with the race-car drivers, observe their way of life, and pick up some jargon and lore. Hawks and Bright did not get along well from the start—their respective life-styles as well as their politics clashed. While Glasmon and Bright stayed at a local dive (dubbed the "Hotel Cesspool") with whores, grifters, and crap-shooting racing drivers, Hawks stayed in a hilltop mansion with auto magnate Fred Dusenberg. One night, while in a crap game, Bright overheard a driver telling about a true-life incident that was to form the basis for the central dramatic episode of *The Crowd Roars*—a jealous driver causing his buddy's death during a race. When Bright phoned Hawks with the idea, drunk and excited in the predawn, an annoyed Hawks hung up.

The next day, according to Bright, he told Hawks his notion at length but encountered little evidence of approval in Hawks's stony, impassive visage. Later, a girlfriend in the local telegraph office tipped off Bright that Hawks had sent a telegram to Zanuck, claiming the new twist as his own invention. Shortly thereafter, a telegram from Zanuck arrived in Indianapolis summoning Glasmon and Bright back to Hollywood, where Zanuck retold the idea to the two screenwriters, loftily claiming it as *his* own. After performing a rewrite, the two were relieved of further work on the project, and filming began—with Hawks expressing vague dissatisfaction with the script's final form.

At this point, young Niven Busch, later a best-selling novelist, arrived in Hollywood under a freshly inked contract to Warner Brothers and was promptly assigned to report to Hawks on location at the Ascot and Ventura racetracks in Los Angeles. There, Hawks would outline revisions and Busch would return to his bungalow, work late into the night, rise at five a.m. and type the spruced-up dialogue, and return to the racetrack with carbon copies of the day's "sides." Without his by-now-customary scenarists, Cagney seemed nervous and involved himself in writing his own altered dialogue—for the first time, apparently; that was something he always avoided if he could, but did assertively when he felt it absolutely necessary. "He [Cagney] didn't like what I wrote for him," Busch recalled. "Cagney would take me into his trailer and say, 'Look, Niven, I can't say this crap.' Then he'd out with some lines of his own. They weren't always usable from my point of view but they were usually better than mine. In this way, I got my start in Hollywood, learning to write dialogue."

The resulting story (with Busch sharing screenwriting credit with main constructionists Glasmon and Bright) operated on several levels—as an acute study of a compulsive competitor, as an exploration of sibling rivalry and sexual jealousy, and as an observation on the fickle, ugly emotions of the grandstand crowds. Joe Greer (Cagney) is the speedway hero of the piece: Dapper and fearless, in a typical Hawks theme he refuses to surrender his vaunted independence to a love affair with a loyal, devoted woman friend (Ann Dvorak, in a sensitive characterization); and he quarrels rabidly with his kid brother (Eric Linden), an aspiring driver, who himself is in love (with Joan Blondell). Fiercely competitive during a crucial race, Greer causes the fireball death of a long-time pal (Frank McHugh) and is so overcome with remorse that he becomes a haggard drifter, haunting the racetracks with his self-pity, until he is rehabilitated at the climax by his forgiving sweetheart.

The Crowd Roars may be Hawks's most obscure sound film, but undeservedly so. Slowly paced, unflamboyant, it was poorly received by critics at the time. But it is emotionally involving and accurate in its detail, coming off as a labor of love for the director (himself an ex-racing driver). One recommendation, among others: *Crowd* has the first pairing of Cagney and Frank McHugh, the chubby, likable character actor who was to dog Cagney's heels as a sidekick in eleven pictures, with an intimacy that echoed their off-screen friendship. (McHugh had been Pat O'Brien's roommate during their salad days on Broadway.) Though McHugh provided comic relief in Cagney's films—he had an odd, squeaky voice that invited laughter—he usually proved a loyal comrade, less a "second banana" than an accomplice, a stand-in for the audience's allegiance. To Cagney's intense, driving rhythm he was a poky counterbalance—a whimpering choreographer in *Footlight Parade*, in contrast with Cagney's barking impresario. When McHugh died in the course of a Cagney film, as in *The Crowd Roars* or *The*

With Eric Linden and Frank McHugh in Howard Hawks's THE CROWD ROARS. (WCTR)

Roaring Twenties, he died violently, and his death always signalled a sharp turn for the worse. When he stayed alive, as in *Footlight Parade, Here Comes the Navy, The Irish in Us,* or *City for Conquest*, he supported the Cagney character with above-call devotion, pledging his faith in Cagney even when everyone else had deserted him.

Because Hawks is widely considered to be an outstanding director of men and masculine themes, his contribution to the developing Cagney persona is an intriguing matter. Unquestionably, he was one of Cagney's most sympathetic directors. *The Crowd Roars* stands out as among the finest of Cagney's early 1930s titles. Cast as the ideal Hawksian hero, a lone-wolf daredevil, Cagney responded with a deeply etched performance. The tendency toward melodrama or theatricality (a tendency fostered by Warners' "tough guy" obsession) is held in check, and Joe Greer emerges as a more rounded character. The scenes in which, downcast and unshaven, Greer wanders through the racetracks seeking employment are gripping. And when he breaks down sobbing into the arms of his steadfast girlfriend (Dvorak) at the film's resolution, the tableaux is poignant.

With Ann Dvorak, loyal to the finish, in THE CROWD ROARS. (WCTR)

Exeunt, Glasmon and Bright

The five movies in sequence that Glasmon and Bright wrote for Cagney early in his career were the most stable and positive relationship Cagney ever had with his Hollywood screenwriters. The Glasmon–Bright stories laid the groundwork for Cagney's persona—the vulnerability as well as the toughness, the child-like emotions, the reckless edge of comedy, the social attitude, the volatile relationship with women. These qualities were streamlined and modified through the years, but they were omnipresent in some variation. If it is true that Cagney eventually rejected the image promulgated by *Public Enemy* and some of his early "tough guy" pictures, if it is true that Cagney had a habit of making disparaging remarks about the Warners' crew of screenwriters, it is also true that he always made an exception for the two fellows from Chicago who were present at the creation.

Yet Glasmon and Bright, luminous in the firmament in 1931, were not to last as a team. For one thing, Bright had burned his bridges at the studio by punching Darryl Zanuck during a hot-tempered argument over the casting of Loretta Young in *Taxi!* Also, Zanuck could not help but be aware of the studio scuttlebutt: that Bright had befriended Cagney and recruited him politically to leftist causes; that Bright had encouraged Cagney to walk out after the success of *Public Enemy*; that Bright had, in fact, recommended a lawyer to Cagney. Besides, Bright had enraged Zanuck by staging a one-man sick-out over his own salary—obtaining a raise for himself and partner Glasmon (who refused to walk out).

That was only part of it. The mentor–student relationship between Glasmon and Bright had long since begun to sour. Bright was no longer so unquestioning of the man, once his employer, whom he had previously held in awe by virtue of his age and worldliness. Increasingly, they found themselves at odds over script ideas. Glasmon was politically conservative, Bright was a radical and a leftist; Glasmon disapproved of his partner's extramural political involvements and union organizing. Their plots and themes became a tug-of-war. Glasmon resented the union rhetoric of *Taxi!* and sided with Zanuck who wanted to introduce gangsters into the plot. When, after *The Crowd Roars*, Zanuck abruptly terminated Bright's contract, giving an interview to *The Hollywood Reporter* claiming that Bright was incompetent and worked well only in partnership with Glasmon, Glasmon did not lift a finger and their partnership lapsed overnight. (Zanuck also told the press that Bright would never work in the industry again. Agent Myron Selznick, who detested Zanuck, took this as a challenge and got Bright a job the day after his firing, writing *She Done Him Wrong* for Mae West.)

In one year alone, 1931, they had written eight pictures—five for Cagney, *Three On a Match* (an early Bogart vehicle), and *Union Depot* for Blondell and Douglas Fairbanks, Jr., all at Warners (and another for Universal, under the table, which shall remain unnamed). In that same year, two of their films, *The Public Enemy* and *Smart Money* were up for Academy Awards. (*The Public Enemy* was nominated for Best Original Story; *Smart Money* was nominated for Best Original Story too, but with Lucien Hubbard and Joseph Jackson receiving the nomination credit.)

Glasmon and Bright were the hottest team in the industry. Their break-up, at the height of their renown, was a scandal. Both went on to a succession of other partners and credits but never, individually, quite regained the success of their youthful combination. Their paths diverged, their friendship dissolved. But in 1938, Bright, organizing for the Screen Writers Guild, volunteered to solicit his old partner Glasmon for membership. As it happened, Glasmon had been prominently mentioned in screenwriting circles as a prospective member of the studio-sponsored union, The Screen Playwrights. The two former partners held an emotional reunion in Glasmon's shuttered Hollywood apartment. Glasmon was pale and, unbeknownst to Bright, had been diagnosed as having a terminal disease. He agreed to pledge the more liberal Screen Writers Guild. Within a week, Glasmon was dead.

Publicity shot for WINNER TAKE ALL. (WCTR)

3
Professional Againster

Newspapers are wondering that James Cagney is quarreling with his high salary. Maybe he doesn't like the parts they have cast him for. Anyone can see that Cagney has gifts the criminal world does not bring out. Maybe it's his life he is fighting for.

LINCOLN STEFFENS
Lincoln Steffens Speaking

As one of the screen's first antiheroes, Cagney commenced a tradition that has persisted from Bogart to Brando to Dean to Nicholson. With *The Public Enemy* was signalled the end of the "pretty boy" as primary star factor. Cagney was *of* the people—urban, Irish ethnic, up from hunger, territorial, outrageously masculine. "He was and continues to be so brilliantly right in his interpretation of a particular type of American male," wrote *The New York Times*, "a type that has been spawned in large numbers out of the slum districts of New York and Chicago, that it is a natural thing to suspect that he is not acting at all."

His politics were an extra dimension of his appeal. Off-screen, too, Cagney was a rebel, a political maverick, a left-wing sympathizer, at one point on the verge of becoming a Communist. In his everyman roles he was pitted against cops and capitalists in movies that were like allegorical indictments of a dog-eat-dog system—and his feelings for the masses were echoed in interviews and public appearances at every opportunity. Especially in the early 1930s, when the first crest of his popularity coincided with the Great Depression, Cagney became a symbol embraced by moviegoers—of hope and guts; of resourceful humanity in ferment.

On the Side of the Downtrodden

Even as a boy in New York City, Cagney was socially aware and politically motivated, more restless and searching than any of his family. In his preteens, he would listen to speakers in Union Square declaim on the subjects of women's

47

rights, anticlericalism, anarchism, pacifism, the international workers movement, and other such dissidence. As an ad copy boy for *The New York Sun*, he moved freely through the newsrooms of the city's major papers and became friends with some of the reporters—many of them proverbially hardbitten and cynical, others liberal or outright socialistic. It was the heyday of muckraking; newspaper stories and books vied to reveal the latest inequity. But Cagney did not have to be reminded of muck or social ills: They engulfed his boyhood and burned into his consciousness. "He [Cagney] couldn't find peace anywhere," remembered William Cagney. "He always found something to be heart-broken about."

Ironically, the settlement house closest to the Cagneys was in the neighborhood at 76th Street and East End, right off the river. But though this particular slum haven had recreational clubs and boxing, it did not have any special dramatic or public speaking programs. And Cagney's mother Carrie Cagney was determined that her children would have a formal education, specifically in speech. As a girl, she had shown extreme promise in this but had had to leave school with that promise never really fulfilled. One of her adult weaknesses was that she could not talk in front of an audience—not that Carrie Cagney hankered after a public life, but it bothered and embarrassed her. So, one by one, she persuaded her sons to take up public speaking in classes at the further distant Lenox Hill Settlement House, which, interestingly enough, also became part of Cagney's political breeding ground.

First, Carrie Cagney coaxed Harry, the eldest, into the drama and speech program at Lenox Hill. Harry was a crackerjack athlete and excelled at practically every sport, but drama was not his forte. He would occasionally perform Shakespearean declamations at home, but the other Cagney boys rode him in derision. Then Carrie Cagney started in on James, who was about 17 at the time. "I was a little boy," recalled William Cagney,

> and I was in that strange position where I could observe things happening and weigh them and think about them. I remember it as if it were yesterday, when Jimmy walked over to the door to leave one time for the evening. She said, "Where you going, son?" He said, "I don't know, Ma." He opened the door. She said, "Son, hey, why don't you go down to . . . ?" He started to shake his head—he knew what was coming. She said, "Now, how is it going to hurt? If you don't like it, leave!"
>
> The next thing I knew he was palling around with all of them [from the settlement house]—and they were all radicals. The lady in charge [Florence James] was radical. Her husband, Burton James, the drama coach, was a socialist. She eventually wound up in Seattle, where she became quite famous. She was very active and indoctrinated all of the boys into being socially active, Mother Russia and all that. Not Harry. But Jimmy—Jimmy was ready to listen to it, because he was listening to it already when he was ten years old.

I think Jimmy was always a true liberal or humanist or whatever you want to call it, and he was dedicated to it, even to the extreme that he raised hell with me one day when I walked across the grass. "Goddammit Bill, that's living!" he said. And he stood over me when I caught a fish and explained to me how that had hurt the fish. Ruined fishing for me for the rest of my life! That's the way he always was about all pain to anybody.

The rancorous four-week Actor's Equity strike of 1919 occurred the year Cagney entered show business, and it introduced him, with its bread-and-butter issues, to unionism and organized labor. When bookings would become scarce on the vaudeville circuit, Cagney and his wife Billie—at the invitation of socialist friend Will Crawford—would spend time at a single-tax colony in Free Acres, New Jersey, an outdoor haven for socialists, anarchists, and philosophical free-thinkers of every stripe. While on the road, Cagney assiduously kept up with national and world affairs. "His buddies were all socialists, from before 1920 to 1930," recollected William Cagney. "They all came out of the Settlement House, vaudeville or the newspapers. When I used to meet Jim when he came back to town we'd always wind up in *The Times* news department, talking with ten or fifteen reporters, all liberal or radical."

By the time Cagney arrived in Hollywood in 1930 he was committed to an active role in social change, and he had pronounced sympathies with the Communist Party. The Soviet revolution was still untainted, and the collapsed United States economy offered the possibility of social upheaval at home. Links were being forged between left-wing political organizers and cultural figures in New York and Hollywood. The first major social protest by literary figures occurred in 1931 when, under the leadership of novelist Theodore Dreiser, a self-appointed committee to investigate injustices inflicted on coal miners by unscrupulous mine owners descended on Harlan County, Kentucky. Members of The Dreiser Committee, as it was known—including John Dos Passos, Edward Dahlberg, Lester Cohen, and a novelist-cum-screenwriter named Sam Ornitz—were arrested on trumped-up charges of criminal syndicalism, which in turn brought increased nationwide protests and publicity for the coal miners' cause.

Ornitz was an ex-New York City social worker and penal reformer whose first novel, *Haunch, Paunch and Jowel*, had become a best-seller; in 1928 he moved to Hollywood. There he met Cagney, who came forward in 1931 with a donation to the Harlan County miner's fund, and they struck up a friendship of mutual admiration. By 1931, Ornitz was a confirmed Marxist, and he and John Bright involved Cagney in all of the key political committees of the era: including the Film and Photo League (an ad hoc Hollywood group striving to apply its leftist principles to movie making); the Scottsboro Boys Committee (a nationwide organization to defend nine black men sentenced to death for allegedly raping two white women on a freight train between Chattanooga, Tennessee, and Huntsville, Alabama in 1931); and the National Committee for the Defense of

Political Prisoners (with specific emphasis on the plight of Tom Mooney, implicated in the Preparedness Day bombing of 1916 in San Francisco, and serving time in prison ever since). Some of these committees were fronted by Communists—indeed, Ornitz and Bright eventually joined the Party. Yet Cagney was a willing participant for monthly get-togethers with conspicuously left-wing agendas, evenings highlighted by newsreel and speakers. The threesome—Ornitz, Bright and Cagney—shared a jaundiced vision of Hollywood, whatever their idealistic view of the world. "Cagney was a poor boy on the side of the downtrodden and the losers," said Bright.

It was Ornitz and Bright who enlisted Cagney into the Mooney cause. Some time after the actor had made his splash in *The Public Enemy*, Cagney was invited to appear at a rally in San Francisco to agitate for Mooney's pardon. Cagney was a sincere Mooney supporter (he in fact waved to Mooney from outside the prison). But part of the attraction for the star was in meeting Dreiser, who was one of the sponsors of the rally; and Lincoln Steffens, the author, lecturer, and noted muckraker, who was the scheduled principal speaker.

The Hollywood contingent of Ornitz, Bright, and Cagney took the train up the coast to meet Dreiser and Steffens before the mass meeting. Then Ornitz, Bright, Dreiser, Steffens, and Cagney had a long, relaxed dinner at John's Rendezvous, a steak house in San Francisco. Cagney and Steffens responded to each other warmly and were later to become very chummy in their lifetimes—Cagney even took a house in Carmel, California, to be near Steffens (who also had a home in Carmel). Throughout the meal Cagney and Ornitz conversed and joked in Yiddish, which amazed Dreiser and Steffens. The five of them lingered so long over dessert and cocktails that they were nearly late for the start of the program at the Civic Auditorium with thousands of people in attendance. Though Steffens was the keynote speaker, Cagney was on the platform along with Ornitz, Bright, Dreiser, and a host of others, including William Schneiderman, state secretary of the Communist party. The crowd recognized Cagney with a roar.

Back in Los Angeles, the press—the Hearst newspaper and *The Hollywood Reporter* being among the most virulent and reactionary—needed little encouragement to go after Cagney. His public left-wing endorsements aroused the same fury as his refusal to knuckle under to standard Hollywood contract terms. Daily, the *Herald*, the *Express*, and the *Examiner* poured out anti-Red and (a favorite target) anti-Mooney venom in news items and editorials. A photograph of Ornitz, Bright, and Cagney at a huge public rally in the company of known Communists at a huge public rally—which was climaxed by the singing of the "Internationale"—was more grist for the mill. When Bright and Cagney returned to work at the studio, the pressure mounted. They were called in by Jack Warner, who raised hell with them about being Communist dupes and demanded that Bright and Cagney back off from their political activities.

The same sort of hell-raising evidently was going on in the privacy of Cagney's home. "All of this was grist to the mill to Cagney's wife, who was relatively conservative, and moved him steadily to the right," observed Bright.

"For every $10,000 [he made], she moved him to the right six more inches. She felt I was ruining his career by involving him in left-wing causes. She hated me for that reason. Though, in the beginning, I was very friendly with her, as time went on she was poisonous in her attitude toward me, Sam Ornitz and, ultimately, Lincoln Steffens."

In the year or two of their closest intimacy, Bright only saw Cagney—usually so reserved, composed and urbane—visibly angry twice. Once was when he was being deliberately goaded by Bright in a conversation about the unfair terms of his contract. The other time was the occasion of a meeting to raise support for the Scottsboro Boys. Executive Secretary of the Hollywood chapter of the Scottsboro Boys Committee, Bright drove to Cagney's home to pick him up (Cagney hated to drive and, when in a car, preferred to travel even as a passenger at a dangerously slow speed). According to Bright, Cagney came to the door and said apologetically, "I'm not going to go." "Jesus Christ," complained Bright, "They're advertising you!" At that point Billie Cagney came to the door and insisted, "He's decided not to go." Remembered Bright: "That's when he [Cagney] flared up. He said, 'You decided that I wasn't going to go.' They got into it—went round and round. And finally, he went."

Warner Versus Cagney

Of course Jack Warner had plenty of grudges against Cagney that had nothing to do with Cagney's communism (or lack of it). The two had been sour enemies since Cagney's first picture, *Sinner's Holiday*. Cagney knew that Warner did not hold him in the same esteem as the well-mannered, gentleman stars of the studio—the George Arlisses.* And Warner was known to gripe in private about the lack of gratitude displayed toward him by his tough-guy discovery, even at one point, according to Edward G. Robinson's autobiography, weeping and carrying on about how unappreciated was his largesse. Warner called Cagney a "professional againster." Yet it is hard to say which of Cagney's extramural activities he disapproved of more—his left-wing affiliations or his contract demands and walk-outs, which, by example, were pioneering the cause of actor's rights.

In the early 1930s Cagney was in the forefront of every major actor's movement in Hollywood. Most historians, for example, place Cagney as a leader of the "actor's rebellion" against the so-called "Merriam Tax." During the 1934 California gubernatorial campaign the major Hollywood studios, Warners included, actively backed Frank E. Merriam, the conservative Republican candidate, against author Upton Sinclair, the opposition candidate, a noted vegetari-

---

*Ironically, George Arliss, formerly a distinguished British stage actor, was a Cagney booster and confidant throughout the 1930s. Cagney would occasionally consult Arliss on career questions. According to Niven Busch, Cagney was offered the lead role in the Warners' production of *Babbit* in 1933, but Arliss advised him to turn it down. It was perhaps just as well: Cagney would have made an unlikely George Babbit, the Midwestern conformist realtor of Sinclair Lewis' novel. The role went to trusty secondary player Guy Kibbee, one of the few starring opportunities of Kibbee's career.

At Screen Actor's Guild meeting discussing possible strike against the studios, with Robert Montgomery (right), then-President, in 1937. (Wide World Photo)

an, muckraker and utopian socialist. The motion picture moguls were understandably alarmed by Sinclair's proposed EPIC (End of Poverty in California) program and by his outspoken criticism of trashy Hollywood filmmaking. Fake newsreels were produced by MGM showing armies of tramps ready to cross the California state line if Sinclair was elected; and a group led by Louis B. Mayer and newspaper magnate William Randolph Hearst reportedly raised a campaign fund of half a million dollars "partly by assessing their high-salaried employees one day's salary," according to one knowledgeable account. Although most actors, writers, and directors in the industry meekly paid their one day's dunning into the Republican war chest, "Cagney and Jean Harlow refused," according to this account, "and led a revolt against the tax."

Sinclair lost, thanks to such power-brokering, but significantly, "his campaign and the producer's tax on studio personnel coincided with the rise to power of the Screen Actor's Guild and the fight of the Screen Writer's Guild for recognition." Cagney was not one of the founding SAG members—by the time he joined the organization there had already been several clandestine meetings, issuance of an actor's bill of rights, and a concerted membership drive. As a result of that drive, a group of the most important stars in Hollywood joined the Guild on the night of October 4, 1933, including (in the order the names appear in the minutes) Groucho Marx, Cagney, Ralph Bellamy, Frank Conroy, Isabel Jewell, Frank Morgan, Jeannette MacDonald, Ann Harding, George Bancroft, George Raft, Eddie Cantor, James Dunn, Charles Butterworth, Chester Morris, Warren William, Robert Montgomery, Fredric March, Otto Kruger, Paul Muni, Lee Tracy, and Adolph Menjou. "No doubt," according to a history of the Guild that appeared in *Films* magazine, "the magic of their names had much to do with the fact that the membership jumped from 81 to four thousand in six weeks."

Once on the rolls, Cagney spearheaded the union action, becoming one of the Guild's acknowledged early leaders, a board member, first vice-president (1934-1939) and eventually president (1942-1943). With lifelong pal Robert Montgomery, Cagney worked out a good-cop-bad-cop routine that helped SAG raise funds and establish ties with other organizations during its crucial early struggle for recognition. Montgomery (who preceded Cagney as a Guild president) was MGM's boyish, all-purpose light comedian, yet his debonair manner onscreen, and his stalwart Republican politics offscreen, belied the fact that he hampered his own career in Hollywood by his forceful representation of actor's rights. "Cagney and I worked it out beforehand," Montgomery recalled for a Guild oral history project,

Cagney with his reputation for being very tough, a very tough fellow and a very tough operator, and I with a reputation for being a very smooth article in those days. And Cagney would simply sit in the room [with potential donors and supporters] while I talked but would keep staring at the man to whom I talked—never took his eyes off him—while I begged and implored him to please give us an ad for one page or half a page or anything in order to raise funds for the organization. Cagney would simply stare at them. Little by little we became an organization."

A Working-Class Hero

As the result of his political efforts, which were highly publicized in fan magazines as well as in the Hearst press, Cagney became a sort of proletarian hero to the American Left—as much to his own embarrassment as Warner's. "Greater than the tragedies he has enacted," effused a writer for the leftist *New Theatre and Film*, is the very tragic situation whose protagonist he himself is—to be such an artist and to have almost every achievement crippled at its climax by the conditions of the industrial background which pays him well but which he cannot control. Everything good he has done has been in an accidental frame. All the memorable moments are fragmenting, in spite of the main direction, and increasingly unrelated to a central pattern. There is nothing so disastrous to the morale of an artist of Cagney's calibre as to have every excellence of his work at the grudging mercy of a chance director or a haphazard choice of the editorial department or the shears of the cutting room. . . . James Cagney, one of the pre-eminent American artists in any field, finds himself in a situation which he can only imagine must be quite intolerable. A living definition of the American working class—the most vital, creative personification of the energy, courage, cleverness and fatalism of vast numbers of American workers, he finds himself not only hamstrung by the contracts of his producers as far as "art" goes, but what is worse, he finds himself forced into testimonials against the best possibilities of that class from which he springs and whose heroic representative he could be.

The (compromised) critical attitude toward American society in Cagney's pictures gave rise to a belief that Cagney attempted to score political points in his scripts. Never mind that the political perspective of Cagney's films was no more extremist (if any different at all) than other Warner's films of the period (or, for that matter, that the socially critical stance vanished almost entirely after Cagney went independent—and shortly thereafter, turned Republican—in 1942). But movies in which he played a common type battling cops and capitalists bore an added sting during the Depression because of Cagney's underdog image and, to a certain extent, because they reflected so accurately his real origins and concerns. Central to his mythopoetics was a movie such as *Taxi!*, which according to Bill Nichols writing in the leftist *Screen* nearly a half century later, was "conceived as part of an international worker's cinema movement," with Cagney listed among the Film and Photo League's "claimed advisors and associates."

Yet there were obvious political flaws in *Taxi!*, especially in its errant second act, and they had to be rationalized at the time. According to Marxist film critic H. A. Potamkin, writing in a 1933 issue of *Close-Up* magazine, "A film like *Taxi!* was not borne along its logical motif of the struggle between the taxi trust and the privately owned taxi. I understand Cagney wanted such a picture but it was rejected as being labour v. capital!" Echoed another contemporary account:

> *Taxi!* could have been a superb picture. As it was, its plot, which started out in a series of fast events surrounding a taxi war with union trouble, was wanly pushed over into boy–girl romance. Cagney was furious that the dramatic significance of the whole idea was deliberately sabotaged by

Cagney as a working-class hero in TAXI! (WCTR)

influence from the Hays Office, whose police fears any mention of industrial controversy. But even in retrospect—Cagney the taxi-driver was an ominous and solid character.

But Cagney's membership in the Film and Photo League was fairly innocuous—and limited to attending a few meetings. Besides, Cagney was not someone who would have argued for injecting politics into a storyline, per se, as much as he might argue for the integral resolution of a drama (which, in the

In training for the boxing scenes in WINNER TAKE ALL with ex-welterweight champion Harvey Perry. (WCTR)

case of *Taxi!*, and quite a few other Cagney films, *would* have meant carrying through with the implicit political themes rather than copping out with some trite, melodramatic deus ex machina). But the role of *Taxi!* coscreenwriter Bright, also a member of the League and someone who was later blacklisted for his extensive left-wing activity in Hollywood, was more central; and he admittedly was sweet-talked by production-head Zanuck into diverting the union struggle into safer territory. According to Bright, the League was *not* formally or informally associated with *Taxi!* (contrary to the account in *Screen*), and the story was hardly conceived as part of any class struggle, except in Bright's mind. Though Bright and Cagney got away with making Hollywood's first explicitly prounion picture—"just by making it exciting and not editorializing with agit-prop," in Bright's words—they had mixed reactions to the finished work: proud of the film, yet disappointed by the dilution of politics and by the gangsterish plot turn that they themselves, ironically, had accepted.

Was Zanuck manipulating them for the benefit of the Hays Office and his own (relative) political conservatism? Yes and no. After the release of *Taxi!*, Bright recalled encountering Zanuck striding briskly along on the lot one day, carrying a copy of *The Nation*, with Margaret Marshall's favorable review of the newest

The gentler Cagney: romancing Marian Nixon in WINNER TAKE ALL. (WCTR)

Cagney picture. "Say," called Zanuck to Bright, "I want to talk to you! Here's a review of *Taxi!* in a magazine I've never heard of—*The Nation*—have you ever heard of it?" "Yes," admitted Bright, keeping pace. "Well," continued Zanuck, "this reviewer says that *Taxi!* has great social significance." "Yes?" answered Bright, waiting. Zanuck asked, "Did you *intend* that?" Bright, "Yes." Zanuck's reply, in perfect innocence: "Well, I'll be a son of a bitch, I thought it was just cops and robbers!"

Winner Take All

Meantime, Cagney continued to escalate his one-man contractual war with Warners. The post-*Taxi!* lull lasted through the completion of just one more picture: *Winner Take All,* a comedy-drama directed by Roy Del Ruth, with a script by Wilzon Mizner and Robert Lord based on a *Redbook* story gathering dust in the Warners files since March 1921.

Lord was a Harvard graduate and ex-*New Yorker* contributor who later became Humphrey Bogart's partner in Santana Productions. Mizner was a legendary raconteur and epigrammist—a veteran of Barbary Coast and Yukon carousing and drinking bouts with all and sundry; he was known as "The Burgomaster of Broadway," and had intimidated the New York literati with his strapping physique and penetrating wit before taking up residence in Hollywood. (H. L. Mencken is said to have admired his line, "I respect faith, but doubt is what gets you an education." Of Mencken, Mizner quipped, "I liked the guy but he talked me out of it.") The first Mizner–Lord collaboration for Cagney epitomized Cagney's "split personality" in so many Warner's films of the early 1930s: by alternating a touching and wholesome love story with loutish comedy and physical derring-do, something (ostensibly) to satisfy both actor and management, audiences and critics. The upshot was superficial on both levels, out of kilter, but deft, fast-moving, comic, entertaining—and commercial.

Winner Take All begins on a bizarre note. Jimmy Kane (Cagney), a prizefighter racked by exhaustion (alcohol? a terrific beating?), is introduced at ringside. Kane is retiring to a health spa, the announcer proclaims, and needs some charity assistance from his fans. "He always gave us more than our money's worth," the announcer pleads, "and we owe it to him." From the rows of bleachers comes a blizzard of coins. Gaunt, forlorn, dodging the hail of cash, Kane stutters a halting appreciation; but unnerved, the pugilist cannot complete his words. "Folks," the voice on the loudspeaker dramatically intercedes, "what he is trying to say is, he thanks you."

After such a prelude Kane is sequestered at Dr. W. Betts Rosario's Ranch and Hot Springs in scenic Arizona, a bucolic setting that allows for the gentler side of the tough guy to be accented in Kane's courtship of sweet-and-nice Peggy Harmon (Marian Nixon). It is not long, though, before the revitalized Kane is lured back to his urban boxing habitats, at which point the movie shifts gears and extracts crude and familiar laughs at Kane's dullard attempts to climb the social ladder and woo showy society dame Joan Gibson (Virginia Bruce, on loan from MGM). The boxing scenes are grimy and realistic—an amateur boxer in his youth, Cagney was the holder of a black belt in karate in his prime and the most physically fit, surely, of all movie stars who impersonated champ fighters. But the choice between the two worlds of *Winner*, and the sweethearts who represent them, is predictable, thematically and otherwise, right down to the moment when Kane plants a kick in the rear of high-society Gibson, who has been secretly planning all along to embark on a romantic ocean cruise with a more well-bred lover.

As Kane, Cagney offered one of his most lumpen characterizations—dense, slangey, thickly Eastern-accented, vain, and unsentimental. One scene—in which he decides to fight a "winner-take-all" match to pay Peggy's rent, while concealing his thoughts from her and conversing about something else—is particularly powerful. Cagney plays the scene with eyes that are hot and feverish, his hands thrust into his pockets, glancing away nervously and talking in spurts, all the while chewing gum mechanically. One curious footnote about this citizen Kane: his black assistant trainer is named Rosebud (Clarence Muse).

When filming of *Winner Take All* ended in March of 1932, Cagney tore up his contract and walked out again—for the second time in two years. His salary at the time was in the neighborhood of $1250 weekly. By comparison, Ruth Chatterton was receiving $7000 weekly and Richard Barthelmess was earning $125,000 per picture—even though Cagney was, by now, the acknowledged box-office star of the lot. "A player," Cagney told reporters, "should be in a position to demand what he is worth as long as he is worth it."

Six months passed while Cagney sent up various smokescreens about his future plans, and lawyers for both sides bickered. "I feel," Cagney informed the press,

> that I have given the best years of my life working for inadequate compensation. My employers can't see my way, so I'm through. I have dispensed with my home here and next week I'm leaving for a tour of America and Europe. While abroad, I'll very probably accept vaudeville offers. Look, give me a break. I received honors, but I could not obey the studio code, so after my return to America I'll write a book called *Luck, Honor and Obey*. I hope you'll like it. After that I'm turning seriously to the study of medicine.

Since two of Cagney's brothers, Harry and Ed, were already physicians, Cagney's threat to enroll in medical school at Columbia had the ring of truth. There was talk of making a film in Europe. A Broadway play was bruited about. Mary Pickford announced she was negotiating with Cagney to costar with her in the romantic *Shanty Town*, to be directed by Frank Borzage. Cagney publicly offered to appear in three more Warner's pictures without additional salary if the company would cancel the remainder of his five-year contract. Still, Jack Warner was as furious and as stubborn as Cagney, and he would not abrogate the contract; one of the industry's top stars remained idle, while critics reviewed *Winner Take All* grievingly, as if it were the actor's swansong.

Finally, in September of 1932, the matter was brought to the Motion Picture Academy for arbitration. Director Frank Capra (a confessed Cagney admirer) chaired the arbitration panel which included Joseph I. Schnitzer, owner and operator of Western Costume Company, and actor Fredric March. Outside the board meeting room, according to Cagney, Jack Warner assured the star that he would not be overburdened with work again, implying that Cagney would not have to act in more than four pictures annually. But, Warner added, he could not stipulate this in the contract for fear of incurring the wrath of his brother, Harry Warner—a staunch anti-Red with a puritanical streak, and therefore no great fan of Cagney's—not to mention the studio's other underpaid, overworked stars. Compromising (Cagney wanted to limit his annual output to three pictures), Cagney agreed—a verbal agreement. The signed legal settlement was for $3000 weekly on a 40-week-per-annum basis, with four yearly options of $500 additionally per week per year. The principals were all smiles when announcement of the truce was made to the press.

*After the arbitration settlement in 1932: (left to right) director Frank Capra,
Cagney, Darryl F. Zanuck, and Jack Warner. (MOMA)*

Even so, there were hints of dark provisos built into the contract, apart from
Cagney's oral understanding with Jack Warner—including admonishments
about Cagney's left-wing activities. In its December 1932 issue, *Photoplay*
gloated, "Another Hollywood Bolsheviki has been converted! James Cagney has
turned from a militant, red-headed, fiery-tongued *red* to a goose-stepping,
silent-tongued, obedient soldier." The magazine noted that a percentage of
Cagney's salary would be held in escrow annually and added,

> if rumors are true, Jimmy gets that bonus *only if* he's a good little boy and
> gives his producers and directors and various other bosses, like super-
> visors, no cause for worry. He's to appreciate the fact that silence is golden.
> He's not to talk to reporters who delight in writing Bolshevistic statements.
> Nor to be late on sets and keep high-priced companies waiting. Nor to "go
> up" on his lines and make numerous retakes necessary. Jimmy can learn
> lines. He's as bright as the proverbial dollar. But perhaps he didn't study
> when he wasn't feeling chummy with the big fellows.

Against All Isms Except Americanism

Certainly there was steady pressure from the media, from the studio, and indeed even from the government for Cagney to diminish his left-wing ties. In August of 1934 Cagney was in the news, branded a Communist by the Los Angeles County "red squad." It seems that Detective Ray Kunz had obtained some correspondence between journalist Ella Winters, wife of Lincoln Steffens (and later on, wife of screenwriter Donald Ogden Stewart) and Caroline Decker, secretary of the Cannery and Industrial Worker's Union, an alleged "local Communist official." The result of a grand jury investigation was 17 indictments issued against suspected radicals by District Attorney Nick McCallister and the naming of several celebrities, including Delores Del Rio, Ramon Navarro, Lupe Velez, and Cagney, as Communist sympathizers. The Winters letter allegedly cited Cagney by name and stated, "I have Cagney's money again. . . . Cagney was fine this time and is going to bring other stars up to talk to Stef about Communism." Cagney, according to the red squad, had offered to supply Decker with typewriter ribbons. In her letter, Winters allegedly noted that "He [Cagney] wrote a piece for the Screen Actor's Guild, which, as you know, is the employee's rebellion against the producers, even though employees get $3500 per week [Cagney's own salary].

Predictably, there was a clamor from the press, but Steffens used his personal prestige to clear Cagney, telling reporters,

> Ella Winters reported the San Joaquin Valley cotton strike a year ago for a national magazine and while she was there she saw a little baby die of starvation—turn black and die in the worker's district. When she told people, including Cagney, of the utter misery she had seen there, he gave some money to help. So did other people who gave food or clothing or money for food or clothing. When they heard those conditions described or saw them with their own eyes. That's all.

For his part, Cagney went on the offensive, denying the charges and defining himself politically as being "against all isms except Americanism." He told reporters,

> If Ella Winters wrote such a letter as has been reported found by the police, and which I can hardly believe she did, then she had no right to do so, because I had never expressed any intention of coming to the aid of anyone trying to upset our government. I am proud to call myself a 100 per cent American. This old country of ours has been pretty good to me. I started with nothing, worked hard and today am very comfortable. I believe that nowhere else is there the same glorious opportunity for anyone to work hard as in America. It certainly would be ridiculous for me to align myself with any Communistic, socialistic, Nazi, white shirts, silver shirts or any

With the "Irish Mafia": (l to r) Spencer Tracy, Pat O'Brien, Frank McHugh, Cagney, and Lynne Overman (standing). (Homer Dickens Still Collection)

other un-American movement because I would be the first to suffer should these radical movements and agitations succeed.*

Despite such external pressures, it would be too convenient to ascribe Cagney's gradual rightward political shift to cowardice or caving in, especially when

---

*The smear tactics of Los Angeles' "red squad" were notorious in the early 1930s, and it was widely suspected by the Left in Hollywood that the Winters–Decker "leak" was set up by a police informant. Though Cagney was drifting away from the Left, it may be that his public statement "against all isms" was itself a deliberate posture to deflect the issue. According to Ella Winters, who left the United States with her husband (screenwriter Donald Ogden Stewart) during the Hollywood blacklisting of the 1950s, Cagney seemed generously unconcerned about the controversy. In her autobiography, *And Not To Yield* (New York: Harcourt, Brace and World, 1963), Winters wrote, "James Cagney was one of a number of Hollywood people who had read [Lincoln] Steffens and enjoyed coming up to Carmel to talk. Some had contributed funds for the [San Francisco maritime] strikers. One morning the Hearst newspapers carried banner headlines: James Cagney had been 'sending funds.' My heart stopped. I had been so protective of all the Hollywood people who had helped. What could have happened? Soon it came out—a police raid on Caroline's office had turned up a note referring to 'Jimmy's money.' I felt physically ill. I saw myself as having ruined Cagney, ending his four-thousand-dollar-a-week salary. I expected him to be justly furious, to break off relations, never again to visit. The telephone rang. I managed to pick up the receiver. It was Cagney. 'Hullo darling.' I heard his cheery, Irish voice, with its peculiar pronunciation of the *r*. 'How are you? I'm all right.' I wept with relief."

there were family pressures and private doubts. Cagney's politcs were more of a romantic attitude from his youth than an ideology. He did not see himself as a symbol, an organizer, a leader—or even as a joiner of a mass movement. Without ego, "he [Cagney] was the least prima donna of any major movie star ever," in John Bright's opinion. He was also uncomfortable and ill at ease among crowds—and when he made his public appearance in San Francisco in the early 1930s on behalf of political prisoner Mooney, he was terrified to encounter a "wild-eyed gang" of Mooney supporters in the rally hall. ("Screaming, yelling, giving vent to God knows what psychotic upsets, and doing everything except what one would consider appropriate to helping their man in prison," wrote Cagney in his autobiography.) Cagney eventually came to resent what he felt was the Left's exploitation and manipulation of his star image. When, in 1936, he viewed a documentary film about Fascist atrocities committed during the Spanish Civil War, he stepped outside and vomited, and then went back inside and wrote a personal check to cover the costs of an ambulance. Organizers for the Republican cause inscribed his name on the side of the ambulance and toured it across America to raise additional funds at other rallies; some of those rallies linked-up to related causes that Cagney did not countenance. "He [Cagney] didn't appreciate that," said William Cagney.

Plus—significantly—nearly all of Cagney's post-1930 Hollywood clique of friends were anti-Communists and politically moderate. None were socialists (as in the New York days of vaudeville and Broadway); a few, such as the Robert Montgomerys, were Republican; most were Rooseveltians who ultimately swerved to the Right. Sam Ornitz, John Bright, and other "fellow travellers" were never welcome in Cagney's inner social circle, partly because of Billie Cagney's vehemence on the subject. That circle was dubbed the "Irish Mafia" by Hollywood pundits. Old stage pals Frank McHugh, Pat O'Brien, and Spencer Tracy formed the core—they initially reunited in the early 1930s for a dinner to sign autographs for a Hartford, Connecticut, church auction and then decided to make their get-togethers a regular occasion. In time they were joined by Lynne Overman, Frank Morgan, Ralph Bellamy, and others (not all of them Irish, incidentally, and none of them leftist). Except for Tracy, the whole group turned Republican after the death of FDR and, even in the 1930s, they were Hollywood's square and decent set. Their evenings together were for laughs and light conversation and discussion about movies and personalities, not politics.

And not only Cagney's wife, but also his brother William Cagney—who was to become his most trusted advisor—was fiercely anti-Communist. The youngest Cagney son arrived in Hollywood in 1932 and was promptly signed by Paramount Pictures to be flaunted as Cagney's lookalike in a string of flea-budgeted quickies. Paramount's ploy did not prove very successful at the box-office, however, and William Cagney did not enjoy acting as much as he relished the business opportunities in Hollywood. He took note of the controversies swirling around his brother's politics, and he felt that Cagney's career was being endangered. Publicly, he said nothing untoward. When approached by report-

Anti-Nazi stars: Cagney was one of 56 Hollywood celebrities to urge, in 1938, that the United States sever economic relations with Hitler's Germany "until such time as Germany is willing to re-enter the family of nations in accordance with humane principles of international and universal freedom." From left to right: Melvyn Douglas, Cagney, and Edward G. Robinson. Back row: Gale Sondergaard, Helen Gahagan Douglas, Henry Fonda, and Gloria Stuart (with fur cape). (United Press International Photo)

ers after the Communist allegations by the "red squad" in 1934, he said indignantly, "When people are hungry and starving, James Cagney doesn't ask them their political beliefs, he helps them." Privately, he—and Harry and Ed—went to work convincing their brother to stay away from leftist political affiliations. As much as possible his brothers decided to insulate Cagney from the influence of the Left. "His brothers kept Jimmy from being destroyed," insisted William Cagney.

The fact is that Cagney's brief flurry of left-wing activism ended almost concurrently with the Glasmon–Bright period of his work and his second walkout, when his career took a new upswing and the various external and internal conflicts resolved themselves in his retreat into privacy and domesticity. By his own admission he remained "a soft touch" for donations for years to come, signing the odd check over to this or that cause. He remained liberal as long as FDR was alive. But he was shielded and swayed by family and friends; and too, his spirit was broken by the course of world events. "Pre-Hitler–Stalin [the Hitler–Stalin pact of 1939]," explained William Cagney, "I think his [Cagney] attitude was that out of the preachments of Communism were coming some of the most humanistic statements in the world, the world needed it, and he would back it. But the Hitler–Stalin pact shattered him. This was terrible. I don't think he could ever forgive Russia for aligning itself with Hitler."

Phony image-making circa mid 1930s: Cagney did not smoke and rarely drank.
(WCTR)

4
Tough Guy

Even the most ascetic cineast will admit that it is impossible to forget how he looked at the height of his popularity. The spring-heeled walk, poised forward on the toes; the fists clenched, the arms loosely swinging; the keen, roving eyes; the upper lip curling back in defiance and derision; the rich, high-pitched, hectoring voice; the stubby, stabbing index finger; the smug purr with which he accepts female attention—Cagney's women always had to duck under his guard before he would permit them to make love to him. He was practically unkillable; it would generally take a dozen Thompson guns and a bomb or two to bring him to his knees; and he would always die running at, not away from his pursuers, in a spluttering, staggering zig-zag, ending with a solid and satisfying thump. He moved more gracefully than any other actor in Hollywood. And he had a beguiling capacity for reassuring while he murdered: he would wrinkle up his face into a chubby mask of sympathy and then let you have it in the stomach. His relaxedness, even when springing, was absolute; he released his compact energy quite without effort. When circumstances forced him to shout, his face would register how distasteful he found it.

KENNETH TYNAN
Sight and Sound, 1951

After returning to Warners, Cagney entered the upsurge of his career, his most concentrated period of work. But it was not to be "hail the conquering hero." Paradoxically, the years from 1932 to 1936 involved a shift away from the experimentation, the idiosyncracy, the novelty of the Glasmon–Bright pictures to generic material and typecasting, whether embodied in action-fests or low comedy. With the exceptions of *Footlight Parade* and *A Midsummer Night's Dream*, all were variants—some ingenious ones—on the tough-guy theme. Not only was Cagney, at this point, one of the most financially risk-free actors in Hollywood, he was also one of the most sincerely admired. Frank Capra's declaration (in his autobiography) that *"all* parts would be perfect for Cagney" was echoed by other directors and studios in town. Yet Jack Warner refused to loan-out Cagney when the offers came in—not once, ever—preferring to keep his top star on a tight leash and to grind out the maximum number of movies and dollars while Cagney was still hot.

Marian Nixon, Virginia Bruce, Evalyn Knapp, Mary Brian, Patricia Ellis, Madge Evans, Alice White, Gloria Stuart, June Travis, Margaret Lindsay—these were his female costars of the period, as interchangeable then as they are faint and forgotten today. Cagney's onscreen relationship with women became moulded after the popularity of his character in *The Public Enemy*. Many of his costars were simply punching-bag specimens a la Mae Clarke. Yet Cagney could be distrustful one moment, tender the next. His screen kisses might be followed by a gentle sock to the jaw that mocked his emotion. It was not always love at first sight. More likely it was love/hate, with Cagney despising any female invading his territory. Later, the female lead might win him over, prove herself tough, equal to his manhood. But such a woman—in the world of Cagney's movies—was rare. And if Cagney was depicted as married, as in *Footlight Parade, White Heat,* or *One, Two, Three* (*Yankee Doodle Dandy* and his independent films are the exceptions that prove the rule), those marriages were either estranged or loveless, as if to reinforce the image of the untamed bachelor.

The studio had a motive for all this, one that was in part good business judgment and in part a self-fulfilling theorem. Cagney was thought to be more popular with male moviegoers (who presumably identified vicariously with his woman-bashing) than with female moviegoers—or at least *equally* popular— which put him in a category apart from most of the other heartthrobs of the screen. Indeed, as *Variety* reported on one occasion:

> The populace, at least that portion attending the Strand [in New York City], are now expectant of this player socking all and sundry including all the women in the cast. There's even a distinct tremor of disappointment through the house when no wallop is forthcoming. . . . And Cagney probably has no more partial gathering than the mob which gathers at the Strand whenever they hang out his name. The boys start to gather early and a peek at 12:30 noon will reveal a good-sized assemblage of 90 percent male. That element which delays deliveries to see a picture and drops over from Eighth Avenue and West, goes in a big way for the manner in which James handles his film women.

Hence the evolution, at times the virtual ossification, of the tough guy. It is to Cagney's credit that he never sloughed his way through the worst of his vehicles, and that the tension he felt offscreen was probably just factored into the oncamera voltage. For indeed, the slow process of extinguishing the yearning artist in Cagney had only just begun.

Hard to Handle

Mizner and Lord provided the script for Cagney's first picture after his 1932 walk-out: a story entitled *Bad Boy*, then changed during filming to *Hard to Handle*. In the words of Jack Warner, the title "was appropriate for both the writer"—Mizner, who died as shooting progressed—"and the actor." The studio played the "comeback" theme for all it was worth in advertisements: "The Movies' Prodigal Son-of-a-Gun Returns" and "All Is Forgiven!" "We sure

With Mary Brian in Mervyn LeRoy's HARD TO HANDLE. (WCTR)

have missed you [Cagney]," read one display promotion, "you, rascal, you! We needed someone to put those hard-to-handle dames in their place!"

Yet *Hard to Handle* was a zany departure from the manhandling Cagney. A raucous, topical, in-joke comedy directed by studio favorite Mervyn LeRoy (who happened to be married to Harry Warner's daughter), it opens with a scene striking for its subject matter that cynically evokes the era: a dance marathon. Allen Jenkins is a histrionic master of ceremonies, Sterling Holloway is among the determined, down-and-out contestants, and Cagney plays Lefty Merrill, an irrepressible swindler who exploits the despondency of the Great Depression by organizing the marathon event and, later, by advertising a fortune in treasure supposedly buried at a fairgrounds. (For authenticity's sake, an actual "gold rush" was filmed by Warners at the Ocean Park Pier in Los Angeles.) But Merrill is himself bamboozled when his partner in the marathon dance fraud absconds with the purse money, leaving the relatively more honest cad to contend with a lynch mob. Worse, Lefty must explain the unwonted development to the exhausted contest winner, a young, fair-haired type (Mary Brian—alas, Carole Lombard was originally set for the role) with whom he has circumstantially fallen in love over the objections of her mother (Ruth Donnelly). After pursuing his true love from West Coast to East Coast, Merrill hits upon the ultimate scam, masterminding a national craze for grapefruit—the link to *The Public Enemy* was simultaneously amusing and publicity rich. At this point in the original story (by Houston Branch) there was an edge of social comment—Merrill's antics somehow caused the accidental death of his own child, and the story ended with a fierce tirade by the Cagney character against rapacious businessmen. But Warners had already left behind the phase of its most disillusioned social filmmaking, movies like LeRoy's *I Am a Fugitive from a Chain Gang* and William Wellman's *Wild Boys of the Road*. So Mizner and Lord chose instead to resolve the story frivolously with farce and courtship.

Hard to Handle was a tremendous hit, proving that Cagney's absence had not adversely affected his formidable drawing power. Besides Cagney's own winning characterization, the film boasts a peppery performance by undervalued comedienne Ruth Donnelly—pepper to Cagney's salt—and smooth, inobtrusive direction by LeRoy. It is among the actor's most enjoyable early comedies. *Hard to Handle* gets a nod, nearly forty years later, when director LeRoy is introduced from the bleachers during the marathon dance contest that figures centrally in the film version of Horace McCoy's *They Shoot Horses, Don't They?*.

Picture Snatcher

Cagney's next film, *Picture Snatcher*, was based on an actual incident in the 1920s, when a *New York Daily News* photographer scooped the competition by strapping a camera to his leg and taking a picture of murderess Ruth Snyder as she died in the electric chair. Cagney played a reformed felon named Danny Kean, an ingratiating mug who retires from the rackets to picture-snatch for *The Graphic News*, a disreputable tabloid. The novice photographer manages some startling scoops: first, by obtaining an exclusive shot of a half-crazed fireman standing armed guard over the smouldering ruins of his own house (while inside, the fireman's wife and her lover are discovered, dead, in each other's embrace); then, by stealthily photographing an electrocution in Sing-Sing (a la Snyder); finally, by conniving his way into the hideout of a former cohort turned

In the newsroom with Patricia Ellis and Ralph Bellamy in PICTURE SNATCHER. (WCTR)

cop killer (Ralf Harolde) just in time to click shots of the bloody showdown with police. An unconventional journalist, to say the least, Kean accomplishes all of his daring assignments by foregoing ethics: lying, cheating, and stealing to picture-snatch, a mode of behavior that is the source of endless tension between Kean, his righteous girlfriend (Alice White), and her dad, a proverbial Irish cop (Robert Emmett O'Connor).

Like many so-called gat-and-gag stories of the period, *Picture Snatcher* neatly sidesteps the dilemma of how to water-down its guts and gore for Hays Office approval by framing the action in the guise of a newspaper yarn, thereby permitting the sex and violence of precensorship days to be experienced by a "legit" reporter. This was a common ploy after the first gangster cycle of the early 1930s, when rampant lawlessness gave way to such noisy newspaper sagas as *Five Star Final* or *The Front Page*. An ex-con named Danny Ahern suggested the *Picture Snatcher* story; ex-newsmen P. J. Wolfson and Allen Rivkin contributed the scenario. Insubstantial though the movie may be, it is well made and briskly entertaining, with humor and suspense to compensate for the lackluster romance. Lloyd Bacon, with the aid of "dialogue director" William Keighley (newly arrived from Broadway), sped the narrative along. Cagney is fleet and brazen if somewhat familiar here, while Ralph Bellamy adds a touch of loutish humor as Kean's boozing editor. If for nothing else, this forgotten picture ought to be remembered for its last words, the unofficial credo of eyewitness journalism, uttered in an ecstasy by Cagney: "Was you there, Charley?"

With Frankie Darro and Madge Evans in the reform-school melodrama
MAYOR OF HELL. (WCTR)

The Mayor of Hell

The Mayor of Hell had the advantage of a canny director in Archie Mayo and a provocative script by Edward Chodorov—based on Isiin Auster's story, which was inspired by a 1931 Russian film *Road to Life*. Only a teenager when he arrived in Hollywood to work on *Rasputin and the Empress* for MGM, Chodorov was later blacklisted during the McCarthy era for his play- and screenwriting on Russo themes and in solidarity with the downtrodden. When he went to work for Warner Brothers writing *The Mayor of Hell*, he was only nineteen years of age.

The youthfulness of the writer was evident in the vitality of the story as well as in its structural deficiencies. The story concerns one Patsy Gargan (Cagney), a piddling hoodlum turned ward heeler who accepts the supervision of a boys reformatory as part of his patronage from crooked politicos. Once ensconced at the juvenile prison, he is attracted to the institution's nurse (Madge Evans) and her visionary scheme to allow the juvenile delinquents to govern their own lives while wards of the state. Identifying with the youths, Gargan dismisses the sadistic superintendent (superbly played with evil banality by Dudley Digges), and the reformatory is turned into a democracy. Even the orneriest kid (Frankie Darro in a chip-on-the-shoulder, film-stealing role) is enlisted in the cause after he is elected mayor of the reformatory by the other boys.

But Gargan reverts to his former self and shoots a rival gangster, crossing the state line to avoid arrest. Then the superintendent returns in a fit of vengeful glory, reinstating the old, harsh methods of prison administration. A well-liked lad is locked in a small, freezing hut for punishment, and the youth, subject to spasms, dies. Aroused, the young hellions go on a rampage, seize the superintendent, and stage a mock trial. When the terrified superintendent tries to escape, he plummets to his death from the roof of a burning barn, cheered on by the mob of juveniles. Gargan arrives too late to halt the killing, but in a stirring, shouting speech above the din he persuades the youths to halt the riot before any more harm is done to the ruling order.

Certain sequences of *The Mayor of Hell* remain grim and exhilarating today. The climax, with the surly superintendent meeting his just desserts impaled on the barbed-wire fence of a pigsty, is as unequivocal and overtly symbolic a moment of political filmmaking as any ever devised on the Warners' backlot. Though Cagney gave a stalwart performance, he was dominated by a scenario that called for him to be absent at critical stages of the plot, in the mood-setting beginning and at the electrifying conclusion. Sidekick Allen Jenkins lent laconic support that helped offset pallid leading lady Madge Evans. But the real heroes, the real stars of *The Mayor of Hell* were the young actors who played the alienated, embittered delinquents, as convincing as a swarm of pint-sized Cagneys. Warners remade *Mayor* as *Crime School* in 1938 starring Humphrey Bogart—but among other shortcomings, Bogart lacked Cagney's street-sassy manner, and the remake paled in comparison.

Footlight Parade

Footlight Parade followed, a dividend of Cagney's 1932 walk-out. Not only was it the ex-hoofer's film musical debut—except for some showoff dance steps in *Other Men's Women* and *Taxi!*—but this backstage musical codirected by Lloyd Bacon and Busby Berkeley was also an industry trend-setter with its fresh formula. Both movie and actor scored a resounding success. Wrote one contemporary reviewer in *Film Pictorial*: "Although he [Cagney] used to be in musicals in his stage days, he sings and dances here in a manner that makes one wonder why his talent in this direction has not been used before."

With off- and on-screen pal Frank McHugh in FOOTLIGHT PARADE. (WCTR)

As Chester Kent, the producer who mounts lavish theatrical prologues for movie theaters, Cagney had his first major law-abiding role as well. Latter-day film critics have seen the iconology of then-President Franklin Delano Roosevelt in Cagney's character, who must overcome a torrent of crises in the plot of *Footlight Parade*—a cinema symbol, as it were, of resilient leadership against crushing odds. (Warners had an affinity for FDR and his policies, and the popular president turned up in many Warners' films, including *Yankee Doodle Dandy*.) In the film, the beleaguered Kent is being hustled by his ex-wife (Renee Whitney) for alimony, betrayed from within by an informer who is passing on his secrets of choreography to competitors, cheated by wily copartners Gould (Guy Kibbee) and Frazer (Arthur Hohl), doggedly pursued by two attractive females (Joan Blondell and Claire Dodd) intent on marriage, and faced with looming, nigh-impossible deadlines for three new theatrical prologues.

A dizzying musical extravaganza with more subplots than a tree has branches, *Footlight Parade* has nary a dull moment, and one of Warners' truly great supporting casts in the effervescent Hugh Herbert as a bothersome relative of one of Kent's "angels"; Frank McHugh as a whining choreographer who must mimic

Dancing the "Shanghai Lil" number with Ruby Keeler in FOOTLIGHT PARADE. (AMPAS)

cats (he detests cats!) for a new feline number; Ruth Donnelly as the mother over-protectress of the male ingenue; and those croon-swoon, shuffle-off-to-Buffalo love-mates, Dick Powell and Ruby Keeler. Blondell has a chance to shine as Kent's secretary, Nan Prescott, and she makes the most of it; a crisp and fetching performance. It is her smartness that is so appealing here. Kent, trusting and slow to learn, does not realize he is being double-crossed by his partners until Prescott blackmails the duo and gaily delivers the withheld payments to her astonished boss. She also unmasks the pretentious Vivian Rich (Claire Dodd), a golddigger with fraudulent society airs, by telling her rival for Kent's affections, "As long as there are sidewalks, *you'll* have a job," delivering the line as a kiss-off with a smug, satisfied smile. The audience understands she is Kent's better half long before he does, for she is trading barbs with his adversaries, grumbling asides, swapping ideas excitedly with the show-biz tyro, and stealing around every corner of the plot, nourishing its weaknesses.

Cagney, meantime, is simply prime. He seems fueled by adrenaline, sputtering orders, moving in rhythm, and even trading punches in two-four time. Almost without exertion, it seems, he surmounts the contrived obstacles of the plot, composing newfangled dance routines and offering pointers on technique while dashing from rehearsal hall to rehearsal hall, from creditor to creditor, keeping pace with his romantic enmeshments and dancing just a tantalizing little. He saves the eye-opener for the "Shanghai Lil" finale, only one of three full-scale production numbers tagged on to the end of the story, splendiferously staged by musical maestro Berkeley. Substituting at the last minute for the drunken lead dancer of his crowning prologue, Cagney/Kent teams up with Ruby Keeler and sweeps the picture into a grand and tidy conclusion with his own glittering, controlled demonstration of song and dance. "He [Cagney] could learn whatever you gave him very quickly," Berkeley once said, admiringly. "You could count on him to be prepared. And expert mimic that he was, he could pick up on the most subtle inflections of movement. It made his work very exciting."

Lady Killer

Why Cagney's spectacular success in *Footlight Parade* was not followed by other Cagney musicals is a mystery and a tragedy; and it was a bitter frustration to the actor. One reason may be the angry departure of swaggering Warners' production head Darryl Zanuck in the spring of 1933 and his replacement by Hal Wallis, who now merged control of First National and Warners. Cagney and Zanuck had always gotten along, but Cagney and Wallis never had anything but a cold relationship. Wallis did not share Zanuck's eagerness for musicals—though he certainly produced his share—nor was he as willing to fool with the sure thing of Cagney's image on the screen as a gutter-bred tough.

In 1933, for example, a proposal by an ex-fan magazine columnist named Rosalind Keating Shaffer for a film called *Fingerman* described "a fellow, grown up in the slums of New York [who] gets to running with a bad gang. He isn't bad, just burning with resentment against the rotten breaks life has handed him and his family." Early story treatments by studio writers Ben Markson and Lillie Hayward, under Zanuck's supervision, depicted the "fellow" as an accomplished tap dancer, struggling for breaks in the New York entertainment world who accidentally gets mixed up with a criminal element. So specifically was the script being tailored for Cagney, under Zanuck, that Markson and Hayward recommended reusing the ending of *The Public Enemy*—the scene in which the mummied figure of Tom Powers falls into the camera—in *Fingerman* to exploit Cagney's climbing popularity. "The use of an actual reproduced scene from *The Public Enemy*," the writers argued in a memo to Warners' executives, "that is still in the memory of everybody, might be a very novel and interesting way of finishing the picture."

This last treatment, dated March 31, 1933, inventively attempted to meld the "tough guy" and the song-and-dance Cagney into the same figure, ergo satisfying both Cagney and presumed audience expectations. But Wallis came aboard

Manhandling Mae Clarke — again — in LADY KILLER.

in mid-April. In notes pencilled in the margin of the Markson–Hayward treatment, Wallis, or one of his subordinates, discarded the basic ''tough dancer'' conceit, rejected the *Public Enemy* idea, and instead ordered *Fingerman* revised to suit Cagney's studio-restricted image. ''Develop tough, hard-boiled, cocksure Cagney—knows it all,'' went the decree, ''Gets start in gangster craze—women like because of roughness—treats everybody as a moll—he must start tough and rough.''

By the time *Fingerman* came before the cameras as *Lady Killer* later in 1933, with director Roy Del Ruth at the helm, the revisions, specifically to enhance Cagney's ''roughness,'' were dramatic. In the film version, the main character, Dan Quigley (Cagney), is no longer a tap-dancer; in fact, Cagney does not dance an iota in the entire picture. Quigley is a brash but lowly theatre usher who, as the story evolves, becomes embroiled with a ruthless gang of con artists when he discovers their flourishing operations and muscles in. When one of the ''pigeons" accidentally dies, Quigley escapes to Hollywood where he changes his name and performs as an "extra"—doing cameos as an Indian and an eighteenth-century romeo—before zooming up to star status, partly on the basis of fan letters he ghosts himself.*

The Hollywood satire is the real grist of *Lady Killer*—which is not to say that Cagney does not thrash his way courageously, unseriously, through the whole episodic storyline. But what is interesting about *Lady Killer* is the degree to which the seeds of excess in Cagney's persona were a matter of studio edict; how that alienated him; and how, indeed, that impaired his movies. In accordance with the studio's insistence that "women [should] like him because of roughness," in the screen rendition of *Fingerman*, the Quigley character was developed into a ruffianish "lady killer"—to the point of absurdity. His extraordinary hostility toward gang moll Myra (poor Mae Clarke—also the victim of *Public Enemy*'s indulgences) may have been justified as action for the camera, but as drama it was poorly motivated. In one scene Cagney drags the actress by her hair the entire length of a room, then bodily tosses her out of his suite. It is without exception the most violent scene in terms of treatment of women that Cagney ever performed. Yet in the movie it is played unabashedly for laughs.

Costar Margaret Lindsay, colorless here as glamour queen Lois Underwood, fared little better in the script. In one key scene, Quigley attends a gala birthday party in her honor. Because she has mockingly requested monkeys, elephants, and a Swiss band as her birthday present, Quigley triumphantly delivers monkeys, elephants, and a Swiss band into the midst of her chic Hollywood affair. Bedlam ensues. The animals run wild. Quigley laughs uproariously as Underwood, the woman he theoretically adores, hysterically bursts into tears. (A coda was written into the script in which the guests join in Quigley's laughter when they finally comprehend the joke—but most likely, it was dropped during filming.) It is a totally irrational scene—which is also intended to be *funny*. Anarchy in Cagney's persona was one thing, but writers, directors, and producers conspired to block all possibility of a serious relationship or screen romance. In this context it is easy to appreciate why so many of Cagney's female costars turned out to be plain, disappointing, and, in advance of the fact, forgettable.

Enter, Michael Curtiz

After *Lady Killer*, Cagney starred in *Jimmy the Gent*, a breakneck screwball comedy that marked his first association with one of the studio's most versatile and consistently entertaining directors, Michael Curtiz. Thus *Jimmy the Gent* is more stylish than average Warners' fare, more free-wheeling. In the Bertram Milhauser scenario Cagney is Jimmy Corrigan, "Personal Contacts," a frenzied, impulsive tracker of missing heirs to unclaimed inheritances—finding the long-

---

*This was supposed to be an "inside joke" in the film colony in 1933, because indeed there were reported to be ex-criminals of every sort making their living under aliases as "extras" in Hollywood.

With Allen Jenkins and Bette Davis in Michael Curtiz's screwball comedy
JIMMY THE GENT. (AMPAS)

lost relatives regardless of whether or not they actually exist. His closest rival in the dubious occupation is the gentlemanly Wallingham (Alan Dinehart), who is just as unscrupulous though he serves tea to his clients. Wallingham's secretary, in turn, is Joan (young, blonde-haired Bette Davis), who used to work for Corrigan before being smitten by Wallingham's pretense of chivalry.

In this early pass at comedy, Davis is too abrasive to be very likeable, and Cagney—looking eerie with close-cropped hair and eyes like dark slits—seems fueled by the friction between them into a hypersonic state. As the story unspools, Corrigan's quest for heirs becomes secondary to his manic search for the proper social graces with which to impress his clients and Joan. ''Ethics! Ethics! Who's got ethics?! Am I a gentleman or ain't I?'' he screams at one point, after being affronted by Joan. Then he slaps his sorry assistant Louie (Allen Jenkins) around like a punching bag and winds up his tantrum by heaving a rock through his own office window. ''Sure, boss,'' the harassed Louie replies, ''you been a sucker for ethics all your life!'' Though Corrigan is reluctant to halt certain of his more unsavory practices, such as paying stoolies in Wallingham's employ, he does allow his secretaries to begin serving tea. And in the blissful ending to

*With Joan Blondell in their last teaming-up, HE WAS HER MAN.
(UCLA Film Archives)*

this giddy tale, Corrigan beats Wallingham to a fortune, unmasks his skullduggery and reconciles with Joan — to be married (!). "Ethics!" he exults, hugging Joan as the picture fades, "I'm just crawling with ethics!"

He Was Her Man

He Was Her Man is the most unusual example of Cagney and Blondell's teamwork, as well as the most serious, the most thoughtful. The story is credited to Robert Lord who, when asked to come up with a low-budget dramatic vehicle for the popular costars, suggested a variation on his own *One Way Passage*, made earlier in 1932 with Kay Francis and William Powell. Tom Buckingham and Niven Busch provided the actual script—which had Cagney as a doomed gangster-on-the-lam, wistfully crossing paths with ex-prostitute Blondell, beginning a new life. "Cagney liked the idea," recalled Busch, "although he liked pictures with a little more action in them and where he came up the winner."

In *He Was Her Man* Cagney decidedly comes up the loser: He is Flicker Hayes, a criminal with a shady past being pursued by vengeful double-crossed rivals. Hayes meets and falls in love with a reformed prostitute, Rose Lawrence (Blondell), who has entered a mail-order marriage contract with a gentle-spirited Portuguese fisherman (Victor Jory). Travelling together, Hayes and Lawrence are drawn to each other gradually, ineluctably, until the moment when Hayes is cornered by his appointed assassins and must spurn her in a pose of bravado to spare her from the line of fire. "You're just trying to let me down easy," she tells him, suspecting his sacrifice, aware of the killers waiting within view. His face betraying no weakness of emotion, Hayes bades her a jaunty goodbye and rides off with the gunmen to the edge of a nearby cliff. "Nice day for it," he mutters. "Nice day for what?" rasps one of the thugs. "The wedding," Hayes answers. As the words escape from his mouth, Hayes is cut down by gunfire, the sound muffled by church bells in the distance—pealing for the wedding of Rose and the fisherman.

Though *He Was Her Man* has its clichéd aspects (the buxom, fawning character of the fisherman's mother, for example), it features a fully assured Cagney and Blondell in a minor key. This, their eighth film together, was also unaccountably their last. Why Warners chose to break them up at this point in their respective careers is yet another riddle—though it may have something to do with Blondell's astute and sympathetic portrayal of a former prostitute and the reaction which undoubtedly fulminated from the Hays Office. Never again did Cagney find such a durable and appropriate female costar. The actresses who followed Blondell were, for the most part, playing meek and complacent women, or worse, characters such as Mae Clarke's to be shoved and tossed around— witness Virginia Mayo in *White Heat*, Doris Day in *Love Me Or Leave Me*, or Arlene Francis in *One, Two, Three*.

Here Comes O'Brien

Here Comes the Navy was a trivial romp that proved so successful it spawned an embarrassment of quasi-sequels. The original is a seafaring comedy–drama with Navy swab Cagney butting up against hard-headed senior officer Pat O'Brien—described by one critic as "the cinema's most skilled exponent of the rapid-fire delivery"—in the pattern-setting first of their eight "you-hit-me-and-I'll-hit-you" films. All the worn ingredients of the Cagney–O'Brien bouillabaisse were introduced at the outset here: the tedious rivalry over the female ingenue (Gloria Stuart), the loyalty to Cagney of froggy pal Frank McHugh, the abundance of slugfests, and the ridiculous heroics that redeem the Cagney character before the end title. It is fun, nothing special, albeit much admired—Oscar-nominated as Best Picture of 1934—in its day. Lloyd Bacon directed, while Ben Markson and Earl Baldwin collaborated on the script. The writers should have been credited for *Devil Dogs of the Air* (the airborne version) and *The Fighting 69th* (the WWI combat version), too, as characters, dialogue, and plot—not to mention a basic idea—were lifted practically wholesale for the imitations.

There was a dichotomy in the Cagney–O'Brien relationship onscreen that was pure and tensile to audiences. Whether as a policeman (in *The Irish in Us*), a priest (*Angels with Dirty Faces, The Fighting 69th*), a military officer (*Here Comes the Navy, Devil Dogs of the Air*), or a banana plantation imperialist (*Torrid Zone*), O'Brien represented scowling authority while Cagney signified contempt for that status quo. O'Brien may have been "top dog"—but the storyline always revealed Cagney to be the "moral" victor. For example, Cagney always "got the girl." Bland and sexless by comparison, O'Brien was never rewarded with the elusive sweetheart when Cagney was around. Not that their pictures together (with the possible exception of *Angels with Dirty Faces*) are profoundly dialectical; more the opposite. Indeed, one critic complained that Cagney's beefs in *Here Comes the Navy* are so easily resolved by the curlicues of plot that he ends up being an "amiable recruiting poster" for the military. But moviegoers got the point anyway.

It is noteworthy that O'Brien joined Cagney as a "hyphenate" the year Blondell disappeared—a tough man substituting for a tough woman. In their banter and camaraderie and in the uneasy fulcrum of their oneupmanship, Cagney and O'Brien captured the essence of many male friendships. The undercurrent was love. Indeed it can be argued that their films are love stories between men, with Warners capitalizing on the bosom friendship between the two actors and Cagney and O'Brien adding touches and nuances to make their closeness palpable to audiences. Cagney has recalled how he embellished his relationship with O'Brien in *Ceiling Zero* by throwing his arm around him at points in the story, hugging him unabashedly—thus accommodating what is generally regarded as a Hawksian conceit of male bonding. That sort of physical attachment between the two also crops up in *The Irish in Us* and *Torrid Zone*. So too do Cagney and O'Brien refer to each other (jokingly, but with affection) as "dear" or "sweetheart" (in *Here Comes the Navy, Devil Dogs of the Air, Ceiling Zero*, and *Torrid Zone*).

With his male costars—among them, later on, Edmond O'Brien in *White Heat*, Dan Dailey in *What Price, Glory?*, and John Derek in *Run for Cover*—Cagney could get away with an intimacy, a warmth, that seemed utterly credible because he had no compunctions about evoking it. In *Here Comes the Navy* Chesty O'Connor's (Cagney) friendship with Droopy (Frank McHugh) is so expansive that Droopy plaintively blows O'Connor a kiss when the miscreant sailor departs the *U.S.S. Arizona* for transfer, prompting a nearby sailor, unnerved by the spectacle, to crack, "Oh swift, what are you two guys, a couple of violets?" Yet that spontaneous exchange, so delightful and so casual, a reflex, a throwaway, was readily understood and acceptable to audiences within the otherwise traditionally male context of a Cagney picture.

Another tension sustained the duo of Cagney–O'Brien through their eight slap-happy pictures—the tension of two stars of parallel stature (although Cagney always received top billing and top money), essentially dramatic actors developing as a tandem box-office attraction. Independent of Cagney, O'Brien

*Authority vs. rebellion: Pat O'Brien and Cagney in their first shouting match,
HERE COMES THE NAVY.*

was a competent though relatively uninteresting performer; it was only when
rubbed against the sandpaper of Cagney that he seemed to gleam and sparkle.
Friends they were, but it *was* a career rivalry, too—and O'Brien eventually tired
of his typecasting (vis à vis Cagney), complaining about it publicly. "Jimmy is
grand to work with," he told a reporter in the early 1940s. "I think one picture a
year with Cagney would be fine. But, as it is, I've been with him in every
uniform—the army, the navy, the police, the marines, the air corps—and it's
always a case of me falling in love with his girl, or him falling in love with mine.
It gets tiresome." Except for *Ragtime*—in which they do not appear together in
the same scene—the advent of the 1940s and *Torrid Zone* spelled the end of their
working partnership; and O'Brien's solo career, while never very stable, finally
began to pay off with his spitfire performance as the legendary football coach in
Knute Rockne—All-American.

St. Louis Kid **and** *Devil Dogs of the Air*

Less successful than *Here Comes the Navy*, and less innocuous, was *The St.
Louis Kid*, also released in 1934. Directed by Ray Enright from the "B" unit, *Kid*

With stock company regular Allen Jenkins in ST. LOUIS KID.

was a weak, confused comedy–drama with Cagney as Eddie Kennedy, a combative, happy-go-lucky truck driver on the St. Louis-to-Chicago milk run who becomes a grinning, unconscionable scab when oppressed dairymen call a strike and set up picketlines. After swapping insults with his leading lady (Patricia Ellis), Cagney/Kennedy takes a bum rap for the company goons who have murdered a striking dairyman—at which point the drama and the political issues involved take a nosedive. Coming at the time of a national "milk trust" scandal, *Kid* could have been timely and influential—but writers Warren Duff and Seton I. Miller were sidetracked by the usual amorphous romantic and underworld fixations. As it is, *St. Louis Kid* is notable mainly for sap Allen Jenkins as comic relief and for an improvised Cagney monologue in which he rhapsodizes about the joys of country life. Otherwise, *Kid* is an embarrassment from any standpoint, distinguished according to *Time* magazine only because "it shows James Cagney receiving a cuff on the jaw from his leading lady instead of giving her one."

Vying with *St. Louis Kid* for the dregs is *Devil Dogs of the Air*, Cagney's next picture, which was coproduced by Cosmopolitan Productions, the William Randolph Hearst affiliated unit situated on the Warners' lot in the mid-1930s. This was ironic, to say the least, considering the Hearst press's vigilance against

Publicity pose for DEVIL DOGS OF THE AIR. (WCTR)

Cagney's politics in its news columns; and because *Dogs* was little more than a flimsy rewrite of *Here Comes the Navy*, a thinly veiled military preparedness tract. The story had Cagney as an arrogant stunt flyer enamored of a local waitress (Margaret Lindsay) and locked in macho competition with Lieutenant William Brannigan (Pat O'Brien) of the Marine Flying Corps. Except for some okay aerial photography, it was already old stuff—O'Brien granite, Cagney the chiseller; Lindsay, insufferably cloying; Frank McHugh, skulking about with a smirk on his face. All of it tied up into a neat package with Cagney's *apologia* at the finis.

Parenthetically, this moment of contrition or apology was becoming an expected and repeated gimmick in Cagney's movies, not unlike the presence of his

Role reversal: on the side of the law with Robert Armstrong in G-MEN. (WCTR)

"mother," for it was seen as another redeeming trait in the psychology of moviegoers. It could take the form of dialogue or action. In *Lady Killer*, Dan Quigley (Cagney) assaults a policeman as he is being jailed, but catches himself and murmurs, "I'm sorry." A near-identical situation occurs in *The Roaring Twenties* when underworld kingpin Eddie Bartlett (Cagney) savagely attacks ex-partner Lloyd Hart (Jeffrey Lynn) after Hart has run off with club singer Jean Sherman (Priscilla Lane). In the midst of his jealous rage Bartlett stops abruptly, murmurs "I'm sorry," turns, and staggers away. The Cagney apologia is carried to extreme lengths by his face-saving martyrdoms in such movies as *Ceiling Zero*, *The Fighting 69th*, and *Captains of the Clouds*. But comparable acts of redemption happen in nearly every Cagney story; indeed, there may not be another major Hollywood star who had to go to jail or *die* so often to keep the moralists happy.

Cagney as a G-Man

The adventures of crime exterminator Melvin Purvis, the FBI agent credited with stalking John Dillinger to his grave, were the inspiration (or lack of it) for *G-Men*, adapted by Seton I. Miller from Gregory Roger's book *Public Enemy No.*

The family ethic: with Frank McHugh, Mary Gordon, Olivia de Havilland, and Pat O'Brien in THE IRISH IN US. (WCTR)

1. Unexpectedly, Cagney did *not* play the Dillinger prototype: In a conversion designed to mollify the Hays Office as well as to inaugurate a new cycle of "reform" gangster pictures, Cagney played Brick Davis, an upright lawyer who joins the ranks of the special forces after an old college buddy turned G-Man is gunned down by ruthless mobsters. The casting reversal was a clever ruse, congenial to Cagney, and milked by the studio for all the publicity it was worth. "Hollywood's Most Famous Bad Man Joins the 'G-Men' and Halts the March of Crime," blared the Warners' advertisements.

Predictably, Cagney made for one cool, confident gangbuster, but the story itself was pat and schematic, with a surfeit of gunplay and felonies to satisfy the action crowd. In his first solo credit as Cagney's director—in filmland—William Keighley proved resourceful in charting the violent choreography of such scenes as the climactic shootout at a rural hideaway in Wisconsin, an incident patterned after one on Dillinger's own road to his demise. And Ann Dvorak, who does a musical turn as a nightclub chanteuse, injects a note of unforeseen pathos as Davis's female acquaintance trapped in her marriage to sullen "public enemy" Barton MacLane. But haughty Margaret Lindsay makes little sense as Davis's romantic counterpart, and Robert Armstrong, stodgy as Davis's FBI superior (who is, conveniently so, Lindsay's "brother"), rides an artificial current of enmity with Cagney into the ground. Whatever its flaws, *G-Men* was regarded as first-rate melodrama in its day. Wrote one reviewer: "*G-Men* is James Cagney's best picture since *The Public Enemy*." One of Cagney's enduring if lesser efforts, the film was rereleased 15 years later, in 1949, on the occasion of the 25th anniversary of the FBI, with a newly-filmed prologue enacted by real-life agents to promote the agency's mythology.

The Irish in Us

Only a trifle like *The Irish In Us*, also released in 1935, could have followed such a conscious piece of solemn good citizenship as *G-Men*—and, conversely, *Irish* is a capriccio whose obvious lack of aspiration somehow pays off in goofy, loose-jointed comedy and ensemble high spirits. Remembered cast member Allen Jenkins: "The script was a weak sister and the director [Lloyd Bacon] said, 'Boys, anything you can think up, put in.' It was an 18-day picture, a B picture frankly, and it made $2 million." Studio records show that numerous writers (among them, Malcolm Stuart Boylan, Seton I. Miller, and Warren Duff) took a whack at the original story by Frank Orsatti—with its title, *The Irish In Us*, too tempting to be passed up by a studio casting department with Cagney, Pat O'Brien, and Frank McHugh on call—before Earl Baldwin, chronically ill, ended up with the screenplay credit between hospital spells. Even so, "the boys" did their share of script embroidery during filming.

The premise was humble: A closely-knit Irish family, composed of a pampering mother (Mary Gordon, of whom *Time* magazine observed, her "brogue is so strong that, to the possible improvement of the picture, half her lines are virtually unintelligible") and three rowdy, quarrelsome "boys" (O'Brien as a cop, McHugh as a fireman, and Cagney as a ne'er-do-well who manages prize fighters), is torn asunder by jealousy over pretty Lucille Jackson (Olivia De Havilland) and by the antics of a Cagney-trained contender dubbed Car-Barn McCarthy (Allen Jenkins), who comes up swinging every time he hears a bell, be it telephone or ringside. What happens? A la *Footlight Parade*, Cagney is called upon to stand in for Car-Barn at the last minute and perform some fancy fisticuffs in the ring—winning the big match, the girl, family respect, and so on and so forth. The whole implausible story is rendered so off-handedly, larded with soft Irish music and sentiment, that the movie is simple, unassuming jollity.

A Midsummer Night's Dream

After *The Irish In Us*, Cagney was enlisted as part of an all-star cast for one of the most lavish and highly-touted Warners productions of the 1930s, *A Midsummer Night's Dream*, William Shakespeare's classic fantasy–comedy. It was one of

Rehearsing for A MIDSUMMER NIGHT'S DREAM in 1935 with (l to r) Joe E. Brown, Mickey Rooney, Dewey Robinson, Arthur Treacher, Frank McHugh, Otis Harlan, Cagney, Hugh Herbert, director Max Reinhardt, and dialogue director Stanley Logan. (MOMA)

the studio's rare, early stabs at committing the great Bard to film and was initiated by the wild acclaim accorded a Hollywood Bowl production of *Dream* by European theatrical eminence Max Reinhardt (who had fled his homeland to escape Hitler) earlier in the decade. At producer Hal Wallis's urging, Reinhardt was approached to mastermind the film version of *Dream*, with his former protegee, German emigrant William Dieterle, cosigned as director, on the theory that Dieterle would help translate Reinhardt's bum English as well as his fine stage techniques into cinema. Besides Cagney, cast as the rapscallion Bottom, the lineup included Dick Powell as Lysander, Joe E. Brown as Flute, Jean Muir as Helena, Hugh Herbert as Snout, Ian Hunter as Theseus, Frank McHugh as Quince, Victor Jory as Oberon, Olivia De Havilland as Hermia, Anita Louise as Titania, Arthur Treacher as Ninny's Tomb, and Mickey Rooney as the fairy sprite Puck.

Prepossessing though it seemed, *Dream* fell short of being an ideal, trouble-free production. "The long association of Reinhardt and Dieterle did little to stop the endless arguing which arose regarding the direction of the players," reported William R. Meyer, writing in *Warner Brothers Directors* (Arlington House, 1978).

After three weeks of shooting, the production was almost shelved when it was discovered that designer Anton Grot's forest could barely be photographed. Grot's Expressionistic creation consisted of trees composed of burlap coated with plaster of Paris, real leaves applied one at a time, and painted silver. The tree branches were so huge that the camera could only pick up small sections in one shot—and the forest ran over two sets. Ernest Haller, the original cameraman, who worked so well with Edmund Goulding [another Warners' contract director], was replaced at Dieterle's insistence by Hal Mohr. Mohr, an expert at lighting, immediately informed [Jack] Warner and Dieterle that the set would have to be severely altered. The following weekend, Mohr and crew proceeded to unclutter the forest, and they substituted a single light source in place of Haller's variety.

With the snarl-ups common knowledge in Hollywood, skepticism and cynicism mounted and supplanted initially favorable expectations, in part accounting for the harsh—at best, mixed—critical reaction greeting the film upon its release in 1935. "Fairly tedious," sniffed Otis Ferguson in *The New Republic*. "The chief fault of this production of *A Midsummer Night's Dream* is that it shows little or no regard for Shakespearean poetry," said *The London Times*. "The rhythm and the verse are for the most part ignored. The lines are so broken up, so disconnected by intervening photographic shots intended to relieve the tedium of speech, that the metre is almost completely destroyed." Yet then as now, critics debated the merits of this work of highbrow culture by Hollywood's lowbrow studio, and the film did have its defenders, chief among them Andre Sennwald of *The New York Times*, who eloquently countered, "Whatever its flaws, it is a work of high ambitions and unflagging interest. Hollywood pursues the shapes and shadows of the unfettered imagination with courage, skill and heavy artillery in Max Reinhardt's film version of *A Midsummer Night's Dream*. . . . For the work is rich in aspiration and the sum of its faults is dwarfed against the sheer bulk of the enterprise. It has its fun and its haunting beauty."

Certainly it is not a Shakespeare for purists, who were no doubt taken aback. The musical arrangements of Mendelssohn's music by Viennese composer Erich Wolfgang Korngold (brought to America by Reinhardt for this purpose), Grot's art direction, the camerawork, the costumes, makeup and special effects, the dance ensembles by Bronislava Nijinska and Nini Theilade—these were dazzling, and there were Oscar nominations for the craft achievements (as well as for Best Picture of 1935). But the technical glitter only served to clash with some of the more neovaudevillian performances and with the "broad stage gestures" of the actors that Cagney, in his autobiography, blamed on the film inexperience of Reinhardt. Cagney came in for the same flak as the other players—more so, considering the anticipation for his performance—so that even someone like Sennwald, one of the film's champions, wrote him off as disappointing. "As Bottom, the lack-wit weaver whom Puck maliciously endows with an ass's head," wrote Sennwald, "James Cagney is too dynamic an actor to play the

Doing Shakespeare with Joe E. Brown in A MIDSUMMER NIGHT'S DREAM. (WCTR)

torpid and obstinate dullard. While he is excellent in the scenes in the wood, in the 'Pyramus and Thisbe' masque he belabors the slapstick of his part beyond endurance.''

But if Cagney's Bottom is a failure, which is arguable, at the very least it is an ''honorable failure,'' in Andrew Sarris's words, and a mesmerizing one. ''As Bottom,'' Cagney says in his autobiography, diffidently, ''I simply had another job to do, and I did it." Yet the key to appreciating his bombastic portrayal is that Cagney played Bottom with the exuberant vulgarity of—well—of part gutter-snipe and part vaudeville clown. It was *Cagney* in a Shakespearean mode. When he spits on his hands before reciting verse in the play within a play, it is a gesture borrowed not from the Elizabethan tradition but from the city streets and tank-town circuitry. Critics who took offense at this *Dream* did not grant that what might be irreverent Shakespeare was, in this case, mighty reverent War-ners. In his autobiography, *Laughter Is a Wonderful Thing* (New York: A.S. Barnes, 1956), cast member Joe E. Brown described the ensemble strategy:

> Some of us were certainly not Shakespearean actors. Besides myself from the circus and burlesque, there was Jimmy Cagney from the chorus and Hugh Herbert from burlesque. At the beginning we went into a huddle and decided to follow the classic traditions in which Herbert and I were brought up. I really believe Shakespeare would have liked the way we handled his low comedy and I'm sure the Minsky Brothers did. The Bard's words may have been spoken better but never bigger or louder.

Frisco Kid

Also released in 1935 was *Frisco Kid*, with Cagney back in form as Bat Morgan, a "dog-eat-dog" Barbary Coast sailor who strongarms his way to rule and riches among the less-civilized denizens of San Francisco in the Gay Nineties. Morgan earns his rep by killing the notorious hook-armed Shanghai Duck (Fred Kohler) in a barroom brawl; then he becomes the top stooge for crooked politico James Daley (Joseph King). Their dynasty of sin is toppled by a gun-toting mob of vigilantes—even as Morgan is being romanced, and proselytized, by a pretty moralist who just happens to be the local crusading newspaper editor (Margaret Lindsay). Dressed in a fancy wing collar, vest, and brocaded waistcoat, his hair curled effeminately, Cagney submitted a portrayal that vacillated between the attitudes of a roughneck and a conscience-troubled hero, taking neither pose too seriously. *Frisco Kid* does have its inducements—atmospheric settings, the scowling performance of Barton MacLane as villain Spider Burke, the anguished dying of pal Solly (George E. Stone) in Bat Morgan's arms, and the extravagant, unruly riot sequence at the finale. But the story (by Warren Duff and Seton I. Miller, who were becoming Cagney's most active scenarists) amounted to little more than boilerplate, and Lloyd Bacon's direction could not compare with the high gloss of the Samuel Goldwyn production of *Barbary Coast*, directed by Howard Hawks, also released in 1935.

Ceiling Zero

The year, 1935, came to a finish for the busy star with the filming of Howard Hawks's *Ceiling Zero*, a Cosmopolitan Production for Warners that involved the

Barbary Coast romance with Margaret Lindsay in FRISCO KID.
(UCLA Film Archives)

proficient ensemble of Cagney, Pat O'Brien, June Travis (an appealing ingenue, daughter of a Chicago White Sox executive, whose motion picture career was fleeting), Stuart Erwin, Isabel Jewell, and Barton MacLane. A prestigious stage hit about courageous pilots who fly air mail missions during dangerous ''ceiling zero''—or low fog curtain—weather, *Ceiling Zero* was penned by Frank ''Spig'' Wead, a well known aviator and athlete who injured his spine in a household accident and thereafter became a writer. (His life was celebrated by director John Ford in his 1957 production of *The Wings of Eagles*, with John Wayne playing ''Spig.'') Hawks brought in noted writer Morrie Ryskind to touch-up Wead's play for film purposes, which gives some idea of the esteem Warners held for the project—but Ryskind goes uncredited because Wead threatened to take the matter to grievance.

The *Ceiling Zero* experience was not an altogether happy one for Hawks, who steered clear of Warners for another five years afterward, returning only in 1941 for *Sergeant York*. For one thing, the Production Code office totted up a list of objections to the script that included Dizzy Davis's (Cagney's) characterization as ''an habitual seducer who cheerfully deserted his victims'' and any indications that Davis commits suicide at the movie's conclusion—both key story points on which Hawks managed to walk a tightrope. In addition, letters with the implied threat of legal action were exchanged between the studio and commercial airline

*With director Howard Hawks on
the set of CEILING ZERO.
(Howard Hawks Collection,
Brigham Young University)*

officials who fretted that "the public will confuse that pioneering, experimental era [of *Ceiling Zero*] with the high safety, comfort and speed of air transport today." This, too, Hawks tactfully handled. But Hawks did not cozy up to Wallis, who was less in awe of the director than Zanuck had been; and Wallis pestered Hawks with memos advising him on everything from June Travis's hairdo to Pat O'Brien's incessant "barking" style of delivery. Hawks preferred to work in a leisurely manner, while Wallis was continually pressing him to speed-up. Memos from Wallis complained (as in one, dated October 14, 1935) that the director was "getting next to nothing in his dailies" and "at this rate we won't finish the picture until Christmas."

The imperturbable Hawks persevered, finishing in six weeks, including one generously alloted to rehearsals. The result was a gutty, perceptive, tension-racked melodrama with Cagney splendid as the flamboyant flyer whose devil-may-care lifestyle causes the air-crash death of a close buddy—as well as, eventually, his own. It is one of the finest Cagney–O'Brien vehicles, as dramatic and emotional in its own way as *Angels with Dirty Faces*. Hawks stripped the duo of some of their more calculated antagonisms and concentrated instead on their characters' deep bond of friendship. The nuances provided by the real-life friends ironically enhanced the "pansy quality" of the story that had been among the objections of the Production Code office. In one scene, for example, as Cagney is talking on the telephone, O'Brien's hand drifts lazily up Cagney's

Do-or-die with Pat O'Brien in Howard Hawks's CEILING ZERO (WCTR)

neck and rests there, stroking his pal as if he were a favorite cat. The two are forever exchanging winks, glances, and knowing smiles at each other's innuendoes and shared secrets. In these scenes, and in the over-all masculine ambience of *Ceiling Zero*, Hawks demonstrated his sensitivity to the Cagney–O'Brien friendship and stretched the boundaries of Cagney's screen persona.

The Looming Confrontation

The tally for Cagney was 15 pictures since his 1932 walk-out, an average of *five* annually—up one from the number that had been guaranteed to him as the limit in private conversation with Jack Warner. It was not a pace *or* a level of quality that gratified Cagney. He continued to be upset about the story choices, the supporting casts, the lesser directors, and the cost cutting. The star was openly derisive about such movies as *Picture Snatcher, Devil Dogs of the Air, St. Louis Kid, Frisco Kid*, and some of the others. But his protests were to no avail; he was under contract. The high-pressure calendar did not abate, however, and when, in April of 1935, Cagney was ordered to appear for night filming for *G-Men*, he simply refused and went home for an early dinner. Lawyers for both sides skirmished on that one, but Warners was forced to back off because Cagney's schedule was too crucial to be interrupted for a suspension. After that, it was only a matter of time before there would be a more substantive confrontation.

The real Cagney: At home reading in the mid-1930s. (WCTR)

5
Grand National

No one can blame me for getting a bit annoyed with this business of striking women in every one of my pictures. It has been going on for some time now. In each succeeding picture, I approach such scenes with a sinking feeling. The film audiences seem to have found it novel when I first did it in The Public Enemy. *They clamored for more. The writers of all my pictures have written it into the scripts, and the directors have followed it up by directing it into the pictures.*
JAMES CAGNEY
The New York Herald, 1935

By 1936 Cagney and Warner Brothers were at swords' points. Despite what he believed were oral assurances from Jack Warner to the contrary, Cagney had been averaging five films annually since the 1932 settlement instead of the agreed-upon four. Though his salary was now up to $4500 weekly, Warners withheld $1250 per week in an escrow account as indemnity against Cagney's illness or bad behavior, meaning that over $50,000 yearly was in abeyance. Other studios offered Cagney as much as $100,000 per picture for his services, but Jack Warner refused to loan out his disgruntled star. When Cagney looked for an attorney to help him break his contract, noted entertainment lawyer W. I. Gilbert told him that he could win the case, but if he did, Cagney would never work in motion pictures again. Cagney's agent George Frank quit when informed of the actor's plans—and was promptly replaced by William Cagney, who assumed management of his brother's affairs.*

The studio hierarchy was a step ahead of Cagney and orchestrated a showdown. One week before Christmas 1935, the actor was assigned to participate in a story conference with director Lloyd Bacon and writers Tom Reed and Robert

---

*Frank, who stood to gain thousands of dollars in agent's fees if Cagney stayed with Warners, subsequently testified against Cagney, his own former client, at the trial. Devotees of the lexicon of Varietyese might like to take note of *Daily Variety's* gleeful double-entendre headline at the time, "Cagney Agent Fings Actor in WB Suit."

Lord for a prison melodrama called *Over the Wall*. Cagney was to play the part of "Bam Craig"—to be followed, according to items leaked to the trade papers, by roles in a musical called *Stage Struck* and *The Adventures of Robin Hood* (in the title role subsequently played by Errol Flynn). Predictably, Cagney did not attend the conference, and he was duly suspended.* Then, in February of 1936, Cagney formalized the breach by filing suit against Warner Brothers, alleging that in his oral agreement with Jack Warner four years earlier he had been deviously seduced into appearing so frequently in motion pictures that it was detrimental to his box-office draw and future earnings ability.

The Cagney lawsuit was unprecedented and sent shock waves through the Hollywood establishment. It came at a time when there was already much union and legal ferment on the scene—with Mae West and Marlene Dietrich, among others, already in court against their employer studios. "While on the surface the [Cagney vs. Warners] legal battle is supposedly just a star vs. studio tiff," *The Hollywood Reporter* noted in a page-one banner headline article, "insiders see it not only as the most drastic legal attack on the traditional option form of contract, but also as the opening wedge for the Screen Actors and Writers Guild to force their long sought standard form of contract on the producers, should Cagney win." Cagney gave interviews to the press, blasting Warners for forcing him into such films as *Devil Dogs of the Air*, "which had no reason to be filmed under any circumstances." Insiders realized that Cagney's demands for approving story, supporting cast, and director hit as hard (if not harder) at the studio's dominion as his financial demands.

The trial opened to much fanfare and world-wide reportage in early 1936. The joke around Hollywood was that the trial boasted an all-star cast, since many of Cagney's witnesses had participated in the Academy arbitration in 1932—including actor Frederic March, who testified in his *Anthony Adverse* plumage, arriving straight from the set. March had been warned by a certain well-known producer that testifying for Cagney would jeopardize his blossoming career, but he bravely took the stand anyway to affirm that he was privy to remarks made by Jack Warner in 1932 to the effect that Cagney would only be obliged to make four pictures a year. Later, Warner was to deny this repeatedly on the stand.

The highlight of the one-week hearing was undoubtedly the appearance of J. L. himself, who was grilled on the witness stand for four hours by attorney Gilbert, coached from the sidelines by William Cagney. The mutual antagonism between Warner and his number-one drawing card was paraded before the world press, which reported that the two "glowered" at each other across the counsel tables. Warner testified that Cagney had been a "headache" to him ever since his arrival in Hollywood in 1930. Red-faced and perspiring, under relentless attack from Gilbert, Warner seemed harassed and took refuge at times in his

---

*When actor-pal Pat O'Brien was substituted for Cagney in *Stage Struck*, he too refused and was briefly suspended. *Over the Wall* was never produced, with the studio claiming that nobody but Cagney could play the lead.

faulty memory. Gilbert alleged that Warner did not specify the number of pictures Cagney would have to make in his 1932 contract, because he was fearful of his brother Harry's reaction, not to mention that of other overworked Warners' players. Warner was flustered but he did not yield, insisting that he had never promised to limit the number of Cagney pictures in an "asserted oral agreement" with the actor.

One week later the judgment was delivered by Judge Charles L. Bogue of the Superior Court in Burbank, and it was a bombshell. The decision was in Cagney's favor. But the court ducked the major issues of suspension, the continuous option contract, and the alleged oral agreement, seizing instead on a billing (i.e. Cagney's formal positioning in the credits) irregularity tacked onto the lawsuit practically as an afterthought, and finding that irregularity "neither casual nor inadvertent." The billing in question ("See 'Ceiling Zero,' the tensely exciting drama of the air starring Pat O'Brien and James Cagney during its simultaneous run at the Warner Bros. Hollywood and Downtown Theaters") gave O'Brien first mention during the run of *Ceiling Zero* at Los Angeles area theaters—a clear violation of Cagney's written contract. Though the court ruling was less than decisive about the larger matters involved, the judge did enjoin Warners from interfering with Cagney so the actor could make deals elsewhere. The Cagneys rejoiced. J. L., meantime, announced his intention to appeal the verdict to the California Supreme Court.

Within a fortnight, Cagney made his first appearance as an "independent," and it was a symbolic one—on a Shell Saturday night radio broadcast of Maxwell Anderson's toney *Winterset*. It would be months before he emoted in front of cameras again, however, for no one in Hollywood wanted to risk the wrath of Jack Warner, who was furious and humiliated. No company wanted to risk being blackballed from the Warner chain of moviehouses. Quietly, the word went out among the studio autocracy: Cagney was to be blacklisted. Talks with Darryl Zanuck at Fox, with Samuel O. Goldwyn and with David O. Selznick went nowhere. "Jimmy was the hottest star in the business," remembered William Cagney, "but nobody would have him. I would get right up to the point of signature with some of these companies and suddenly they'd run screaming from the room they were so frightened." An account in *The New York Times* read, "Though rated among the top box-office draws of the time, Cagney remained inactive for a year and it was generally believed in Hollywood that other studios were reluctant to hire him lest they be placed in the position of encouraging a 'rebellious actor.'" It was common knowledge in the industry, the *Times* reported, that "other players, notably Bette Davis [who later sued Warner Brothers herself], were eyeing Cagney's efforts and should the Cagney situation work out, it's possible that there will be considerable contract jumping."

Meanwhile, reaction built in the global press. The court suit seemed to be hurting Cagney not just in actual dollars, but also in the distortion of his motives. Fan magazines took sides, and few were bold or perceptive enough to side with

Cagney. Martin Quigley's conservative *Motion Picture Herald* pontificated,

> It is the day of loud temperamental outbursts by the stars in Hollywood, the reverberations rocking the walls of both studios and courtrooms as some of the really recalcitrant players plaintively air their so-called "grievances" in the open. . . . Outstanding in the star-versus-studio fracas is the case of "Bad Boy" James Cagney who hauled the Warners into a courtroom and a public trial to abrogate his contract. Mr. Cagney pitifully pleaded that the brothers are overworking him—at $4,500 a week!

When Ann Dvorak left Warner Brothers over a similar contract dispute, *Screenland* snidely accused her of "Doing a Cagney?" and the magazine gloated, "James Cagney, the rebel who won screen fame so swiftly is still, at this writing, 'resting.'"

An admiring profile of Jack Warner in the December 1937 edition of *Fortune* assessed the situation as a dispute of obedient vs. obstinate workers: "In Dick Powell, O'Brien, Blondell, Glenda Farrell, George Brent, Kay Francis and others," the *Fortune* writer opined,

> Jack has assembled a sort of permanent stock company who fall efficiently [note the business terminology] into each new role with an easy feeling that they have seen it before and will get home for dinner. But when he gets hold of a star with the authentic afflatus, Jack is likely to have more than his share of trouble. He had most with Cagney, who got sick of being typed as a girl-hitting mick and of making five pictures a year instead of four. He expressed his dissatisfaction in such ways as growing a moustache, talking to Jack in obscene Yiddish and finally suing his way out of his contract on a technical breach of the billing clause. Jack is still after him in the courts.

The belief that Cagney's third, conclusive walkout would have a ripple effect in Hollywood was widespread—and proved, in time, to have foundation. In her memoirs, Bette Davis attributed her own inclination to desert Warners to Cagney's influence. "I was beginning to understand," she wrote, "why Jimmy Cagney was on suspension for refusing to play a certain part. Our contracts were outrageous and the security I dreamed of on Broadway had become the safety of a prison. I was being handed crumbs by the studio, financially as well as artistically."

Great Guy

When the major studios declined to oppose the will of Jack Warner, Cagney once again flouted conventional wisdom by signing with Grand National Pictures, a "B" company that made its bow in late 1936 on the premises of General Service Studios. Cagney was its only "name" star. For his services, Cagney

*First story conference for GREAT GUY, with producer Douglas MacLean (at left)
and author/screenwriter James Edward Grant.*

received a down payment of $100,000 cash and the essential stipulation that he
could reject any story that did not suit him. Only two movies resulted from the
short-lived arrangement—but the story choice in each case was significant; both
were departures from his Warners image. Because Cagney sat in on all story
conferences, the resulting pictures proved to be personally thematic works.
They are not his most fully realized films by any stretch of the imagination, but
they do give the flip side of the tough-guy image and attest to the individual
sensibility of a major motion picture star estranged from the system.

Rumors were that the first picture, *Great Guy*, based on the Johnny Cave
stories by James Edward Grant in *The Saturday Evening Post*, would never be

completed. The resentment in Hollywood against Cagney was being fanned by Jack Warner. Production problems, including the difficulty of persuading another studio to loan out a leading lady, ominously delayed the shooting schedule. Mysterious lab problems threatened the footage. "When the picture was about to go into production," recalled William Cagney,

> I went to [producer] Doug MacLean and said to him, "You'd better send somebody through the lab with your film because they'll sabotage you." He looked at me and said, "My god! Tch-tch." I said, "You poor stupid bastard, you don't know what these people will do to you!" The next morning I came in and asked, "How do the dailies look?" They said they had had trouble at the lab. "What do you mean, trouble?" I asked. "Struck by lightning," they said. I said, "Didn't I tell you to send somebody through the lab?" "Oh, you're dreaming, Bill, you're dreaming." Then it happened again—two nights in a row. Finally I said, "Notify everybody we're suing—and not just for dailies, but for collusion."

The eventual release of *Great Guy* (or *The Pluck of the Irish*, as it was titled in England) came at the end of 1936, and it was worth waiting for—a personal postcard from the star in self-exile. Though the budget of Grand National was painfully shoestring—and the script was patched together by no less than five scenarists (with hardboiled writer Horace McCoy contributing dialogue)—*Great Guy* was ably directed by silent-era veteran John Blystone. It emerged as a lean and crackling comedy–drama that, pointedly, placed Cagney squarely on the side of the law—as meat inspector Johnny Cave, a congenial crusader in a metropolitan Bureau of Weights and Measures who singlehandedly battles a ring of grafters who are defrauding shoppers by cheating on grocery weights. Besides Cagney, the movie boasted a cluster of Irish troupers including James Burke, Edward C. McNamara, Edward Brophy, Ed Gargan, Mary Gordon, and—as Cagney's female costar, interestingly enough—Mae Clarke. (Joan Blondell was originally sought for the role but Warners refused to release her.) As Johnny Cave's girlfriend, a role very unlike her moll specialty, Clarke essays a sweetly comic performance. Thus is the grapefruit beneficiary of *The Public Enemy* repaid by Cagney for his impolite, historic gesture. And Clarke's casting was only one of the subtexts of *Great Guy*, which, in the words of *The New York Times*, "bears unmistakable evidence of that Hollywood rarity, complete cooperation of the director and the story and casting departments."

The title itself was an obvious inversion of Cagney's tough-guy monicker at Warners and derived, symbolically, from the last line of *G-Men*, where Jeff McCord (Robert Armstrong) grudgingly admits of Brick Davis (Cagney) to his sister (Margaret Lindsay), "Take care of him, sis, he's a *great* guy." In his newborn autonomy, therefore, Cagney chose to associate himself with a law-abiding film such as *G-Men* rather than with the gangster-groundbreaking *The Public Enemy*. In reversing the conventions of the typical tough-guy story, fur-

Filming the cafeteria scene in GREAT GUY with Mae Clarke. (MOMA)

thermore, *Great Guy* was true to its title. In a meaningful reverse, for example, it is Cave's girlfriend Janet Henry (Clarke) who dominates the romantic angle in the picture. She, for instance, decides where they will dine (in a simple cafeteria rather than in an elegant restaurant, as Johnny Cave prefers). Then, while shuffling through the cafeteria line, she tells Johnny Cave just what and how much he should eat. Not only is she *not* manhandled a la the Cagney–Clarke relationship of past movies, but she wins every argument with force.

By the same token a considered point against the violence prevalent in so many other Cagney films is registered in the *Great Guy* script. At the beginning of the story, for example, the intrepid Cave is commanded by his superior to make his arrests and pursue his investigations without resorting to fisticuffs, the accepted tough-guy manner. Conscientiously, Cave abides by this advice until, deceived by a gas station attendant who purloins some useful evidence, he flashes a sudden, right-fisted punch. Then, gazing regretfully at his clenched fist, he murmurs sorrowfully, ''Aw, I promised. . . .'' This becomes a recurrent riff in the narrative—one of the ways in which Cagney was attempting to recast his persona in terms more compatible with his own self.

Bearing in mind Cagney's own political disposition at the time, it is interesting to note the progressive political perspective of *Great Guy*, which is in keeping with the most forward-looking films of the Warners' tradition. Like other movies of the era, such as Warners' own *Bullet or Ballots*, released the same year, *Great Guy* is candid and uncompromising in its condemnation of larcenous businessmen and thieving politicians. Even the local mayor in *Great Guy* proves to be a crook. In one scene, Johnny Cave lectures a roomful of Weights and Measures agents, warning them (and, by extension, the audience) about dishonest merchants and big-money price fixing. Bribes to grocery owners, he cautions, are an everyday occurrence. Ironically, scenes like this one in *Great Guy* prompted production code complaints of a far dissimilar nature to those provoked earlier by the underworld Cagney. "The depiction of James Cagney as an honest, capable and competent employee in the Department of Weights and Measures in a great city," wrote Raymond Moley in his authoritative *The Hays Office* (New York: Bobbs–Merrill, 1945),

> was the signal for vehement outcries from retail grocers and gas-station owners who insisted the picture cast a reflection on their honesty (curiously enough, it never seems to have occurred to these protestors, as Joseph Breen pointed out, that the very existence of such departments as a Department of Weights and Measures indicates the acknowledgment, by the community itself, that there is a need for the supervision of weights and measures in retail stores, including grocery stores and gas stations).

Cagney's performance, meanwhile, was lightsome, discernibly different in temperament from most of his previous work at Warners. In one brief, distinctive sequence, Cavanaugh (Robert Bleckler), the villain of the piece, laughingly derides Johnny Cave after having had the deputy inspector falsely arrested and interrogated for a robbery he did not commit. Silent, brooding, Cave endures the ridicule, revealing only by his darting eyes a comprehension of the set-up. Warners' Cagney would have replied blindly with his fists. The wiser "great guy" weathers the abuse with abundant poise. Indeed, Johnny Cave yields to an all-out fistfight only once in the film, at the finale, when he locks an astonished policeman (Edward C. McNamara) out of a room while, inside, he trounces the top hooligan. The scene is played for laughs. "Unlock this door or I'll break it in," barks the cop, listening to the sounds of the thrashing going on inside. Then, as his face relaxes into a smile and he pulls out a smoke, he adds, "As soon as I finish this cigar."

Something To Sing About

Cagney's second Grand National feature was a musical comedy, *Something To Sing About*, which depicted an unassuming bandleader named Terry Rooney (Cagney) who sojourns to Hollywood and is chewed up by the star-making

With brother William and sister Jeanne on the set of SOMETHING TO SING ABOUT. (WCTR)

machinery. The original story and music were contributed by the director Victor Schertzinger—a songwriter and orchestra leader of minor renown who later directed Bob Hope–Bing Crosby "road" pictures. The prospects for Cagney's first musical since *Footlight Parade* were exciting. But *Something To Sing About* turned out to be less consistent and fulfilled than *Great Guy* and was weakened by Grand National's deteriorating production values. The settings and stage dressings were embarrassingly plain. Of the cast, only affable William Frawley, as Rooney's chatterbug agent, is first-rate—excepting Cagney, although it has to be said that, as with *Great Guy*, his role is as deserving of notice as is his performance.

The story has New York City bandleader Rooney trapped by Hollywood stardom. Awarded a movie contract, Rooney relocates in Hollywood where he is informed by ebullient producer B. O. Regan (Gene Lockhart) that he will soon be the nation's newest acting sensation—despite Rooney's insistence that he is really a song-and-dance man at heart. A ridiculous procession of makeup specialists, wardrobe experts, and diction tutors prepare the bandleader for the plateaus of stardom. Already perturbed by his phony image making, Rooney

A chorus scene from SOMETHING TO SING ABOUT: To the left of Cagney is Johnny Boyle, who choreographed his dances in YANKEE DOODLE DANDY, and to his right is Harland Dixon, another much-admired hoofer of the era. (Homer Dickens Still Collection)

explodes on the set when a bit player irks him during the filming of the final scenes of his first picture. A full-pitched brawl ensues on the set; then Rooney stalks off the lot and sets sail on a honeymoon cruise with his newlywed wife (Evelyn Daw). Upon his return, Rooney discovers to his consternation that he is a genuine star, America's brand-new rage, for the shrewd director of his film had kept the cameras rolling during the unrehearsed fracas. Now fans are enamored with the rip-roaring tough-guy find. The trusting bandleader is coaxed into signing a lucrative contract, with one catch: He must masquerade as a bachelor so as not to disappoint fans or detract from his box-office glamour. When gossip columnists float rumors of his supposed amorous entanglements with other stars, his jealous and heartbroken wife withdraws to New York. Angry and resolved, sick of irresponsible press agents and nutty producers, Rooney also flies homeward to New York, where he is reconciled with his wife and his former nightclub orchestra just in time for a joyous musical finale. Like the actor who portrays him, Rooney is presumably permanently disaffected from the dream factory of Hollywood.

Coming as it did in the midst of his own voluntary separation from the Hollywood establishment, *Something To Sing About* could not help but be interpreted on several levels by Cagney followers, the most obvious being a categorical attack on Hollywood excesses and the star syndrome. Producers, especially, bear the brunt of Cagney's animosity here. Studio magnate B. O. Regan (whose initials provide one of the running gags) is an empty headed, deceitful blowhard who, in one key scene, conspires to trick Rooney into a substandard and catchpenny contract. Not that the satire here is any more devastating than in other Hollywood projects, such as, say, Cagney's own *Boy Meets Girl* released the following year, but it carried extra weight because of the immediacy of Cagney's involvement, and because the character he played was the antithesis of his recognized image—although, ironically, closer to his real self.

The musical elements of the film are disappointing when compared with such pictures as *Footlight Parade* and *Yankee Doodle Dandy* or even *West Point Story*. Actually, Cagney does not sing a single note in *Something*—there is a running joke whereby the lyrics are "stolen" out of his mouth every time he begins to warble. And the dancing is less magnificent than elsewhere, the choreography loose and tossed off; one zippy routine with a chorus of sailors aboard an ocean liner seems almost improvised. But that chorus included famous dancers Harland Dixon and Johnny Boyle, whom Cagney revered—Boyle later served as his personal choreographer for *Yankee Doodle Dandy*—and the spontaneity of their interplay with Cagney is a precious high point of an otherwise flawed picture.

Whatever its demerits, critics of the day were generous toward *Something* and expressly pleased to see Cagney in another change of pace. "*Something to Sing About*," wrote Frank S. Nugent in *The New York Times*, "is an amusing piece, sardonic and frolicsome, and it slows down only when Mr. Cagney steps off stage. The best of the film is the satirizing (obviously meat to Mr. Cagney who feels that way about the place) of the Hollywood star-building methods." Even more appreciative was the viewpoint of a British critic who wrote that the film "shows us an entirely new James Cagney, one we had never seen before, a bandleader, a song and dance man, a film star who guys the Hollywood routine with all the flair of a born comedian and a born dancer who seems to outdo Fred Astaire at his own game. There is no one in Europe with such snap, speed and skill, who is at the same time capable of attuning all these gifts to the triumph of the social principle."

Return to Warner Brothers

At least two other Grand National features were in the works—a story variously called "Dynamite" or "Oil," with a script by Horace McCoy, about a Texas oil worker whose job is transporting nitroglycerin; and a gangster melodrama by

On the town with radio broadcaster Lowell Thomas, Richard Barthelmess, Joan Blondell, Billie Cagney, and brother William Cagney in the early 1930s. (WCTR)

Rowland Brown, the author of *Doorway to Hell*, called *Angels with Dirty Faces*. But things were not going well for Cagney at Grand National—for one thing, he and producer MacLean, a former actor, clashed over Cagney's relatively gentle-spirited "great guy" characterization in a disagreement that echoed his persistent differences with Warners' producer Hal Wallis. Also, Grand National could not hope to match Warners in its distribution and promotion abilities, and in 1937 Cagney slipped from his customary niche on the theater-owners' list of top-ten box-office attractions. His career was clearly suffering. When, in late 1938, premature rumors of Grand National's insolvency (the company was actually to survive into the 1940s) swept through the company, the Cagneys were ready. Armed with affidavits from ex-Warners' employees about the existence of a "blackball" against Cagney, and threatening another lawsuit, William Cagney made behind-the-scenes overtures to Jack Warner.

Warner had been heavily criticized by the trade papers and by his own executive peers for ousting his top money-making star and, in effect, cutting off his nose to spite his face. Now the studio chief was prepared to drop hostilities.

He sweet-talked the Cagneys by acceding to their every demand and by pro-claiming to them that Warners was where they belonged. The contract that William Cagney negotiated for his brother remains a model of its sort. Cagney agreed to make eleven pictures for Warners—two or three per year for the next five years, plus one to fulfill the previous contract. In return, the actor was to receive $150,000 per picture plus 10 percent of the grosses over $1,500,000. Twelve weeks of continuous vacation—Cagney's cherished summer sojourn back East—were guaranteed. William Cagney was assured an assistant produc-ership (on brother Jimmy's pictures). And the Cagneys were given story refusal as well as an option to submit ideas of their own—one of which, the contract specified, was going to be a "biopic" of Revolutionary War hero John Paul Jones, who was one of Cagney's favorite historical figures.

But the most remarkable portion of the document was a "happiness clause" (in the words of William Cagney), whereby Cagney could cancel his Warners' contract after any motion picture or at the end of any given year if his relation-ship with the studio was determined to be "obnoxious or unsatisfactory to him." This was a breakthrough, to say the least. Thus did Cagney return to filmmaking at Warners with a contract that was the envy of every motion picture star in Hollywood. Ironically, the ruling in the Cagney–Warners' lawsuit was reversed by the California Supreme Court in early 1937, but the hatchet had already been buried; the Cagneys had privately agreed to allow Jack Warner to "save face" with a reversal, and Warner Brothers did not press to settle further the account of Cagney's long absence.

Cagney aboard his schooner MARTHA circa 1938. (WCTR)

6
The Happiness Clause

"Mr. Cagney can do nothing which is not worth watching. One knows what to expect and he seldom disappoints: the lightweight hands held a little away from the body ready for someone else's punch: the quick nervous steps of a man whose footwork is good: the extreme virtuosity of the muted sentiment and his magnificent unconsciousness of the camera."

GRAHAM GREENE
Graham Greene On Film

In a certain sense William Cagney was his brother's alter ego. The star was actually a shy introvert, the other Cagney was a romeo and a partygoer. James was an artist—an actor, a hoofer; William was an astute businessman who made his fortune in real estate, buying early into property in Beverly Hills, Newport Beach, and elsewhere in Southern California. James was a left-liberal (at least until the late 1940s); William was apolitical or conservative, depending on the subject at hand. James and Jack Warner reviled each other. When J. L. materialized on a set for one reason or another, James would rush out of his trailer and abuse him in Yiddish. William, on the other hand, had a "strange affection" for his brother's nemesis, the studio chief. After a preview in Burbank, with Cagney scowling in the background, J. L. would call William over to his limousine, and they would ride together back to Los Angeles, William cueing J. L. in the singing of sentimental, popular songs. James, of course, was a happily married homebody who rarely went out in public—except to boxing matches—and resisted attending his own previews. William, contrarily, relished the Hollywood nightlife and chummed around with an eccentric lot, including Howard Hughes and director-cum-restauranteur Preston Sturges. Romantically linked with a succession of pretty starlets (not always when he was unmarried), it was William—not his more famous brother—who was among the Hollywood celebrities spotted in a predawn police raid on a Sunset Strip "locker club" in the 1940s. When, in 1945, his first wife, the beauteous Boots Mallory, filed for divorce, among the reasons cited were William Cagney's "frequent and unexplained nocturnal absences from home."

Yet they were as close, as attached, as two brothers can be. No longer, by the advent of the 1940s, was William his brother's lookalike; he enjoyed eating too much and was less successful than James at losing weight. But they were soulmates with a deep family bond. They shared the same sense of humor. Both were witty raconteurs who could expertly mimic the foibles of any Hollywood figure. It was not unusual to discover the two Cagneys, at lunchtime, rolling around on the floor of James's trailer, convulsed in laughter at some private joke. Every night, for years, they telephoned each other ritually to chat and say goodnight. "Sam" or "Johnny" they would call each other, just to vary the conversation, tiring of plain old "Jimmy" or "Bill." Still, there was much they rarely discussed—politics, for example. And they rarely discussed the pros and cons of James's career, which they were both of one mind about, instinctively.

In fact, James was growingly indifferent to his career by 1938, and William was sensitive to inflaming him by bringing up specifics about this or that prospective project until the details had been smoothed out. Cagney had one of the best financial deals in Hollywood—in 1941, his salary would amount to $362,500 annually, second only to Bing Crosby's. But Cagney was not materialistic, and was already comfortably rich. He continued to distrust and dislike Hollywood. Knowing this, in 1939, William helped him and Billie, his wife, build a knotty-pine house in Coldwater Canyon, an almost rural area in the hills above Hollywood, bringing in some horses and Rhode Island reds to lend it a country air. But Cagney still longed for the last days of filming when he would pack up his luggage, reserve a drawing room on the train, and head back East to Martha's Vineyard, to his yacht and to the colonial estate he had bought in the mid-1930s. A good part continued to tempt him—but increasingly he believed that a motion picture he would be lastingly proud of was not likely to emerge from the Hollywood system.

It was at this point in Cagney's career that William became his advisor and—more than his advisor—his booster and mentor, someone who believed in Cagney enough to devote himself to making the best possible Cagney pictures for the better part of the next two decades. There were times when William believed in Cagney pictures more than James did. James could now sequester himself back East between movies; William would fight the studio battles. Writers, especially, were a sore point with the Cagneys (and the Cagneys attitude toward some writers was a sore point with those writers). According to William Cagney, "Warners specialized in a group of guys who didn't mind going over the last pictures and picking out the identical scenes and putting them in the next picture. I thought I was looking at the last picture one time when I went to see Jimmy and Pat O'Brien in a follow-up picture. Same scene, same restaurant. Sez you, sez me." First-class directors were now expected; the post-1938 properties had to be more than just tough-guy vehicles. "What I was after in all

With Dick Foran, Pat O'Brien, Ralph Bellamy, and Marie Wilson in BOY MEETS GIRL. (WCTR)

of these movies," remembered William Cagney, "was to get the impression of Cagney changed from a sez-you, sez-me roughneck, which was what he was playing. I wanted things to happen to Jimmy for a change, not for Jimmy to *cause* things to happen."

With brother William agitating behind the scenes, and with the happiness clause as leverage, Cagney's next period of work at Warners was to prove—despite disappointments—one of the most fertile of his career.

Boy Meets Girl

A sensation when it was originally produced on Broadway, *Boy Meets Girl* was purchased by Warner Brothers for Marion Davies and intended to be directed for the screen by theatrical magnate George Abbott. Regarded as a prestige property, the stage hit by Bella and Sam Spewack (who also did the screen adaptation) was rewritten to accommodate Cagney and pal Pat O'Brien as the first step of

Cagney's post walkout settlement deal. It was a good faith gesture from Warners—strictly comedy, without any tough-guy overtones. But when Marion Davies was dropped from the project, reportedly because she quarreled with the script, Lloyd Bacon came in as director, and the whole treatment became more pedestrian. This was to become a pattern—an interesting project dangled in front of Cagney, then cheapened in the making. Warners showed its reluctance to promote Cagney as other than a gangster type in England where *Boy Meets Girl* "was held up" until after the release of Cagney's next feature, *Angels With Dirty Faces*, according to *Film Pictorial*, "because Cagney is making a comeback after his quarrel with Warners and it was thought that English audiences would rather see him in one of his customary tough roles before they saw him in a broad comedy."

Boy Meets Girl certainly has its devotees today, but it is a movie that has worn badly with time. The pacing is frenetic, the staging confused, and too many of its relentless stream of one-liners are unfunny. ("While we were making it [*Boy Meets Girl*]," Cagney relates in his autobiography, "Pat and I were harassed by the producers' insistence on more speed. . . . we knew the absolute need for pacing, letting air in at certain spots to prevent it from being unadulterated rush. We fought the Warners' brass on this and at the points where they won, the results for the picture were sad.") Cagney and O'Brien play Robert Law and J. C. Benson, two wacky Hollywood scenarists who concoct a scheme to elevate a cute baby named "Happy"—the offspring of a studio commissary waitress—into overnight stardom. In the film, Happy pictures become the national rage. The little tyke even stars as the hero of shoot-'em-up Westerns ("from the story by Wm. Shakespeare—out of the plains and into your heart"), upstaging the studio's doltish, swell-headed screen cowboy (Dick Foran). Ralph Bellamy is buffoonish as producer C. Elliot Friday; Frank McHugh plays a shifty lawyer; and Marie Wilson (substituting for Marion Davies), as the commissary waitress, endows her characterization with an ethereal naiveté. But Cagney and O'Brien are out of control, racing through their parts (playing multiple roles in their own proposed screenplays) without proper guidance, complementing (pun intended) each other in the dialogue. "New!" exclaims Law. "Brand new!" echoes Benson. "How!" exclaims Law. "And how!" echoes Benson. It sounds good on paper—and it has its moments. But *Boy Meets Girl* deserved a classier handling, and what was hoped to be a change of pace for Cagney instead became a failed exercise in howling farce.

Angels with Dirty Faces

At the behest of William Cagney, *Angels with Dirty Faces* was originally acquired for production at Grand National, where he was poised to make his debut as a producer. The story of a dramatic friendship between a hoodlum killer and a parish priest, *Angels* was written by Rowland Brown, an erratic and rambunctious Hollywood figure who, besides writing the *Doorway to Hell* story, had directed a much-admired gangster picture called *Quick Millions* in 1931. Brown was also set to direct the planned Grand National version of *Angels*. When the Cagneys left Grand National, they took *Angels* with them. While the story conferences with Brown continued apace, William Cagney kept *Angels* separate from the Warners settlement, and tried to shop the movie around Hollywood independently. It almost became a David O. Selznick production until, at a crucial meeting, a Selznick minion warned, "Mr. Selznick, it [*Angels*] doesn't fit in with your image," and William Cagney stalked out of the room in a furor. Thus, in time, *Angels* was brought to Warners for consideration, where its reception was at first tepid. After reading the Rowland Brown scenario, producer Sam Bischoff complained (in a studio memo dated January 14, 1938), "It's about the worst thing I have ever read." Staff producer Lou Edelman concurred, "In its present form I wouldn't touch *Angels With Dirty Faces* with a thirty-foot pole." Nonetheless, William Cagney championed the basic storyline to Jack Warner, and *Angels* was duly negotiated as the follow-up to *Boy Meets Girl*. But Brown, considered a risk by the studio, was dropped as director *and* screenwriter—he was to receive only story credit, much to his anger and dismay. And though William Cagney fully expected to be assigned as producer, he was not. Instead he was reduced to volunteering suggestions from the sidelines, while the project he had nursed along for years was developed by studio hired hands.

One damaging hurdle to this development was the piqued interest of Joseph Breen, censor-successor to Will Hays, who was alert to Cagney's return as a gangster character at Warners and who wrote studio executives that the watchdog office of the industry regarded *Angels* "as the gravest problem that has confronted them in years." The Breen organization dictated a long list of exceptions to the *Angels* script. Words such as *snotty, lousy, sissy, punks, helluva,* and *stink* had to go. (And it must be mentioned, lest the Breen office be considered merely puritanical, ethnic slurs such as *nigger* and *shyster* were also targeted for omission.) All gunfire had to be kept to a minimum, there was to be no actual, observed passing of money in the gambling sequences and all killings had to occur off-screen. Flippant references to God or to priests—one of the key gimmicks of the story—were to be avoided. To many of these complaints, Warners surrendered or compromised, watering down the street authenticity of the original story in the process, but the most ironic of the Breen objections had to be the censor's insistence that the actual electrocution of the hoodlum killer occur off-screen. Though Warners painstakingly reconstructed California's death chair for the sake of authenticity—and publicity—the execution of the Cagney character was not directly shown, thus giving the screenwriters their motive to devise, instead, that long, effective walk down the corridor of death by Rocky Sullivan (Cagney) and Father Connelly (Pat O'Brien); and the killer's electrocution evoked by shadows.

The writers assigned to *Angels* were Warren Duff and John Wexley. The former

With The Dead End Kids (Billy Halop, left; Leo Gorcey, lower left; Bernard Punsley, right; and Gabriel Dell, far right) in ANGELS WITH DIRTY FACES. (WCTR)

was a prolific film writer who had begun his career as an actor in San Francisco—and whose Warners' credits included several pre-*Angels* Cagney vehicles; the latter was a well-known social consciousness playwright, author of the prison melodrama *The Last Mile* and a stirring investigation of the Scottsboro Boys case, *They Shalt Not Die*. Duff was okay, but the Cagneys both grew to dislike Wexley intensely, not for his politics, but for what they believed was the wordiness and phoniness of his writing. The shooting script of *Angels* depressed both Cagneys. "When I picked Jimmy up at the train station, he said, 'How's the script?'" William Cagney recalled.

I said, "It's awful." He turned pale. He said, "Then, we'll walk again." I said, "We can't, nothing would look so ridiculous as walking out again. It'll be us who look wrong, not Warners." He said, "Goddammit, what are we going to do?" I said, "We're going to rewrite it on the set. Put back all the things that made you approve it in the first place." Now, that's easier said than done. Although Jimmy would do it partly, anyway—even if it was a good script. Jimmy was expert at what he called "dropping in certain things." When he wasn't working with you that way you didn't have Jimmy Cagney. Back when Darryl Zanuck was in the front office, he would call Jimmy in and say, "What's the matter, Jimmy?" Jimmy would say, "They tell me I have to shoot the script the way it was written. If that's what you want, that's what I'm going to give you." Darryl would say, "Aw, Jimmy, fer chrissakes. . . ."

Evidently, to some extent that (dropping in certain things) is what transpired during the filming of *Angels*. "Like so many of the catch-as-catch-can pictures we made then," recalled Cagney in his autobiography, "it [Angels] had an insubstantial script that the actors patched up here and there by improvising right on the set." Cagney, O'Brien, Bogart—all participated, trimming and revising dialogue, and coming up with their own bits and phraseology. Hungarian-born director Michael Curtiz (nee Mihaly Kertesz) was a workaholic who was not averse to a little script tinkering as long as it did not interfere with his own obsessive visual dynamics. (Said to be unfamiliar with the language of his scripts anyway, Curtiz' mangling of the vernacular was popular Hollywood lore. One example: "Smile with the coat buttoned.") But Darryl Zanuck was no longer captaining the ship; Hal Wallis was in charge now, and Wallis did not encourage improvisation on the set, even from Cagney. Wallis and Cagney continued to fuel their adversary relationship. Not only was Wallis issuing memos against ad-libbing, but also equally unappreciated were his memos to Curtiz advising the director to play up Cagney's "menacing" qualities (Cagney figured his menace was a *given*, and he preferred to underplay it). Not that Wallis was simply an interloper here. For one thing, it was he who had the notion of integrating the Dead End Kids so completely into the story. He was assertive about the relationship between the Cagney and Bogart characters ("You should get the feeling every time these two meet that the air is charged with dynamite and that anything can happen," he advised director Curtiz in a memo), and he conceived of the "wild soundtrack" of Rocky Sullivan's garbled screaming that so climaxed the execution scene.

Despite all of this pulling in opposite directions, or perhaps because of it, "if there is one Cagney film to place in a time capsule, in order to understand his appeal and import, it just might be *Angels With Dirty Faces*," in the words of Andrew Bergman, writing in *James Cagney* (New York: Pyramid, 1973). "Not merely one of his truly virtuoso performances, the role of Rocky Sullivan is a kind of summation of the appeal of the gangster to American audiences of the Thirties." The *Angels* story: Notorious gangster Rocky Sullivan (Cagney) returns to the neighborhood of his youth where he is idolized by the Dead End Kids, a gang of punk teenagers, and romanced by a street-wise girlfriend (Ann Sheridan). Rocky's friendship with Father Jerry Connelly (O'Brien) dates back to their own boyhood run-ins with police, but now the parish priest fears that Rocky's presence in the neighborhood, and his renewed criminal activities, might nullify the priest's attempts to mould the boys' characters. In a pleading

With priest-pal Pat O'Brien, as Cagney heads for the electric chair in
ANGELS WITH DIRTY FACES. (AMPAS)

voice, Father Connelly asks Rocky to give up his life of crime. "Whatever I teach them [the Dead End Kids], you show me up," he implores. "You show them the easiest way." When Rocky refuses, Father Connelly vows to campaign against crime, even against the exploits of his boyhood chum. "Go to it," Rocky tells him warmly, and they shake hands. When Rocky murders rival James Frazier (Humphrey Bogart), a crooked lawyer, he is captured by police and sentenced to die in the electric chair; and Father Connelly begs Rocky to feign cowardliness before he dies to deflate the hero-worshipping of the neighborhood youths. "You're asking me to crawl on my belly—the last thing I do in life?" answers the gangster. "Nothing doing." But in his defiant reply is a hint of fondness and concession. And en route to the electric chair, Rocky suddenly erupts in a blood-curdling seizure of fear. Real or faked? "I think in looking at the film," wrote Cagney in his autobiography, "it is virtually impossible to say which course Rocky took—which is just the way I wanted it. I played it with deliberate ambiguity so that the spectator can take his choice." Whichever, Rocky goes to his death a coward in the eyes of the neighborhood delinquents, but a martyr and a hero to his friend, the parish priest.

From the opening—a long dolly shot moving from the headlines of a newspaper ("Harding Nominated for President") to a sweeping view of the brimming tenements of New York's lower East Side, to the galvanic image near the end (the writhing outline of Rocky Sullivan as he is dragged toward the electric chair), Curtiz' crisp direction crackles with emotion and suspense. Though Humphrey Bogart and "Oomph Girl" Sheridan got the buildup for marginal roles, both were satisfactory. The Dead End Kids (Billy Halop, Bobby Jordan, Leo Gorcey, Bernard Punsley, Gabriel Dell, and Huntz Hall) made for an exquisite flock of wisecracking simpletons. There are the usual gangster acrobatics— gunplay and action scenes aplenty—but the heart of *Angels* is to be found in the unusual relationship between Rocky and Father Connelly, prime Cagney–O'Brien. O'Brien had his most complex role as Cagney's foil, and he responded with urgency and feeling. Cagney's performance was hard grain to perfection, modeled in part, according to his autobiography,

> on a fella I used to see when I was a kid. He was a hophead and a pimp, with four girls in his string. He worked out of a Hungarian rathskellar on First Avenue between Seventy-seventh and Seventy-eighth streets—a tall dude with an expensive straw hat and an electric-blue suit. All day long, he would stand on that corner, hitch up his trousers, twist his neck and move his necktie, lift his shoulder, snap his fingers, then bring his hands together in a soft smack. His invariable greeting was "Whadda ya hear? Whadda ya say?" The capacity for observation is something every actor must have to some degree, so I recalled this fella and his mannerisms and gave them to Rocky Sullivan just to bring some modicum of difference to this roughneck.

For his characterization, Cagney won the Best Acting prize from the New York Film Critics in 1938 and his first Academy Award nomination (losing, in this instance, to another priest characterization, the more "respectable" choice of Spencer Tracy in MGM's *Boys Town*).

The Oklahoma Kid

The next Cagney–Bogart pairing, in 1939, "was always regarded within the studio as a sort of campy satire," reported coscreenwriter Robert Buckner. Not so according to Cagney, however, who described it in his autobiography as yet another instance of Warners shortchanging him. A writer by the name of Edward E. "Ted" Paramore had conceived of a story about mountain men, focusing on Kit Carson. "We researched it," in the words of Cagney, "and I came up with some things I wanted to do, pretty exciting things, I thought. Warners, without warning, pulled Paramore off the script [substituting Warren Duff and Buckner], and without a word changed directors [to ever-ready Lloyd Bacon]. When I got the final script it had as much to do with the actual history as the Katzenjammer Kids. It had become typical horse opera, just another programmer." Eventually

On the set of THE OKLAHOMA KID with William Cagney, Mrs. Carolyn Nelson Cagney (his mother), and Jeanne Cagney. (Wide World Photo)

called *The Oklahoma Kid*, the story pitted Cagney as Jim Kincaid, the redoubtable outlaw son of a reform mayoral candidate during the Oklahoma land rush era, against a heavy named Whip McCord (played by Bogart). Rosemary Lane did duty as Cagney's love interest.

Dressed in good-guy white ("Cagney looked like a mushroom under a huge Western hat," Bogart once quipped), the gunslinging Cagney makes for an unexpectedly engaging cowboy, especially when he interrupts saloon chatter to sing a few bars of "I Don't Want To Play in Your Yard," punctuating his melody with a few well-aimed pistol shots at the burly, disapproving companions of Whip McCord. In another scene he cradles an infant in his arms and sings "Rock-A-Bye Baby"—two versions, English and Spanish. "The script was so typically predictable that the actors were reduced to cuffing it," said Cagney in his autobiography, "ad-libbing where we thought it would do the most good." In this category is Cagney's oft-twitted exclamation of "feel the air!"—"reaching up to feel the air as I said that line"—and a twist in the customary romantic clinch before riding off into the sunset at the picture's conclusion. Cagney

His song interrupted: with Trevor Bardette, Ward Bond, Ray Mayer, and Humphrey Bogart in THE OKLAHOMA KID.

viewed *Kid* as another setback, but it carried with audiences and critics—thanks to a fine supporting cast, superior technical values (James Wong Howe's cinematography and Max Steiner's jaunty score) and a romping atmosphere. "There's something entirely disarming about the way he [Cagney] tackled horse opera," wrote Frank S. Nugent in *The New York Times*, "not pretending a minute to be anything but New York's Jimmy Cagney, all dressed up for a dude ranch. He cheerfully pranks his way through every outrageous assignment his script writers and directors have given him." Wrote *Time* magazine: "Typical shot: Cagney—whose Bowery accent lends an admirably exotic touch to his impersonation of a badlands sharpshooter, blowing complacently through his pistol barrel when he shoots someone."

Each Dawn I Die

When William Cagney informed the Warners' front office that his brother would *not* play the gangster role in *Each Dawn I Die*, the bureaucracy was taken

With cobilled tough guy George Raft in EACH DAWN I DIE. (WCTR)

aback. Instead, Cagney wanted to play another part in the film, that of muck-raking journalist Frank Ross, whose idealistic faith in the machinery of justice is destroyed when he is framed by a crooked district attorney and sent to prison. The Cagney brothers' choice for the part of hardened lifer Hood Stacey—who befriends Ross and escapes with a vow to find the man who framed the reporter—was George Raft, whom Cagney had also vouched for before Raft was assigned a dancing cameo in *Taxi!* Cagney's friendship with Raft, an occasionally moody actor who had just been released from his Paramount contract, dated back to their hoofing days together on Broadway.

Once Warners committed itself, it turned out to be an inspired match-up, with as much spark and chemistry as any of the Cagney–Bogart pairings. Like Cagney, Raft projected his own personality on the screen; his acting was minimalist. He trimmed his dialogue and always preferred to *react* rather than to speak or act, conveying emotions by a mere flicker of the visage. There is a scene in *Each*

Dawn I Die during which Frank Ross's fiancée (Jane Bryan) beseeches Stacey for help, telling the fugitive con that the newspaperman has gone to the "hole" in prison rather than reveal the pact of their escape plans. "You're a slum kid who never had a chance," she says. "But so is Frank. He hates crooked . . . and rotten politicians as much as you do. The only difference is you chose crime— the easy way. He's spent his life fighting." Stacey/Raft remains silent during the harangue; coolly, calmly smoking a cigarette. In that pointed, informational way of his, he betrays his compassion by only the slightest ripple of expression. At his best, as here, Raft, still-faced and scratchy voiced, had a sense of himself that was commanding on the screen.

With the demonstrative Cagney in *Each Dawn I Die*, Raft was sublimely paired. Cagney played it hard as nails, without any comic implications; and he is breathtaking in the convulsive scenes in which, unnerved by prison life, stir-crazy from solitary confinement, he wilts into a sobbing paroxysm. His relationship with Stacey is so believably developed, in the Norman Reilly Raine–Warren Duff–Charles Perry script (based on Jerome Odlum's novel), and the action moves so efficiently under the tutelage of director William Keighley ("the least sentimental director of gangster careers," in the appraisal of critic Manny Farber), that the film's maudlin coda is almost plausible. Once on the outside, Stacey learns that the guy who framed Ross has just been sent to the very prison from which he himself has escaped. Loyal to his promise, Stacey takes a taxi back to prison and strolls through the front gates, then engineers a suicidal break-out. After coercing a confession from the stoolie, within earshot of the warden (played by George Bancroft), Stacey perishes in a volley of gunfire. Ross is cleared of all charges. As he is leaving the prison, exonerated, the warden hands him a photograph inscribed by Stacey before the fatal fusillade: "To Ross, I found a square guy."

The Roaring Twenties

Cagney bade farewell to the 1930s—and also, for ten years, to the gangster picture—with his next feature, a grandiose, rise-and-fall Prohibition epic called *The Roaring Twenties*, a movie cherished by buffs nowadays but regarded at the time, by many of the involved parties, as a dubious proposition at best. Ex-newsman Mark Hellinger provided the original story (called "The World Moves On") and grandiloquently introduced the film as "a memory of the past" with a montage (assembled by budding director Don Siegel) of news clips and simulated history. Indeed, by orchestrating publicity that prominently linked his name with the picture, Hellinger ensured that the movie became widely known, then as now, as Mark Hellinger's *The Roaring Twenties*. This was the cause of no little resentment and derision on the Warners lot, where, after the picture opened to surprisingly good reviews and box office, associate producer Sam Bischoff and Hellinger got into a shouting match and near fistfight in the private

Publicity shot for THE ROARING TWENTIES: Frank McHugh, Cagney, and Humphrey Bogart.

studio dining room over who deserved more credit for the picture's success. Certainly, there was a surfeit of names to choose from—apart from Bischoff's and Hellinger's—for studio records reveal that no less than ten contract writers took a crack at Hellinger's thinly drawn story at one point or another, including Robert Lord, John Wexley, Earl Baldwin, Frank Donoghue, Niven Busch, Howard Koch, John Huston, Jerry Wald, Richard Macaulay, and Robert Rossen (with the latter three receiving screen credit, and Rossen doing yeoman revisions during filming). Even at that, it was "one of the worst scripts I ever saw" before shooting began, remembered William Cagney. According to William Cagney, director Raoul Walsh met secretly with him before the start date and begged him, "Don't let Jimmy do it, Bill. Don't let Jimmy do it." But William Cagney assured Walsh: "Don't worry, I'm going to tell Jimmy to rewrite it as much as possible on the set."

Studio files indicate that, truly, there was extensive pruning and shearing on the set. William Cagney recalled, "Each night, Bogart, McHugh, and Cagney would go over the next day's shooting, with the script girl writing down the dialogue and with each person in the scene ad-libbing." It drove producer Wallis crazy, this "ad-lib quality," and he complained about it in memo after memo to director Walsh, arguing that Cagney was once again subverting the toughness of the tale by softening his own characterization. "I notice," he wrote to Walsh on July 26, 1939, during filming,

> that you are still changing lines occasionally, and particularly when Cagney is involved in the scene. For example, the other night in the scene in the garage where he hires the three mugs out of jail, you cut out the speech at the end of the scene where Cagney told the three men never to try to pull anything on him or he'd take care of them—or something to that effect. I assume that it was cut because Cagney didn't want to be the tough guy again, but you must insist on keeping these things in because they are necessary for his characterization. He is a very nice guy all through the story and if he occasionally has a scene where he has to be tough, you must insist on having it done that way in order to keep the characterization correct.

Walsh incorporated Wallis' best advice or, when he could, dodged the memos, while the story became the genuine collaborative effort of all involved. "There was no heart in that goddammed script," recollected William Cagney. "It was a typical Republic script, the worst kind of Monogram cheapie. But there was *heart* in the picture. Somehow or other heart crept into it with all their ad-libbing."

The Roaring Twenties unspools with a flashback: Three WWI soldiers who shared a foxhole cross paths after the armistice. Cagney is Eddie Bartlett, a former garage mechanic who finds honest employment scarce and instead becomes a bootlegger, teaming up with old trench buddies George Hally (Humphrey Bogart) and Lloyd Hart (Jeffrey Lynn) in a lucrative partnership of crime. The three are befriended by a nightclub hostess named Panama Smith (Gladys George, in a role patterned after the real-life 1920s nightclub madame Texas Guinan). When Bartlett falls in love with a young, would-be singer (Priscilla Lane)—who rejects him for conscience-ridden Hart, now a lawyer—his racketeering empire begins to crumble. His spirit broken, Bartlett becomes an anonymous taxi-driver. One day, years later, his passenger turns out to be the singer, now happily married to Hart, who has become the local crusading district attorney. She tells Bartlett that Hally, still reigning as a vicious vice lord, has threatened to kill Hart, and she begs Bartlett to intercede. On New Year's Eve, the drunk, raggedy ex-kingpin visits Hally's luxurious quarters to ask Hally to spare Hart. A shoot-out erupts, Hally is killed, and Bartlett escapes, mortally

With Humphrey Bogart (and henchman) before the final shoot-out in
THE ROARING TWENTIES.

wounded, after a bloody exchange of gunfire with Hally's henchman. Bartlett's
balletic, physically drawn-out death is reminiscent of the gutter dance of *Public
Enemy* (and inspired, Cagney has said, by his memory of a Frank Buck film in
which the hunter killed a giant gorilla that died in a slow, amazed way). Stunned
and injured, he stumbles along the sidewalks of the city, knocking over a
garbage can, gasping for breath, still pursued by Hally's thugs. Bent, contorted,
he zig-zags in retreat, climbing the great steps of a cathedral, seeking refuge,
almost straightens, then falls, spins and sprawls motionless in the shadow of the
church. Panama Smith (who has been loyally waiting for him in the taxi) runs up
to the body and cradles Bartlett in her arms, just as a nameless cop races over.
"How were you hooked up with him?" the cop asks, strictly businesslike. She:
"I never could figure it out." Cop: "What was his business?" Panama (her voice
choking with emotion): "He used to be a big shot." Fade-out.

Unoriginal, yes—superficial, yes—but flaws notwithstanding, *The Roaring
Twenties* is superb; exciting spectacle, moving, lifelike drama. Besides Jeffrey

Death on the cathedral steps: with Gladys George in THE ROARING TWENTIES.

Lynn and Priscilla Lane, who did their best with bland, one-dimensional roles, the supporting cast includes the luminous Gladys George ("who has breathed piognance into the stock role of the nightclub hostess who calls her customers 'chump'," in the words of *The New York Times* reviewer) and the always-welcome Frank McHugh (in his typical role as Bartlett's dim but devoted sidekick). Cagney digs deep under the skin of Bartlett to capture his raffish "menace" and romantic obsessiveness without ever losing sight of his moral equilibrium. *Roaring Twenties* provides moviegoers with the best opportunity to inspect Cagney and Bogart at fair odds, the one capping his 1930s gangsterdom and the other emerging as the principal antihero of the 1940s. As the two mobsters vie for control of the liquor rackets, so too do the actors vie for dramatic focus and acting honors. Bogart seems intimidated by the more complex and profound Cagney portrait, which is evident even before their square-off in the final sequence. In that crucial scene, Cagney goes for the heartstrings while Bogart, malignant at first, ultimately "is called upon to cringe and howl for his life to be spared," in the words of critic David Thomson. "But he cannot admit cowardice and his writhing is embarrassingly inept." Some of that impotency is caused by the role itself—Bartlett is an infinitely more vivid character—but some is owed to Cagney's embroidery. As a performer, Cagney was simply more intense, more physically volatile; and in *The Roaring Twenties*, as in their other two pictures together, he tended to automatically subdue the more impassive tough guy, Bogart.

Roaring Twenties, it is worth noting, was the first Cagney picture to be directed by Raoul Walsh, a silent-era veteran who began his long and estimable career as an actor in *Birth of a Nation* for D. W. Griffith. They were to do four pictures together—three among Cagney's finest—one of the actor's most profitable associations with any director. Walsh tried to give the city battleground of *Twenties* a majestic scope, and alone among Cagney's directors he seemed to grasp the tragic as well as noble dimensions of the Cagney persona, the conflict between the modern world and a man rooted in the past. They were two of a kind, Walsh and Cagney—not intellectually, but they sprang from the same turn-of-the-century, New York City upbringing. "Raoul Walsh never spoke to the actors and if he did, whatever he said was incomprehensible," asserted William Cagney. "Yet I never saw a picture of Walsh's that did not have an added dimension that was not measurable. A masculine integrity, perhaps. Even if the actors were inclined to be terribly soft, they were inspired under him to be forceful. Same words, same everything—but with a jolt to it."

Directed by William Keighley

Meanwhile, William Keighley was fast becoming Cagney's most prolific director—replacing not only the Ray Enrights, who were persona non grata according to the 1938 settlement, but the Del Ruths and the Bacons, who also were understood to belong in another, less elevated league. Keighley was more meticulous and more attuned to acting than either Del Ruth or Bacon, and he had Cagney's confidence by virtue of their New York theater days in the 1920s. Not that Keighley's material was always to be envied. Such was the case with Cagney's first release in 1940, *The Fighting 69th*, a prevaricating account of the exploits of Manhattan's famed First World War "fighting Irish" regiment, with Cagney as a swaggering coward named Jerry Plunkett, spurred to eventual heroics by troop chaplain Father Duffy (Pat O'Brien). As usual, Plunkett/Cagney is martyred after penitence and reformation, but *69th* was a pale imitation of the earlier Cagney–O'Brien uniform pictures, "with all its obvious theatrics, hokum and unoriginality," in the words of *The New York Times*. Cagney was seduced into participation by the patriotic Irish subject matter and by the cast: George Brent, Jeffrey Lynn, Alan Hale, Frank McHugh, Dick Foran, Henry O'Neill, Sammy Cohen, Tommy Dugan, and TV's future "Superman" George Reeves. O'Brien did his pious routine, Cagney did his ignominious one. The battle

As a coward in the ranks of THE FIGHTING 69TH. (WCTR)

panoramas were big budgeted but no less so than the advance promotional campaign, which included a widely publicized meeting in New York City between Cagney and O'Brien and the real Father Duffy and surviving members of the "Fighting 69th." Five thousand fans greeted the stars at Grand Central Station. And the film was a box-office hit—though admittedly not up to the level of its antecedents.

Keighley's next Cagney assignment was a melodrama called *Torrid Zone* about romance and revolution in a banana republic. There was only one hitch—acting on his brother's behalf, William Cagney rejected the script. In a memo (dated December 13, 1939) to Hal Wallis, William Cagney expounded, "This is just the type of story that made Cagney want to leave the studio upon expiration of his last contract. There is no real substance or importance in the entire 103 pages, and I know that Jim will only be enthused by plot and development that is worthy of his talents." Cagney's brother continued: "*Torrid Zone* is what has been known for so long as a typical Cagney vehicle and that is just the reason he would refuse to do it—the only difference being that it is set in a banana country. I personally feel that it is about as good a vehicle for George Raft as I have read in a long time, and feel too, that with nothing of importance to start with, the folks who have worked on it have done a very good job."

The "folks" doing such valiant work were Richard Macaulay and Jerry Wald, who cooked up their story to (among other things) launch Ann Sheridan in a steamy opus a la Jean Harlow in *Red Dust*. Claude Rains was in mind for the part of the banana plantation manager, and when Cagney, then Raft, refused to do the picture, both Fred MacMurray and John Garfield were considered for the part of the foreman. The Cagneys rejected a host of other projects in the meantime (including *Brother Orchid* because of its "gangster angle"), hoping that the John Paul Jones saga might somehow spring into fruition. Warners intended to stall forever on the risk and expense of a naval historical epic, however—and Wallis continued to want Cagney for *Torrid Zone*. So director Keighley, working with Macaulay and Wald, began to tailor the script in Cagney's direction. The implication in the original story that Lee Donley (the Ann Sheridan character) is a prostitute was dropped, and she became a vagabond torch singer and card shark. Rosario (the George Tobias character), originally a simple bandit, became a revolutionary "with a sound reason for all his actions"—including (at this stage of the writing) dying for his cause. Nick, Cagney's character, was brush stroked with comedy, and all "criminal" innuendo vanished. And Pat O'Brien, a trump card in the casting, was brought in as Case, the plantation manager. The improved script was sent off to "the Master and Squire of Martha's Vineyard," as Keighley dubbed him, and they awaited his go ahead.

At this point an additional pressure influenced the evolution of the script—one that could not have been foreseen. The United Fruit Company, hearing of the prospective Warner Brothers picture, threatened behind the scenes to take legal steps to discourage any intimation in the story that the company corrupted local officials, killed rebels, behaved cruelly to natives, or operated as the de facto law of the land in certain Latin American countries. "Now, of course, I do not know what United Fruit has actually done in Central America," mused Morris Ebenstein, a Warners lawyer, in a memo on the subject, "Like everyone else, I have heard a lot of stories on the subject." Correspondence between Warners' lawyers and United Fruit representatives suggests there were mutually agreed-upon script revisions, with overseas distribution (among other veiled threats) hanging in the balance. Thus, the script was sanitized, and brought further along the path of comedy and unreality.

As it happened, *Torrid Zone* was played almost entirely for laughs. Except for a few pick-up shots at the height of harvest on the United Fruit plantation in Honduras (one of the perks of the United Fruit–Warners arrangement), its authenticity was limited to a seaport, banana grove, and tropical jungle constructed on Warners' 30-acre annex (albeit exotically photographed by James Wong Howe). As realistic melodrama, it is intentionally preposterous, yet as

With card shark Ann Sheridan in TORRID ZONE. (WCTR)

such, it is a rapturously synthetic—hilariously under-rated comedy. "There is a punch line a minute," wrote one reviewer,

> some of them so close to the borderline that they must have necessitated the use of a Hays Office censorial slide rule. . . . As the foreman, Mr. Cagney again shows that he has more tightly muscled energy as an actor than half the Hollywood leads put together; Mr. O'Brien is scowling, loud-mouthed and credible, and there should be special mention of Andy Devine's dim-witted Number One Boy and George Tobias as the loveable revolutionist who is nearly shot a week ahead of schedule to forestall an untimely demise by hunger strike. But if the males are two-fisted, Miss Sheridan meets them blow for blow, line for line.

Torrid Zone was the last film Cagney and O'Brien made together at Warners— and an unabashedly wacky one. As Steve Case, the cigar-puffing banana plantation imperialist beset by an elusive revolutionary, a female con artist, and his old wife-stealing pal, O'Brien is at his most fidgety and profane. Case tries hard to disguise his affection for new-arrival Nick Butler (Cagney), but he fails miserably. As he hungrily devours a string of "collect" telegrams from Nick—"Meet me down at the boat, sweetheart!"—he angrily issues orders that no more are to be accepted. Furiously he crumples the telegrams, spits insults about Butler and then schemes madly to keep the maverick administrator on hire as his plantation foreman. They are wonderfully in stride in *Torrid Zone*, Cagney (in a smoothie role) and O'Brien, one instant at each other's throats and winking at each other—and the audience—the next. Finally, their deal is swung, the chase is on to capture Rosario, and in the benevolent climax to the yarn (an ending United Fruit did not appreciate, perhaps), Case gets Butler, Butler gets Lee Donley, and Rosario escapes to revolutionize yet another day.

Ann Sheridan was just about the only actress since Joan Blondell to rival Cagney in his ever-lopsided on-screen battle of the sexes. "One of the great screen teams," argues David Shipman in his *The Great Movie Stars: The Golden Years* (Crown, 1970). "It wasn't written up at the time, and as far as is known, legions of fans didn't write in to ask Warners to reunite them. . . . They complemented each other perfectly, he all bombast and bounce, she more knowing, sharp and disillusioned." Wry and deadpan, her voice guarding her emotions, she traded barbs with Cagney and O'Brien with a female élan sorely missing since *Blonde Crazy*. "Why don't you send that mind of yours out and have it dry cleaned?" asks an exasperated Butler at one point. "What's the use?" replies Lee, a faint smile telegraphing her punch line, "Look at the company I'm in." When Nick ultimately falls in love with Lee (natch), he grudgingly pays her the ultimate Cagneyesque compliment: "You know, you'd be a pretty nice guy if you weren't around so much at the wrong time." Expressed in explicitly male terms, his phrase underlines the implicit sexual thesis of all Cagney/Warners (Cagney/Hollywood) works: Only a woman who is tough (tough like Cagney, tough like a man) is a fitting mate for the male hero. Cagney's cinema was—as it had been since *Public Enemy*—plainly a man's world.

City for Conquest

A film version of *City for Conquest* had been on the back burner for the Cagneys ever since 1935 when, homesick for the bustle of New York City street life, William Cagney stayed up all night reading Aben Kandel's novel, mesmerized by it. "Aben Kandel was a kind of gutter poet," said William Cagney. "He could write like hell." When Cagney's brother inquired about the story rights, he learned that they were owned by Columbia. It wasn't until much later, in 1941, that he persuaded Jack Warner to acquire the property for his brother. William would serve, officially now, as associate producer. It was going to be a dreamed-of undertaking for the Cagneys—this compassionate story of a blinded

Hedda Hopper and Cagney talk during a break in filming of CITY FOR CONQUEST. (AMPAS)

With Frank McHugh and future director Elia Kazan in CITY FOR CONQUEST.
(WCTR)

boxer and his starry eyed kid brother musician who composes a "City for Conquest" symphony. But enchanting as the movie is for contemporary audiences, its execution was regarded as a major setback by the Cagneys, and its memory never ceased to rankle them.

There were two main wrinkles from the Cagney viewpoint. One was the screenwriter—John Wexley, again—who did the bulk of the construction (with William Cagney supervising), with Robert Rossen coming in for revisions. The Cagneys continued to dislike Wexley, and cooperation with him during story sessions reached a low point. Again, there was ad-libbing on the set, particularly from Cagney who made a point of correcting the fight truisms. The other complication was the director Anatole Litvak, a Russian emigre who had studied filmmaking under Pudovkin before laboring for an interval during his lengthy and capable career at Warners in the 1940s. Litvak was a caring director but his authoritarian manner rubbed Cagney the wrong way. According to William Cagney, "Jimmy and Litvak didn't get along very well because Litvak was inclined to take actors and push them around by the arm." Litvak himself later claimed, "He [Cagney] was playing a character he'd never played, a weaker man than he was used to playing, and he couldn't quite adjust to the part, and I came to an impasse with him." As Cagney himself later confided to Hedda Hopper: "I

Heartrending finale; with kid brother Arthur Kennedy and devoted pal McHugh in CITY FOR CONQUEST. (WCTR)

was born nervous. Won't even go to previews of my own pictures. The last one I ever saw was *City for Conquest*. When it was over, I sat there thinking, 'Was that what it was about?' It didn't add up to the hours and days of work that had gone into it. It was alright, but it didn't represent the effort we'd all made. Now, I figure when I've finished a picture I've done as well as I can so I let it go.''

That said, it must also be said that *City for Conquest* remains, despite poetical pretensions, one of Cagney's most beautifully realized films. It is not a specimen of gritty realism by any means, more like soap opera with a dash of naturalistic fervor, but it is ripe in urban detail, authentic in its boxing spectacle,* zestfully acted and heartfelt. Cagney plays Danny Kenny, an ordinary guy content with

---

*Once again Cagney, over forty, sparred with former contenders during training and then did all of his own boxing on-camera. ''Some wise guys think all movie fights are faked,'' he told a reporter during filming. ''I'd like to have had them with me. I trained hard for this, with Harvey Perry—otherwise, I couldn't have taken it. Had five weeks of roadwork, up at 5:30 every morning. Worked up by easy stages to ten miles, with sparring partners riding alongside on bicycles. It made me feel like knocking their heads off, which I tried to do in the ring. That's what they hoped I'd try. I took the works—bag punching, wind sprints, rope skipping, shadow boxing, wrestling. Mushy Callahan, ex-welter-champ of the world, the technical director, says I trained as hard as any pro ever did for the title. I was baked out, steamed out, tired out—reduced ten pounds, slept ten hours every night. It made me feel great.''

his workaday life as a truck driver. But his ambitious girlfriend (Ann Sheridan), herself glory bound as a dancer on the theatrical circuit, goads him into a boxing career. Hair pulled back and eyebrows arched, alternately ingenuous and worldly wise, she smoothly manipulates events to her satisfaction. On board the Staten Island Ferry, she leans longingly over the boat railing and in a day-dreamy voice urges Kenny to make a name for himself in the world. "Aw, c'mon," he answers nonplussed, "get off that express and take a local." "But Danny," she insists in a convincing tone, "I don't want you to do it for *me*, I only want you to do it for *yourself*."

They are well suited—she the yearning romanticist, he the pragmatist. But she loses him altogether when he is blinded in the ring during a championship match; when an opponent splashes a burning chemical into his eyes and then grinds it in with his fists. An optimistic scrapper, the blinded Kenny continues to sell newspapers on a streetcorner for his livelihood and encourages his disconsolate kid brother (Arthur Kennedy) to finish his symphony composition. The picture concludes with a gorgeously sentimental passage reminiscent of Chaplin's last scene in *City Lights*. At his newsstand, Kenny is listening with one ear cocked, a smile on his face, to the radio broadcast from Carnegie Hall of his brother's "City for Conquest" symphony, which is dedicated to him. Then he hears the faint, nearing footsteps of former sweetheart Peggy Nash (Sheridan)—she too, down on her luck, jobless, teary-eyed and guilt-ridden by her role in Kenny's tragedy. With blurred vision and misty eyes, still smiling, Kenny extends his hand to her. "I knew you'd come by this corner some day," he says simply. "You'll always be my girl, Peggy."

It may be that Litvak's magisterial, European style of directing (recalling Max Reinhardt's for *A Midsummer Night's Dream*) gnawed against Cagney's rattling pace and American demeanor. The director's insertion of certain trendy film gimmicks nearly undermined aspects of the melodrama, to be sure. In this ruinous category can be placed Litvak's dreadfully obvious superimposition of Kenny's smiling figure during the triumphant Carnegie Hall performance and his adoption of *Wonderful Town* narrator Frank Craven as a sort of omnisicient old-timer in the narrative (Craven's part was drastically edited to cryptic proportions before the film's release). But the performances are nothing less than captivating; not only Cagney's, who loved the Aben Kandel novel and invested the material with the fiber of his own life—and Sheridan's—but also those of a lustrous cast that includes Donald Crisp, George Tobias, Arthur Kennedy, Frank McHugh (as Kenny's worshipful tagalong), and Anthony Quinn as the satanic dancer who nearly whisks Peggy Nash away. Future director Elia Kazan has a small but eye-catching part as "Googi," Kenny's boyhood chum, who grows up to become a suave gangster. Googi has the misfortune to be killed in the line of his criminal duty midway through the story, managing to gasp surprisedly before he folds, "Gee, I never figured on that."

The Strawberry Blonde

The Strawberry Blonde was a rarity for the Cagneys—a blessed experience, a movie in which all things turned out as intended, and one of Cagney's most lyrical comedies. It was William Cagney's "baby" from the beginning; indeed, James balked at the script at first ("for no particular reason," recalled William, "just to be contrary, as he could sometimes be"). The James Hagan play *One Sunday Afternoon*, which provided the basis for *Strawberry Blonde* was a property that William had fondly tracked over the years. His friend, Lloyd Nolan, had starred as the pugnacious Biff Grimes in the New York cast. Then, when the play was being mounted in Los Angeles, its producers made a pass at most of the good-looking male ingenues in the industry, including William Cagney, who craved the part of Biff Grimes but lost out in the competition. The joke around Hollywood was that the *first* movie version of *One Sunday Afternoon*, Paramount's picture of the same title with Gary Cooper in 1933, was the only Gary Cooper picture ever to wind up a loser at the box-office, so badly was Coop miscast. William Cagney was certain he could turn the story into a success with his brother as the lead. At his instigation, Warners purchased the rights, and Steven Morehouse Avery did a preliminary in-house draft, faithful to the play, with a bucolic setting.

William Cagney's notion was to refashion the story as a valentine to his mother Carrie Cagney—who spent more and more time in Los Angeles in her declining years (she was to die in 1945) surrounded by her children, all of whom had moved to the West Coast by 1941—and to the "romantic memories" of her youth. Thus the title change and the use of the musical chestnut, "Casey Would Waltz with the Strawberry Blonde (And the Band Played On)." "I remembered my mother singing that song when I was growing up," recalled William. "When she was a young girl she was the 'strawberry blonde' of her neighborhood and she had a boyfriend named Casey." Actually, in the film, the "strawberry blonde" was supposed to be Ann Sheridan, on whom William Cagney was sweet at the time (though he also happened to be married). But when Sheridan went out on one of her periodic suspensions from Warner Brothers, the casting was switched to Rita Hayworth.* To achieve that strawberry blonde look (even though the picture was to be shot in black and white by James Wong Howe), Hayworth's auburn hair was dyed light red and her brow moved back an inch to form a widow's peak. It was Hayworth's first plum role.

It was William's inspiration to engage the Epstein brothers, Julius J. and Philip G., to revise the screenplay. The Epsteins were identical twins with a reputation in Hollywood as intelligent and witty screenwriters whose specialty was doctor-

---

*William had nurtured a crush on Hayworth too, ever since he, like his brother, had taken tap dancing lessons at the school in Hollywood owned by her father, Eduardo Cansino, in the early 1930s, when young Rita was still a strikingly beautiful teenager.

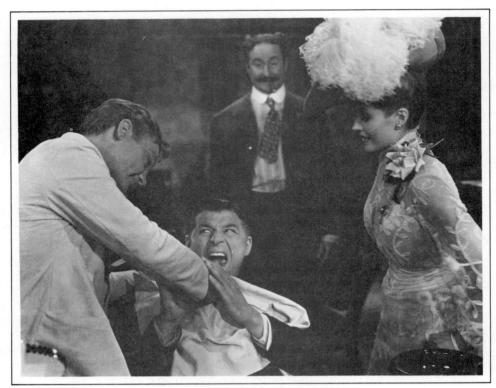

Sweet revenge: Cagney the dentist, Jack Carson, George Tobias (in background), and Rita Hayworth in THE STRAWBERRY BLONDE. (WCTR)

ing any ailing script. They came to Hollywood from New York in the late 1930s and were highly regarded for their stage and literary adaptations, although, ironically, their only Oscar was a shared one (with Howard Koch)—the Best Original Screenplay for *Casablanca*. Very popular on the lot, the brothers kept up a running stream of patter and jokes in story conferences and proved to be the right choice for such an airy diversion as *Strawberry Blonde*. They switched the locale to the city (lower Manhattan), built up the Gay Nineties atmosphere, and ladled on the broad comedy and straight, honest sentiment. Then, as Julius J. Epstein recollected, director Raoul Walsh shot their script verbatim. According to Epstein, ''Walsh said, 'Boys, I think there are a few too many titles'—by which he meant dialogue, because he came from the silent era. So we trimmed the dialogue and then he shot it word for word, one of the rare experiences like that we had.''

Cagney played the Biff Grimes part, a dentist who has learned his craft by correspondence, a tough but gullible plug whose boast is that he ''don't take

With Olivia de Havilland playing his wife in THE STRAWBERRY BLONDE. (WCTR)

nothin' from nobody" because "that's the kind of a hairpin I am." As the story opens, Biff has just been released from prison for crimes of an undisclosed nature. A flashback reveals his flaws: a lifetime of yearning for the elusive strawberry blonde of the neighborhood and of being a fall guy for his conniving pal, Hugo Barnstead (Jack Carson), who married her. Though Biff has himself been lucky in love, marrying the strawberry blonde's friend, Amy Lind (Olivia de Havilland), a free-thinker type, he has always regarded his wife as a plain Jane and never adequately appreciated her fine, subtle qualities. When the story returns to the present, Biff gets an unexpected opportunity for revenge when Hugo Barnstead drops by in emergency circumstances "one Sunday afternoon" to have his tooth pulled. But the years in prison have given Biff time to reflect, and the renewed encounter with Hugo and the now-shrill strawberry blonde enlightens him about his own stupidity: no longer will he take himself, or *Amy*, for granted.

There are tragic underpinnings in this story of a man who cannot surrender his fantasies, and director Walsh fully accented them. In later interviews Walsh was to cite this neglected comedy as one of his favorites of his sound period, saying, "It brought me back to my childhood." Usually such a robust director, here he orchestrated his own dream-like memory of the past, a flip side as it were of the gritty *Roaring Twenties*, a rollicking and romantic, ultimately bittersweet nostalgia for the turn of the century. On the Warners' backlot were conjured ingredients evoking that bygone era: suffragettes, horseshoe pitching, beer tents, moonlight rendezvouses in city parks, and the fabled, enigmatic strawberry blonde. The stock company of Warners was in full flower: "man of many accents" George Tobias as Biff's stoical pal, Nick Pappalas; Alan Hale as Biff's rapscallion father (whose death scene was movingly dramatized); Jack Carson, blustering his way through an exquisitely insufferable characterization; and Rita Hayworth, appropriately ravishing and frivolous in her hoopskirts.

Cagney's performance is blithe, comic, effortless, and Olivia de Havilland proves an adept and spirited comedienne. The movie is laden with Cagney's touches—as when Biff Grimes, garnering his first buss from the strawberry blonde, vaults ecstatically into a handspring and kisses a nearby horse. But the relationship between Biff and Amy provides the interplay at the story's heart, and it is a delight as it develops in three distinct stages: adversaries, sweethearts, and dutiful marrieds. The "topper" is saved for the film's end, when Amy confides to sheepish husband Biff that she is pregnant. It is an awkward moment. Both are embarrassed. Suddenly, impetuously, Biff kisses her, and when she protests, blushing because they are in public view, he exclaims: "When I want to kiss my wife, I'll kiss her anytime," [gesturing with his arm] "anyplace," [broader], "anywhere," [his arm sweeping the horizon]. "That's the kind of a hairpin I am," he says, punctuating his words with emphatic finger-jabbing. A wide smile underlines his obvious satisfaction, and the credits roll. It is the closest the on screen Cagney ever came to being domesticated by romance.

Brides and *Captains*

Ever since *Jimmy the Gent*, Cagney and Bette Davis had wanted to team up in another motion picture, something more substantial—and at various points during their respective battles with the Warners' front office they were promised, as a sop, a prestige property, something on the order of Eugene O'Neill's *Anna Christie*. Instead the studio saddled them, in 1941, with another screwball comedy *The Bride Came C.O.D.*, with a script by the Epstein brothers, based on a story by Kenneth Earl and M. M. Musselman. The premise sounded attractive: A Texas oil tycoon (played by roly-poly, gravelly-voiced Eugene Pallette) hires a charter flyer (Cagney) and offers him ten dollars per pound for the air-freight delivery of his own daughter—"unmarried." Seems the spoiled heiress is about to wed an obnoxious bandleader (Jack Carson), and Big Daddybucks objects. Abducted on the eve of an elopement that is to have been broadcast globally

On the set of THE BRIDE CAME C.O.D.: (l to r) director William Keighley, Cagney,
Bette Davis, and actor Harry Davenport. (Homer Dickens Still Collection)

by an enterprising radio broadcaster (Stuart Erwin), the heiress and her flyer–
kidnapper crash-land in the desert where they seek refuge in a spooky ghost
town and find themselves, gradually, against all resistance, falling in love.

But where *The Strawberry Blonde* is infectious and easily paced, *The Bride Came
C.O.D.* is comedy gone amuck—brittle, strained, exaggerated by the truculence
of its two stars, the studio's bitch and tough guy, mismatched. The rest of the
company is deft and daft: Pallette, Carson, Erwin, George Tobias, William
Frawley, and Harry Davenport. But Davis is so bristly (wrongly cast here as a
light comedienne, not her forte) and Cagney so likewise that what should have
been a light concoction collapses from constant overdrive. Wrote *la Bette* in her
autobiography:

It [*The Bride Came C.O.D.*] was called a comedy. It had been decided that
my work as a tragedian should be temporarily halted for a change of pace.
Jimmy, who had made the gangster artistic, Jimmy, who was one of the
fine actors on mine or any lot—Jimmy, with whom I'd always wanted to

With Bette Davis in the bristly comedy THE BRIDE CAME C.O.D. (WCTR)

work in something fine, spent most of his time in the picture removing cactus quills from my behind. This was supposedly hilarious. We romped about the desert and I kept falling into cactus. We both reached bottom with this one.

Not quite—bottom was yet to be reached for Cagney with *Captains of the Clouds*, filmed in 1941 and released in 1942, starring Cagney as Brian MacLean, a cocksure American northwoods bush pilot who joins the Royal Canadian Air Force and winds up fighting Nazi sky raiders in England. Though *Captains* is directed by Michael Curtiz, the story is but a warmed-over military prepared-ness sermon, much like *Here Comes the Navy*, et al., sans partner Pat O'Brien (whose solo career, thanks to *Knute Rockne—All-American*, was finally taking off), and redeemed only by some praiseworthy Technicolor backwoods scenery and aerial photography. (It is Cagney's first color picture.) The first half of the drama takes place in the forested wilds of (on-location) Canada where adventuresome pilot MacLean filches flying jobs from competitors; the second half of the tale shifts awkwardly and implausibly to RCAF pilot heroics—including Cagney's

Left to right: Dennis Morgan, Alan Hale, and Brenda Marshall with Cagney in CAPTAINS OF THE CLOUDS.

proverbial, sacrificial death (as in *Ceiling Zero* or *The Fighting 69th*) where he proves his character by kamikazeing during a sky battle with Nazi planes. Neither trusty secondary players George Tobias nor Alan Hale—not one thousand genuine RCAF cadets who are awarded their wings by World War I flying ace and Air Marshall William Avery ("Billy") Bishop in a cameo sequence—bolster the movie sufficiently. Though Cagney "is much better than his thankless role," in the words of *Time* magazine, the picture was a throwaway.

Though Cagney could be wheedled into a movie if its theme was anti-Nazi or its costar Bette Davis, the results continued to be a letdown. The scorecard since the 1938 settlement, though an improvement, was a case of too little too late from the Cagneys' point of view. They still rejected story after story proffered by Warner Brothers and waited in vain for something like the John Paul Jones saga or a Eugene O'Neill adaptation to materialize. Both James and William knew that they were marking time, and they grew restless.

Cagney rehearsing rigorously for the dance numbers of YANKEE DOODLE DANDY. (AMPAS)

7
Yankee Doodle Dandy

It survives as his masterpiece, a manic punchinello Uncle Sam, arse out, head forward, strutting his way through routines as if he had reinvented dance. Only this ferocious animation could have tamed the jingoism of the film; as Cohan, above all, Cagney seems to be driven by non-human forces, like a toy running wild. . . .

DAVID THOMSON
A Biographical Dictionary of Film

The story behind the making of *Yankee Doodle Dandy*, one of the most upbeat, right-minded pictures ever produced in Hollywood, is one of bad blood, ulterior motives, deliberately rose-colored biography, and irony upon irony. It begins several years prior to 1941—for the idea of a biopic based on the career of Broadway showman George M. Cohan had been kicking around the studios for years. The aging Cohan, stricken with cancer, was eager to preserve his legacy and anxious to sell the rights to his life story. When, in late 1938, Cagney pal and Cohan confidante Edward C. McNamara approached the Cagney brothers with the idea of Cagney playing Cohan, Cagney demurred, politely informing McNamara, "Cohan doesn't like me, he'd never agree to it." In fact, Cagney had met Cohan only once, in 1926, when the immortal song-and-dance man was casting one of his plays. ("I was in and out in a great hurry," Cagney was to recall years later, "Cohan holding I was not the type he was looking for.") Too, Cagney had seen and marvelled at Cohan's performances on stage in *Ah, Wilderness!* and *I'd Rather Be Right*. But Cagney had a visceral dislike for Cohan, dating back to Cohan's siding with the producers during the Actor's Equity Strike in 1919. It went against the grain for Cagney, a strong unionist, to glorify a reactionary.

Then, in 1940, something happened to alter the equation. Cagney's name cropped up again in the grand jury testimony of one John R. Leech, said to be the former "chief functionary" of the Los Angeles Communist party. Making the most of Cagney's known associations and sympathies, Leech named him as well as Humphrey Bogart, Clifford Odets, Frederic March, Jean Muir, and others as Communist members, sympathizers, and contributors of the Communist party; Leech alleged Bogart contributed $50 monthly. On the face of it, it was a preposterous accusation—indeed, Cagney had flirted with the party, was a friend of certain party members. But he had never joined, and his own left–liberal activism had already begun to wane. In his autobiography, he dates his disillusionment from contact in the early 1930s with that "wild-eyed" crowd of supporters for Tom Mooney in San Francisco. Also, the Hitler–Stalin pact and the line toed by party followers in Hollywood hit Cagney hard. The struggles of the early 1930s were fading into the past, as were such friends as John Bright and Sam Ornitz, replaced now by the Irish Mafia and his brother.

Regardless, the Communist accusation was relished by the press. *The New York Times* printed the charge on page one (but the eventual retraction wound up on page 21). The allegation was taken up by Buron Fitts, who was campaigning for re-election as district attorney of Los Angeles. When the Communist accusation hit the newspapers, James was back East on vacation and it was William who was called on the carpet in the office of Harry Warner. At that precise moment in history, Hitler was conquering Poland—among other things, hurting Warners' overseas distribution—and the Hitler–Stalin pact "looked very bad with the Jews in Hollywood," according to William Cagney. Harry Warner was on the warpath against pro-Reds. "He [Warner] told me in no uncertain terms," remembered William Cagney, "that if my brother didn't clean his skirts of this charge, he was going to destroy him." Warner suggested the Cagneys file a defamation lawsuit; but William Cagney had an alternate idea—to take the issue directly to Martin Dies, the flamboyant chairman of the House Un-American Activities Committee (HUAC), and to play off Dies against Fitts.

As it happened, Dies was scheduled for a stopover in Los Angeles within a few days, at which time William Cagney—accompanied by "B" producer Bryan Foy, Humphrey Bogart, and others—met privately with Dies and his assistants at the downtown Biltmore Hotel. William Cagney made the case for his absent brother while Dies listened in silence. Afterward, according to William Cagney, Dies asked, "But where *is* your brother?" "In Martha's Vineyard," came the reply. In the full color of his Texas accent Dies countered, "Well, where *ah* come from, somebody call you a son-o'-bitch and you do nothin' about it, you're a son-o'-bitch. I'll tell you somethin'. I'm goin' to Sacramento from heah. You get your brother up there and have him testify to our satisfaction and I'll give him a clean bill of health, y'heah?"

Shortly, William Cagney called James in Martha's Vineyard and urged him to cut his vacation short and fly back to California. Cagney was reluctant to cooperate. "He [James] was mixed up," recollected William Cagney, "because he knew me so well that when I said either he would have to do this or Harry

Cagney with HUAC Chairman Martin Dies who, in 1940 after testimony in Sacramento, cleared him of accusations of being a Communist. (Wide World Photo)

Warner would destroy him he knew there was no equivocation." There was another stumbling block—Cagney had never flown before, swore he never would. Yet the arguments of William Cagney prevailed. "To his credit," remembered William Cagney, "Jimmy got on the plane, which is probably the hardest thing he ever did in his life." Cagney flew to Los Angeles, and from there, with his brother, to Sacramento where, behind closed doors, he testified for fifteen minutes about his politics. Upon emerging, he told the press he had donated money to the San Joaquin Valley strikers, the Salinas lettuce strikers, the Motion Picture Relief Fund, the Hollywood Guild, the Scottsboro Boys Defense Fund, the Community Chest, and other organizations "whose work I have never considered un-American." Charges that Hollywood is permeated with Communists are, said Cagney, "so exaggerated they are ridiculous." For his part, Martin Dies delivered a statement to reporters clearing Cagney.

On the plane back to Los Angeles, William Cagney was thoughtful. He believed the label of pro-Red would continue to damage James's career, and that something had to be done to combat it. He turned to his brother and said, "We're going to have to make the goddamndest patriotic picture that's ever been made. I think it's the Cohan story." Cagney nodded in agreement. All his early opposition to the Cohan biography withered away. The Cohan story was, in time, to replace the John Paul Jones saga in his imagination and to become his most personal, fulfilling, triumphant role.

The Script's Progress

From the outset, with Jack Warner suggesting that the Cohan picture be called *Son of Yankee Doodle*, *Yankee Doodle Dandy* shaped up as a constant battle between the Cagneys and the Warners' front office. When Hal Wallis was assigned to oversee the production, the Cagneys anticipated trouble; they did not like Wallis very much and had clashed with him regularly over the years. James's differences with Wallis dated back to the early 1930s and the resentment felt by the Zanuck production unit at Warners when young Wallis at First National was favored by Jack Warner with more prestigious stage and literary properties, while the Zanuck squad was forced to originate its own story material. Later, Wallis' ceaseless stream of memos advising screenwriters and directors on how to "toughen" up Cagney was not appreciated—nor were his dictives urging Cagney to accept this or that inferior picture assignment. Already, by the time of *Yankee Doodle Dandy*, Wallis had earned James's undying enmity. In his autobiography, Cagney refers to Wallis, deprecatingly, as "front office." For his part, in his autobiography, *Starmaker: The Autobiography of Hal Wallis* (New York: Macmillan, 1980), Wallis had to admit, "He [Cagney] and I never became friends. He was cold to me and I wasn't particularly fond of him."

Some at the studio—Wallis included—resented William Cagney's de facto producership, which was ironclad per James's contract. William Cagney was no-nonsense about his position; he had firm ideas about what was advantageous for his brother. More than once he had threatened to pull Cagney off a project unless there were suitable concessions; he ran interference for his brother and insulated him from the day-to-day problems, summarily rejecting tough-guy vehicles submitted to Cagney as a matter of course. Consequently, brother William had enemies in the studio bureaucracy, and he was systematically denied his rightly deserved publicity and credits. Though he was active behind the scenes on every Cagney picture since *Boy Meets Girl*, William Cagney was not officially credited as associate producer until *City for Conquest* in 1941. (It was common practice at the studio in the 1930s and 1940s to credit higher-up executives, even Jack Warner in some cases, as being "producer" of a particular picture. It was not until mid-1942 that Warners production supervisors, of which William Cagney was one, were awarded their rightful producing credits.)

The first bone of contention between Wallis and the Cagneys was over Wallis' choice of screenwriter: It was an odd one, Robert Buckner, a former journalist, humorist, travel essayist, and short-story writer who had worked briefly on *The Oklahoma Kid*, and whose most recent assignment for the studio had been

The Four Cohans: With Jeanne Cagney, Rosemary De Camp, and Walter Huston. (WCTR)

another successful biographical picture, *Knute Rockne—All-American* in 1940. Buckner had never written a musical, nor had he ever seen Cohan perform on stage. Indeed, Buckner seemed to have little confidence in the assignment and tried to beg off the task on several occasions, certain that Cohan's life offered little dramatic potential, especially considering that Cohan himself intended to monitor the script's progress. But Buckner's attitude improved after he met Cohan in New York City and passed muster with the song-and-dance entertainer. They developed a warm rapport over the three months or so they conferred at Cohan's Fifth Avenue apartment. Buckner and Cohan took long walks daily, and Buckner would serve as an entranced audience of one as Cohan, joined by his surviving pals (including ex-partner Sam Harris), sang and danced his old routines and acted out highlights of his career. Together they would pore over clippings and scrapbooks while Cohan proferred script advice and suggestions—at one point, Cohan even came forward with his own lengthy and rambling screenplay draft (which was diplomatically accepted by Buckner and then bypassed). If the Cagneys were not ecstatic about Buckner, at least Cohan was. "Cohan had some anti-Semitic prejudices to combine with his Hollywood ones," reported Buckner, "and he had reasons that he explained to me during the three months or so I worked with him in New York. He was also a solid Catholic, if occasionally lapsing, and he liked the screenplay I wrote on the life of Knute Rockne. This, together with the fact that I am a Gentile was, I believe, the determining factor in my selection."

Cohan's primary concerns were historical accuracy (especially regarding vaudeville life and incidents that reflected negatively on himself) and the depiction of his romantic affiliations. Cohan had a "prudery about screen romance," according to Cagney, and he desired there be no mention of his first wife or his having been married twice. The first Mrs. Cohan, a vaudeville headliner named Ethel Levey who quit as Cohan's leading lady after their bitter divorce, was said to be observing the preparations for *Dandy* with growing anxiety; in fact, she later sued for invasion of privacy (and lost). The wife predicament was solved in the final draft—not by Buckner, but by the Epstein brothers—by a composite character named "Mary." As for Cohan's ban on love scenes, that was fine with Cagney. "This taboo on love scenes didn't bother me," the actor later recalled,

> for the way I do a love scene, it's never a necking party. To me, a panting and grappling love scene is embarrassing when I see it on the screen. So when I sang 'Mary' to the girl who played Cohan's wife [Joan Leslie], I just told her the lyrics as she played the melody. I poured coffee, put sugar into it, stirred it and handed it to her. Then I sat down, drank the coffee, and she sang the lyric back to me. The way we did it, it was an effective love scene without any lashings of goo!

Buckner was responsible for the frame–flashback structure of *Dandy* and much of the plotting. But William Cagney was deeply involved in the story sessions too, and he and Buckner did not get along. William Cagney felt that Buckner was being too obsequious to Cohan, too literal in transcribing the man's story. Again and again, Buckner and William Cagney found themselves at odds, and when Buckner went to Wallis for support, William Cagney one-upped them both by threatening his brother's withdrawal. When the Cagneys were away on location in Canada for *Captains of the Clouds*, Buckner rushed through a final draft, and Wallis gave it his stamp of approval and a start date. When William returned from filming, he was outraged and confronted Wallis, "How are your dancing shoes, Hal?—because you're going to have to play the part!" The preliminary shooting script was sent to Cagney at his retreat in Martha's Vineyard, and in his autobiography he records his reaction: "I read it with incredulity," he wrote.

> There wasn't a single laugh in it, not the suggestion of a snicker. And this was a script purporting to be about a great American light entertainer, a professional humorist, a man who wrote forty-four Broadway shows, only

Cohan (Cagney) and partner Sam Harris (Richard Whorf) "meet cute" and get bankrolled by "angel" S. Z. ("Cuddles") Sakall. (WCTR)

two of which were not comedies. I said to brother Bill, "It's no good. I won't touch it. But I'll tell you what I'll do. I'll give it a blanket O.K. now if you put the Epstein boys on it to liven it up and inject humor.

Buckner's script was simply unfunny. With Cagney holding out, Buckner was now dropped from the writing, and the Epstein brothers—Julius and Philip, who had so pleased the Cagneys with their work on *The Strawberry Blonde* and *The Bride Came C.O.D.*—were approached. The bathos and the flag-waving of *Dandy* were not the Epsteins' cup of tea, however, and they said no, adamantly, recommending instead a friend who needed work, a gagman named Edmund Joseph, whose career credits included service on several Abbott and Costello features. Joseph, a free lancer from outside the studio gates, was duly hired on; but though he sprinkled a few jokes into the script, he did not complete the chore. William Cagney persisted in his overtures to the Epsteins until they finally relented, as a favor to him, coming on the project in November before Thanksgiving as filming of the musical numbers was already due to

Conferring with director Michael Curtis on the set of YANKEE DOODLE DANDY. (AMPAS)

begin. The enlistment of the Epsteins was the final rebuff to Buckner, whose influence on the picture was diminishing.

As it happened, the Epsteins revised and tinkered throughout filming in November and December of 1941 and January of 1942, and their contribution (with Cagney adding his own "touches" throughout) pervades the script of *Dandy*. Among their enrichments: They resolved Cohan's relationship with Mary and turned it into a sweet, old-fashioned romance; they wrote the delightfully comic Dietz and Goff interlude; they expanded the role of Josie M. Cohan; they created a deathbed scene for George M.'s father; and they kept up with the headlines by writing the "Over There" coda after the bombing of Pearl Harbor. The nostalgic feeling for the turn-of-the-century period, the overall sense of comedy, and the character of George M. Cohan were all substantively enhanced by the Epsteins' participation. But curiously enough, their names were left off the final credits, which read, "Original Story by Robert Buckner, Screenplay by Buckner and Edmund Joseph." For as the production was being filmed, Buckner threatened to go to arbitration over credits, claiming that 90 percent of the construction and 70 percent of the dialogue were his. As the Epsteins were diffident about the project in the first place, they bowed out, allowing that "four names would clutter up the screen," and secured a credit for their pal Joseph as a compromise. (Actually, *five* names deserve mention on the screen—for a writer by the name of Jack Moffitt wrote the flavorful narration during postproduction.) Yet the matter was not blithely forgotten. In interviews, the Cagneys always belittled Buckner's work, and Buckner always belittled William Cagney, more privately, in kind. Lawsuits were bruited about (but never materialized). The private dissension became public shortly after the premiere of *Dandy* when the Cagneys paid for a full-page advertisement in the Hollywood trade papers pointedly thanking the Epsteins for their saving involvement. "Although we were grateful," recalled Julius J. Epstein, "it was embarrassing to us and it was demeaning to Joseph and Buckner."

Cagney as Cohan

The casting was crucial. Seventeen-year-old Joan Leslie, fresh from her appealing debut in *Sergeant York* in 1941, was set for the pivotal role of Cohan's wife, Mary. Casting Jeanne Cagney, James's sister, by now a magna cum laude graduate of Hunter College who had worked her way up the ladder of the business through summer stock, radio drama, and "B" pictures at Paramount, was director Michael Curtiz' idea. Rosemary DeCamp was to play the elder Mrs. Cohan (a bit of casting approved by Mrs. Cohan's real-life grandson, Fred Niblo Jr., a screenwriter on the Warners' lot). And after much discussion, Walter Huston was finally prevailed upon to play the supporting role of Cohan's father. Huston's resistance to playing a lesser role was worn down after William Cagney promised him a show-stopping death scene—which James Cagney proceeded to steal with a spontaneous outburst of tears that "just seemed to do the finishing off of what was in the script" (Cagney's words).*

Arriving from Martha's Vineyard, Cagney threw himself into the Cohan characterization. "Psychologically, I needed no preparation for *Yankee Doodle Dandy*, or professionally either," he wrote in his autobiography. "I didn't have to pretend to be a song-and-dance man. I was one." For two months prior to actual filming, Cagney rehearsed the dancing sequences. With his sister Jeanne, he practiced for four hours daily and then, during production, from seven to nine in the morning and for two hours every night after filming—brushing up on intricate wings, cramp rolls, and buck dancing. Cagney's instructor was Johnny Boyle, who had danced in the chorus of *Something to Sing About* and who was to later choreograph Cagney's routines in *West Point Story* as well as in *Dandy*. Known to aficionados as "the dancer's dancer," Boyle was undoubtedly one of the finest technical dancers of his era. He had worked on Broadway in the Cohan–

---

*Of the deathbed scene, Julius J. Epstein recalled, "Curtiz kept saying, 'Give me the tear in the eye' Finally my brother [Philip] said, 'Let's give him the tear in the eye.' So we wrote the death scene with the Cohan trademark—'My mother thanks you, my father thanks you' and so on. We thought it was hilarious. We thought they would never use it. But they did and it was one of the best scenes in the film."

Harris revues and had staged dances for Cohan, so he knew the Cohan mannerisms—his stiff-legged technique and his run up the side of the proscenium arch.
More recently, Boyle had gravitated to Hollywood where he found steady work
as a choreographer and specialty dancer. It is possible that Boyle was involved
somehow in Cohan's only "talkie" musical, *The Phantom President* of 1932, in
which there is a scene where Cohan, wearing blackface, sings a ditty entitled
"Maybe Someone Ought to Wave the Flag," then tap dances on the apron of his
minstrel show trailer with steps copied nearly step for step, later, for the
"Yankee Doodle Dandy" number in *Dandy*. Likewise, there is a brief, uncanny
moment in *Something to Sing About*, in which Cagney tap dances merrily down a
long flight of steps—just as the character of George M. Cohan does in the finale
of *Dandy*.

The rehearsals of *Dandy* were so arduous that, according to Cagney, Boyle
hurt "one foot badly enough to be virtually incapacitated for dancing for the rest
of his life." Still, despite all the rehearsals, Cagney did not feel quite ready when
the cameras rolled. Perfectionist that he was, Cagney fretted that his dancing
was not up to par with Cohan's. The first production number to be filmed was "I
Was Born in Virginia" (seen in the montage sequences), and Cagney "went onto
the shooting stage not knowing entirely what I was going to do" (in the words of
his autobiography). "It got by, but I didn't feel right about it." Then Curtiz shot
the memorable "Yankee Doodle Dandy" number excerpted from the play *Little
Johnny Jones*, a spectacular high point of *Dandy*. Cagney once more did not
measure up to his own rigorous standards. "Again, not enough rehearsal and
again apparently nobody noticed it, but I did. There was a rigidity in certain
areas of the number because I wasn't always sure of what the next step was
going to be."

The challenges of evoking Cohan in the nonmusical sections of *Dandy* were
dissimilar. Cagney was an expert mimic who could easily imitate gestures,
dialects, and individual quirks; and not only did he remember Cohan from the
stage, but he also screened *The Phantom President* so he could register the
mannerisms—the New England drawl, the monkey-like stance (not unlike Cagney's own—from a lifetime of lifting weights), Cohan's habit of leading with
his chin.

One night Cagney decided to consult with the Irish Mafia at their regular
dinner party gathering. Some of those who were present that night had worked
with Cohan in New York in their pre-Hollywood days. Besides Spencer Tracy
(once a Cohan protégé), the list of guests included Frank McHugh, Ralph
Bellamy, and character actors Frank Morgan and Lynne Overman. Cagney asked
whether he ought to use the Cohan mannerisms full force offstage as well, or
whether that would overemphasize the trick. Cagney recalled, "When it was
announced that I was to play Cohan, I told the boys what my plans for him
were. I did play him as straight as I could, in the offstage sequences, and used
his mannerisms only when the opportunities presented themselves, without

Cagney as Cohan, in the "Little Johnny Jones" number. (AMPAS)

dragging them in unnecessarily. Apparently that worked, because they all agreed that was the sensible approach."

Meantime, with filming in full throttle, the Cagneys seemed to be caught in a veritable crossfire of competing egos and differing artistic views. Buckner, isolated from the Epsteins, was bad mouthing their revisions in a series of secret memos addressed to the front office, warning the studio that Cohan's endorsement was being jeopardized by the Cagneys' steam rolling. Indeed, Cohan's own representatives in Hollywood were kept in the dark until filming was completed and a "rough cut" could be assembled—and lawyers on both sides were nervous. "I was fighting treachery every step of the way," remembered William Cagney. "You didn't know, every time you stepped on a plank, whether or not you would drop 4000 feet and disappear. The scheming was Byzantine." Apart from Buckner's intrusions, the studio seemed to be nit-picking about the budget—one squabble involved the expense of using a real horse in the "Little Johnny Jones" dance number (the Cagneys won); producer Wallis took every opportunity to side with director Curtiz when minor disagreements arose on the set (again, the Cagneys usually prevailed). When, early in the filming, choreographer Seymour Felix went to Wallis and demanded that Johnny Boyle be fired—Felix was jealous and resentful of Boyle's relationship with Cagney—it was *Felix* who was fired, that afternoon. Ironically, most of the dances were already staged—by Felix. But an innocuous cover story was given to the industry trade papers, and LeRoy Prinz finished up, consolidating his reputation by basically directing on-camera the singing–dancing sequences that Felix had so painstakingly devised.

William Cagney managed to hold the line, under duress. There was no final straw, just a point of no return. A couple of weeks into the filming of dialogue scenes, William Cagney found his brother in his trailer sitting for makeup with Perc Westmore. After walkouts and lawsuits and now this incessant backstabbing, he felt he had had enough. He walked in and tossed a legal document in front of Cagney. "What have you got there?" asked Cagney. "Cancellation of both our contracts," replied William. There was only the briefest pause—they had not discussed such a move. "This," said Cagney, taking out a pen, "ought to start a riot." He signed the document, calling quits to his long, embattled relationship with Warner Brothers. He looked up and remarked, "I'm tired of fighting, fighting, fighting and then finally getting what I want." *Yankee Doodle Dandy* was to be their last picture under the 1938 contract—the Cagneys were finally activating their "happiness clause." Consequently, the studio backed off, and the Cagneys completed *Dandy* under rare conditions of freedom. *The New York Times* reported, "As a result [of this action], they were left alone to do exactly as they pleased with *Dandy*. The Warners were 'prepared to make any concession.' They let William spend nearly $1,500,000 getting the picture exactly as he wanted it. James backed him up all the way." The next step for the brothers was to be the formation of their independent company, Cagney Productions.

A Tour-de-Force of Make-Believe

Actually, *Yankee Doodle Dandy* is more hagiography than biography, a fantasy concoction based ever so loosely on the real story. Cohan's setbacks and tragedies, his repugnant elitism during the Actor's Equity Strike of 1919, and his humiliating rejection by Hollywood later in life—these were discreetly glossed over in the script in favor of an abundance of cheap sentiment and knockabout comedy. The movie cleverly unfolds in flashback, so that the story begins as a Congressional Medal of Honor is being bestowed on the venerable Cohan by the president of the United States (FDR-soundalike Captain Jack Young). Then, with hurtling speed, the film traces Cohan's celebrated career from its humble vaudeville origins to its many Broadway conquests. Extravagant musical routines fill in the thematic gaps. The intimate numbers (such as the one where Cohan and partner Sam Harris "meet cute," or Cohan's lovely rendering of "Mary") linger in memory as keenly as the beaming musical extravaganzas (particularly "Give

"My mother thanks you, my father thanks you, my sister thanks you, and I thank you." (AMPAS)

My Regards to Broadway'' and ''Yankee Doodle Boy''). All the ingredients jelled—a topflight supporting cast and gallery of bit players; a condensed score of Cohan's best-loved tunes and authentically styled routines; crisp cinematography by James Wong Howe; and buoyant direction by Curtiz, who wore the love of his adopted country on his sleeve.

Curtiz' visual strategy was to fix on Cohan at all points in the story, thereby consolidating the movie around Cagney's performance. Bravura, tour-de-force—all superlatives apply. It was, is, Cagney's greatest attainment as an actor, and the fact that it is such an anomaly in his career makes it all the more brilliant. As Cohan, Cagney staggered critics and moviegoers who heretofore had regarded him as little more than a crude movie gangster type, demonstrating conclusively for posterity, as he had only insinuated in *Footlight Parade* and *Something to Sing About*, that he was a consummate song-and-dance artist too. He sang with a Yankee-clipped, sonorous staccato; he danced with a fury that belied the subtle intricacy of the steps. He began the piece as youthful, overweening George M., advanced to middle age, and wound up as a restless codger

The spectacular "You're A Grand Old Flag" number, a production high point.
(AMPAS)

who taps down the White House stairs in rhythm with soldiers marching off to World War II. The aging never struck a false note—for Cagney believed in himself as Cohan as much as audiences did. A proud and a feverish characterization, it was as if Cagney were vengefully dispelling his gangster past, as if, too, he were reconciling aspects of the tough guy in Cohan. As critic Andrew Bergman wrote in his book *James Cagney* (New York: Pyramid, 1973), "He [Cagney] caught more than a touch of Cohan's self-love, but managed to make the character a good deal more sympathetic than Cohan was in actuality."

The premiere of *Dandy* was moved up from July 4, 1942, when Cohan's cancer began to spread. The opening night benefit in New York City on May 29 raised an estimated $4,750,000 in war bonds for the Treasury Department. For a nation immersed in jingoism, the patriotism of *Dandy* could not have been better timed. The critics were rhapsodic. "*Yankee Doodle Dandy*, the story of George M. Cohan, actor, songwriter, author and producer, is as perfectly timed for 1942 as *Sergeant York* was for 1941," wrote Archer Winsten of *The New York Post*. Howard Barnes of *The New York Herald Tribune* observed that:

> The latter came to a nation moving reluctantly into war, matched its objections with a famous conscientious objector of the last war, and solved his and our problems in a magnificent real life display of heroism. The

As Cohan, receiving his Congressional Medal of Honor from FDR (Captain Jack Young).

former, now showing at the Hollywood Theatre, comes as our soldiers and sailors depart to fight on the seven seas and five continents. What could be more timely than to have recalled for us the career of America's lustiest flag-waver, the author of "Over There"? The magic of *Yankee Doodle Dandy* is conjured up by the consummate Cagney portrayal. He even looks like Cohan at times and he has the great man's routines down cold. The point is that he adds his own individual reflections to the part, as should certainly be done in any dramatic impersonation of a celebrated figure. He has given many memorable and varied screen performances in the past, but this is nothing short of a brilliant tour-de-force of make-believe.

The film was nominated for eight Academy Awards: Best Picture, Best Supporting Actor (Huston), Best Original Story (Buckner), Best Director (Curtiz), Best Editing (George Amy), Best Sound (Nathan Levinson), Best Musical Scoring (Heinz Roemheld and Ray Heindorf), and Best Actor (Cagney). The outpouring of praise for Cagney's performance was crowned by his second New York Critic's prize for best acting and his first—and only—Oscar as Best Actor. (In a year dominated by MGM's *Mrs. Miniver*, Levinson, Roemheld, and Heindorf were the only other *Dandy* winners.) "Sensible people who attended the Academy dinner say Hollywood reached a new high in sappiness that night," re-

Cagney accepts his Best Actor Oscar at the Academy dinner in 1943. Presenter (standing behind him) was Gary Cooper, Best Actor winner for 1941's SERGEANT YORK. (Wide World Photo)

ported a contemporary magazine. "Actresses wept unconvincingly, and pushed other actresses around when those other actresses, also weeping unconvincingly, tried to hog the stage. It was a night of speeches in which some of the biggest people in motion pictures behaved as though they were bereft of their senses. . . . Only two speakers seemed to return a sense of balance. One was Irving Berlin and the other was James Cagney." When Gary Cooper, the previous year's honoree, tore open the envelope and announced Cagney's name, the ovation was thunderous. Cagney's acceptance speech was succinct. "I've always maintained," he told the crowd, "that in this business you are only as good as the other fellow thinks you are. It's nice to know that you people thought I did a good job. And don't forget that it was a good part too." The following day, Cagney placed the Oscar statuette on brother William's desk to acknowledge his gratitude.

A movie that so avidly salutes the flag, the family, and the American ethic of drive and ambition, *Dandy* is one of Cagney's most personal films, his favorite, the one he always preferred to be remembered by. As such, it is fascinating to note the parallels to his own life that enriched his participation. Like Cohan, Cagney launched his career in vaudeville and only after years of hardship rose to the pinnacle of his profession—for Cohan, Broadway and the theater; for Cagney, Hollywood and motion pictures. Like Cohan, Cagney surrounded himself with members of his family during his life, both before and pursuant to his success. And like the fictional Cohan of *Dandy*, Cagney was married early in his life to a show business hoofer who "retired" after their union while his career blossomed. The conclusion of *Dandy*, meanwhile, is strangely prophetic. When hip teenagers tell the aging Cohan, sequestered on his farm, that they have never heard of the once-famous star, the scene evokes Cagney's own lifelong love affair with rural existence and foreshadows his own spell of retirement into near oblivion in the 1960s.

The Liberty with Facts

Meantime, George M. Cohan had been cut off from the production since the unceremonious departure of Buckner, and he and his lawyers were anxious, to say the least, about the liberties with facts. In late April 1942, a projector, screen, and print of the movie were delivered to Cohan and his wife (the second Mrs. Cohan) at their summer home in Monroe, New York, where they viewed *Yankee Doodle Dandy* in a hall above the town firehouse. Both were in wheelchairs—Mrs. Cohan had not walked in years. During the screening, Cohan had to be escorted from the room several times to relieve himself, so badly was he now suffering from cancer of the bladder. Among Cohan's fears: his wife Agnes' reaction to the character named Mary. What happened afterward may or may not be apocryphal, but it is an anecdote that the Cagneys, who were not present, always relished telling. When the lights went up, Mrs. Cohan *rose* out of her wheelchair and walked over to George M., saying "Oh, George, you were fine"—adding sweetly, "And I always *knew* I was 'Mary' to you." According to Cagney: "She had accepted me as George . . . completely." Shortly thereafter, Cagney received a telegram from Cohan: "Dear Jim, How's my double? Thanks for a wonderful job. Sincerely, George M. Cohan." Within the year the original "yankee doodle boy" was dead.

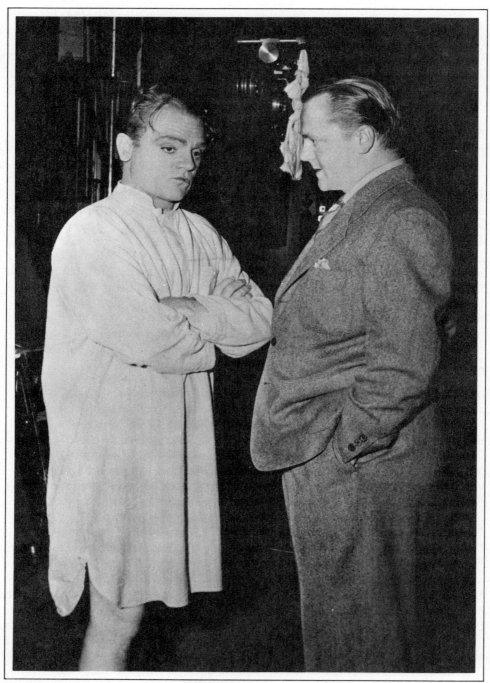

With brother William on the set of JOHNNY COME LATELY. (WCTR)

8
Cagney Productions

I am not the characters I play. I believe that, in order to do anything well, you must have perspective, a certain amount of objectivity, of detachment. This is necessary in order to give a clear portrait of a character. If I were a "tough guy," I couldn't play one even as well as I do. It has been more valuable to me to stand on the sidelines and, with a certain degree of impersonality, register the reactions I have noted. The idea of playing oneself is essentially fallacious. The fact that I am supposed to be a tough guy in real life doesn't bother me in the least. It's amusing. It doesn't matter.

JAMES CAGNEY

The years immediately following *Yankee Doodle Dandy* should have been an upward spiral of ever greater glory for Cagney. After all, he had now earned the Academy Award for Best Actor. He and his brother had left Warner Brothers and incorporated as Cagney Productions, thus finally establishing the actor's vaunted independence in the form of a small family production unit. And Cagney was in the prime of age, at the zenith of his popularity.

Yet circumstances always seemed to conspire against the Cagneys: Resistance to their independent endeavors was tirelessly fanned in Hollywood by another pair of brothers, Harry and Jack Warner; World War II intervened with its priorities; and, above all, Cagney's "steam" for motion pictures was evanescent, and he seemed all but spent by the struggles over making *Yankee Doodle Dandy*. In the next seven years he was to star in only four pictures; though they included his most personal, his most magical characterizations, it was in general a period of lulls.

"The Best Deal in Town"

Characteristically, in 1943, when William Cagney finalized the production–distribution contract for Cagney Productions, he pronounced it "the best deal in town." And certainly it was—on paper. The financing came from Banker's Trust

163

in New York City and Security-First National on the West Coast, with Cagney Productions agreeing to produce nine pictures to be distributed by United Artists, the company founded by Mary Pickford, Douglas Fairbanks, Charles Chaplin, and D. W. Griffith. Eighty percent of the production costs would be borne by the banks; the Cagneys would defer their equal salaries of $150,000 each until after profits; and each brother kicked in a sum of $45,000 for preproduction costs for the first film.

The clincher was a "favored nation's" clause in the distribution terms, whereby the Cagneys would receive the best sliding-scale distribution percentages available to United Artists clients—equivalent to those received ʰ ex-MGM producers Hunt Stromberg and David O. Selznick. In principle, ₍ meant that Cagney Productions would cede 25 percent of the first $800,000 gro. of every picture to UA but only ten percent above $800,000, so that on the firsᵉ two independent pictures—which averaged $1.5 million at the box-office domestically—the Cagneys were paying only 17 percent for distribution, a low mark for that era.

But where to begin? With *Dandy*, the Cagneys felt they had achieved a synthesis of the tough guy with a newborn Cagney; now they were faced with the problem of how to top the role of George M. Cohan. The matter was complicated by the Warners' continued animosity and by the Cagneys' belief that agents of story material were being privately warned to steer clear of doing business with Cagney Productions.

"I think it was the success of *Yankee Doodle Dandy* that made it so difficult for us to find a vehicle to follow it up with," explained William Cagney.

Everything we read was just pale. Vanilla. We couldn't get a goddammed story. We were sweating for a year, trying to find a vehicle. But nobody was submitting.

If you had read the papers at the time Cagney Productions was forming, you would see what I mean. It wasn't that they were seething with it every day, but once a week you would see someone gratuitously summing up how certain it was that Cagney Productions, or any independent production, was doomed to failure. They cited Charles Ray, Gloria Swanson, Buster Keaton, a line-up of twenty top stars who went broke [as independents], and it was quite convincing.

They were also doing everything they could to make sure we didn't get the stories we needed to be a successful producer. The brokers, the agents, didn't work with us. They never came near me. Later on, I was able to work with a few of them. And I can't even claim that this was an active conspiracy other than, why weren't they there? We had money to spend. In a certain sense, we had the top actor of that period. And he had just won the *Yankee Doodle* [Academy] award.

After the first year passed, the Cagneys had significantly *less* money to spend. And though publicity churned out by the company proudly indicated that the

*The formation of Cagney Productions: William Cagney (left), Ed Raftery
(president of United Artists and George M. Cohan's representative in
Hollywood), Cagney, and unidentified person. (WCTR)*

brothers had rejected some 400 scripts in their quest for "the right one," the
truth is that very few screenplays were seriously considered. Cagney Productions did not have the capital to be developing more than a couple of stories at
any given time—besides, it was not their style—and the front burner was as
vacant as the back. As their cashflow dwindled, Howard Hughes, another
maverick and a carousing buddy of William Cagney's, dispatched his right-hand
man, Johnny Meyers, with the missive, "The genius wants to buy a piece of your
company." The wealthy Hughes offered to sink $1 million into Cagney Produc-
tions in return for a 30 percent interest in the outfit.

But William Cagney was wary. He knew that Hughes had been remanded out
of a controlling interest in any motion picture studio during wartime because he
was also in the business of manufacturing bombers, infrared detectors, and
other military hardware. This offer was Hughes' way of keeping a finger in the

pie. But, with Hughes, you could never be sure that it would not turn out to be two fingers—or more. In a session at Hughes' Bel-Air residence—with the eccentric billionaire spiffing up for the occasion in a blue suit and college tie—William Cagney cautioned Hughes that if his largesse was accepted he would not have anything to say about *anything* in Cagney Productions. Hughes simmered for a while, then piped up, "I can vote! I'll have a third of the stock!"

At that foreboding remark, William Cagney departed, without ever returning Hughes' persistent phone calls. Three months later, according to William Cagney, Hughes showed up in the producer's living room and demanded, "Why didn't you ever call me back on that deal?" Cagney replied, "You want the truth, Howard?" Hughes: "Sure." Cagney: "I just figured that one morning at 3:30 I'd be sound asleep, there'd be a knock on the door, I'd get up kind of bleary-eyed, open the door and there'd be a doll with bazooms out to here. And she'd say, 'I'm your new leading lady, Howard sent me.'" Years later, William Cagney recalled with a chuckle: "Hughes blew his top because he knew it was true. He was addicted to bazooms. If everybody in the world was looking for him, a pair of lovely bazooms would find him."

Thus, the Cagneys maintained their precarious independence—albeit without a movie to show for it. Then along came a book by Louis Bromfield called *It Takes All Kinds*—known variously by such other titles as *You Get What You Give* and *McLeod's Folly*—a picaresque small-town fable about political corruption and crusading journalism. Bromfield was a well-known author of the period, and his novel had been bouncing from story department to story department in Hollywood since its publication in 1931. It was a wispy sort of story, more Capraesque than Cagneyesque, but at the time there seemed to be no other options. "Sadly to say," recalled William Cagney, "I think I was taken. I think Warners sent me *McLeod's Folly* through a friend of theirs and had that friend press it to the hilt. They knew we had no story, so they set me up with something they tried to lick and never could lick. The story was likeable, but dreary in the sense that there were no explosions. We had to manufacture the explosions."

To manufacture the "explosions"—the necessary plot crises and machinations—William Cagney called on British dramatist (and latterly, Hollywood scenarist) John Van Druten, an artful constructionist whose comedies for the stage (many of them filmed in various incarnations) included a version of Christopher Isherwood's *I Am a Camera* (later adapted as *Cabaret*), *Old Acquaintance* (updated for the screen as *Rich and Famous*), *The Voice of the Turtle*, and *I Remember Mama*. Van Druten was so facile that, after brainstorming in story sessions with William Cagney, he would step into his office and return 20 minutes later with a finely polished scene fresh from his typewriter. "A magnificent writer," recalled William Cagney, "so much so that when he really got going he'd say to me, 'Watch it, Bill! I'm bewitching you!' It [the Bromfield story] was hard to whip but he worked like hell."

Hiring a director was a trickier proposition. "We looked all around for a

*On the DANDY set with brother Edward Cagney, mother Carolyn Nelson
Cagney, and Jeanne Cagney. (Courtesy of Jeanne Cagney)*

director," recollected William Cagney, "and somehow or other they weren't
there. I think there was a total conspiracy to see that we didn't succeed and I
think they got the word to directors: 'Don't work for the Cagneys.'" Finally,
William Cagney settled on William K. Howard, who had been blackballed by the
major studios and was on the last legs of a once ambitious but now erratic career.
Howard had come from Ohio, getting his start in distribution before establishing
himself as an important director in his heyday in the early 1930s; but he was an
iconoclast, outspoken against the studio chiefs and the studio system, and a
drunkard. Furthermore, the studio heads had promulgated the gossip—vehemently denied by his friends—that Howard was anti-Semitic, which was anath-
ema to his motion picture career.

All of these details were left, in the main, up to William Cagney. Bromfield—
James Cagney admired; the story appealed to the actor, with its poet–artist–
vagabond hero, more so that it did to his producer–brother. The director Howard was an old acquaintance. But as usual, Willaim Cagney packaged the
ingredients while the star heeded the progress and assented from the sidelines.

''I usually didn't bother Jimmy with any of the details,'' explained William Cagney.

My procedure, in almost every deal I made for Jimmy, whether it be for acting or productions, was to proceed generally with no long discussions about what we were going to do; just keep him advised of who I was working with. Purposely, I didn't get into any details about terms or conditions because he would take a position on something and I'd have trouble on the thing. My problem was to keep him open until I could recommend something at 100 percent so there could be no fluttering around the deal.

Johnny Come Lately

With its puzzling new title of *Johnny Come Lately*, the maiden Cagney Production was launched in September of 1943—a month in which papers were dominated by news of the Italian surrender, bulletins from the Russian front and dispatches from the offensive in the Pacific—a year dominated by such war-themed pictures as *Casablanca, Watch on the Rhine, So Proudly We Hail, In Which We Serve, North Star, Action in the North Atlantic, Destination Tokyo*, and *This Land Is Mine*. If, a year previous, with war clouds gathering on the horizon, *Yankee Doodle Dandy* had seemed perfectly on target, now *Johnny* seemed untimely, anachronistic. Partly because Cagney played a tramp on the road of life, partly because Cagney played the role so whimsically, *Johnny* evoked the work of Chaplin in its shiny, emotional positivism. But it was a Chaplin miscalculated, out of sync with headlines and out of favor with critics, and a movie that consequently never received its proper due.

In any year *Johnny* would have been an unusual movie, a special one, which is apparent from the opening moments of the story. The camera floats along the streets of a picturesque small town, pausing to catch the drift of conversation between hoboes and observing the yawning movements of the citizenry. Underneath a town statue, chuckling to himself, absorbed in a volume of Dickens, is Cagney, playing a happily out-of-work reporter named Tom Richards. In his hand a pencil is poised to underline memorable Dickensian passages. Of Richards' past, nothing is known or learned. It is hinted that he is recovering from a sad romance. He implies that he once had weighty principles as a journalist. When he is jailed by the town magistrate as a vagrant, he refuses to be written down as a transient, explaining that he merely prefers travel to regular employment.

Richards is befriended by an elderly newspaperwoman named Vinnie McLeod (veteran stage actress Grace George in her only motion picture role), who is a guardian angel to the town's homeless and who enlists Richards in her crusade against local corrupt politicos. Despite her husband's death, her competitor's

With Grace George in the maiden Cagney Production, JOHNNY COME LATELY.

threats, and the reluctant pawning, piece by piece, of her estate, McLeod intends to carry on the good fight in her editorials. Her ideals rub off on Richards, whom she defends in court, she informs him simply, "because you were reading Dickens."

Working for McLeod's small press, Richards proves himself an able journalist and—like the actor who plays the part—an artist. He sketches bold caricatures, stimulating a sharp upswing in circulation, and seems barely interested in the romantic tension between himself and Vinnie McLeod's niece (Marjorie Lord), preferring to lavish his attentions on the lady publisher, her sultry cook Aida (Hattie McDaniel), and saloon madam Gashouse Mary (Marjorie Main), a cynic who will not join the clean-up campaign until her old pal McLeod is nearly slain by a nocturnal assassin. In time there is a great, grassroots uprising, and Richards must prove himself capable with his fists as well—but this element is perfunctory in the script and unnecessary for such an otherwise quixotic character.

Indeed, the liberties taken with Bromfield's original novelette suggest that Van Druten and the Cagneys were intentionally toying with Chaplinesque associations. In Bromfield's version of the story, the character (Tom Richardson) is 29,

With Marjorie Main in JOHNNY COME LATELY. (WCTR)

Boston-bred but living in New York City, a "cold and stiff" fellow who is "writing a series of articles on how badly the wandering honest fellow out of work is treated." (Bromfield's novel was originally published, remember, during the Great Depression.) None of this definition remains in the film: Therefore, Richards becomes nomadic, samaritan, mysterious, heroic. Without any means of subsistence, he hops a train as the film ends, onward to another destination, another fate—like Chaplin, vanishing into the distance. A fellow bum recites a verse entitled "Open Road to Freedom" as the two ride along through the scenic countryside in an open boxcar—and points out that some fellow named Richards wrote it. The only reaction from Richards/Cagney is an enigmatic smile.

What Van Druten's amiable and leisurely scenario lacked in explosions it made up for in its collection of small-town types who parade their tics with flourish and enchantment. Grace George is a revelation, dignified and radiant; Hattie McDaniel, rowdy and flirtatious; Marjorie Main, bedecked in satins, earthy and comical as the town tart who insists, "I run a straight place." Among the film's other enticements are Edward McNamara as a crooked political hack (who sings nonsensical rhymes to himself); timid legislator Robert Barrat (whose engagement to Gashouse Mary breaks up over the issue of ketchup); Margaret Hamilton and George Cleveland as the Fergusons, lifelong McLeod employees (he, a tippler and bumbling; she, old-biddyish); and even a little mouse "who comes around every lunchtime for his food." The first-class technical contributions include Leigh Harline's lilting score; setpieces—director Howard loved maneuvering around elaborate setpieces—by Jack Okey; and photography by Theodore Sparkuhl. William Cagney spent an additional $50,000 to have the film stock custom printed by Pathé lab, an uncommon practice that added to the texture of the movie.

Manifestly, *Johnny* was an "expert effort of application," in William Cagney's words, but so atypical of Cagney, so uncategorizable, that critics sent up a hue and cry. *Johnny Come Lately*, wrote John T. McManus in *P.M.*,

> is almost the kind of business that might result if Jimmy Cagney, the immortal Hollywood movie star, had returned to play the lead in the annual production of his old high school's Masque and Film Club. . . . *Johnny Come Lately* is so palpably amateurish in production and direction, so hopelessly stagey, uneven and teamless in performance, and so utterly pointless that it is bound to cause raised eyebrows wherever it is shown.

Echoed Archer Winsten in *The New York Post*: "To put it bluntly, it is an old-fashioned story told in a very old-fashioned manner. Please, Mr. Cagney, for the benefit of the public, yourself and Warners, go back where you made pictures like *Yankee Doodle Dandy*."

There were dissenting voices—particularly James Agee, who was sensitive to what the Cagney brothers were attempting during this period—but they tended to be drowned out by the chorus of critical nays.* Eloquently wrote the critic for *Time*:

> Grace George seems effortlessly to have learned what so many transplanted Broadway actors ache over—how to project her touching elegance in a medium new to her. James Cagney, who in his time had to plant fists or a grapefruit on young ladies faces and shoes on young ladies behinds, here develops his tenderest relationship with middle-aged ladies (the Misses George, Main and Hattie McDaniel), and each of them is worth a

---

*One of Cagney's most articulate admirers, Otis Ferguson, film critic for *The New Republic*, was killed in action at sea during World War II. The loss of Ferguson's passionate voice—in 1943—was a profound one for the Cagneys, not to mention for the critical community at large. As for Agee, writing in *The Nation*, he conceded only that "the Cagney brothers' first independent piece, *Johnny Come Lately*, seems to persuade many people that the Cagneys (and others) should stay dependent. I do not agree. The film shows a fatal commercial uneasiness and, I half suspect, radical loss or atrophy of cinematic judgment. But *Johnny*, before it breaks down into a panic of melodramatic and comic propitiation, does give a gentle and leisured if not very memorable first hour whose tone and pace would never have survived a big studio; there is a very appealing performance by Grace George; and there is a general ambience of hope and pleasure about the production, which, regrettably, loses its glow. The hazards of independence are great unless you have daring, brains, ability, and a basic unconfused carelessness about whether you go bankrupt or not; but with very few exceptions I believe that anything good in films which comes out of this country, at all soon, is bound to come from the independents."

dozen average love scenes. . . . These pleasures would have been all but impossible to manufacture in any of the larger studios, for they are given their warmth and life by the pleasure that the Cagney's large cast and the whole production outfit obviously took in doing a job as they wanted to do it. Bit players who have tried creditably for years to walk in shoes that pinched them show themselves in this picture as the very competent actors they always were: There has seldom been as good a cinematic gallery of U.S. small-town types.

Though audiences took *Johnny* to heart—the film easily passed $1 million in profits, according to William Cagney—the few understanding reviews did not compensate for the shock of the volley of negatives. The Cagneys were convinced that Warner Brothers had somehow gotten to the press and persuaded reviewers to say, in William Cagney's words, "Look, tell Cagney to come back home; his pictures stink." The critics took a harsh toll. "What broke out hearts," remembered William Cagney,

was the way the press went after us and tore us to pieces. They went out of their way to tell us how terrible it [*Johnny Come Lately*] was. Don't forget, Jimmy was spoiled in the best sense, because the press had been devoted to Jimmy. And here they were suddenly taking this other position, telling him what a terrible mistake he's made. Don't forget too, it was the start of our own company. To be blasted that way was very disheartening."

Yankee Doodle Cagney

It would be two more years before the next Cagney Production. Meantime, Cagney occupied himself in other arenas: His presidency of the Screen Actor's Guild (SAG) came during this period (1943–1944) and with it his "home front" activities on behalf of United States troops in World War II.

Before Pearl Harbor, Cagney had leaned toward pacificism—indeed, in 1940 he had appeared on a radio broadcast version of Dalton Trumbo's *Johnny Got His Gun*, playing the armless, legless war veteran who symbolizes the victims of militarism. But America's entry into World War II meant an embrace of patriotism and soldiery. As a leader of SAG, Cagney was instrumental in involving stars in bond sales and mass rallies. He donated his services for such short subjects as *You, John Jones*. He raced "exhibitions" at the Roosevelt Raceway in New York to promote the war effort, and donated the use of his Martha's Vineyard estate to the Army for practice maneuvers. In 1942, he performed a three-week whistle-stop tour with some of Hollywood's biggest names to raise defense funds. The all-star bill included Bing Crosby, Laurel and Hardy, Groucho Marx, Cary Grant, Bob Hope, Pat O'Brien, Frank McHugh, Joan Blondell, Claudette Colbert, Bert Lahr, and Charles Boyer. "The show was so big," recalled Frank McHugh, "that someone like Marlene Dietrich could join us

With Ann Sheridan (left) and Edgar Bergen (right) on an NBC Radio program on behalf of a War Loan Drive.

for a few days, as she did in Washington, and you wouldn't know she was there." Cagney performed George M. Cohan routines for the crowds. In 1944, he spent three months entertaining troops in Europe, performing a reported 12 shows a week as an Irish jig and clog dancer.

Too old to serve in uniform, Cagney loyally served at home. But though the 1940s was a transition period for him politically, he remained a steadfast Rooseveltian as long as FDR was alive. The two-year Hitler–Stalin pact had expired in 1941 when German armies invaded the Soviet Union—and it was a time, in Hollywood, when Communists served alongside Republicans on a plethora of victory committees, united in the war thrust. Still liberal, Cagney objected when immigrant Japanese and Japanese–Americans were herded into detention centers as part of the wartime hysteria—and when cinematographer James Wong Howe, who was born in Kwantung, China, was forced to wear a button proclaiming "I Am Chinese," Cagney wore one too. On presidential-election eve in 1944, Cagney was among the stars who turned out for a national radio broadcast endorsing FDR. With Groucho Marx and Keenan Wynn, Cagney

With wife Billie Cagney in the 1940s celebrating the 20th wedding anniversary of the Robert Montgomerys. (WCTR)

sang a rendition of "In the Good Old Hoover Time" that melted into a version of "The Old Red Scare It Ain't What It Used to Be."

Ironically, there was one war measure that cut into the momentum of Cagney Productions—a confiscatory war tax of 91 percent aimed at persons in the top income tax bracket. "By operating his own independent production company," wrote Tino Balio in *United Artists: The Company Built by the Stars* (Madison: University of Wisconsin Press, 1976), "a producer, director or actor in the top income-tax bracket could reduce his effective tax rate from 90 to 60 percent. Moreover, under certain conditions, an interest in a completed picture could be sold as a capital asset, making the profit from such sale subject to a 25 percent capital-gains tax."

But the high tax rate minimized the economic incentives for free-lancing. Moreover, it kept other top stars from affiliating with Cagney Productions. "We could not get people to make pictures for us," noted William Cagney. "I'd call up Bob Hope or one of the top actors in the business and tell them I had a vehicle for them and they'd say, 'No, thank you, I've made my picture this year.' They figured, why make another picture if I'm going to have to pay 91 percent to the government? Everyone slacked off, including my brother. I couldn't successfully argue with Jimmy to leave his beloved farm."

Economically, there was another hidden deterrent. The Cagneys' distribution deal with United Artists was *too* good, as it turned out. William Cagney first grew nervous when he made the rounds with UA sales representatives in New York City and heard them grumble about the Cagneys' percentages. Then, when the returns for *Johnny* began to trickle in, William Cagney realized that his preferential contract interfered with UA's willingness to hard-sell the Cagney product. Cagney Productions audited the company books, which caused constant friction with the UA management. And though checkers were employed to monitor box-office receipts in the major markets, those checkers had relations with theatre owners that predated their assignment for Cagney Productions. "That's one of the reasons why I wasn't too anxious to grind out pictures," recalled William Cagney, "because waiting for me was this tainted checking and tainted selling. You don't get too anxious to hand something to somebody that they're gonna slough."

Not that James Cagney was itching to leave his beloved farm under any circumstances. After his SAG term ended, after the disappointing reception for *Johnny Come Lately*, Cagney faded from the Hollywood scene and spent more and more time on Martha's Vineyard. Generally, the belief around the movie industry was that Cagney would only star for Cagney Productions. Still, William Cagney continued to act as his brother's agent and to entertain "loan-out" offers. A steady stream of such offers came from Twentieth Century-Fox— where ex-Warners' head Darryl F. Zanuck was encamped—including one for a never-realized Nunnally Johnson script for a Jean Renoir film called *Venezuela* or *The Day the Earth Shook*, a melodrama involving an earthquake and a prison break. But this and others Cagney refused. "As far as Jimmy was concerned," explained William Cagney,

> Jimmy wanted to be on Martha's Vineyard cooking Mulligatawny stew. I remember one time I called him. I had a deal worked out with Zanuck who wanted Jimmy for a picture. I got him approval of director, approval of script, approval of leading lady, approval of everything, and the top price ever paid at that time to my knowledge—$350,000. And it was to be shot in 42 days, six weeks.
>
> I locked it up, called him on the phone and said, "Sam, you ready to go to work?" He said, "What do you think?" I said, "Here's the deal I got for you," and I summed it all up. Then I thought I had the clincher: "You don't have to report for three more weeks." He said, "Can you smell that Mulligatawny stew on the stove?" I said, "You mean, screw it?" He said, "Screw it!" That's the way he felt. He didn't want to work. He wanted to be on the farm. He was only happy on the farm. Good scripts were so few

and far between. And everything conspired against your getting a good script because there was a dedication to seeing that we did not succeed as a production company.

Blood on The Sun

When the Cagney brothers finally plunged back into production, it was with a movie property far more typical of Cagney than *Johnny Come Lately*—Cagney as a battling American newspaper editor in Japan in the 1920s who discovers the secret "Tanaka Plan" by Japanese militarists to conquer China. The story was rather a blatant attempt to cash in on the anti-Japanese war fervor in the United States. "We reached for dynamite," admitted William Cagney, "We were desperate when we reached for *Blood on the Sun*. Because we knew there were forces against us, and we had to hit a home run."

The Cagneys once again came up short of director prospects. Warners refused to release Michael Curtiz, so William Cagney signed Frank R. Lloyd, once an Oscar-calibre director, now a man who was aging, slow, and weary. Cagney had an abiding affection for Lloyd, for whom the actor had reportedly stinted as an "extra" in MGM's *Mutiny on the Bounty* in 1935, during one of his walk-outs. Art director Wiard "Boppo" Ihnen (who was married to costumer Edith Head) did the meticulous, stylish scene design—with camera angles so specific that Lloyd was expected to follow them, and did. To add to the beauty of the surroundings meanwhile—more so than to any high tones in the melodrama—William Cagney induced Sylvia Sidney to make her comeback as the female costar. Sidney ("gowned gorgeously and photographs ditto," according to *Variety*), who had retreated to Broadway after being labelled "box-office poison" by exhibitors, played the Eurasian Mata Hari-ish double spy who aids in exposing the Tanaka Plan.

Garret Fort wrote the original story.* But it needed extensive rehauling, and for that task William Cagney hired Lester Cole, well known to him and to others in Hollywood as an activist for the Screen Writer's Guild and a Communist Party idealogue—apart from as a swift and competent constructionist. If this partnership seems improbable today, it merely seemed egalitarian to William Cagney at the time. But soon enough, William Cagney, staunchly on the right wing of the political spectrum, and Cole, staunchly left wing, came to odds over the interpretation of the story. And the Cagney–Cole "split" became something of a cause célèbre in the film industry in the 1940s, partly because Cole (later imprisoned as one of the Hollywood Ten) took the rare tack of publicizing his gripes with the Cagneys: first, in an article entitled "Unhappy Ending" in the first issue of the *Hollywood Quarterly* (later to become *Film Quarterly*), then resurrecting

---

*Though uncredited on the screen, Frank Medford also receives a story credit in Writer's Guild records.

With Sylvia Sidney in BLOOD ON THE SUN. (Copyright © 1945. William Cagney Production. All rights reserved. Released through United Artists Corporation.)

the controversy in his autobiography, *Hollywood Red* (Palo Alto, CA: Ramparts, 1982).

William Cagney felt that Cole was an astute screenwriter but one who "wrote with one objective in mind and that was to promote Communism. He'd get going on a scene and then he'd stop it all to make a speech about Sun-Yat-Sen and the rights of man, and when he got through the scene was gone, out the window. I have nothing against the rights of man, but I just didn't want our picture turned into a tract." According to William Cagney, Cole's basic script outline was good, but the speechifying, which was integrated throughout, had to go—and the two of them came to an impasse over revisions.

Cole's version of events differs. According to Cole, writing in the *Hollywood Quarterly* at the time, "The departure from the screenplay written by me involved only the final sequence and two or three minor dialogue exchanges earlier in the script which led up to this climactic sequence. But in the elimination of my ending and the substitution of another, the entire meaning of the film was destroyed." Briefly, Cole accused William Cagney of substituting an ahistorical, "unhappy ending" for his own, more authentic (but equally apocryphal) one—and of keeping this ending from him until the world premiere of *Blood on the Sun* in San Francisco, which was timed to coincide with the World Security Conference. At that premiere, Cole was "shocked" to discover the alterations.

Cole's ending had the Cagney character, newsman Nick Condon, escaping from Japan and delivering the militarist document to the Chinese delegation of the League of Nations. This precipitates the sudden and dramatic withdrawal of the Japanese government from the world council, with Matsuoka, the Japanese delegate, smug in the knowledge that lack of global unity will keep individual nations from interfering with the Japanese plans.

"The screenplay then showed the dismay and chaos which followed that historic act [Japan's withdrawal from the League of Nations]," wrote Cole in the *Hollywood Quarterly* six months after the film's release in 1945.

> The characters portrayed by Cagney and Sidney move through the milling crowd of diplomats, disheartened by the failure of their mission. Noting the fear and the shame reflected on the faces of various delegates, Sidney asks Cagney if Japan's withdrawal from the League does not mean a future war. To which Cagney replies, "No, not a future war—the war started ten minutes ago."
>
> Arriving at the door leading out of the building, they stop to observe an American, his wife, and ten-year-old boy attempting to gain admittance. The American, a typical tourist of that period, is arrogantly demanding an explanation for the guard's refusal to permit him to enter; was he not an American taxpayer? The guard politely retorts that perhaps Monsieur is not aware of it, but America is not a member of the League of Nations. At which Cagney remarks to the discomfited tourist, "Very embarrassing, isn't it?" Then he stares hard at the American boy of ten, shakes his head soberly, and says, "Good luck, soldier." The American tourists gaze in bewilderment at their son—and the picture ends.
>
> Substituted for this sequence was the following: The girl escapes with the document, through Cagney's ability to hold off the armed might of the Japanese police force. Where she goes remains a mystery. Cagney then is pursued by the police as he seeks sanctuary in the United States Embassy. Arriving there, he is ambushed by innumerable armed Japanese. He makes a final dash for the Embassy door. A tremendous volley of shots is fired; he falls to the ground; the Japanese close in on him. An American diplomat emerges from the Embassy and Cagney gets to his feet. He is not dead after all. The Japanese police captain, faced by the American State Department, swiftly backtracks. He makes apologies. It has all been an error. Surely the Americans, who are very generous, will forgive them. To which Cagney retorts, "Sure, sure. We'll forgive you; but first we'll get even." There the picture unhappily ends.

According to Cole, the insidious political cop-out of the revised ending involved the tacit endorsement of William Randolph Hearst's campaign "for a

With Jack Halloran (behind Cagney) in BLOOD ON THE SUN.

negotiated peace with Japan as opposed to the U.S. official position for unconditional surrender." This is obliquely implied in Cagney's threat to "get even." "Evidently," estimated Cole, "Hearst's politics were Bill's." (No surprise there.) As for the star, James Cagney, Cole said only, "After the preview I told Jimmy Cagney that it wasn't just me he sold out, but the American people, and he would hear more about it. Always a decent guy, he seemed embarrassed."

More likely, Cagney was embarrassed at Cole's harping on what must have seemed to him to be such a niggling—and arguable—plot detail. If there was a more progressive "message" in Cole's ending, as opposed to the Cagney's, it must have been as coded and obscure then as it is now.* To say the least, the screenwriter's outrage—still, forty years later—over not being allowed to side with the "official" U.S. policy of unconditional surrender is ironic, especially in light of the atomic blasts that eventually constituted the coupe de grace of that policy.

*Allegorical theme work was Cole's pride as a screenwriter. He once boasted to Party members, apropos of *The Romance of Rosy Ridge*, that he had managed to politically dissect the issue of returning war veterans in his latest screenplay. But as *Rosy* happened to be set in the post-Civil War era, its "message" about alienated, neglected, and jobless World War II veterans did not necessarily impact on contemporary audiences.

For what it is worth, according to William Cagney, the ending of *Blood on the Sun* was always regarded as the weakest part of the story. It was rewritten "ten or twenty times" during the course of the production by Nathaniel Curtis, an ex-radio comedy writer on staff at Cagney Productions (who is credited with providing the "additional scenes"). The producer says he never approved Cole's ending—which was thought to be too downbeat and expensive—nor was he especially satisfied with Curtis', as it turned out.

But there is a further annotation to the controversy surrounding *Blood on the Sun*, which would seem to taint Cole's version of events. Ring Lardner, Jr., another Communist (and like Cole, also one of the Hollywood Ten), also worked on the screenplay. He was brought in by William Cagney specifically to edit and revise Cole's version, on the theory that one comrade might nudge the other in a less rhetorical direction. According to William Cagney, Lardner, Jr. was less emblematic in his writing, sensitive to the Cagneys' story needs, and deserved a coscreenwriting credit. Yet he remains uncredited, and it is curious that in neither of his accounts does Cole mention Lardner, Jr.'s involvement.*

All of this would amount to a picayune footnote to the making of *Blood on the Sun* were it not for the sour impact it had on the Cagneys. Once again they felt burned. It was another nail in the coffin of Cagney's waning leftism and in the widening split in Hollywood between the extreme right and left. The publication of Cole's original article was a notorious incident in Hollywood in the 1940s, and Colonel Wilkerson of *The Hollywood Reporter*, for one—latterly, in the Cagney camp—used it as an opportunity to blanketly attack Cole and Communists in general.

Even more ironic, considering this to-do, *Blood on the Sun* is one of Cagney's least auspicious films, the most hackneyed one to fly under the banner of Cagney Productions. In retrospect, the Fort–Medford–Cole–Lardner–Curtis screenplay is hardly worth the claims upon it. The Japanese were characterized

---

*The precise details behind the writing and rewriting of *Blood on the Sun* remain murky. Accounts and recollections vary. When informed by the author, forty years later, that Lardner, Jr. had worked a bit on the screenplay, Cole expressed astonishment—"negatively." William Cagney insists that the two were in a room together with him at one point to hash out revisions; Lardner, Jr. says that is "very likely"; Cole says absolutely not. In any event, Lardner, Jr. says he was only in on a limited number of discussions, and that "I certainly did not do enough to deserve a credit. I think William Cagney exaggerates my participation in that regard."

Lardner, Jr. was on the Cagney Productions payroll to write the script for *Bugles in the Afternoon*, a Civil War Western culminating at the Little Big Horn, originally intended as a starring vehicle for Cagney. Ironically, Lardner, Jr. eventually had his own political differences with William Cagney, which help shed light on the period. "He [William Cagney] told me I had treated the Indians [in the *Bugles* script] like a race of oppressed Jews and that I had treated Crazy Horse better than General Custer, which was true, since I had treated Custer like the idiot he was. But this was in the book [the source material for *Bugles in the Afternoon*]; I merely chose to accent it." Lardner, Jr. continued, "He—or maybe it was Jimmy—encouraged me to take a liberal point of view in the script [of *Bugles*]. Then he [William Cagney] became quite scared of it. I had the impression they [the Cagneys] were going through a period then of being highly nervous, either about politics or worrying about Jimmy's career." Lardner, Jr.'s script was eventually tossed out, revisions made, and *Bugles in the Afternoon* produced in 1952 with Ray Milland in the lead.

With Sam Jaffee (foreground), on loan-out from Cagney Productions in Henry Hathaway's 13 RUE MADELEINE. (Copyright © 1947 Twentieth Century-Fox Film Corp. All Rights Reserved. Courtesy of Twentieth Century-Fox.)

with a near-racist tinge. Sydney is adequate in her part, but Robert Armstrong, in Oriental make-up, bald and monocled, is hopeless as Colonel Tojo, the conniving Japanese militarist, while Jack Halloran is amateurish as the slow-witted villain of the piece. Playing Nick Condon, a masterful Judo expert capable of felling countless Japanese with his gyrations, Cagney approaches his part complacently, which is about all it deserves.

The more discerning critics of the era were unimpressed. But *Blood on the Sun* did have its desired effect on moviegoers. "The Japanese were kicking the hell out of us all over the world," said William Cagney, "and the reaction from audiences when Jimmy sailed into them was electrifying." *Blood* was the second Cagney Production to make over a million dollars in profit.

13 Rue Madeleine

Three years were to elapse before the release of another Cagney Production, and in the meantime Cagney agreed as a favor to Darryl Zanuck to star in a picture for 20th Century-Fox. His contract stipulated $300,000 for eight weeks of work as Bob Sharkey, a leader of the wartime Office of Strategic Service in a story called *13 Rue Madeleine*, written by John Monks, Jr. and Sy Bartlett, and directed by veteran Henry Hathaway.

Described in the script as "this wonderful tough guy from Minnesota," Sharkey is a sharp-nerved American spy who is martyred by his own forces behind enemy lines while on a desperate mission to gather intelligence and neutralize a German double agent. A mock documentary, modelled after producer Louis de Rochemont's *March of Time* series and de Rochemont's previously successful collaboration with director Hathaway on *The House on 92nd Street, Madeleine* is slickly assembled and competently acted by a cast that includes Annabella, Richard Conte, Frank Latimore, Sam Jaffe, and Blanche Yurka. But *Madeleine* is one of Hathaway's minor films, and it is marginal to Cagney's career except for an ending that is curiously prophetic. Sharkey is captured by the Germans and tortured for the secrets he has been privy to as a top spy; he confesses nothing. But the Allies order the demolition of the German spy headquarters at 13 Rue Madeleine, where Sharkey is imprisoned, so the patriot and his secrets will be blown to smithereens. As the walls crumble around him, Sharkey laughs maniacally, gleeful in the face of certain death, knowing that his enemies will perish with him. That final scene foreshadows Cagney's similarly eruptive death as Cody Jarrett in *White Heat*.

The Time of Your Life

Cagney Productions had not been entirely idle. The company had laid the groundwork for filming *The Stray Lamb* by Thorne Smith, author of the *Topper* stories, after purchasing the rights to the offbeat fantasy from the John Barrymore estate in 1943. Another slice of whimsy—a sort of love story between a girl, a guy, and a horse—the eccentric project was cast with Robert Montgomery as Mr. Lamb and Cagney ("a fey character by nature," in the words of William Cagney) in a secondary role as the Russet Man. Elaborate sets were designed and constructed at the Goldwyn Studio. The adaptation was provided by Nathaniel Curtis. Britisher Richard St. John was to direct and steeped himself in preproduction. The choice of leading ladies was narrowed. The Cagneys were only two or three weeks away from the start date, in 1947, when word hit of a pending carpenter's strike—one of many labor strikes convulsing Hollywood in the post-World War II era.

Certain the strike would shut filming down, William Cagney asked the Goldwyn management for an extension on their space allotment. For reasons the Cagneys never quite fathomed (though meddling from Warner Brothers was suspected), they were told to begin shooting on the appointed date. In good conscience they could not. So William Cagney made the decision to dismantle the sets, move everything over to General Service Studios, and cancel the production, paying off the director's salary and amassing a half-million-dollar loss in preproduction costs. To the Cagneys' amazement, the Goldwyn man-

With William Bendix (at left) and James Barton in William Saroyan's THE TIME OF YOUR LIFE. (AMPAS)

agement filed a lawsuit against Cagney Productions and pursued damages in court for years—relenting only in 1953 when the Cagneys returned to the Goldwyn site to film *A Lion Is in the Streets*.

Crushed, William Cagney hastily looked around for a more manageable property, preferrably a one-set story, and *The Time of Your Life*, the famous play by William Saroyan, came to mind. At first William Cagney did not have any special attraction to the Saroyan idea other than its logistical simplicity—all of the action takes place in one San Francisco waterfront saloon. In some ways the antithesis of his good-souled characters, Saroyan was a curmudgeonly sort in person—humorless, Cagney described him in his autobiography. Saroyan's previous brush with Hollywood had been a nasty one; Louis B. Mayer had beguiled him into writing *The Human Comedy* for MGM on the pretext that Saroyan would direct it, only to turn the reins over to contract director Clarence Brown when the screenplay was finally in. (Saroyan had the last laugh, though, publishing a novel based on his script to precede the film's release in 1943.) But when Saroyan was contacted by the Cagneys, he professed to like their small-

With sister Jeanne Cagney and Wayne Morris in THE TIME OF YOUR LIFE. (AMPAS)

shop approach; and he accepted $100,000 as a seven-year lease on his noted property.* Forthwith, the adaptation was turned over to reliable Nathaniel Curtis.

The Cagneys decided to adhere strictly to the play. When German emigrant director Henry Koster balked at that, disagreeing with William Cagney, he was dismissed on the eve of filming, and H. C. "Hank" Potter, an American with stage and comedy background, replaced him. Casting was William Cagney's forte, and he assembled the outlandish habitues of Saroyan's slice-of-life saloon. Cagney, of course, was Joe, the tavern philosopher. William Bendix played Nick, owner and bartender, gruff but loving. Wayne Morris was little-boy naive as Tom, Jeanne Cagney showed her range as melancholy ex-hooker Kitty Duval.

*The unusual limited-duration clause in Saroyan's contract with the Cagneys is the reason why *The Time of Your Life* is the rarest-seen Cagney film. Only two "legal" copies exist—one in the Library of Congress and one in the Cagney Productions' vault. After seven years the film rights reverted to Saroyan, and after his death in 1982, to his estate. From time to time, the Cagneys made noises—and efforts—to rerelease the picture. But Saroyan was obstinate and litiginous, and for 30 years William Cagney feared to screen his own copy—which, unlike the release version, has Saroyan's original ending—for friends. This, even though the Saroyan picture ranks "second" in Cagney's career according to the family estimate, second to *Yankee Doodle Dandy.*

Broderick Crawford and Ward Bond swagger in to sip beer and trade arguments. James Barton is crustily magnificent as Kit Carson, the great pretender of the Wild West, who spins tales so tall even he does not believe them. Paul Draper is Harry, the mercurial dancer, and James Lydon makes an ingenuous Dudley, the young gallant who cannot reach his girlfriend on the phone. Blick, the icy villain of the story, is played with brute force by an obscure actor named Tom Powers (shades of *The Public Enemy*!).

It was a much more elaborate picture than anyone had realized at the outset. The Cagneys lavished care and expense on the sets (by Wiard Ihnen), the lighting, and the camerawork (by James Wong Howe). The budget of less than $1 million doubled to $1,800,000. The 40-day shooting schedule crept up to 75 days. But something had happened to the Cagneys—to William and James, to Jeanne, to Doctor Ed, who was aboard as assistant production manager. They had become enamored of Saroyan, addicted to his quirky rhythms and homespun philosophies. His parlance—"No foundation, all the way down the line"— entered the Cagney family parlance. And though they knew they were digging themselves deeper into a gamble, they were entranced, and they continued.

The spirit was contagious among the rest of the cast, the exhilaration palpable on the set. "Everybody was so much in love with what they were doing," remembered Jeanne Cagney, "that we were counting our Oscars beforehand." Then there were two disastrous previews, one in Pasadena and one in Santa Barbara. In Santa Barbara, recalled Jeanne Cagney, the audience reacted to *The Time of Your Life* as if it were a Chaplinesque comedy, laughing throughout *until* the ending. "The original ending just went off like a sweet, sad song," remembered Jeanne Cagney. "There was no resolution of any kind. It was very avant garde for the period. And the audience was spun by it. You could have heard a pin drop in the theatre. There was a kind of sense of, what is it? I just don't think audiences were ready for a philosophical play."

Stung by the reaction of the preview audiences, the Cagneys decided to refilm the ending with more of a slam-bang finish, "a bit of Cagney action," in William Cagney's words. In Saroyan's play, Blick is disposed of off-stage by the voluble Kit Carson. In the Cagney Productions' version, Blick is thrashed by Joe/Cagney until the thug collapses into an unconscious heap. When Blick revives, Nick tosses the bully out of the saloon, and Joe and Kit Carson return to boozing and swapping yarns as the film fades. The rewrite gave Cagney an opportunity to use his fists, a nod to his tough guy lineage. Two favorite screenwriters—the Epstein brothers—contributed the revise as a favor to the Cagneys, gratis.

Even so, this slight departure from pure Saroyan was unnecessary—and as far as it went, unsuccessful. The rest of *The Time of Your Life* still anticipated by 30 years the work of such directors as Robert Altman with its mosaic of characters, "its random turmoil and coincidence" (in critic David Thomson's words), its attitudinizing. The shock of seeing Cagney almost totally removed from his Warner Brothers' context could not be tempered by a mere cirlicue in the ending. In France the reviews were headlined: "The Tiger of the Screen Sits Down." This

Cagney and Eleanor Roosevelt at the premiere of THE TIME OF YOUR LIFE to benefit New York's Wiltwyck School, of which the president's wife was an executive board member. (WCTR)

was a reference to the fact that Cagney's character as Joe, never budges from his vantage seat at a table near the bar. (Indeed, Joe is asked to dance twice and demurs, explaining, "I don't even like to walk.") On top of everything else that was different about *The Time of Your Life*, audiences were asked to accept a Cagney—normally so physicalized, his entire body moving and twitching within the frame—reduced to expressing himself with his eyes, his voice, his putty face.

American critics were unusually tentative in their response, sensing the boldness of the work for the most part, and agreeing with James Agee (lately of *Time*) that, despite gaps, "those who made the picture [*The Time of Your Life*] have given it something very rare." Indeed, *Time* was a "reach" for all involved. It exudes the warmth and love invested in it. And it has to be counted among the most wistful, the most fanciful, the most anomalous of Cagney's films. His character is a gentle thinker, no tough guy. Like Tom Richards, Joe is a man of mystery and impulse—cheerful, inquisitive, vagarious, "spiritually luminous" (in the words of *The New York Times*)—a man who is as serious about chewing gum as he is about quaffing champagne and issuing philosophic dictums. This was Cagney as he viewed himself, and he gave it his utmost in a film that remains singular and enchanting.

"Early one morning two or three weeks ago," wrote the hard-to-please Saroyan in a letter to Cagney Productions,

> I stood in line at the United Artist Theater and bought a ticket to the first showing of *The Time of Your Life* in San Francisco. I did this because, as you know, I wrote the play and wanted to find out as quickly as possible if my kind of writing could be made to mean anything at all in a movie. The people came into the theatre and sat down and finally the lights dimmed and the movie started. It wasn't more than three minutes until I had forgotten that I had written the play. I was too busy enjoying it to care who wrote it. Before I knew it the film was over, and as far as I was able to tell, everybody in the theatre was sorry it was over. That bar was just naturally a good place to visit. All by way of telling you I think you have made one of the most original and entertaining movies I have seen. Furthermore, I have no intention of pretending that it's my fault that you have made such a film, for I think the truth of the matter is this: that you and your associates have expertly edited and translated into the medium of the motion picture a most difficult and almost unmanageable body of material. I send you congratulations, profound thanks and all good wishes.

For such actors as William Bendix (who went on to star in TV's *The Life of Riley*) and Broderick Crawford (who would be cast as the lead in the film version of Robert Penn Warren's *All the King's Men*), *The Time of Your Life* proved a career springboard. For Cagney Productions, despite the imprimatur of Saroyan and the bon mots of critics, *The Time of Your Life* proved its deathknell at the box-office. The movie registered a loss of over a million dollars. Coupled with the abortive *Stray Lamb* production and the harassment of the Goldwyn lawsuit, that loss spelled the eventual demise of the Cagneys' production company.

The box-office failure of *The Time of Your Life* precipitated the return of Cagney to the Warner Brothers' fold for *White Heat*. When Cagney signed his 57-page contract with the Burbank studio he was guaranteed $250,000 per starring assignment for three Warners' pictures over the next three years. But, importantly, there was a clause in Cagney's contract that allowed for the filming of one Cagney Production feature per every Warners' picture and for release and distribution of that feature through the Warners' system. Cagney Productions intended to pay its bank debts rather than declare bankruptcy. And the company intended to survive.

"Maybe I'm gilding the lily," recalled Jeanne Cagney, "but we never felt that Cagney Productions was a failure, not at the time certainly. It was a time for holding our heads high. It was kind of a triumphant time for Bill and Jim. They paid their bills. They tried interesting things. And there was vitality to everything Cagney Productions did."

Cagney making his "comeback" as gangster Cody Jarrett in WHITE HEAT.

9
White Heat

A climb-to-success in the great American tradition—the carnage piling up at the bottom of the ladder—White Heat is also genuine black comedy as are few other films (Bunuel's El is another) which lay claim to the title. Black comedy will not come of "irreverent" spoofs on "taboo" subjects (like The Trouble With Harry or The Loved One), but rather from a vision so outrageously terrible that one has to laugh at its very extremity: one must laugh in order to bear it. White Heat commands such a vision and does so with such absolute integrity that (because it's not by Bunuel or someone of similar intellectual repute) one can never be sure that the film's makers even know what they're doing. Unlike Bonnie and Clyde, no one nudges you in the ribs.

I don't know where on earth one can get to see White Heat now off of Forty-second Street; probably, its violence would proscribe it even from television, where most of what was great in the American film now writhes under the cutter's knife. And yet it is among the best films made in this country, and one with much to tell us about the kind of country—its marriages, family life and corrupting aspirations—in which it was made. This it does with so utter a lack of pretension that its casual brilliance almost seems accidental—surely, since the film was made in Hollywood and doesn't have subtitles, they couldn't have known what they were doing, could they?

WILLIAM S. PECHTER
Twenty-four Times a Second

If *White Heat* resuscitated Cagney's career—and Cagney Productions—it was also in some respects a bitter pill to swallow; a return to being the tough guy. Only Cody Jarrett was an uglier, more antisocial character than Tom Powers, and graying and potbellied at that. For Cagney, *White Heat* was not simply a comeback, but his redefinition as a gangster type to a new generation of moviegoers. Worse, it was to become an acknowledged cult classic in his lifetime, haunting him with its acclaim and its revivals. Along with Tom Powers and George M. Cohan, Cody Jarrett became the role with which he was most often identified. As time went on and his own view of his career narrowed, he found the movie more and more objectionable, an opinion many reviewers had put forth when *White Heat* was first released. As the later acclamation grew, so too did Cagney's revisionism and disparagement. In his autobiography he went so far as to label *White Heat* a "cheapjack" job (complaining, parenthetically, that longtime pal Frank McHugh should have been cast as Jarrett gang member Tommy Ryley). To liven up the dull script, Cagney claimed, he himself introduced the psychological angle and the "mother complex"—claims that are unworthy of him in their extravagance and that, furthermore, are not borne out by an examination of the script drafts. "The original script of *White Heat* was very formula," Cagney wrote in his autobiography, "the old knock-down-drag-'em-out again, without a touch of imagination."

Ivan Goff and Ben Roberts

In point of fact, the *White Heat* script generated tremendous excitement at Warners in 1948 and 1949, and at the time its grotesquery appealed to Cagney. His later downgrading of the screenwriters is especially ironic, considering that Ivan Goff and Ben Roberts were—apart from Glasmon and Bright and the Epstein twins—practically the only screenwriters Cagney ever admitted to valuing wholeheartedly. Indeed, he went on to employ them for three other pictures in the twilight of his career: *Come Fill the Cup* in 1951, *Man of a Thousand Faces* in 1957, and *Shake Hands With the Devil* in 1959. Goff, whose strength was dialogue, was an ex-reporter and transplanted Australian; Roberts, the better constructionist, was Bronx-born, a New York University graduate. Both were veterans of separate pre-World War II stints in Hollywood. They met in the Army and formed a partnership that was to prove long and fruitful, in television as well as in motion pictures. In 1948, after performing a rewrite for Warners on a B picture called *Backfire*, they were given contracts by the studio; their maiden assignment—*White Heat*.

Working from a sketchy treatment about the Denver mint robbery of Christmas week, 1922 (written by an ex-Los Angeles newspaperwoman named Virginia Kellogg), Goff and Roberts began to assemble their screenplay in November of 1948. They decided to manipulate the gangster genre and write a variation on the Ma Barker story, synthesizing her several sons into one. They would give the son a mother complex and accentuate the Freudian implications; and then, in the words of Roberts, would "play it like a Greek tragedy." Most likely it was Roberts, an omnivorous reader and classics buff, who was instrumental in furnishing the mythological underpinnings of the story—the Achille's heel of Cody Jarrett's headaches; his Oedipal complex; the Trojan horse heist (with its double-edged theme of the imposter, Fallon, in the belly of the Jarrett gang). Fans of Cagney, Goff and Roberts wrote with him in mind from the beginning and they lobbied with the Warners' front office to cast him in the part. From production head Steve Trilling came this response: Jack Warner did not want Cagney back on the payroll. "They fight like pit bulls," explained Trilling. But when the screenwriters persisted, Warner had to concede the box-office prospects, and Cagney was signed to return to the studio of his heyday.

"When he [Cagney] came into the project, he came into our office," remembered screenwriter Roberts.

Ivan Goff (seated at typewriter) and Ben Roberts at work on the screenplay of
WHITE HEAT. (courtesy of Ivan Goff)

He lay down on the couch, like he always did, and he said, "What are you going to do, fellas?" We said, "Jimmy, we're going to keep it moving, and we're going to make him [Cody Jarrett] a really interesting character—the study of an evil man, but we want the audience to understand *why* he is evil. We see that behind his state of cruelty is a man who is driven, who is really sick, who is driving himself toward destruction. We don't want to compare ourselves with Greek tragedians but it is, in a sense, about a man who is destined to die, who knows it, and who wants to get where he wants to go before it happens. Everyone who is in his way is thrust aside, and ruthlessly." Cagney said, "Well, it sounds interesting. Sounds like it will be fun to play." We said, "We'll give you some scenes to play that we think will be pretty hairy." He said, "Whatever you say, fellas." Jimmy was marvelous that way. It was always like that with him on the pictures we did with him. He would say, "What are you going to do, fellas?" Then— "Whatever you say, fellas."

The script was six months in the gestation, and when completed it unfolded in three distinct acts like a well-made play. Act one encompasses the bloody mail train robbery engineered by the Cody Jarrett gang, which was set outside a railroad tunnel in the Rockies (based on an actual holdup in the low Sierra Madres), as well as the depiction of Jarrett's sympathy-engendering headaches and his mother complex. The second act centers on Jarrett's term in prison, the relationship between undercover "roper" Hank Fallon/Vic Pardo (Edmond O'Brien) and Jarrett, the conspiracy between "Big Ed" Somers (Steve Cochran) and Jarrett's wife Verna (Virginia Mayo), and the news of Ma's death that triggers Jarrett's escape. The screenwriters needed a "topper," or climactic sequence, and they hit upon an idea while scouting locations around Los Angeles. The swirling pipes, retorts, Hortonspheres, coils, and tubes of an oil refinery suggested "mother earth in metal" (in Goff's words) to the writers and inspired act three, which depicts the "A-B-C" police tailing method (an innovative and unpublicized surveillance technique), the abortive Trojan horse payroll robbery at a southern California oil-cracking plant, and Cody Jarrett's spectacular demise.

It was an ingeniously crafted script, what with its various "white heat" motifs and "surrogate mother" replacements (or, looking at it from another perspective, with Edmond O'Brien as an insidious Pat O'Brien substitute). Inarguably, *White Heat* made inroads for the genre. With such pictures as *High Sierra*, it helped shift the locale of the outlaw jungle from the urban east to the snow-capped mountains and arid desert terrain of the dying frontier. Not only was the degree of violence unusual, but so was an *outlaw* whose criminality was overtly pathological or psychological.* The old Warners had always conscientiously stressed the social context of its gangster figures—especially Cagney. But the post-World War II breed of screenwriters had no such compunctions; the war had darkened hopes and given rise to *film noir*. Other movies of the era, notably 1947's *Kiss of Death*, also presented deranged gangster types in *noir* situations, but *White Heat* had the greater shock value. Cagney had been the cinema's Everyman: Now he was robbed of his social conscience and surrendered to a death that could not help but evoke the Hiroshima-Nagasaki blasts.

*Goff preferred to describe Cody Jarrett as an *outlaw*, not a gangster; and indeed he and Roberts briefly flirted with *The Last Outlaw* as a working title.

*Director Raoul Walsh and Cagney, around the time of THE ROARING TWENTIES.
(Homer Dickens Still Collection)*

Cagney's Interpolations

Filming occurred in May and June of 1949. The director was Raoul Walsh—Cagney's most virile and understanding director. Whatever Cagney's later misgivings, indications are that the actor was profoundly involved at the time in interpretation of the Cody Jarrett character. His interpolations—his "touches," or "goodies," as he was so fond of calling his contributions to a script or role—are manifest throughout the narrative of *White Heat*. The most indelible moments of the movie—Cody being comforted by Ma; Cody's prison freakout; the fiery Hortonsphere climax—are all developed virtually shot for shot from the Goff–Roberts screenplay. But Cagney had a gift for underscoring the motifs of that screenplay at every crucial juncture.

The scene in which Cody Jarrett sits abjectly on Ma Jarrett's lap is one of *White*

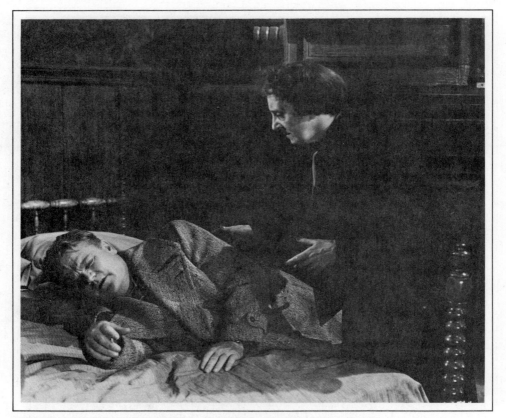

The mother complex: Cagney and Margaret Wycherly in WHITE HEAT. (WCTR)

Heat's most justly famous. In interviews conducted before his death, director Walsh claimed that this precious bit of business was his suggestion on the set. It is more likely that Cagney, who also claimed to have devised the moment, improvised it on the spot, thereby perfectly depicting the Oedipal complex of Cody Jarrett. (Walsh, a superb action–adventure director and a speed demon at work on the set, was not known for conversing with his actors about details of their performances unless, perchance, a cloudburst interrupted filming and afforded some time to kill.) As Cagney explained in his autobiography, "To get in the Ma Barker flavor with some pungency, I thought we would try something, take a little gamble. Cody Jarrett is psychotically tied to his mother's apron strings. I wondered if we dare have him sit in her lap once for comfort. I said to the director, Raoul Walsh, 'Let's see if we can get away with this.' He said, 'Let's try it.' We did it, and it worked."

Mother surrogate: Cagney and Edmond O'Brien in prison scene from WHITE HEAT.
(WCTR)

The lap-sitting detail was *not* in the script. As screenwriter Roberts recalled,

Jimmy stopped by the office one day [after filming] and said, "I just did something startling, I don't know if it will work—Raoul thinks it will." We said, "What did you do?" He said, "I sat on Mama's lap." We just looked at each other and thought, it'll be sensational if it works. Without saying anything, it's what the picture is about—the Oedipal thing—he reverts to the child who needs his mother. Then when we saw it on film it was marvelous, because it was so simply done."

Added collaborator Goff, "The audiences [of the time] were startled but they knew they were looking at something awfully personal. And it was a great moment because of that."

The vulnerability as well as the perverse cruelty of Cody Jarrett was a trait that

Cagney instinctively amplified. The excess and theatricality of the character tickled him, for it was never his preference to play a scene *down*. "He [Cagney] may ask you what you want him to do, but he already knows how he wants to do it," said screenwriter Roberts. "He's hoping you won't say, 'Play it *down* here, Jimmy.' He'd rather go high and *really* do it and get to the guts of the scene." Understating or playing it safe was not his method as an actor. Instead Cagney liked to take a scene one notch higher than expected and play it *in extremis*, adding a twist that unleashed another shade of meaning or reaction.

For example, the brief scene in which Verna informs Cody that Ma is out shopping for strawberries for her on-the-lam son concludes unsatisfactorily in the shooting script with Cody throwing Verna a withering glance. On the set it just was not enough. Director Walsh stopped the filming and asked Cagney for a "topper." Cagney suggested that Cody knock Verna down, but Walsh thought it might be too clichéd. Then Cagney suggested that Verna stand on a chair, which Cody would kick out from under her in a snit after her sarcastic crack. And that is how the scene unreels in *White Heat*—just a tiny detail but one that makes an otherwise insignificant scene click.

The prison scenes of *White Heat* were filmed in Warners' own authentically styled steel cell block, patterned after San Quentin, Folsom, and other California prisons (and recognizable in countless other Warners' features). One of the most unforgettable scenes in *White Heat* is the one in which Cody Jarrett, learning of his Ma's betrayal and death, goes uncontrollably berserk in the prison mess hall. Ironically, that was a scene Jack Warner tried to excise from the script for budgetary reasons. The screenwriters, director Walsh, and contract producer Lou Edelman were summoned to Warners' inner sanctum in the executive suite and chastised for the exorbitance of shooting a single scene with 600 extras and only a couple of distinguishable lines of dialogue.

According to Roberts,

> Jack [Warner] called us in and he said, "The script's pretty good but it's expensive. That scene in the mess hall—can you play it in the chapel?" We said, "Jack, what's Cody Jarrett doing in the chapel? Praying? And seriously, the whole point of the scene is to have a lot of noise that goes absolutely dead silent when he makes his first animal-like scream. All the rattling knives and forks suddenly go dead silent—that's the terror of the scene. It'll make the hair on your scalp prickle. But if you put it in the chapel, it'll already be quiet because nobody will be saying anything." As I recall, Raoul Walsh finally said, "Give me three hundred extras and the machine shop, which we'll convert into a mess hall, and we'll be out by noon so the men can go back to work." Warner said, "You got it." So Walsh did it in three hours and was out for lunch. One take.

Before undertaking the scene, Cagney conferred with Goff and Roberts, asking them, "How crazy do you want *that*?" Roberts recalled that he said,

Cody Jarrett (Cagney) and wife Verna (Virginia Mayo) in WHITE HEAT.

"You're the actor, Jimmy, we just put it down on paper. If you want to make people's spines tingle, so much the better." The set was jammed with visitors the day the mess hall scene was filmed, with the writers and William Cagney among the onlookers.* For director Walsh and the sake of camera placements,

*Cagney was not the sort of actor to shy away from audiences during crucial emotional scenes—indeed, he seemed to relish visitors; on the days in which he was "electrocuted" in *Angels With Dirty Faces*, the set was crowded with junketing reporters, and Cagney gave dozens of interviews.

Cagney walked through his paces. Nobody was quite sure how he was going to play the drama until Walsh yelled, "Roll 'em!" Instantly, Cagney went into a terrifying transformation, as if utterly crazed. It was—and is on film—frightening; it was frightening for the visitors and it was frightening for the writers themselves, who experienced the scene as they had written it played to the hilt. The extras, wholly unprepared, were momentarily stunned, and believed for a second that they had truly witnessed a famous movie star go insane—it was that credible.

In his autobiography, Cagney explained diffidently,

> Not long ago a reporter asked me if I didn't have to "psych" myself up for the scene in *White Heat* where I go berserk on learning of my mother's death. My answer to that question is that you don't psych yourself up for these things, you *do* them. I can imagine what some of the old-timers would have said in answer to that question. They would have laughed aloud at the idea of an actor pumping himself up with the emotional motivations to do a scene. The pro is supposed to know what to do, then go ahead and do it. In this particular scene, I knew what deranged people sounded like because once, as a youngster, I had visited Ward's Island where a pal's uncle was in the hospital for the insane. My God, what an education that was! The shrieks, the screams of those people under restraint! I remember those cries, saw that they fitted, and I called on my memory to do as required. No need to psych up.

The memorable climax was filmed in the industrial district south of Los Angeles, near Torrance and the Signal Hill oil wells on the grounds of one of southern California's largest chemical and oil refinery plants. Again, Cagney went with the flow of his inspiration, albeit carrying through the basic intentions of the script. "That he [Cagney] will do all the time," acknowledged screenwriter Roberts. "When he feels something, he just keeps going, and it's usually very good." In the scene, Cody Jarrett is crouched atop the Hortonsphere, surrounded by legions of police. He suffers his final burst of insanity and—giggling and shrieking with laughter—is brought down by a hail of bullets and a blazing explosion. That bizarre element, the mirth of Cody Jarrett as he destroys himself, is *not* in the script. The giggling and the laughter were among Cagney's touches on the set, a detail that somehow magnificently capped the movie.

"Made It, Ma! Top of the World!"

The two movies that bookended the 1940s for Cagney could not be more unalike—indeed, there is probably not another film actor whose abilities and persona could span the gap between *Yankee Doodle Dandy* and *White Heat*. For that matter, there is a world of discrepancy between the original "public enemy," Tom Powers, and his more brutal counterpart, Cody Jarrett. Times were changing and so were Cagney and his image. Only vestiges of the once-irresistibly charming tough guy of the 1930s remained. The comic glimmers were gone (only to surface, extemporaneously, in scenes such as the one in which Cody Jarrett absentmindedly munches on a leg of chicken as he shoots a double-crosser through a car trunk). Paunchy (for the first time Cagney deliberately did not lose weight for a role), no longer juvenescent, Cagney had changed physically too, which meant that he was no longer a romantic commodity. It soured his character's relationships with women—not with Ma, certainly—but with his own wife Verna.

Most importantly, *White Heat* was a disavowal of the progressive political stance that had been a Warner Brothers tradition in the 1930s and 1940s, the studio outlook that seemed to absolve gangsters by indicting the wrongs of the social system. (Warners' proud motto was enscribed on a billboard that used to stand across the street from the studio: "Good Pictures Are Good Citizenship.") But Cody Jarrett is lunatic, not impoverished by class. He is beset by maddening headaches and a psychotic mother complex. His loot is laundered in Europe by a high-finance gentleman. There is little rationale for Jarrett's behavior, no social explanation for his remorseless killing. In the twisted context of the story, not even the cops are heroes. The Treasury agents tinker with the modern technological devices like high school science whiz kids; the undercover roper, Hank Fallon/Vic Pardo, shows no guilt in betraying someone who has become his intimate. The script is devoid of reference to history or mass conditions. Thus, *White Heat* is Warners' official goodbye to its social consciousness gangster works of the 1930s and 1940s. For Cagney it was also a brusque severence of that aspect of his image, that segment of his past.

As for Ma, she is a holdover from *Sinner's Holiday*, as vicious and lacking in compassion as Cody Jarrett. Cagney's early "mother" films formed a foundation for the unholy affinity between Cody and Ma in *White Heat*. Here, the tough woman/mother dependency discovered in many Cagney films swells to ludicrous proportions. Ma Jarrett synthesizes all the sturdiest traits of Cagney's women, producing a female who is not only motherly but manly. Indeed, Ma Jarrett symbolically becomes a "man" when Cody is sentenced to prison, and she is designated titular head of the Jarrett gang. She dominates the group in Jarrett's absence until she is shot dead, treacherously, by a bullet in the back (fired by Verna). Her violent death (although her demise occurs off-camera, it is the first and only time that Cagney's mother dies in a picture) marked the end of prominence for Cagney's mother and coincided with his 1950s maturation. Now, understandably, he was too old to have a mother on the screen. But the point had already been scored through years of filmwork: This boy gone wrong—witness his mother's trust—was really okay.

The stunning climax of *White Heat* brought all of these familiar parts of Cagney's persona into a shrill cacophony. The wailing laughter of Cody Jarrett, as police circle him like buzzards, belongs to the 1930s Cagney, the charmer, out of place and out of time. It is like some weird proof that Cody has finally teetered over the brink. Cody shrieks with laughter; Fallon (the Judas) aims and shoots. Cody shrieks again, Fallon shoots again. Stumbling, still laughing, Cody stands erect, unafraid, and points his pistol at the gas tank—the world—below. He fires. An explosion, the flames envelop him—yet it is not the formulaic cops-and-robbers death, but a suicide, a blinded Samson tearing down the columns of his enemies, a willful farewell to the 1930s Cagney. Above the din is heard his voice with its perverted salute to motherhood: "Made it, Ma! Top of the World!" Never was the Freudian signature so overt. And, strangely, it seemed as if Cody Jarrett were still laughing.

In his definitive book on Hollywood directors, *The American Cinema* (New York: E. P. Dutton, 1968), critic Andrew Sarris approvingly quotes the *Time* reviewer who "perceptively observed that Raoul Walsh was the only Hollywood director who could have got away with a shot of James Cagney sitting on his mother's lap." Sarris continued, "The principle of counterpoint operates here. Only the most virile director can effectively project a feminine vulnerability in his character." Yet it is apparent that the *Time* reviewer and Sarris never viewed *Sinner's Holiday* nor did they take it adequately into account in their analysis of Cagney's—not Walsh's—career. The famous lap scene as well as the mother complex are duplicates of scenes in Cagney's debut movie 20 years earlier and in other Cagney movies in the interim. What Walsh did was not to dictate the Cagney persona, but to usefully employ it in telling the story of Cody Jarrett. The feminine vulnerability, the mother dependency—these were Cagneyesque qualities, inherent and true in the actor.

The Critical Reception

White Heat remains one of Cagney's hallmark performances. He understood the neurosis as well as the ruthlessness of Cody Jarrett, and both were given intensity and conviction. The rest of the cast measures up to that corrosive level: Ex-Shakespearean and ex-Shavian actress Margaret Wycherly as Ma Jarrett was evil yet oddly affecting; ex-Goldwyn Girl Virginia Mayo as Verna, in the ascendancy of her career, was icily transparent, dumb comic relief; Edmond O'Brien was appropriate as Fallon/Pardo; and Steve Cochran (as "Big Ed") and Fred Clark (as the Trader) were staunch in key supporting roles. Cinematographer Sid Hickox, a career Warners' cameraman, filmed the story in a dark, newsreel style, "as though he deliberately stained the camera with sand pebbles," in the words of screenwriter Roberts. And director Walsh, in his element with action, crime, and Cagney, kept it all moving, visceral and driven.

Yet if audiences flocked to Cagney's comeback, many critics (except the astute *Time* reviewer and some few others) were not as ardent about the tough guy's return, and *White Heat* was largely a movie without honor in its day. It was passed over for Academy Awards (except for an Original Story nomination to

"Made it, Ma! Top of the world!" (WCTR)

Virginia Kellogg, a credit that Goff and Roberts rued having surrendered to her) and neglected by the New York critics circle as well, usually a partisan Cagney camp. Among critics the movie revived the periodic gripes about Cagney's insidious social influence, the complaints about his tough-guy portrayals that had lain dormant for nearly a decade. One magazine pronounced: "In *White Heat*, you are subject to an unending procession of what is probably the most gruesome aggregation of brutalities ever presented upon the motion picture screen under the guise of entertainment." Typical of the breast beating was the viewpoint of Bosley Crowther of *The New York Times*, whose first review of *White Heat*, on September 3, 1941, called it "the acme of the gangster–prison film" with a "brilliantly graphic" performance by Cagney. One week later, responding to pressure from church and civic organizations, Crowther took the unusual step of revising his opinion, writing a second review. This time he called Cagney's comeback role ironic and just a little sad. It isn't sad, mind you, from the viewpoint of the avid thriller fans—nor from the point of view of the Warners who will reap a vast harvest with this film. . . . For the innocent thrills and amusement—yes, amusement—which a well-designed *White Heat* can give to large segments of the public are balanced, we feel sure, by the unhealthy stimulation which such a film affords the weak and young. And the notions it spreads of moral values are dangerously volatile.

Interestingly enough, this backlash by the good-citizens brigade had its flip side in the reaction of Hollywood's left wing, which saw in *White Heat* Cagney's final abandonment of his avowed social principles. Hollywood's (alleged) Communist party members and left–liberals were being vociferously attacked by cold warriors under the umbrella of HUAC, the House Un-American Activities Committee (the same committee whose then-chairman Texan Martin Dies had cleared Cagney of pro-Red charges a decade earlier). Many of Cagney's former friends and coworkers were eventually blacklisted, their careers interrupted for decades or their lives broken. The accused included writers John Bright, Sam Ornitz, Lester Cole, Ring Lardner, Jr.—the latter three who went to jail rather than give testimony before the committee—John Wexley, Edward Chordorov, director John Cromwell, and fellow star John Garfield (who appeared as an extra in *Footlight Parade*).

To Cagney's credit, he did not actively involve himself in the blacklist; indeed, his politics were still in flux at this early stage of the McCarthy era, his conservatism not yet hardened. But he was one of a number of stars who quietly supported Olivia De Havilland when she attempted to have a strongly worded anti-Communist resolution passed after World War II by the Hollywood Democratic Committee (a Hollywood "united front" political action organization that backed FDR, the United Nations, racial tolerance, and other left-liberal causes—including, ultimately, condemnation of the HUAC witchhunt in Hollywood). When that resolution was strategically bottled-up in executive committee, Cagney and a "B" star named Ronald Reagan were among the "name" performers who joined De Havilland in resignation. After FDR's death, when anti-Soviet and anti-Stalin sentiment was fanned to a pitch by reactionaries in Hollywood, the fragile alliance between Hollywood left–liberals and party types shattered. When, in 1947, director John Huston sought Cagney's enlistment in a Committee for the First Amendment delegation to Washington, D.C. to protest the HUAC investigations in Hollywood, Cagney made himself conspicuously unavailable.* In 1948, the year *White Heat* was being prepared for filming, Cagney voted Republican for the first time—for Thomas Dewey.

This backdrop was duly noted by John Howard Lawson, a screenwriter, who

---

*Among Cagney's reasons: Humphrey Bogart, who later embarrassed the delegation by publicly denouncing the Committee for the First Amendment, was prominent in the group, and Cagney mistrusted the sincerity of Bogart's politics.

with Ornitz, Cole, Lardner, Jr., and the rest of the Hollywood Ten, was jailed for refusing to testify about his alleged membership in the Communist party. Lawson had also been an executive board member of the Hollywood Democratic Committee—and one of those who had stonewalled De Havilland's anti-Red statement. A Marxist, Lawson viewed *White Heat* at a Saturday night showing with other prisoners while incarcerated in a federal institution. The essay Cagney's movie inspired Lawson to write (reprinted in Lawson's *Film in the Battle of Ideas*, [New York: Masses and Mainstream, 1953]) signalled a sort of official repudiation of Cagney by the American left that had once, in the early 1930s, been so much a part of his aura and following. Sensing the "new," rightist Cagney here, Lawson wrote that the "anti-social message" of *White Heat* made an "unforgettable impression" on the inmates. "There are many decent, well-intentioned people in prison," wrote Lawson,

> many who recognize that the forces which drove them to vice or crime are inherent in our present social system. Related to this partial understanding is a deep bitterness, a feeling that the individual has no chance in a jungle society unless he adopts the way of the jungle.
>
> *White Heat* idealizes this code of the jungle and advertises it as a way of life. It made a strong impression on the prison inmates, especially on the younger men. There were long discussions after the showing: One would insist that Cagney is characterized as a madman in the picture. But Cagney is a famous actor. The prison audience—and this is probably true of any audience—associated the fictitious character with Cagney's reputation. The spectators saw him as an attractive symbol of toughness, defending himself against a cruel and irrational society; at least, it was said, "he has the guts to stand up and fight back!"
>
> This emphasis on the individual's total depravity in a depraved society rejects the possibility of rational social cooperation. Man is doomed to prowl alone, a beast in the jungle.

Publicity photograph, circa late 1950s.

10
The Fifties

We met him at Martha's Vineyard and we were sitting on his boat, which remained moored most of the time, if not always. He said, "I'm thinking of giving it up, fellas, it just isn't as much fun as it used to be. Maybe this [Shake Hands with the Devil] *will be my last film." I said, "Jim, if someone sends you an exciting script, you're going to do it." He said, "Something has happened. The firebell just doesn't go off anymore, I just don't want to go to the fire. And it's too tough on me physically. I have to lose fifty pounds before every picture." I said, "You're an actor, you're a great actor. How can you not respond to something exciting—something no one else could do?" He said, "Well, I'm also getting past the age when I'm Jimmy Cagney. I can only play certain roles now, you know."*

BEN ROBERTS

After *White Heat*—and the virtual collapse of Cagney Productions by 1953—Cagney's appetite for making motion pictures was further diminished. The career typecasting, the demise of his own independent company, and the shifting political winds disillusioned him. As he grew older, he was less and less willing to undergo the strict weight-loss regimen he demanded of himself for each new role. The parts no longer beckoned so alluringly. Middle aged, he was no longer ripe for the romantic roles of yore and too old to play the mama's boy. No studio was churning out Cagney-type social consciousness pictures in the witch-hunting atmosphere of the Cold War (and Cagney, a full-fledged Republican, was as likely to pop up on one side of an issue now as the other). So it was a double bind: He was trapped both by Hollywood and by his own inertia.

He could still be tempted into a project: by song and dance (as always); by patriotism (as with *The Gallant Hours*), by location filming (in the South Pacific for *Mister Roberts*; in Ireland for *Shake Hands with the Devil*), as a box-office favor (playing himself in *Starlift* or George M. Cohan in *The Seven Little Foys*); or as a director, for the first time (in *Short Cut to Hell*). But Cagney's image was now cemented as a tough guy, not only in the view of his legion of fans, but in the perception of writers and directors as well; at times his roles were cartoonish reductions of his previous work. Thus Cagney ended up playing *Cagney* in such

With Virginia Mayo and director Roy Del Ruth during rehearsals for
WEST POINT STORY. (MOMA)

movies as *Starlift* and *Seven Little Foys*, as well as such pictures as *West Point Story* (a Warners' retread stitched together on "inside" Cagney jokes) and Billy Wilder's *One, Two, Three* (whose humor is based almost entirely on Cagney career motifs). This image dilemma is a classic one for aging Hollywood stars. The wonder is that in Cagney's case the 1950s proved a decade of such interesting and peculiar variety, with highs to match the lows—and that, still, the work did not satisfy.

The *West Point Story*

Cagney always maintained a special affection for *West Point Story*, an affection out of proportion, perhaps, to its over-all quality. The first picture to emerge from the Warners' docket after *White Heat*, it is a full-scale musical about an out-of-work Broadway impresario (named Elwin Bixby) who becomes a West Point cadet to stage the annual academy variety show. Johnny Boyle was still around to oversee Cagney's dance numbers, and Virginia Mayo gave the frustrated song-and-dance man a sexy, leggy ingenue to toss around as his musical

Dancing with Virginia Mayo in WEST POINT STORY. (WCTR)

partner. His song-and-dance routines have an élan worthy of Cagney at his youthful best ("some of the best dancing I ever did," he proudly recalled in his autobiography). His spotlight number with Mayo, "Brooklyn," a tune by Julie Styne and Sammy Cahn, is a droll and angular, ersatz adagio—with taps. "It's still a pleasure to look at," recalled Cagney, "because it showed some versatility and humor, things I prize highly and always strive for."

Unfortunately, the rest of the vehicle is disappointing. The subplot of Cagney wooing cadet Gordon MacRae to the greener pastures of Broadway becomes tedious and the cadet shenanigans likewise. Though the movie reunited Cagney with director Roy Del Ruth for the first time since the early 1930s (Del Ruth had gravitated from urban comedy–dramas to musicals), Del Ruth never had the pizzazz of a Curtiz, especially with such flimsy material. The supporting cast of MacRae, Doris Day, Gene Nelson, and Alan Hale, Jr., is amiable enough but is sacrificed to the creaky plot. Head closely-shaved, Cagney gives a riotous, bellicose performance as Bixby, whose challenge it is to single-handedly whip the cadet variety show into shape. At one point he throws a *White Heat*-like fit when the cadets cannot learn to step in chorus unison. He stamps his feet, bellows, leaps up and down, and kicks a nearby piano. Then, bulging inside his West Point uniform, he demonstrates the proper method of footwork, bounding and stepping barbarously. "The measure of Mr. Cagney's impact upon the whole tenuous show," wrote Bosley Crowther in *The New York Times*, "is patently indicated when he is not on the screen. For then the thing sags in woeful fashion. The romance becomes absurd and the patriotic chest-thumping becomes so much chorus-boy parade."

In its aping of earlier Cagney films, *West Point Story* set the tenor for much of Cagney's work in the 1950s. As in earlier Cagney features (such as Del Ruth's own *Lady Killer*), there is a running gag here about Bixby's hot-tempered, right-fisted punch—he slugs his producer whenever he settles a contract; and, shades of General Patton, he is almost expelled from West Point when he wallops a cadet. When Bixby's secretary (Mayo) explains to West Point personnel that Bixby's grudge against the military began "when he asked for a size eight shoe [in the Army] and they gave him a twelve—and he hasn't been the same since," she is echoing dialogue that was used nearly verbatim twice before in the Cagney films *Here Comes the Navy* and *The Fighting 69th*. And when Bixby is forced to dance the "Brooklyn" finale as a last-minute substitute for the show's lead dancer (Nelson), whom he has inadvertently KO'd, it is a precise parallel to the climax of *Footlight Parade*.

Kiss Tomorrow Goodbye

For every Warners' release there was to be a corollary Cagney Productions' feature—per the *White Heat* contract. The first of these was the adaptation in 1950 of a seamy crime novel by Horace McCoy titled *Kiss Tomorrow Goodbye*, with Cagney as its violent protagonist Ralph Cotter. Today the motion picture enjoys a devout following among film noir devotees. Among them is writer–director Paul Schrader who, in his days as a film critic, acclaimed *Kiss Tomorrow Goodbye* as the logical, sordid follow-up to *White Heat*. According to Schrader's notes for a noir retrospective at the Los Angeles County Museum of Art, *Kiss Tomorrow Goodbye* is kindred to *White Heat* in that it orgiastically celebrates a psychotic Cagney as noir antihero. British critic Raymond Durgnat reserved special mention for *Kiss Tomorrow Goodbye* in his widely regarded "The Family Tree of Film Noir," published in the August 1970 issue of England's *Cinema*. Classifying the movie under "Crime as Social Criticism," and placing it under the cryptic subhead "Prohibition-type Gangsterism," Durgnat called the movie "quiet but astonishing" and compared it to George Stevens' *A Place in the Sun*, also released in 1951. (Both films employed the same scenarist, Harry Brown.) Schrader and Durgnat contend that *Kiss Tomorrow Goodbye* fulfills the basic criterion for true film noir: dark, pessimistic, corrupt, and relentlessly cynical (Durgnat's phraseology).

Off camera with Barbara Payton (center) and Helena Carter (right) on the set of KISS TOMORROW GOODBYE.

Yet *Kiss Tomorrow Goodbye* has to be one of the most misunderstood pictures Cagney ever made; it needs to be perceived in the context of the actor's strivings as an independent. Far from being in the vein of *White Heat*, it was intended as the flip side of *White Heat*. The former is uncompromisingly violent, voyeuristic, and exploitative of criminal degeneracy, but *Kiss Tomorrow Goodbye* is deliberately structured as an ethical, socially principled work. Though the major figures of both stories are homicidal paranoiacs, and the plotline of both concerns a jailbreak and an act of treachery, there the similarity ends. The villain of *Kiss Tomorrow Goodbye* is not as sympathetically tinged as Cody Jarrett, the script neither Ma-oriented nor peppered with mythological references. The film is actually a fairly conventional one and a relative embarrassment from the point of view of both the screenwriter (Brown) *and* the Cagneys.

McCoy was a writer the Cagneys had known in their short-lived days of independence on the Grand National lot; his novels, among them *They Shoot Horses, Don't They?* (later made into an Oscar-winning film), were very much in vogue during his lifetime. William Cagney's enthusiasm for the property was partly a holdover from his acquaintance with McCoy, partly a hope that the lead character might give his brother's tough-guy image a twist. In McCoy's novel, Cotter is a complex personality—a Phi Beta Kappa with a John Dillinger hang-up; a native-born Southerner (no dialect is used by Cagney in the movie) who once played in an orchestra; a dancer (no hint of this in the movie) whose brother is Reverend Steven C. Apperson, "the biggest minister in the U.S."; an amateur philosopher and guilt-ridden psychopath who, as a child, murdered his grandmother(!). One thing Cotter most assuredly is *not* is socially conscious— true to Cagney's revised 1950's image. Indeed, one could hardly imagine the Cagney of the 1930s assuming a role in which the character brags, as Ralph Cotter does in McCoy's book:

> I didn't grow up in the slums with a drunk for a father and a whore for a mother and come into crime that way. I hate society too, but I don't hate it because it mistreated me and warped my soul. Every other criminal I know—who's engaged in violent crime—is a two-bit coward who blames his career on society. I need no apologist or crusader to finally hold my lifeless body up to the world and shout for them to come and observe what they have wrought. Do you know one of the first things I'm going to do when I get some money? I'm going to have Cartier make me a little gold thing for my wrist, you know, that identification thing the army guys wear on a solid, gold chain, and do you know what I'm going to have inscribed on it? Just this: "Use me not as a preachment in your literature or your movies. This I have wrought, I and I alone."

Primarily, though, it was financial necessity that drew the Cagneys to one of McCoy's lesser works. Warner Bros., easily sold on any Cagney-as-a-gangster film, agreed to a deal "whereby they would give the banks (where we owed money for the loss involved in *The Time of Your Life*) the first five hundred thousand dollars the picture made," Cagney wrote in his autobiography. The picture could be quickly and cheaply produced—with the director, Gordon Douglas, a no-bull practitioner, recruited by William Cagney from the Warners' "B" stable.

Harry Brown's script labored to cleanse McCoy's brooding opus of its *White Heat*-like aberrations. The movie opens with a scene uncharacteristic of film noir: A straightforward courtroom sequence with a group of Ralph Cotter's cohorts in custody and on trial. Cotter is already dead—the narrative proceeds in flashback. That scene, which does not occur in the Horace McCoy novel, ought to clue the perspective for what follows. The aroused oratory of the district attorney informs the audience from the outset that Ralph Cotter is a despicable no-good who deserves little compassion. These remarks preface the ensuing events—the bloody prison jailbreak, the daring blackmail and robbery scheme involving the city constabulary.

In McCoy's book, Holiday, Cotter's would-be moll, is a hellraiser, "full of vinegar," with her own mottled past and a multitude of lovers, depraved and unsympathetic. In the film, as played by Barbara Payton, Holiday has the demeanor of a high school cheerleader. Therefore (and this is important to the Cagneys' theme) she does not deserve the maltreatment she receives from Cotter—who, in one noteworthy scene, swats her viciously with a bundled bathroom towel; and who, throughout the second half of the story, cheats on her

With (from left) Barton MacLane, Steve Brodie, and Ward Bond in Horace McCoy's KISS TOMORROW GOODBYE.

with heiress Margaret Dobson (Helena Carter). There is not much shading to either Payton's—or the other ingenue's—characterization. And the same holds true for the rest of the cast, an adequate assemblage of old friends in stock situations: Ward Bond in swarthy, snarling portrait of a cop on the take; the esteemed Luther Adler as a shyster lawyer; and, in bit parts, William Frawley, Matt McHugh (Frank's brother), and Barton MacLane (as a subordinate detective).

Cagney's characterization is dulled by the script and by his own emotional uninvolvement. The split personality of McCoy's Cotter is given only half-hearted presentation, and Cagney plays the character mostly on one note: the short fuse. Stocky, graying now, he erupts in a breakfast scene that grotesquely mocks the more famous one in *Public Enemy*, when Holiday provokes him by her bickering. "No cream?" he yells, tossing a cream pitcher at her. "How about some sugar?" he adds, flinging a sugar bowl. Then, suddenly, inexplicably, the two lovers fall into each other's arms, laughing and kissing crazily. Later, it is Holiday, blinded by jealousy, who shoots and kills the sadistic gangster. "You can kiss tomorrow goodbye," she tells him (supplying McCoy's title), as he pleads in vain for mercy. Dying, he groans and twists spasmodically on the floor of her shabby apartment, the fair victim of her revenge. The message of the movie, plainly, is that Cotter rated it all along.

White Heat, remember, concludes with that cataclysmic suicide whereby a laughing, jeering Cody Jarrett destroys himself rather than succumb to police: a no-win finis. The conclusion of *Kiss Tomorrow Goodbye* is less equivocal. And there is a coda: The courtroom scene is reintroduced, and the final witness of the case is ushered to the stand. Lest there be any doubt about the theme of Cagney Productions here, the final testimony is given by Cotter's brother, once described in the narrative (by Cotter) as being "one of the few honest men left in the world." The crowning irony is that Cotter's brother is played by William Cagney, longtime co-conspirator in the struggle to reform Cagney's screen image. The district attorney spins a phonograph recording of the local cops taking payola, and Cotter's brother (William Cagney, with his back to the camera) nods perfunctorily to confirm that it is Ralph Cotter's voice on the recording. The evidence is sealed, Cotter is damned in his grave, and the string of accomplices are slated for punishment. Seen from this angle, *Kiss Tomorrow Goodbye* emerges not as a grisly and graphic masterwork of film noir, but instead as a flawed, hurriedly-made genre piece, striking for its traditional morality.

Come Fill the Cup

Gordon Douglas also directed *Come Fill the Cup*, Cagney's next picture in 1951, a sob story about alcoholic newspapermen based on a novel by Harlan Ware and scripted by Ivan Goff and Ben Roberts. Cagney played the lead role of Lew Marsh, the ace newspaper editor and ex-alcoholic who is nursemaid to a bevy of reformed drinkers—and the drama was beautifully acted by him and his crack supporting cast. As such, *Come Fill the Cup* was a partial success. But the dramatic construction was undermined by Jack Warner himself, according to the screenwriters, when the studio boss made a couple of grievous demands upon the story.

First, the part of veteran reporter Charley Dolan, the rehabilitated lush who is Lew Marsh's roommate, was originally written to be portrayed by a black man. But Warner objected, according to Goff, saying, "You think Cagney's gonna be under the same roof as a nigger?" (The irony is that Cagney, as a lifelong foe of racial discrimination, would have relished the screenwriters' ploy.) Instead the role went to old pro James Gleason, who played it with magnanimity. Warner also protested the casting of Gig Young as Boyd Copeland, the newspaper publisher's egocentric pianist–nephew, another ex-lush—but the writers prevailed in that argument, and Young later earned an Academy Award nomination as Best Supporting Actor.* But Warner refused to back down from his worst transgression: a demand that the scenarists hatch a gangster angle for the story to meet his clichéd expectations of what a Cagney picture should be. "The book, as I recall," remembered screenwriter Roberts,

*Under his real name, Byron Barr, the Canadian-born actor who changed his name to Gig Young had appeared in a bit part in Cagney's *Captains of the Clouds* in 1942.

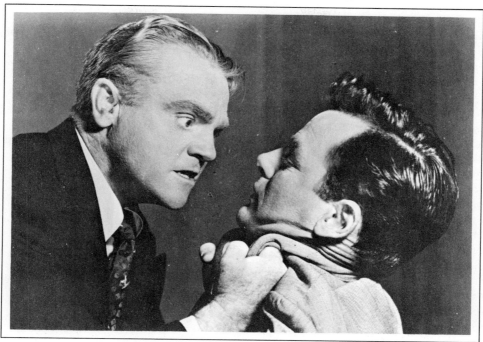

With Gig Young in COME FILL THE CUP. (WCTR)

has no gangster in it, and we wrote the story without a gangster. The bottle was the gangster. We were talking about a story like *The Lost Weekend*. Jack said, ''You can't tell a Cagney story without guns and gangsters.'' We said, ''Why not?'' He said, ''Because that's what the audience expects.'' We said, ''We don't know how to put a gangster in this picture. It'll be bullshit. The story's going to switch tracks.'' He said, ''Well, that's what I want, and if you don't give it to me, I'll put someone else on it.'' We tried to save the film. The first half was so wonderful. But we wrote this gangster character, he got Sheldon Leonard to play it, and the whole thing went right out the window. The last forty minutes of the film isn't watchable.

Indeed, the first half of the movie is sturdy melodrama, good stuff, with Marsh and pals fighting the temptations of booze in their private lives while crusading against crime and corruption on the front page of their newspaper. The gangster–revenge angle is introduced midway, after the mob-arranged highway death of old-timer Dolan. Absurdly, the liquor–lure subplot meets the gangster subplot in the climactic moments of the story, when the underworld chieftain (Leonard) finds Marsh and Boyd Copeland at the mercy of his gun barrel and asks sarcastically: ''What is this—an AA meeting?'' Then he orders the two ex-souses to down slugs of bourbon—to disguise their impending deaths as suicides. Gripping the shot glass with a wry look (after having spent the entire story in an effort to sober up), Marsh hoists the glass for a toast, splashes it suddenly into the gangster's eyes and, in the ensuing tumult, conquers the crime czar as well as, presumably, his thirst.

Whatever the movie's demerits, Cagney's performance is a riveting one. A nondrinker, Cagney incorporated some of the peripheral mannerisms of habitual drinkers in his impersonation, including "this thing of the walk," in the actor's words. In his research, Cagney discovered that "this is what happens to alcoholics—they lose muscle tone, and in order to keep their legs working, they've got to keep them practically stiff . . ." Particularly effective are two sequences: one, early in the story, in which Marsh is on a drinking spree—and groggy, unshaven and pale, he lurches into the path of a careening car; in the other scene, when Marsh learns of his friend's "fatal accident," his eyes well up and he begins to sob. Then he shuffles over to Boyd Copeland, whose carelessness has evidently helped cause Charley Dolan's death, and he erupts— slapping Copeland across the face, choking back a half-laughing, half-crying sound and sputtering a train of enraged recriminations. That threatening edge of disintegration was the pervasive quality of Cagney's performance in *Come Fill the Cup*.

Starlift

Cagney's other 1951 release was just a piffle, a celebrity-studded musical for the Korean War effort—and, ironically, his last picture to be directed by Roy Del Ruth. Along with an ensemble of other stars, including Doris Day, Gordon MacRae, Virginia Mayo, Gene Nelson, Ruth Roman, and Gary Cooper, Cagney made a cameo appearance, which predictably called upon him to utter a few tough-guy phrases during a visit to Travis Air Force Base. "*Starlift* was Hollywood's ill-starred project of ferrying troupes of movie performers to Travis Air Base, north of San Francisco, to entertain replacements bound for Korea and wounded veterans on their way back to U.S. hospitals," wrote the reviewer for *Time*. "But *Starlift* is guilty of its worst breach of good taste when it takes a low bow for Hollywood's patriotic gesture, makes the project seem exclusively Warners', includes in its cast some stars who never troubled to fly up to Travis Air Base."

What Price Glory?

Originally, the 1952 remake of *What Price Glory?* was supposed to be a musical version of the pacifistic stage classic for Twentieth Century-Fox had commissioned the new script by Phoebe and Henry Ephron which was originally going to be retitled "Charmaine." The Maxwell Anderson–Laurence Stallings World

Cameo appearance with Dick Wesson, Ron Hagerthy, Doris Day, and Ruth Roman in STARLIFT.

War I play about trench warfare in France had stirred audiences on Broadway in 1924 and then had been made into a classic silent picture in 1926, directed by Raoul Walsh with stars Victor McLaglen, Edmund Lowe, and Delores Del Rio. "Despite all these favorable antecedents," wrote Cagney in his autobiography,

> *What Price Glory?* never struck me as being anything up my street *until* I heard it was going to be made as a musical. I warmed to that idea immediately and decided to take it on. Then, when John Ford was brought in as director, he vetoed the idea of a musical. "What's wrong with the original?" he asked. That's a question that can only be answered negatively, but I was recruited on the basis of its being a musical, and I wouldn't have done it otherwise. Still, I was committed at that point, and I did it, but not, in Shakespeare's phrase, "for my ease."

Nor for anyone's, it might be added. The updated version of *What Price Glory?* is one of John Ford's least-distinguished films—he arguably the greatest American director to emerge from the first generation of sound. The screenplay lacked

With director John Ford on the set of WHAT PRICE, GLORY? (UCLA Film Archives)

the bawdy vitality and antiwar sensitivity (which would have been relevant to the war raging in Korea) of the original. Director Ford had produced the play on stage in Hollywood in 1949 as a charity benefit for the Military Order of the Purple Heart. Now he clashed with producer Sol C. Siegel and the Ephrons; out of step with the folly-of-war theme, he chose to emphasize the story's histrionic humor. And unhappy with Cagney's casting—though he never allowed as much—Ford simply lost interest in the filming.* Under these circumstances, Cagney acquitted himself as honorably as he could, playing the Captain Flagg character who squares off against Sergeant Quirt (Dan Dailey) for the affections

---

*According to John Ford's biographer, Andrew Sinclair, "His [Ford's] Korean experience, however, had made him unhappy with the message of the play [*What Price, Glory?*]. He was also out of temper because Cagney was given the lead role instead of [John] Wayne, who had played for him on stage. He quarreled with the screenwriters, Phoebe and Henry Ephron, because they did not know his values or understand his rough sense of humor. On the set of the French village on the Fox back lot Phoebe Ephron remarked that there were a lot of Catholic churches for one small French village. 'Don't you think there are a lot of synagogues in a Jewish village?' Ford replied, sending off both screenwriters forever, deeply insulted. They were too green and thin-skinned to survive Ford's normal testing of a newcomer's responses, and they presumed bigotry when they were only enduring his trial by their error. As he could not work on the screenplay with his usual trained writers, Ford barely consulted it when he shot the picture."

With Dan Dailey in John Ford's remake of WHAT PRICE, GLORY? (Copyright © 1952 Twentieth Century-Fox Film Corp. All Rights Reserved. Courtesy of Twentieth Century-Fox.)

of an innkeeper's daughter, Charmaine (Corinne Calvet). But the comedy was rantingly off pitch, resulting in a lot of noise that signifieth nothing. "The total result is deplorable," wrote Archer Winsten of *The New York Post*, "which is shocking, when you see the name of John Ford as director." Alton C. Cook of *The New York World-Telegram and Sun* agreed: "James Cagney and Dan Dailey have lowered their acting standards in keeping with the spirit of the vehicle."

A Lion Is in the Streets

Except for an amorphous corporate association with Robert Montgomery and *The Gallant Hours* in 1960, *A Lion Is in the Streets* was the final independent Cagney Production—ending the experiment with a whimper instead of a bang. Truly, by now, the company was a family undertaking with Edward Cagney moved up to story editor, Jeanne among the supporting cast, William as producer, and James as the star. This story of a Huey Long type of swamp peddler who becomes a political leader and upholder of sharecropper rights, until he is exposed as a fraud and assassinated, was potentially the most provocative of Cagney's independent films. The novel by Adria Locke Langley, on which the

movie was based, was a best seller in the 1940s, when the Cagneys first purchased the story rights. But in 1948 Columbia Pictures beat them to the punch
with a film version of Robert Penn Warren's similarly themed *All the King's Men*,
which garnered critical acclaim and took the sting out of the story's novelty.

Still, William Cagney believed in the project and bided his time. In 1952 a
writer by the name of Luther Davis, on loan from MGM, did an "intermediate
draft" of the script, and William Cagney began shopping around for a classy
director, "someone thoughtful, not action-oriented" (Davis's words), like a
Wyler or a Zinnemann. Again there was a hope of turning the story into a
semimusical.

Circumstances intervened. Davis's script culminated in a dramatic riot set in a
New Orleans square that made the movie seem "almost like a leftist tract," in
William Cagney's words. The Cagneys were still maverick enough, but they
were not suicidal; this was at the height of the McCarthy Era—scarcely judicious
timing for such a theme. Among others, Harlan Ware, one of James's good
friends, tried to talk the actor out of producing the story. At least one director,
William Wellman, rejected the assignment on political grounds. Warner Bros.,
meantime, refused all extensions of Cagney Productions' contract, as much for
economic reasons (*Lion* was big budgeted for location filming in the South) as
political ones, and the studio ordered shooting forthwith on a cut-rate schedule
on the sound stages of Sam Goldwyn Studios. Expeditiously, Raoul Walsh was
approached, and Walsh agreed to direct the movie, provided he could toss out
the final third of the script wholesale. "My guess is," recalled William Cagney,
"he [Walsh] gave it [the script] to somebody he trusted who told him to do that,
because it was unlike Raoul to make story demands. It was too bad—the ending
would have been startling."

Warners and Cagney Productions were at the fag end of their on-again,
off-again relationship. According to screenwriter Davis, his "intermediate draft"
("more than a first and less than a final") was rushed into filming to accommodate the financial demands being made upon the Cagneys by the studio. "I
admire Walsh," recollected Davis,

> but I think he did a terrible job on the picture. The final third of the script,
> Huey Long's degeneration into power, which was the whole point of the
> novel, was tossed out on the theory that there wasn't time to shoot it. I'm
> sure Walsh never even read the book. One day, in fact, he came up to me
> and said, "Kiddo, is it your idea that at the end, Jimmy becomes kind of a
> shit?" Huey Long! I don't think Walsh had ever heard of him. He said, "I
> don't like the idea of Jimmy becoming a shit." That's why he directed
> Jimmy so well—he directed him like a leading man. It was just plain old
> line shooting from Walsh's point of view: here are the jokes, get it in the
> can and on to something else.

There was another mitigating consideration: Cagney was not fully engaged in
the role. He gave one of his rare sloppy characterizations, slurring from the

With Barbara Hale in Raoul Walsh's A LION IS IN THE STREETS.

Southern dialect ("That would be plummmb fascinating!") to pure New Yorkese and back again without paying much heed. Ten years earlier Cagney had been fascinated by the populist side of Huey Long; now—after his Republican "conversion," after the Hollywood onslaught of the House Un-American Activities Committee, after the Cold War had set in—he saw Long only as a Stalinist demagogue. "I wouldn't be surprised," suggested William Cagney,

> if certain things hadn't happened in his [James's] mind from the inception [of *Lion* in the 1940s] until the time we shot the picture. Because Jimmy had this quality of being able to do anything—I don't care what it was—and the audience would be in sympathy with him. Even if they momentarily thought that what he did was abominable, when the picture closed, they liked this guy and they were glad they had spent that time with him because he was colorful. I tried to get him—it always had to be done very subtly, you couldn't act like you were telling him how to work—to go back

to the original thing that he saw in the character, which was this likable quality. But he was emphasizing a lousy quality, with the result that he wasn't saving the scenes like he always did. Jimmy just did not give. I think it was deliberate. I think he was so out of tune with Huey Long, who he was playing—he hated him so—that he did not get the audience to go along with him like he could when he was playing the worst killer. As a result, you didn't want to walk down that street with him. That was the difference—the difference between whether the audience was enchanted or not.

To say the least, *Lion* is an erratic production. The opening sequence (with ravishing Technicolor photography by Harry Stradling) features Hank Martin (Cagney) doing a merry, childish prance in a monsoon-like rain, singing "Oh, I met the girl I love, the girl I am going to marry" to Verity Wade (Barbara Hale). After marrying Verity, he plunges into a romance with a backwoods siren named Flamingo (Anne Francis) and a sensationalistic clash with wild alligators in the wetlands. Shortly thereafter, Martin begins his abrupt political rise—and fall. The continuity is annoyingly sketchy. The cast—Hale, Francis, John McIntire, Lon Chaney, Jr., Jeanne Cagney, Frank McHugh in his last (unlikely) appearance with Cagney as the movie's "heavy,"—never seems very assured and often manifestly awkward.

Although an inferior movie, *Lion* ultimately upholds the tradition of the democratic themes promulgated by Cagney Productions throughout its brief history, albeit with a nod to the changed times. Gunplay resolves the villainy of *A Lion Is in the Streets*, not the peaceful, free persuasion of such earlier independent films as *Great Guy* or *Johnny Come Lately*. Sister Jeanne Cagney is the appointed assassin who shoots her actor–brother in the crucial scene. Mortally wounded, Cagney's Hank Martin eyes his murderess disbelievingly and mounts his odds-and-ends wagon for a fantasy getaway. "I told you I'd lead you to glory," he sputters to the encircling crowd before plummeting to the ground. "You told on me, sweetface," he gasps to his wife Verity, just before he dies. Then, a relevant postscript: The image of the Lincoln Memorial is flashed on the screen, and Lincoln's famous maxim is writ before the viewer: "You can fool some of the people some of the time . . ." and so on. In a final flourish of its founding spirit, the farewell words of Cagney Productions are Abraham Lincoln's.

There would be no more Cagney Productions—excepting two cavalry pictures, *Only the Valiant* and *Bugles in the Afternoon*, both produced by William Cagney without the participation of brother James, finalizing the *White Heat* deal. William Cagney simply lost heart and dropped out of the business, handling only the fine print of James's contracts thereafter. The brief saga of Cagney Productions does not amount to much in actual number of movies produced— more, it is the chronicle of aborted projects and box-office disappointments. The promise of *Great Guy* and *Johnny Come Lately*, it must be said, was muted in *Kiss*

Tomorrow Goodbye and *A Lion Is in the Streets*. But the small-shop idea was one that deserves a footnote in any Hollywood history, as much as Cagney's own, for the ground it broke for independent filmmaking, for the risks it took, and for the modest credo of quality it upheld throughout its existence.

The Comeback of 1955

Cagney did not appear in any motion pictures released in 1954. So, when four Cagney movies flooded the market in 1955, critics spoke reverently of a comeback. "Comeback, hell," Cagney said with a snort in interviews, "I've never been away." The four: director Nicholas Ray's *Run for Cover*, Cagney's first Western since *The Oklahoma Kid*; the Ruth Etting musical biopic with Doris Day, *Love Me or Leave Me*; a film adaptation of the stage hit *Mister Roberts*, with Cagney as the tyrannical Captain; and Bob Hope's comedy *The Seven Little Foys*, with Cagney in a vignette reprising his most famous role as George M. Cohan.

Despite its thematic pretensions—the discernible 1950s crosscurrents of allegiance and paranoia—*Run for Cover* is not much superior to the average cowboy yarn. In the movie (based on a story by Harriet Frank, Jr., and Irving Ravetch, with screenplay by William C. Thomas), Cagney plays Matt Dow, a survivor of years of wrongful imprisonment who heads West to bury his memories. After he strikes up a chance acquaintanceship with orphan Davey Bishop (John Derek), a posse ambushes Dow and Bishop, believing them responsible for a local train robbery. Bishop is wounded in the leg, crippled for life. Dow is nursed back to health by a farmer's daughter (Viveca Lindfors) and remains in town to become the sheriff, with Bishop as his deputy. Yet Bishop is traitorous, bitter about his injury. He joins a gang of bank robbers and helps ambush his friend, Sheriff Dow. Wounded, the tenacious Dow catches up with the robbers and shoots Bishop—just as the conscience-stricken youth has aimed his gun at another bandit, saving Dow's life. Bishop dies in Dow's arms.

As with *High Noon*, the prototypical Western allegory of the 1950s (and *Run for Cover* even has a similar and recurrent theme song), director Ray tried to imbue the story with a resonant social comment about the excesses of the McCarthy era. Cagney is the moral centerpiece, haranguing the townspeople for their shortcomings ("What kind of man are you," he accusingly asks the town sheriff, "to hang a man without a trial?") and sermonizing to Bishop about the vicissitudes of life ("There's a lot of people in this world who had a rougher time of it than you. . . . the only difference is they don't run for cover"). Yet the most affecting moment of the movie occurs at the climax when, realizing he has killed the repentant Bishop, Dow weeps openly and poignantly before the camera. The honesty of Cagney's acting here only points up the self-conscious philosophizing of so much of the rest of *Run for Cover*—a movie notable, primarily, for Cagney's graceful romance with Viveca Lindfors (making *Run for Cover* one of the few 1950s films in which Cagney does not abuse his female costar); and for reuniting Cagney with old Warners' war-horse Grant Withers (Cagney's costar in *Sinner's Holiday* and *Other Men's Women*), now playing a seedy bank robber.

Cagney's hopes that *Run for Cover* would be "offbeat" were dashed. "We've always seen Cagney as the tough little squirt throwing a grapefruit in a girl's face or taking on somebody twice his size and kicking hell out of him," director Ray once observed in an interview. "But Jimmy has not only a great serenity, such as I've not seen in an actor, outside of Walter Huston at times, he has a great love of the earth, and of his fellow man, an understanding of loneliness. I wanted to try and use all that. The vehicle itself wasn't strong enough for it and we didn't have the time to be as inventive as we would have liked."

Cagney always rated his next picture, *Love Me or Leave Me*, among his top five favorites—and understandably so. Everything about this musical biography, which tells the unhappy story of 1920s singer Ruth Etting and her Svengali-like relationship with Chicago laundry racketeer Martin "The Gimp" Snyder, is first class. As Doris Day has commented, "It was a picture that could not have been made at Warners, where musicals were done as quickly and cheaply as possible. The time, money and expertise that MGM devoted to the film were what gave it its look of quality." And not just a *look* of quality; *Love Me or Leave Me* has the

With Doris Day in MGM's Ruth Etting biopic, LOVE ME OR LEAVE ME.

advantage of a pungent, mature, and ultimately tragical script (by Daniel Fuchs and Isobel Lennart) as well as a sentient director in Hungarian-born Charles Vidor, who adhered to the grim realism of the story while interposing wry humor. (A sign in Etting's dressing room, for instance, announces that "the management will not tolerate rough stuff or fighting in this dressing room.") It was another irony of Cagney's career that it was MGM, not Warners, that provided him with his deserved last hurrah as a gangster—and perhaps his most wrenching, tortured, compassionate portrayal.

Dazzling, brilliant, fascinating—these were the superlatives critics applied to Cagney's performance, which garnered the actor his third Academy Award nomination for Best Actor.* Like the real Snyder, Cagney played the role as if physically deformed (as well as emotionally stunted): club-footed and bent. He walked with an ugly limp, spoke with a vainglorious sarcasm, and manifested his anxiety and hurt by nervous knuckle-cracking and bestial outbursts. "Now, look here, you stupid little broad," Snyder screams at Etting at one point, "do you know who I am? Do you think I let dames talk that way to me?" Their

---

*Cagney lost—to Ernest Borgnine's performance in *Marty*. *Love Me or Leave Me* logged in with five nominations, yet won only for Daniel Fuchs in the category of Best Original Story.

At ease with codirector Mervyn LeRoy (at right) and producer Leland Hayward during the filming of MISTER ROBERTS. (WCTR)

marriage is nothing but a loveless combat, and so Snyder ultimately loses Etting to her pianist Johnny Alderman (Cameron Mitchell). But the beauty of Cagney's performance is that he lets the audience in on the inner pain as well as the sadism and obnoxiousness of the Gimp.

Unpredictably, Doris Day matched Cagney tit for tat and proved his best-suited female costar of the decade. Against type, she gave a guileless, dramatic performance, showing how wasted her talent had been, heretofore, in the peppy musicals in which she had specialized. (Her own marriage to agent Marty Melcher had unfortunate parallels to the sordid relationship between Ruth Etting and the Gimp.) A vibrant singer, Day robustly imitated Ruth Etting with a score of memorable standards, including ''You Made Me Love You,'' ''Ten Cents a Dance,'' and ''I'll Never Stop Loving You.'' But she was equally in form during her free-wheeling confrontations with the Gimp. During one especially heated argument, he smashes a vase on her dressing-room floor and she, grasping his hollow bluff, waves away the hysterics with, ''Don't go into dramatics.''

Following *Love Me or Leave Me* was *Mister Roberts*: It had been a best-selling novel and later a smash-hit Broadway play. Director John Ford offered Cagney a couple of weeks' vacation in Honolulu with old chums Spencer Tracy and Henry

As the Captain, with Henry Fonda in MISTER ROBERTS.

Fonda and a newcomer named Jack Lemmon. Tracy never showed up (William Powell took his place) and Ford and Fonda (who had carried the title role for months on the stage) reportedly feuded and scuffled over the interpretation of the screen adaptation. Director Mervyn LeRoy came aboard to reshoot scenes and complete the movie. Cagney stayed apart from the infighting. "I did it [*Mister Roberts*] for a lark," he later said, "and it was one of the easiest pictures I ever made. Everyone else had to jump and holler all the time. I just pulled my cap over my eyes, walked on deck, barked a command or two, and then went home."

Extremely popular in its day, *Mister Roberts* received three Academy Award nominations, including Best Picture. As the cranky Captain whose tyranny provokes a near mutiny on a naval vessel shuttling between islands in the backwaters of the war in the South Pacific, Cagney was "simply great," according to *Variety*. *Cue* called his portrayal "a gem of choleric characterization." *The New York Herald Tribune* described it as "another remarkable portrait." And the rest of the cast—Fonda (as "Mister Roberts," the buffer between the captain and crew), Powell, Lemmon, and remnants of the Ford stock company—also came in for due praise.

A break in shooting: with James (Jimmy) Cagney, Jr., Bob Hope, Billie Cagney, Cagney, and Kathleen Cagney on the set of SEVEN LITTLE FOYS.

Yet, partly because of the brouhaha between Ford and Fonda on the set, one must add that the movie has suffered by revised estimate in the years since its original release. It tends to be scoffed at in the Ford camp as innocuous and regarded (even by Fonda) as somewhat of a disappointment. Though it is supposed to be a "drama with comic overtones," in Cagney's words, it comes off more like a comedy with dramatic overtones, albeit well crafted by LeRoy (who once estimated that 90 percent of the finished movie is his). Certainly Cagney played *his* part for peppery comedy, with an ease that betrayed his familiarity with the role of petty tyrant.* Though Fonda always went out of his way to laud Cagney's performance, original stage director (and coplaywright, coscenarist) Joshua Logan weighed in with a rare demurral in his memoirs, *Movie Stars, Real People and Me* (New York: Delacorte, 1978), complaining that Cagney upset the story's tone by playing the Captain "like an old New England bumbler, without any hatred, without darkness, without threat . . . a kind of Walt Disney character."

*Interestingly, the comparison might be made between Cagney in *Mister Roberts* and Humphrey Bogart's more eerily insane tyrant of a ship captain in *The Caine Mutiny*, released the previous year.

Obviously, Cagney's final release in 1955, Paramount's *The Seven Little Foys*, offers an extreme example of Cagney catering to his own image: For it is a movie in which he makes a brief reappearance in his Oscar-winning role as George M. Cohan, tap-dancing on a table top at a Friar's Club dinner with vaudevillian Eddie Foy (played by Bob Hope). It is the high point of an otherwise too-typical Hope vehicle. Cagney did it as a gesture of friendship to Hope and as an excuse to lose weight during the dance rehearsals. "When I'm taking lard off for a hoofing picture," Cagney told reporters, "and the piano is thumping, I usually wear a sweat shirt. Over that I pull on a rubberized silk thing. On my head I wear a kind of beret teamed up with the sleeves of another sweat shirt that I wrap around my neck. I can work up quite a sweat that way and the blubber pours off me." After rehearsing vigorously with Cagney, Hope told the press, "The man is a horse, a workhorse. Here he was doing this thing free and working like a demon. Why, he danced ten pounds of suet right off me. And I'll bet he lost a good fifteen pounds himself."

Tribute to a Bad Man

Spencer Tracy and MGM were nearing the end of their quarter-century association. On location for a western in the mountains of Colorado, Tracy was ailing and disgruntled by the script; and after a nasty tug-of-war with MGM it was mutually agreed that he should leave the project. His replacement was an old friend who assumed his role to smooth matters over: Cagney. And yet *Tribute to a Bad Man*, directed by Robert Wise from a Michael Blankfort screenplay, may have been better suited to Cagney in the first place. It is a dreary, routine western, given technical lustre by Robert Surtees' color photography and Miklos Rozsa's sweeping score. But the title of the story—which is a grudging salute to an aging tough guy, one Jeremy Rodock (Cagney), a horse rancher and pioneer who mercilessly defends his holdings—is a metaphor for Cagney's entire career.

The story begins with Rodock's hiring of an Eastern tinhorn named Steve Miller (colorless Don Dubbins) who promptly falls in love with Jocasta (Irene Papas, in her first American movie), Rodock's erstwhile mistress. Both hired-hand Miller and Jocasta are shocked by Rodock's murderous frenzy when he is confronted by an occasional rustler or horse thief in the lawless frontier of the 1870s. Begged to go easy on one band of would-be robbers, Rodock instead forces the gang to tread barefoot over miles of hot and dusty, rocky terrain. Not that Rodock lacks a decent side—as is to be expected with a Cagney characterization. In peaceful moments, the hard-bitten rancher puffs on a pipe, plays the piano, and sings a few off-key notes. And he lavishes attention on Jocasta, though ultimately surrendering her to the callow Miller when it seems that she cannot abide his periodic "hanging fever." Away in a buckboard she rides with the young cowboy. Then, torn with regret, she returns—alone. Jubilant and forgiving, the "bad man" asks her to marry him (inconceivably) as the film ends.

Substituting for Spencer Tracy in TRIBUTE TO A BAD MAN.

These Wilder Years

Dubbins, a sort of Cagney protegé, also appeared with Cagney in *These Wilder Years*, originally titled *Somewhere I'll Find Him*, also produced by MGM in 1956. But the key attraction was costar Barbara Stanwyck, a female counterpart worthy of Cagney. Regrettably, the story itself is maudlin soap-opera fare, although Cagney and Stanwyck give it some backbone. The narrative follows the quest of wealthy steel tycoon Steve Bradford (Cagney), who invades an adoption home called "The Haven" (motto: "Anybody's child is everybody's child") to locate the illegitimate son he fathered in his wanton youth. The administrator of the home, Ann Dempster (Stanwyck), refuses to accept Bradford's excuse for the late-blooming interest in his own offspring—"I got older and I got lonely"—and goes to court rather than break her own personal code of ethics by divulging the youth's whereabouts. Though the resolute industrialist loses the judicial decision, he encounters his long-lost scion, now happily married and content to be a foster child, in a bowling alley. Placated and all the wiser, Bradford instead adopts a young orphan (Betty Lou Keim), who herself has just given birth to an illegitimate child. Thus Bradford becomes a father and

With Barbara Stanwyck (in doorway) and Betty Lou Keim in publicity still for soap
THESE WILDER YEARS.

a grandfather in one fell swoop—and, as the story concludes, he has patched up his quarrels with Miss Dempster, hinting that he may soon become a husband, too.

Besides Stanwyck, who contributed her usual staunch and fiery portrayal, the cast included Walter Pidgeon as Bradford's attorney, blustery Edward Andrews, and the two newcomers with fleeting motion picture careers, Dubbins and doe-eyed Keim. Cagney's portrait of the rash millionaire businessman was finely etched: polite, unfeeling, and powerfully obstinate, a lead portrayal so steady and accurate that it almost subverted the platitudinous homilies of the script. (Sample: "Don't cry about tomorrow—wait until it's yesterday.") But if director Roy Rowland's style was unpretentious, it was also plodding and pictorially dull, and the musical background (by Jeff Alexander) was syrupy and intrusive. As most critics viewed it, *These Wilder Years* was made with lofty intentions, with "restraint and goodwill," in the words of Bosley Crowther of *The New York Times*—but it was not half as much fun, certainly, as the Charleston, the black bottom, the tango, and the maxie that veteran dancers Cagney and Stanwyck practiced together, off-camera, between takes.

Man of a Thousand Faces

The life of silent film star Lon Chaney—who impersonated freaks and personified evil during a decade-long reign on the screen during the 1920s, in which he appeared, in one movie or another, as armless, legless, paralytic, hunchbacked, one-eyed, blind, dim-witted, or deranged—offered Cagney one of the most challenging and extraordinary subjects of his career. Cagney assumed the task with what was now rare passion and commitment, telling director Joseph Pevney that he profoundly empathized with Chaney's chaotic upbringing as the son of deaf-mute parents as well as with the great performer's vaudeville background. Indeed, *Man of a Thousand Faces* is similar to another Cagney film with a show business milieu and vaudeville focus, *Yankee Doodle Dandy*, only with a level of horror and suffering that the earlier picture deliberately skirted.

The original script by R. Wright Campbell (based on a story by Ralph Wheelwright) did not satisfy Cagney, who backed out of filming just before the scheduled start date, insisting that Universal employ the trustworthy Goff and Roberts to revise the screenplay and capture more of Chaney's troubled personality. With Cagney adamantly on their side, the two screenwriters wrangled a deal for $1,000 a day, writing against the clock. "In that instance," remembered co scenarist Roberts,

> Jimmy knew what we could do for him, which was to put emotion into the film. It lacked the emotion of a man whose past triggered his future. He [Chaney] was the son of deaf parents—he deaf-signed as a kid and other kids naturally made fun of him—and that colored his whole career, his whole personality. Well, you never saw that [in the original script]! Jimmy just knew instinctively what the story was lacking, and he understood we knew how to do it for him, how to use the Cagney quality and make it work.

Goff and Roberts often found themselves at odds with producer Robert Arthur over the revisions, but Cagney, comfortable with his two *White Heat* screenwriters, sided with them by rote. "We did the script in three weeks," recalled Goff.

A lull in the filming of MAN OF A THOUSAND FACES, with makeup artists Bud Westmore (left) and Jack Kevan (right). (Marc Wanamaker/Bison Archives)

Jimmy would be around in case we needed to try anything out on him. Every night we'd wind up in Robert Arthur's office, going through the day's work. Because Jimmy would be tired—he would have spent the day working out—he'd curl up on a couch while Ben and I, invariably, would get into slangey shouting matches with Robert Arthur. If we weren't able to bring him over to our point of view, one of us would say, "Well, let's ask Jimmy." So Bob would go over to the couch and shake Jimmy and ask, "Jimmy?" And Jimmy would say [Irish accent], "Whatever the boys want!" This is a writer's dream, by the way. We had a sense of enormous power.

As Lon Chaney, with young Rickie Sorenson in MAN OF A THOUSAND FACES.

Cagney's impersonation was magnificent. He combined a reasonable physical likeness to the master of disguises and his own pride in mimicry with a tenderness and understanding of Chaney's private turmoil. The actor used the hand-sign language of the deaf (which he learned for the production) casually and with natural authority, which is especially heartrending at the climax when Chaney, near death and unable to speak, must revert, ironically, to the silent communication of his parents. Other highlights: Chaney/Cagney in blackface, tap-dancing in pantomime with a broom and shadow in a glimpse of vaudeville reminiscent of *Yankee Doodle Dandy*; Cagney as "old Lady Murgatroyd," in wig, granny glasses, and shawl, "sewing" his fingers together to amuse pint-sized son Creighton Chaney (Rickie Sorenson), who later was to take the name of Lon Chaney, Jr.; Cagney, his body twisted in contortions, crawling, imploring the blessings of a faith-healer and then straightening up, cured, as Chaney did in a scene from 1919's *The Miracle Man*; and Cagney, hairy and animalistic, crying out in pain as he is being tortured, duplicating Chaney's performance in the original screen version of *The Hunchback of Notre Dame*.

Unfortunately, whenever Pevney's camera strays from Cagney's verisimilar characterization, the story lapses into tawdry melodrama. When Chaney escorts his wife-to-be (Dorothy Malone) home to meet his family, without telling her of his parents' deafness, the scene ends with the fiancée rushing from the table and weeping in an upstairs room, hiding from the accusing silence of the family meal. The attempted suicide of Chaney's first wife (Malone), the chance reunion with girlfriend Hazel Bennett (Jane Greer), the ghosts of the past that haunt Chaney with stagey coincidence—these elements of the story strain credulity. Except for Celia Lovsky, touching as Chaney's deaf-mute mother, the Universal contract cast—Roger Smith, another male ingenue whom Cagney liked; Jim Backus; Jack Albertson; future Hollywood producer Robert Evans in the role of legendary MGM producer Irving Thalberg; and silent era comedians Hank Mann and Snub Pollard in bit parts as waiters—is uneven under Pevney's direction. Jeanne Cagney makes her last film appearance with her brother, playing (appropriately) Lon Chaney's sister. Goff and Roberts (along with Campbell and Wheelwright) were eventually nominated for an Oscar for Best Original Story and Screenplay, losing to George Wells's script for the less-well-remembered *Designing Woman*.

Short Cut to Hell

In anyone's career *Short Cut to Hell* would be an oddity, but it is especially so in Cagney's. The only motion picture he ever directed, it is a low-budget remake of Paramount's *This Gun for Hire*, which was loosely based on Graham Greene's novel *A Gun for Sale* (with the Albert Maltz–W. R. Burnett screenplay from 1942 updated, for the Cagney-directed version, by Ted Berkman and Raphael Blau).* In his Warners' heyday, Cagney might have played the lead role of Kyle, the cruel, perverted killer. But as a favor to a friend, Paramount producer A. C. Lyles (one of the Republican circle), Cagney agreed to direct the movie for free—rapidly, disinterestedly, and with a stylistic signature that was practically invisible.† Not that Cagney's name wasn't adequately exploited for publicity—the film tried to capitalize on Cagney's behind-the-scenes presence in a unique prologue. Seated in a director's chair, with his name grandiosely emblazoned on the back, Cagney turns to face the camera. *Short Cut to Hell* is his first directing endeavor, he explains. Further, he is "thrilled" to introduce two "exciting" new

---

*But Albert Maltz's name does not appear among the credits for *Short Cut to Hell*. One of the Hollywood Ten, jailed for his refusal to testify about his politics, Maltz was blacklisted in Hollywood after serving his one-year prison term. This brings to at least five the number among the Hollywood Ten with whom Cagney had a personal or professional relationship: Sam Ornitz—a former friend and political associate; Dalton Trumbo, for whom Cagney had appeared in a radio version of *Johnny Got His Gun*; Lester Cole and Ring Lardner, Jr., coscreenwriters of *Blood on the Sun*; and now Maltz. According to most accounts of the era, Maltz's name was deleted from the remake of *This Gun for Hire* at the instigation of producer Lyles and Paramount Studios. Even so, it is the only recorded instance of Cagney cooperating with the blacklist, if inadvertently.

†In his autobiography, Cagney says the 20-day shooting schedule "was long enough for me. Directing I find a bore; I have no interest in telling other people their business."

With Robert Ivers, directing SHORT CUT TO HELL.

actors—Robert Ivers (as Kyle) and Georgann Johnson (as Glory Hamilton). That said, Cagney turns away and the story begins.

And what a trite and monotonic rendering it is. The strange killer with his devotion to cats; the killer's pathetic romance; the rich muckamuck who has been cheating on building specifications—these plot components are basically owed to original scenarists Maltz and Burnett and novelist Greene. Little about *Short Cut to Hell* is distinctly Cagneyesque. There are obligatory manhandling, killings, chase scenes—but filmed as though the life were drained out of the action, with nothing much to suggest Cagney's usual energizing influence. Maybe if he had been younger, if he had been given the opportunity to direct in the flush of his rebellion in the 1930s, the results would have been different. As it is, the inexperience and the indifference—as well as the weak cast and the script's being a genre piece that must have no longer piqued him at this point in his life—took their toll. At best, *Short Cut to Hell* is a half-hearted experiment from an actor who, in his own words, would try anything once. *The New York Daily News* saw "crisp flashes" of the old Cagney in its review, and *Time* said the novice director "manages to beauty-spot a few of the bare places with some characteristic Cagney touches." But even so faithful a Cagney follower as *The New York Times* simply declined to give the movie a review.

*Cagney and Charles Lederer,
writer–director of
NEVER STEAL ANYTHING SMALL.*

Never Steal Anything Small

Never Steal Anything Small, written and directed by Charles Lederer for Universal in 1958, is vintage 1950s Cagney: a tough guy musical that tinnily exploits the canon of the actor's career. The picture opens with a prologue not only trumpeting Cagney's starring role in the film but establishing a rightward political framework for the story that is sorely different from the Warners' Cagney of such earlier pictures as, say, *Taxi!* "This picture," according to the prologue, "is sympathetically dedicated to labor and its problems in coping with a new and merry type of public enemy . . . the charming, well-dressed gentleman who cons his way to a union throne and never needs to blow a safe again." Even more vehemently antilabor than *St. Louis Kid*, *Never Steal Anything Small* was especially ironic, as a peek at Cagney's current political disposition, considering his past reputation as a union activist and his support for Tom Mooney in the 1930s.

The storyline was taken from an unproduced play, *The Devil's Hornpipe* by Maxwell Anderson and Rouben Mamoulian. Cagney played Jake MacIllaney, a hoodlum stevedore who empties company and union coffers alike and who rigs the dock elections to become president of the stevedores' union. The cast included (again) Roger Smith, with Shirley Jones in the chirpy ingenue slot. The only bright spot is a song-and-dance number called "I'm Sorry, I Want a

With Shirley Jones in a scene from the motion picture NEVER STEAL ANYTHING
SMALL. (Universal 1959) Courtesy of Universal Pictures

Ferrari,'' with Cagney and Cara Williams executing their paces on a treadmill, tossing off the lyrics almost tongue-in-cheek. The rest of the tunes are negligible, alas, in this, Cagney's fifth and farewell motion picture appearance as a song-and-dance man.

With John Breslin (left) and Don Murray (center) in SHAKE HANDS WITH THE DEVIL.
(Copyright © 1959. Troy Films Limited. All rights reserved. Released through
United Artists Corporation.)

Shake Hands with the Devil

As the end of the decade loomed, Cagney's interest in acting grew faint, even as his waistline expanded. Yet there were a few distinctive enticements about *Shake Hands with the Devil*—it was to be filmed in the countryside of Dublin, Ireland, and the cast included members of the Abbey Theater and other Dublin repertory companies. Though the story was based on a famous Irish novel by Reardon Conner, Goff and Roberts were summoned to perform their customary surgery on the screenplay (working from an adaptation by Marian Thompson). By the time they switched the period from World War II to the freedom struggle of 1921 against the British Black-and-Tans, and other adjustments were made, "not one line or situation from the novel still existed" (in Roberts' words). True, *Devil* put another gun in Cagney's hands—and the story provided him with a mania a la *White Heat*—but it was a clear-cut message of the corrupting power of violence; and what was more relevant to his thinking, the futility of *political* violence.

"We went to Martha's Vineyard before we left for Dublin to complete our research, our scouting of locations, and our writing of the script," remembered Roberts.

Cagney as an IRA revolutionist in
SHAKE HANDS WITH THE DEVIL.
(Copyright © 1959. Troy Films
Limited. All rights reserved. Released
through United Artists Corporation.)

We said, "Jimmy, this is a tough part. American audiences are going to find it hard to understand your character—that he is a revolutionary who is dedicated to the revolution. That there is no *give*, none. The research we have done indicates to us that Ireland is full of these men and will be, forever. So," we said, "it's not a very crowd-pleasing portrayal, to wind up killing a woman because you have vowed to have no compassion [as Cagney's character does in the story], but that is what this man will do." He said, "I understand the problem. I'm going to play it straight down the line. I'm not going to soften it any, and maybe if people see that, they will understand someone has to *give*, someone has to soften, eventually there has to be a meeting of the minds.

The Irish proverb that provides the film's title is "those who shake hands with the devil often have trouble getting their hands back"—an aphorism pertinent to the actions of a Cody Jarrett or a Ralph Cotter as well as a Sean Lenihan, Cagney's role in *Devil*. A respected surgeon who is also an underground revolutionist, Lenihan is so obsessed by his desire for Irish independence that he will not compromise when a settlement treaty is tendered. Despite the signed truce, he prepares to execute a member of the royal family (Dana Wynter), even as his fellow IRA members beg him to desist. Lenihan denounces his comrades as

With lifelong friend Robert Montgomery, who directed Cagney in THE GALLANT HOURS in 1959. (Wide World)

traitors, whirls to fire the deadly shot, and is cut down in his path by a bullet fired by an American, Kerry O'Shea (Don Murray), who has been trying to stay aloof from the conflict. Like Fallon/Pardo in *White Heat*, O'Shea had been Lenihan's friend; now he becomes his executioner.

Much praised at the time ("one of the fastest, toughest and most picturesque melodramas about the Irish Revolution," in the words of *The New York Times*), *Shake Hands with the Devil* seems a bit pat and workmanlike today, especially in light of the escalating history of the Irish strife in the years since the movie's release in 1959. The plot is slow to gather steam, the payoff predictable. Still, the Irish–British contingent (Glynis Johns, Michael Redgrave, Sybil Thorndike, Cyril Cusack, etc.) is daunting, and it is good sport to watch Cagney evolve from an apparently gentle-spirited physician lecturing to a class of medical students in flowing doctor's robes, to a rabid and pitiless warrior. Among other infringements, some of the non-Abbey actors, Cagney included, forgetfully slip in and out of their brogues, evidently unnoticed by director Michael Anderson.

*As Fleet Admiral William F. "Bull" Halsey, Jr., in THE GALLANT HOURS. (Copyright ©
1960, Cagney-Montgomery Productions, Inc. All rights reserved. Released
through United Artists Corporation.)*

The Gallant Hours

Finally, in 1960, Cagney found his long-awaited opportunity to work with old friend Robert Montgomery who, besides producing his own television series (*Robert Montgomery Presents*, on which Cagney made a rare appearance in 1956), had busied himself during the 1950s as television advisor to President Eisenhower. Only now Montgomery was going to *direct* Cagney. The film, *The Gallant Hours*, was to be a "labor of love" (Cagney's words) for both, telling the story of the crucial five-week period in the life of Fleet Admiral William F. "Bull" Halsey during which Halsey commanded U.S. naval forces at the battle of Guadalcanal in 1942. It would be an expression of patriotism—for Montgomery and Cagney—and also a family occasion, because Cagney's son Jimmy and Montgomery's son Bob, as well as Montgomery himself, took cameo roles in the film—and because Cagney Productions was resurrected, in name only, to share co-production billing with Montgomery Productions.

The two-hour-long film unfolds in documentary style, beginning with Halsey's retirement and proceeding, with a flashback, to the drama of his World War II high command, using narrated reminiscences and newsreel footage. The script (by Beirne Lay, Jr., and Frank D. Gilroy) concentrates on the solitary agony of Halsey's awesome responsibility as fleet commander, rather than giving the actual battle scenes any protracted (and expensive) coverage. As such, the focus is almost continually on Cagney, who gives a low-key and crusty performance—showing Halsey as a contemplative leader, given to outbursts of emotion and temper, but calm within and dignified throughout. In one otherwise inconsequential scene, during a conversation with junior officers, Cagney's Halsey pauses during a stream of orders to—of all things—pick a hair from his teeth. That subtlety might be lost on the indiscriminate moviegoer, but it indicates the reflection and detail that Cagney brought to the characterization, humanizing Halsey as well as exalting him.

Yet the film is laboriously paced. The narration, obvious in its overstatement at times, is one of the weakest parts. The Roger Wagner Chorale provides a soundtrack of bombastic hymns, punctuating grave crises with a discomfiting score. And Cagney—graying, jowled, and heavy around the middle—was growing either vain or lazy about his physique. One scene betrays his condition. Four Navy officers in swimsuits are sunbathing on the beach. Halsey/Cagney runs up to the group and enters the frame, back to camera. Swiftly he dons a full-length beach robe. The implication is distressing but clear: The aging tough guy is concealing his fat.

Directed by Billy Wilder

The fastest-paced movie Cagney ever made has to be *One, Two, Three*, directed by Billy Wilder in 1960 (and released in 1961). As scripted by Wilder and longtime collaborator I.A.L. Diamond (based, loosely, on a one-act play by Ferenc Molnar), the story explodes with an onrush of gags and punchlines, chase scenes and shouting matches—a jewel of lickety-split comedy. Though much of the Cold War jesting is patently obsolete (Cagney: "I wouldn't touch the Russians with a ten-foot Pole—and I wouldn't touch the Poles either!"), the jokes fly so fast and furious that one can overlook the percentage of clinkers. Cagney was over 60, but hyper with energy—and up to his role as the beleaguered C. P. MacNamara, a Coca-Cola executive juggling business, romance, and politics in West Berlin. Chubby, his bulbous face, under a homburg, giving him a look akin to a flesh-and-blood Mr. Magoo, Cagney gave a performance that was fashioned by Wilder as his showcase—metronomical, accelerando—without any hint of cobwebbed age. One shot tracks MacNamara's feet as he ascends a flight of stairs to confer with a passel of Soviet diplomats. The legs bounce with freedom and muscle, dance-like, as if director Wilder were giving audiences a privileged

On the ONE, TWO, THREE set with Lilo Pulver and director Billy Wilder. (Marc Wanamaker/Bison Archives)

glimpse into the song-and-dance man behind the mask of characterization.

Thematically, *One, Two, Three* appropriately rounded out the 1950s for Cagney. The actor was cast as a capitalist, an anti-Communist, a Cold Warrior, bringing his image full circle from its earliest incarnation. Antisystem slum delinquent Tom Powers had metamorphosed into prosystem, corporate-climbing MacNamara, whose main hurdles in life included chaperoning a spoiled Southern teenager named Scarlett (Pamela Tiffin) and subverting her marriage to a young Marxist East Berliner (Horst Buchholz). Cagney's ruthlessness here is reduced to socially acceptable standards. Yet, though dressed in gentlemanly attire of suit, tie, hat, and cane, MacNamara nonetheless suggests a gangster in his pile-driving ambition to rise up the company ladder, in his brutal deprogramming of the overzealous Communist youth, in his trampling of every obstacle in sight. MacNamara may not be a gangster, per se, but he delivers his dictums in rapid-fire lingo, as if addressing a gang of underlings. And though he is married (to Arlene Francis), MacNamara's marriage has turned sour, so he dallies with his pretty secretary (Lilo Pulver), 40 years his junior. MacNamara behaves contemptibly to his wife, so badly, in fact, that she nearly leaves him, taking the children with her as the film is about to end. MacNamara redeems himself just in time with an abject speech of contrition—that valuable, time-honored apologia is still handy to acceptance of the Cagney persona.

There may be irony in MacNamara's incessant defense of Americanism, but derived more, one suspects, from the European-born Wilder than from resurgent patriot Cagney. Certainly there was deliberate dabbling with Cagney's image. In that sense, *One, Two, Three* is like the comic underside of *White Heat*, with citations from other Cagney films as part of the scheme of humor. A wall clock cuckoo waves a flag and sings a version of "Yankee Doodle Dandy." A brash young military officer (Red Buttons) performs a brisk Cagney imitation ("Oookay, Buster!"). Cagney himself cocks his arm, holds a grapefruit menacingly in his hand, and warns Otto Ludwig Piffl (Buchholz), "How would you like a little fruit for dessert?!" There are plenty of other movie references, as is usually the case in Wilder's films: A hotel is named Potemkin and MacNamara/Cagney, in one fit of desperation, cries out, "Mother of Mercy, is this the end of Little Rico?", an homage to another Warners' tough guy, Edward G. Robinson (in *Little Caesar*).

One, Two, Three is one of director Wilder's least-revived comedies, which is a shame, because Cagney (who is almost never offscreen) goes on a rampage of nutty farce. But critics, then as now, have taken exception to the film's overbearing patriotism, icy morality, and rampant sexual humor. "Plenty of speed but not much pace," sniffed Penelope Gilliat in London's *The Observer*. "Cagney, I fear, has done Wilder an ill service," wrote the critic for *Saturday Review*. "He shouts his way through the entire movie, bellowing and bowling over all the opposition. After a while I found myself flinching every time he gathered his breath. A man just can't keep that up without strain to the vital organs."

From Cagney's point of view, if there was any disservice done by *One, Two, Three*, it was done by Wilder. The director and his star did not warm to each other during filming, mostly on location in West Berlin and at the Bavaria Studios in Munich. Wilder—like Anatole Litvak—was more precise and authoritarian a director than Cagney was accustomed to. Among other things, they clashed over the nonstop kineticism of the pacing, which reminded Cagney (negatively) of *Boy Meets Girl*. One sequence required 50 takes. The scene called for Cagney, according to one account, "to deliver at trip-hammer speed several pages of complicated monologue that he had been given only the day before," rattling off a long speech while selecting an assortment of clothing designed to remake Piffl into an acceptably-garbed (American-style) youth. The actor stumbled several times on the line, "Where's the morning coat and striped trousers?" The usually patient Wilder blew his temper. Other actors began to miss their cues. Not until after some 50-odd takes did the scene finally go right.*

Cagney never bothered to see *One, Two, Three*. That excruciating experience of filming was the last straw in his inevitable decision to retire—a decision that was unequivocal and meant to be unalterable. There was no formal announcement to the press. Cagney simply retired to his several estates—in Coldwater Canyon, at Martha's Vineyard, and in upstate Dutchess County, New York, where he raised cattle and bred Morgan horses. All scripts submitted to him for the next 20 years were simply returned, unread, refused.

"While I was shooting *One, Two, Three*," he told Charles Champlin, a film critic for *The Los Angeles Times*, years later,

> I loaned my boat to three of my pals and their wives for a cruise, and while they were out they had a picture taken of the six of them standing on a deck holding drinks and toasting me. They sent me a print of it and they wrote on it, "Thank God you are gainfully employed." And didn't they look smug and happy.
>
> It showed up on a day when we were shooting some last interiors at Goldwyn. And it was a beautiful day, a gorgeous day. I was standing outside, catching the sun and the blue sky and the clouds and the assistant director came out and said, "We're ready for you now, Mr. Cagney." Well, I went back inside that black cavern and right then I said to myself, "That's it baby," and it was. No more. I'm owed $1500 in bets from pals who said I wouldn't stick to it. One guy at 500–1 odds; wait'll I catch up to him. I was always whaddya call it, a journeyman actor, I never gave a damn about the rest of it. Do the job and run. I don't need the applause. My feeling always was there was so much more living to do, outside the industry. By the time I'd finished each job, I'd had my reservations to get out of here [Hollywood]. There was all the nonsense going on here, and I figured the days aren't long enough for doing all the things that are fun and interesting.

*Said Cagney: "The mechanics of learning . . . one line can bug you. I did a play once with Mary Boland. One night she blew a line. The next night, worrying about her line, I blew my own following line. After that, I had trouble with the line every night. It's the rhythm."

Right turn: Cagney reading WALL STREET JOURNAL in scene from ONE, TWO, THREE.

James Cagney in 1982 at age 82. (Alen MacWeeney/Courtesy of ROLLING STONE)

11
The Far-Away Fella

I like where I am. Why interrupt it? All I could ever see were the great gaping holes that weren't filled.

> JAMES CAGNEY
> *The New York Times,* 1974

Cagney kept his vow of retirement—almost. Of all the parts offered to him during the 1960s, only one gave him a "slight tug" of temptation: that of Alfred P. Doolittle opposite Cary Grant's Professor Henry Higgins in the planned film version of the Lerner–Loewe musical *My Fair Lady*. It would have been dream casting. Jack Warner, his old nemesis, offered him one million dollars to take it on. Director George Cukor besieged him with telephone calls. But Cagney eventually said no, a reluctant but vehement no, and the parts went to Stanley Holloway and Rex Harrison, who had possessed them on the stage. As Cagney put it in his memoirs, he just could not summon the interest.

The star whose acting had been defined in such sheer physical terms became only a disembodied voice-over for the remnants of his career throughout the 1960s, emerging only to narrate a few special projects for which he nursed a partisan interest. For example: Anti-Communist venom brought him to work for the government in 1962, narrating a propaganda film produced by CBS entitled *Road to the Wall*, a bloody newsreel of Communist take-overs and purges. "James Cagney Narrating" is the deferential credit that precedes the film, giving some idea of the prestige the Department of Defense attributed to Cagney's participation. A bluntly phrased Cold War exhortation (with Cagney intoning, "Each new threat must be met, force with force, as in Korea"), *Road* was declared obsolete by 1972.*

Yet *Road to the Wall* was revealing as Cagney's most explicit public political statement in years—here, the patriotic, anti-Red themes of *One, Two, Three* were

---

*An interesting comparison might be made between Cagney's narration for *Road to the Wall* and John Ford's direction of *Vietnam! Vietnam!*, sponsored by the U.S. Information Agency. See Joseph McBride, "Drums along the Mekong," *Sight and Sound*, Autumn 1972.

dished up point-blank. Cagney's wealth and reclusion, the fluctuations of history, and the distance he had put between himself and his roots had him now clearly ensconced in the fold of the political far Right. In his book, *Tracy and Hepburn: An Intimate Memoir* (New York: Bantam, 1971), Garson Kanin relates how Cagney's lifelong friendship with Spencer Tracy "practically fell apart" over their widening political differences. "Cagney had grown extremely rich," wrote Kanin,

> as the result of unceasing work and judicious investments. ("No actor," Tracy said, "has a right to be *that* rich!") Spencer observed that the richer Jimmy became, the more right-wing and intolerant he became politically. In his youth, Cagney had been more left-wing than Spencer who, throughout his life, steered a middle political course. The war came, and McCarthyism, Red Channels, and blacklisting, along with all the ugly apparatus of the super-patriots in vindictive action with questionable motives. On many issues, Tracy and Cagney found themselves seriously at odds. The phone calls grew shorter, the time between visits longer, and eventually they saw little or nothing of each other.

Ecology and conservation remained Cagney's passion, something he could reconcile with his Republicanism. A lifetime member of the Audubon Society, he would pop up at congressional hearings on natural resources or be among those raising his voice against further development of Martha's Vineyard. He hosted several radio programs on soil conservation. When, in 1955, he was awarded an honorary doctorate in humanities at Rollins College in Winter Park, Florida, the actor astonished school officials and the student body with a lengthy, fact-filled discourse on—not Hollywood—but environmental issues. And conservation, as it were, provided the impetus for Cagney's second major foray into narration, in 1966, when he lent his voice to General Electric Theatre's *Ballad of Smokey the Bear*, produced in cooperation with the U.S. Department of Agriculture. Cagney was the voice of Big Brother Bear on the animated television special, first aired in 1966, then repeated in 1968 and 1969.

Two other narrative chores: In 1968, Cagney as an act of friendship supplied the prologue for producer A. C. Lyles's *Arizona Bushwackers*, an unexciting "B" Western about captured Confederate soldiers assigned to federal troops patrolling the frontier. No publicity—and only an unassuming credit tipped-off audiences to the fact that the unexceptional words introducing the picture came from the mouth of James Cagney. Then, five years later, in 1972, Cagney narrated (but again did not appear before the camera) the special Academy Awards tribute to former colleague and costar Edward G. Robinson (who had died a few months before the belated honor).

Otherwise, the great, staccato voice was silent, the compact body absent from public view. Cagney did not have to work—with his brother's help he had invested wisely, acquiring (among other things) a shopping center in Newport

Gentleman farmer, photographed in the 1950s. (WCTR)

Beach and 400 acres of desert land near the California community of Twenty-Nine Palms. He alternated between his residences on both coasts, and was said to be happy collecting guns (which he never fired), antiques (especially American furniture), silver, cowboy bronzes by American sculptor Charles Marion Russell, and bric-a-brac. He enjoyed his relaxation and stayed at home mostly, read, listened to Debussy, and practiced his watercolors under the tutelage of a Santa Monica artist named Sergei Bongart. As he had always done, he wrote simple verse.

> Writing verses I cannot help,
> As a pig furrows her brood to whelp,
> Each must come in its given time,
> So there's naught to do but write and rhyme.

But in more ways than one, Cagney had become the far-away fella—as Pat O'Brien once dubbed him—a person who would drift off in conversation or in gatherings, daydreamy and seemingly far away. Now, except for his family and closest friends—O'Brien, McHugh, Montgomery, Ralph Bellamy, Roland Winters, and others dating back to his childhood—Cagney saw few outsiders. "He's a very retiring person," Ralph Bellamy explained to *Rolling Stone* magazine,

> and he's inclined to a kind of melancholia that he's had to strain to overcome. Crowds, I think, have always frightened him, and they were an aspect of this business that he always hated. He never really liked the business much, especially the corporate side. "They can't level with you," he'd always say, very hurt. But show business has kept him in touch with the outside world. He's always there for his close friends, but he's not outgoing.

"His [Cagney's] alienation from the world was a deliberate choice," said screenwriter Ben Roberts. "He was never part of the Hollywood scene. He was rarely seen in public. When this was a nightclub town, he was never there. He and Bill [his wife] just lived quietly. He liked music, art, books—he loved books. He loved good talk. He was really an intelligent Irishman who kind of fought his way up [in the world] to where he wanted to be."

Like a male Garbo, Cagney was rarely glimpsed, rarely photographed. In Los Angeles he would not leave his Coldwater Canyon house for a haircut or to purchase a coat, for fear of being recognized. He saw just four movies in ten years—*My Fair Lady, Oliver, The Lion in Winter,* and *Patton*—and the man who so nettled the Hays Office in the 1930s with his intimations of sex, violence, and rebellion raged in private about pornography and hippies. His own movies were less often revived than those of Bogart's, a more limited actor with a larger cult. Cagney's appeal seemed lost on the younger generation. He was rumored to be dead or grossly fat.

With (l to r) Nancy Reagan, then-Governor of California Ronald Reagan, and wife Billie Cagney at the American Film Institute's Life Achievement Award banquet in 1974. (Wide World Photo)

The Test of Time

Then suddenly in 1974, here was Cagney facing an onslaught of reporters and giving interviews for the first time in a dozen years, being poked and examined and categorized as if he were a rare tropical bird in an aviary, in the words of one reporter. Cagney had been convinced by A. C. Lyles to cooperate with a Life Achievement Award career tribute being planned by the American Film Institute as a fund-raiser for future film scholarship and archival preservation. At 75, the retired actor was reasonably trim and feisty. Indeed, he told the press, he continued to tap-dance every day, working off his early morning stiffness by dancing to Frankie Carle's ragtime music and exercising by jogging in place during television commercials. The AFI's Life Achievement Award, a three-dimensional, six-inch-high silver star, was given to "one whose talent has in a fundamental way advanced the film art; whose accomplishment has been acknowledged by scholars, critics, professional peers and the general public; and whose work has stood the test of time." The only previous winner of the newly instituted award had been director John Ford, who received it five months prior to his death in 1973.

Five distinguished artists: (l to r) Agnes De Mille, Leontyne Price, Cagney, Leonard Bernstein, and Lynn Fontanne; honored at the Kennedy Center in Washington, D.C. for their "lifetime achievement in the performing arts," 1980.

The awards banquet was held at the Century Plaza Hotel in Los Angeles on March 13, 1974, and it was a star-studded gala. Not only were youth culture icons such as John Lennon and Mick Jagger there to pay their respects, but so was an overflowing crowd of Hollywood's old and new guard, including Cicely Tyson, Paul Newman, Clint Eastwood, Steve McQueen, Mae West, and then-California Governor (and future President) Ronald Reagan and wife Nancy. Frank Sinatra emceed the evening, which included a montage of Cagney clips and spoken accolades from Doris Day, John Wayne, George C. Scott, Bob Hope, and others. Frank Gorshin, George Segal, and Kirk Douglas performed a musical take-off of Cagneyisms. The night was not without its gaffes: When Jack Lemmon rambled on a bit too long in his laudatory speech, he was jeered from the back of the dining hall by director Sam Peckinpah (an embarrassment excised from the later CBS television broadcast of the awards ceremony). In general, however, it was an evening of gratitude, an effusive coming-out party with Cagney surrounded by admirers, friends, and family. Among the ex-confreres in attendance: Joan Blondell, Loretta Young, Ruby Keeler, Brenda Marshall, Rosemary DeCamp, Mae Clarke, George Raft, Ralph Bellamy, Frank McHugh, Allen Jenkins, directors Mervyn LeRoy and William Wellman, and screenwriters Ivan Goff and Ben Roberts.

When the preliminaries were over and the applause had settled, Cagney bounded to the stage and muttered, "I'm a wreck!" Continuing, he said, "And about that award, I'm grateful for it. But why don't we just say for now that I'm merely the custodian, holding it for all those wonderful guys and gals who worked over the years to bring about this night for me." He went on to quote his favorite definition of art, taken from William Ernest Hocking's book, *Strength of Men and Nations*. "Art is life plus. Life plus caprice. Where the simple declarative sentence becomes a line of Shakespearean poetry, where a number of musical notes strung together become a Beethoven sonata. Where a walk, done in cadence by a Freddie Astaire or Edward Villela or Patricia Farrell, becomes an exciting dance. That's art." He also read from a poem by John Masefield, the English poet laureate, adding afterwards, "I like that."

Conspicuous by his absence from the representation of Cagneys (including sister Jeanne and wife Billie, along with sundry children and grandchildren) was brother William, who was gravely ill and, it seemed at the time, fighting for his life. But William Cagney was not forgotten in the litany of names Cagney invoked, in appreciation, from the podium. Mentioning Jack Warner—who "gave me a name I shall always cherish—affectionately, mind you—'The Professional Againster'"—Cagney paused, emotion-choked, and added, "But we're old now and full of understanding and that's water over the dam. Am I right, Bill?"* Nor did Cagney forget "the names of my youth: Lager-head Quinlavan, Artie Klein, Peter Leyden, Jake Brodkin, Specks Torpocer, Brother O'Meara, Picky Houlihan. Were all part of a stimulating early environment which produced that unmistakeable touch of the gutter without which this evening might never have happened at all." It was as honest, as moving, as difficult a monologue as Cagney had ever delivered in his career.

So warmly, so smoothly did the AFI event go that Cagney was said to be ecstatic, and it gradually eased him out of his Howard Hughes/*Citizen Kane*-like hermitage. He was more willing to circulate in public now, to appear at other testimonials and functions. He became acquainted with some younger, ardent admirers: with Russian ballet defector Mikhail Baryshnikov, whom he taught some vaudeville era jazz-tap steps at the old Gower Gulch studios in Hollywood one day. And with John Travolta, a Cagney fan since childhood, who phoned

---

*Warner, himself in ill health, was not in the audience, but representing the Warners ex-hierarchy was Cagney's old adversary, producer Hal Wallis, with wife Martha Hyer.

Cagney every Father's Day and informed reporters, "Before I ever met him [Cagney], my mother would threaten me, 'If you don't take the garbage out, I'm going to call and tell Cagney.'" Finally in 1976, there came an unexpected (and much-debated in Cagney family circles) act of revelation: Cagney wrote his autobiography, *Cagney By Cagney* (New York: Doubleday & Co., 1976). He dictated it into a tape recorder on one of his cross-country automobile trips between the West and East Coasts (he still refused to fly). Afterwards, he barely looked at the galleys—in-laws did the polishing. Lamentably, it is an anecdotal, tossed-off reminiscence that glosses over the riddles and frustrations of his life. In it, he describes himself politically as an "arch-conservative."

The film offers predictably were renewed. Jack Lemmon's *Kotch*—refused; the much-bruited-about film version of *That Championship Season*—refused; Sergio Leone's planned epic of *Once upon a Time in America*—refused. Director Francis Coppola flew up in his private jet plane to visit Cagney at his simple one-story stone-house retreat overlooking a six-acre lake in Dutchess County to discuss a possible role in *The Godfather: Part II*. They had a country breakfast (fixed by Cagney) at sunrise, hitched up a pair of horses, and went for an hour's ride through the woods, admiring the beautiful fall foliage; then they inspected Cagney's prized stock of Morgan horses. They drove to the airport together without ever having mentioned the movie prospects. "Mr. Cagney," Coppola said, "I came here to talk you out of retirement, to come and do this thing with us. But—what am I going to tell them, that I haven't talked you out of retirement—you have talked *me* into it?"

Ragtime

In the late 1970s Cagney was diagnosed as a diabetic—but it was a belated diagnosis, and his movement and agility were already curtailed. He was plagued by sciatica as well. Then in 1977 he suffered a mild stroke and, according to accounts, he grew profoundly discouraged, lost his fortitude, and told his wife Billie, family and friends, "That's it, I'm finished." He sold his beloved yacht and his Martha's Vineyard estate. If it wasn't for the firm coaxing of Marge Zimmerman—a retired restaurateur who became his personal secretary and aide-de-camp—and her husband Don, a civil engineer—Cagney might have lapsed into his armchair, fatally depressed. Instead, for exercise purposes a swimming pool was installed adjacent to the New York farmhouse, and Cagney was eased back into his habitual woodland strolls. And his doctor told him: Go back to work.

As it happened, emigre Czechoslovakian director Milos Forman lived across the state line from Cagney in Connecticut, and the two met fortuitously and struck up a rapport. Forman was preparing to direct *Ragtime*, the "belle epoque" best-selling novel by E. L. Doctorow that was originally to be directed by Robert Altman before that director had a falling-out with producer Dino de Laurentiis.

With director Milos Forman filming RAGTIME in 1980. (Copyright © 1981 by Dino De Laurentiis Corporation/Paramount. All Rights Reserved.)

Doctorow's turn-of-the-century tapestry of an America in social upheaval—interweaving true-life characters such as Theodore Roosevelt, Henry Ford, Harry Houdini, Emma Goldman, and Booker T. Washington with fictional ones, in particular a bourgeois New Rochelle family and a young black piano-player named Coalhouse Walker, Jr., who turns to violence after suffering racist indignities—was tailor-made for Cagney. The swarm of immigrants, the beaux arts, the nickelodeons, and the ragtime music were the fabric of his boyhood. One of the central incidents of the story—the murder of celebrated architect Stanford White by millionaire playboy Harry K. Thaw, whose wife, Evelyn Nesbit, had been White's mistress—was a major press sensation in 1906 when Cagney was a kid. Later, in fact, in 1920, Cagney played on a vaudeville bill with Nesbit who by then was capitalizing on her notoriety on the tank-town circuit. *Ragtime* was Cagney's time. Though Forman was kidding him at first when he prodded Cagney about making his comeback in the movie, the director dropped his jaw one day when Cagney asked, which part? "Any part," Forman replied, "Evelyn Nesbit, if you like!" After reading the screenplay adaptation by Michael Weller, Cagney told Forman, "Well, I could do this, this, or this—you make the decision." They settled on a key role: New York Police Commissioner Rheinlander Waldo.

To sweeten the experience of filming, oldest of chums Pat O'Brien and his wife, Eloise, were offered feature parts (as Thaw's attorney and Thaw's mother, respectively). Preproduction work on the streets of New York demonstrated that the Cagney name had lost none of its magic—crowds applauded each time Cagney appeared for a take, and items about his comeback dotted newspapers and magazines. In the fall of 1980 the Cagneys and the O'Briens sailed for London where most of their scenes (none together) were filmed at Shepperton Studios—where New York City's Victorian landmarks, including the J. Pierpont Morgan Library, site of the film's finale, had been recreated in fine detail. Though he had been retired for 20 years, Cagney was nervous only until he spoke his first line and then, "I felt as if I'd done it the day before." His legs were weak and his action blocked accordingly; yet the reports back from the shooting were that the octogenarian star had onlookers and younger cast members in awe of his patience, stamina, and good humor—offcamera—as well as his bristle and timing on: "Watching Cagney's performance was remarkable," screenwriter Weller told the press. "The guy knows how to conserve his energy perfectly. Sometimes when the camera started to roll he looked as if he didn't know what was going on, but the second he was supposed to say his lines he was right there." In interviews director Forman repeatedly called him "some kind of genius." Is that a joke?" demanded Cagney of one reporter when the remark was repeated to him. "Just a job," he preferred to say, "It was easy."

Easy for Cagney, a tad unwieldy for Forman—when the director's $32 million undertaking clocked in at over three hours in length, producer Dino de Laurentiis demanded that the picture be cut to two hours and thirty-six minutes, which would allow for additional theater showings. Novelist Doctorow was summoned and voted with de Laurentiis for the wholesale excision of the pivotal Emma Goldman character (played by Mariclare Costello) as the most expedient course of action. The Goldman character ended up on the cutting-room floor, but Police Commissioner Waldo (at Forman's insistence) escaped the scissors. Structurally, this did not improve what was already (as it was in the novel) an intricate and dizzying continuity ("years appear to pass, but the children don't age," complained one film critic); and it put an unfair burden on Cagney, whose Rheinlander Waldo character dominates the final third of the movie in a standoff with Coalhouse Walker, Jr., and his hooded gang of followers who have invaded the J. P. Morgan library with its priceless antiquities, flaunting dynamite and a list of grievances. Despite the generous screen time, Forman could not conceal Cagney's slowness and his physical limitations; during action or movement the actor was filmed from behind, from the waist-up, or replaced by a stand-in.

Thus when *Ragtime* opened in November of 1981, it garnered decidedly split reviews—some raves, some raspberries, some intelligently mixed. Perhaps Forman's film suffered a bit in comparison with Warren Beatty's kindred epic *Reds* (same epoch, with an Emma Goldman character of its own), released at Christmastime in 1981. With *Ragtime*, at least, critics such as Joy Gould Boyum, whose review in *The Wall Street Journal* was headlined "Didn't Anyone Read the Book?", could play the old "but-the-book-was-better" game. Though Richard

As New York Police Commissioner Rheinlander Waldo in RAGTIME by E.L.
Doctorow. (Copyright © 1981 by Dino De Laurentiis Corporation/Paramount.
All Rights Reserved.)

Corliss of *Time* found Cagney "cool as a leprechaun sphinx in the role of a wily
New York City Police Commissioner," he wrote, "By taking 155 minutes to tell
less than half of Doctorow's 270-page pageant, Forman and Weller have created
an impressive but strangely lopsided movie." Vincent Canby of *The New York*
Times agreed, adding his own reservations: "It's good to see Mr. Cagney back on
the screen as feisty as ever and doing a lot with very little. The manner and the
humor are undiminished, though he has been handled so gingerly there are
times he doesn't seem to have been photographed at the same time as the other
actors in the same scene." Canby added, "*Ragtime* is a major disappointment,
but it's a lively, provocative one. It takes a long broad view of America, which
most of our films see only through a keyhole."

   Yet—cinematic flaws granted—what an opulent, ambitiously themed, magnificent, kaleidoscopic vision of turn-of-the-century America Forman's *Ragtime*
is—what a fitting zenith to Cagney's career—with more than enough pleasures
to compensate for any and all cavilling. Production designer John Graysmark's
dazzling replication of 1906, the lush cinematography by Miroslav Ondricek, the
Twyla Tharp choreography, Randy Newman's ragtime score—these provided

the rich texture of Forman's achievement. Except for Cagney, many of the principals were relative newcomers or nonprofessionals, including author Norman Mailer, starchy and distinguished as architect Stanford White; Elizabeth McGovern, sparkling as Evelyn Nesbit; Mary Steenburgen, James Olson, and Brad Dourif forming the superb triad of Mother, Father, and Younger Brother, respectively; and Howard Rollins, fierce and dignified as Coalhouse Walker, Jr. The smaller parts were no less well cast and acted, with dozens of finely-tuned character bits (chief among them Kenneth McMillan's virulently racist fireman, who ignites the plot) among the movie's recommendations. Justifiably, *Ragtime* turned up on many critics' "best lists" for 1981, and was nominated for eight Academy Awards.*

Onscreen in *Ragtime*, Cagney's magnetism was intact, evident from his first peeking vignette in the opening scene—a bacchanalian feast hosted by Stanford White, at which the guests, including Police Commissioner Waldo (with a curly orange moustache), are surrounded by belly dancers and festooned in wreaths. Cagney played Waldo like a sly old fox, half-irritated, half-amused by the challenge of Coalhouse Walker, Jr., his eyes twinkling with detachment while his one-liners drip with sarcasm. Though he was physically constrained, Cagney did much with his face and inflection and his reading of the riposte to Willie Conklin—"and people keep telling me you're a worthless *slime!*"—is a classic. It was a role he played as if enjoying the ironies, the paradoxes of James Cagney playing a Police Commissioner at the end of his long career. Coalhouse Walker, Jr., was like a young, black Tom Powers, a variation on the "public enemy." The gentle and rollicking Irish of *The Irish in Us* are the beery racists of *Ragtime*. And oddest of all, for a man who had so staunchly backed Ronald Reagan in his right-wing campaign for the presidency in 1980, who had in fact written a venerating foreword to Reagan's paperback "Letters to Children," *Ragtime* was as left-of-center a piece of social consciousness filmmaking as Cagney had ever done. As Andrew Sarris put it in *The Village Voice*, *Ragtime* was like waving "a red flag in the face of the Reaganites."

Postscript

In the flush of receptivity for *Ragtime*, there was talk of Cagney starring in another movie, this one tentatively called *The Eagle of Broadway*, about the last days of gunfighter Bat Masterson, who in his retirement became a sportswriter for newspapers in New York City. It would be another perfect vehicle for

---

*Though Cagney received a Best Supporting Actor campaign in the trade papers, he was not nominated—youngsters McGovern and Rollins *were*, also in the supporting category. Still, the old pro gathered up an abundance of honors for his *Ragtime* comeback—receiving a special citation from the National Board of Review, a tribute from the New York Press Club, a ceremonial key to the city from the mayor of New York, the "Man of the Year" award from Harvard's Hasty Pudding Club, and other special awards (including being the first entertainer to throw the ceremonial first pitch in the 1981 World Series).

Cagney—and it would be directed by Milos Forman's fellow Czech emigre, Ivan Passer. Yet financing was a sensitive proposition with Cagney's health so delicate, and—though it was even rumored that Cagney's legs would be ''animated'' to give the actor the illusion of greater mobility—at this writing no company has come forward with the guarantees.

There was also talk, as there had been for years off and on, of adapting Cagney's life into a biopic a la *Yankee Doodle Dandy*. Travolta was keen on the idea, and Baryshnikov told reporters he coveted the part, despite the insurmountable barrier of his Russian accent. Director Burt Kennedy worked on a script for a spell before coming to an impasse. The Cagney legacy hardly depends on a biopic, though one will almost certainly be made some day. It should not be written as too much of a success story when it is. The rags-to-riches element is there, to be sure, but so are the private scars, and they are part of the life of a great actor who might prefer to be remembered, simply, as a song-and-dance man.

12
The Actor as Auteur

The movies have not produced any Hamlet parts for us, but they have raised a crop of people whose movie legend and cumulative work are almost of that stature. James Cagney is one of them, and it is hard to say what our impression of the total American character would have been without him. He is all crust and speed and snap on the surface, a gutter-fighter with the grace of dancing, a boy who knows all the answers and won't even wait for them, a very fast one. But underneath the fable: the quick generosity and hidden sweetness, the antifraud, straight-as-a-string dealing, the native humor and the reckless drive—everything everybody would like to be, if he had the time sometime. But always this, always: if as a low type he is wrong, you are going to see why. In spite of writers, directors, and decency legions, you are going to see the world and what it does to its people through his subtle understanding of it.
OTIS FERGUSON
The New Republic, 1939

What now, the *actor* as auteur? Consider: When critic Andrew Sarris first submitted his auteur theory in 1962, he did so conditionally, not as a "short cut to film scholarship" but as an alternate view of film history. Sarris was writing about motion picture *directors*—which sparked a furor among scenarists and gave rise to a rival theoretical camp that justly balances the equation by celebrating the contributions of the screenwriter. Stating the case for the dominant creativity of actors promises to be no less popular among screenwriters *or* directors. But because the stars in Hollywood exude such mystique and exert such bargaining force, a theory of actor as auteur deserves to be advanced in the same "modest, tentative, experimental manner" Sarris originally offered his. To paraphrase Sarris, certain actors—like certain writers and directors—have conclusively imposed their personalities on a life's output of filmmaking: for example, the Marx Brothers, Garbo, Astaire, John Wayne (with the connivance of directors John Ford and Howard Hawks), Clint Eastwood.

Take Fred Astaire—a good example and one of which Cagney, an Astaire admirer and friend, would approve. Astaire certainly did not write his scripts; nor did he direct his movies. In most cases he exercised little control over, or interest in, the niceties of the screenplay or the frailties of the director. At RKO, first, and later at MGM and other studios, he allowed himself to be packaged according to studio formulas that his own films came to epitomize. Yet Astaire knew that his movies existed in the main for *Astaire*, for those moments when he transcended their dull plotting. He simply cared less about their framework than about their essence. He reaped the advantages of a star arrangement that subordinated his writers and directors to an expression of his screen personality. His movies reflected his sensibility, primarily. Inarguably, Astaire is their auteur.

So too with Cagney's career—Astaire and Cagney were different artists, to be sure; and different sorts of actor–auteurs. Cagney's work has thematic currents that the work of Astaire's, more the stylist, the purist, lacked. To study Cagney's life and career over the decades they spanned is to wonder at how his films converged on paths of history, reflected history, even perhaps influenced it. From the Everyman fable of *The Public Enemy* to the FDR symbolism of *Footlight Parade*, from the patriotic clarion call of *Yankee Doodle Dandy* to the isolation and paranoia of *White Heat*, from the youthful sympathy for Communism to the Cold War jitters of *One, Two, Three*—Cagney's social consciousness dovetailed with film cycles that mirrored the great tides of modern U.S. history. Fittingly, when Cagney returned to the screen after an absence of 20 years, it was in *Ragtime*, a story that combined a nostalgia for the past with a radical vision of the future—with Cagney, in a final career twist, playing a cop, the only major character in the story impervious to change.

Screenwriters—well, Cagney had a fount of inferior scripts to cope with during his career, and a bad memory when it came to giving screenwriters their due. Glasmon and Bright, the Epsteins, Goff and Roberts—these were his most frequently mentioned favorites; to which he might add John Van Druten, Nathaniel Curtis, Daniel Fuchs, Wilder and Diamond, and Michael Weller, who adapted E. L. Doctorow's novel. But since it so often happened at Warner Bros. that three or four or more writers patched a script together (*ten*, in the case of *The Roaring Twenties*)—one who specialized in plot, perhaps, one for structure, one for character detail, and one to toss in a few gags—why should Cagney, especially in the pre-Guild days, develop a swollen opinion of the integrity of the screenwriting profession? After all, he rarely worked with the first rank, and he always improvised liberally, colloquializing, trimming, adding dialogue, phraseology, and bits of business. There is no question that he liked and respected writers; he counted many among his friends. And every Cagney Production, with the exception of the fouled-up *Blood on the Sun*, was completed with a single credited screenwriter.* But Cagney believed that, in Hollywood,

*Scenarist Harry *(Kiss Tomorrow Goodbye)* Brown remembers that being released by Warner Bros. to stint on the payroll of Cagney Productions in 1950 was akin to having a vacation from a concentration camp. The Cagneys' story sessions were informal; the work routine, flexible and relaxed. The writer enjoyed a pre-eminent status. All of the Cagneys—"a genial, overweight Irish clan," in Brown's words—participated in story conferences at one point or another, with Doctors Harry or Ed or Jeanne far more likely to stop by and toss in an idea than the nominal star of the company, brother James.

the script realized according to the intentions of the writer is a rare one; and in his career, that was certainly a truism.

His directors, meanwhile, were—more often than not—inauspicious craftsmen employed to project his personality onto celluloid to the best of their capabilities. The sameness of pictorial style in his earliest films, those that introduced and moulded the screen Cagney, is as striking as the spectrum of characterization the actor managed to convey. Under the more skilled Warners' directors—Wellman, Curtiz, or Walsh—Cagney excelled. But it was under the more workaday taskmasters that he honed the Cagney persona. Before *Yankee Doodle Dandy*, Cagney's most regular directors were the workhorses of the lot: Roy Del Ruth, Lloyd Bacon, and William Keighley. Among them they directed *20* Cagney pictures, nearly one-third of his films.

And who were these three illustrious figures? Bacon was the son of actress Jane Bacon and actor–writer Frank Bacon; he had been an actor with the old Essanay Film Company, playing a villain for "Broncho Billy" Anderson before moving up to gagman on two-reel comedies. An incongruous dresser, known for wearing loud, flashy clothing and dark glasses, Bacon could occasionally be inspired as a director—brooding and provocative, as with the 1930 version of *Moby Dick*, starring John Barrymore. But mostly he was a single-take aritst, reputed to be "faster than anybody in Hollywood," according to a profile in *The New York Times*, holder of the studio record for filming 47 different scenes in an eight-hour day for *Knute Rockne—All-American*. The studio prized him for *always* coming in under budget.

Bacon was prized by Cagney for another reason; he never deigned to read the entire screenplay, preferring to peruse only the pages of the day's filming; and he gave his actors free reign. "His [Bacon's] technique was to *trust* the actors," Cagney once told an interviewer, "and it worked. Bacon once said to me, 'I tried for two years to make a go at acting, and I couldn't figure it out. How the hell am I going to tell you what to do?'" The Cagney–Bacon pictures were the actor's laboratory: They are alike in their unmistakable allegiance to the Cagney character, in their professional but uncomplicated exposition, in their feeling of spontanaeity that is the consequence of the hurried pace of filmmaking.

"We did pictures like [Bacon's] *Picture Snatcher* in fifteen days," Cagney told a writer for *Films and Filming* in 1959,

and this is perhaps why people today think they move so fast. . . . Lloyd Bacon actually shot rehearsals. I heard the cue come [in a scene with Ralph Bellamy and Patricia Ellis] and I walked through the door, went up to the desk and did the necessary. As I was working out what I was going to do for the scene and got all the business done I heard Bacon say, "Cut. Give me that one." So I said I was rehearsing. He said, "Fine. Over there." And we started on the next scene.

Bacon directed *nine* Cagney pictures, all before 1940. Del Ruth directed six—including the four that were crucially propellant early in Cagney's career, two of them written by Glasmon and Bright—and the two, *West Point Story* and *Starlift*, that represented Del Ruth's later relegation to musicals. An ex-newspaper cartoonist and reporter from Philadelphia, Del Ruth was weaned in Hollywood on Ben Turpin and Harry Langdon comedies, which may explain why his Cagney films are highlighted by brisk comic tidbits. He could be more precise, more urbane than Bacon—but overall, he was "more a trend follower than a trend setter," in Andrew Sarris' opinion. John Bright recalled him as an arrogant studio hack who was rude to his secretaries but obeisant to the stars. To Cagney, Del Ruth was someone appreciated for not interfering with the actor; they never clashed.

Keighley is the most problematic of the three. Associated with Cagney on the stage in New York, he joined the Warners' crew in the early 1930s in time to serve as "dialogue director" for such Cagney films as *Picture Snatcher* and *Footlight Parade*. Unpretentious and well liked, as well as being economical and reliable, Keighley was dubbed a "talk expert" because his dialogue scenes raced by so fast and furiously. Ironically, his reputation was developed as the gritty, hardboiled director of such films as *G-Men* and *Each Dawn I Die*, although off-camera he was well educated (in France), genteel, and noted for establishing a mood of whispered intimacy with his actors. Like Bacon, Keighley is a relatively unresearched director—neither are mentioned in Sarris' exhaustive *The American Cinema* (New York: Dutton, 1968). But it seems that he had as little passion for Hollywood as Cagney; he quit directing in the early 1950s, at the top of his form, and retired to travel and dabble in photography. Before that, Keighley had spent almost his entire career at Warner Bros. and directed five Cagney features—plus, before being replaced by Michael Curtiz, scenes for *Captains of the Clouds*.

Parenthetically, Cagney seemed to fare best with his most laissez-faire directors; sparks flew whenever he was thrown together with more authoritarian ones: Anatole Litvak, Billy Wilder, and, to a certain extent, John Ford. Not that the more tightly vised films are Cagney's worst by any means—Litvak's and Wilder's are among his best. Hence, the argument can be made that Cagney would have made greater films with greater directors, however authoritarian—and indeed Cagney was the first to make that argument, in 1932, two years after arriving in Hollywood, when he demanded story and director approval as terms to end his second walkout. Yet Cagney suffered at Warners because of his in-house rebellion, and invariably he was stuck with lesser directors and abbreviated shooting schedules. And the fact of the matter is that for the bulk of his career he worked with "B" directors or with "A" directors on their least-personal projects.

Thus Cagney was unimpressed with most Hollywood directors and scornful of their prestige. As often as not, he believed, cameramen appointed the angles,

With director Lloyd Bacon, unidentified actor, and (at far right) Donald Crisp on the set of THE OKLAHOMA KID in 1939.

and few directors "knew what they were doing when they got in front of a camera to demonstrate [acting]." He liked to tell this anecdote about director Michael Curtiz:

> One of my directors, Mike Curtiz, had been an actor in the Hungarian and German theatre. He arrived one day on the set with a very specific idea of how a particular scene should be played. I said, "Go ahead, Mike. Show me how you want it." He went in and played it with all the old fancy European techniques—brushing off the cuffs with a flick of the finger, reaching fussily for a cigarette and lighting it with a flourish, then putting his foot up on a bench, and proceeding to talk with one hand on the hip. "Alright, Mike," I said, "Now, I'm going to do just as you suggested. I want you to watch closely." I'm a fairly good mimic, so I got before the camera and did it exactly as Mike had worked it out. When I finished, I asked him what he thought. "I guess I'm a pretty lousy actor, huh, Jimmy?" There was nothing further to say.

Yet Cagney is not an actor–auteur merely because he second-guessed his directors or penciled his scripts—although he did. ("Empty lines are his most violent hate on the set," reported one 1930s fan magazine. "Any number of directors can tell a tale of how Cagney had said, 'No dice. The guy's only speaking words.'") Nor because he suggested camera angles or dictated those angles by the trajectory of his movement—which he did.* Nor because he steeped himself in story sessions and casting, whenever possible, and contributed ideas ranging from scene drawings for *City for Conquest* to new stanzas to the World War II song, "Bless 'Em All," which he eventually sang in a barroom duet with Alan Hale in *Captains of the Clouds*. Obviously, when in the mood, Cagney could be helpful in nearly every department. But everything apart from acting was incidental to Cagney: incidental to his total immersion in the role, out of which sprang his pervasive intrusions and involvements.

On camera Cagney knew what was right for Cagney. He felt this deeply and with confidence. He arrived on a set, customarily, fully prepared for the day's filming, having read the script and prepared his characterization, his dialogue, his blocking, and his gestures. He was not rigid—he might have details worked out beforehand or add some unpredictable flourishes while the cameras rolled. Director Howard Hawks remembered that "Cagney was so much fun to work with because you never knew what Cagney was gonna do. When I work with Cary Grant, I can go home and write a scene for Cary and know how he's gonna handle it the next day, but Cagney had these funny little attitudes, you know, the way he held his hands and things like that." After discussing Cagney's character with him before shooting began on *Ceiling Zero*, Hawks conceded, "Your ideas are better than mine. Let's shoot it."

To pinpoint the character, or just for variety's sake, Cagney would often fix on an intonation or physical quirk that appealed to him. He showed up on the set of *Ceiling Zero* sporting a roguish moustache; for *Jimmy the Gent*, he appeared nearly bald, with a stark, close-shaven haircut—and director Curtiz, taken aback, was nevertheless forced to begin shooting on schedule. For *St. Louis Kid*, he bandaged his fists and decided to punch adversaries with his forehead. As he wrote in his autobiography, "I went around hitting people with my head, all of this in a specific attempt to vary the old punching formula. I can still hear the reedy voice of *St. Louis Kid*'s producer, 'When are you going to take those bandages off and start punching right?'" What the producer did not understand was that Cagney was determined to play it according to Cagney. In the words of Elia Kazan, "He [Cagney] was not servile with directors, rather the opposite,

---

*One example among others: The prison-cell scene between Cody Jarrett (Cagney) and Fallon/Pardo (Edmond O'Brien) in *White Heat* was written by Ivan Goff and Ben Roberts to be played in an edited sequence of camera shots. On the set, director Raoul Walsh set up the scene to be filmed with a master shot, individual shots, and over-the-shoulders shots. According to screenwriter Roberts, Cagney approached Walsh, saying, "That's a lot of movement. What are you doing that for, Raoul? The camera's going to jerk around—this is supposed to be a confidential scene. Why don't you just start back and move in and we'll play the whole scene." Walsh said, "Sure, if that's what you want." Added Roberts: "It was much better, because it kept the two guys riveted like that."

Guitar-playing during a camera break on the set of EACH DAWN I DIE.

kept his own counsel, listened, nodded, walked away, did it. And directors, producers, co-stars, financiers, studio heads, he feared no one.''

Rhythm, Mimicry, and Daring

Cagney was always humble and unassuming about his ''art,'' a word that amused him. In 1974 he told an interviewer,

> Acting was a job to be done and I liked doing it. Apparently, whatever equipment I had seemed to lend itself to the job and it worked, and inasmuch as it worked and the pay was good, why not? I had no idea of performing high art. The axiom for me has been this very self-evident truth: that you're only as good as the other fellow thinks you are because

he buys the tickets. You leave all that to him; you don't sit in judgment on your own work. You hope it's right, and if it isn't, too bad.

When, in 1933, brother William asked him for some acting advice at the beginning of his own fleeting motion picture career, Cagney told him, "There's not much to tell you about acting, but this: Never settle back on your heels. Never relax. If you relax, the audience relaxes. And always mean everything you say."

"Never relax"—a catch-phrase, but one that helps explain the febrile energy of every Cagney performance. On camera, he never relaxed. And that quivering intensity became a film's overall tempo, pulse, musicality, whether expressed in the song-and-dance of *Yankee Doodle Dandy*, the suspense *tremolando* of *White Heat*, or the tick-tock hilarity of *One, Two, Three*. Even when his pictures are not tightly edited, they seem paced at a blur, for Cagney is nearly always operating at an upper velocity, his movement swift and choppy, his words spilling out in a staccato rush. A fanatical dancer, he skipped lunch hours to rehearse old steps; on the screen, he displayed the strut, the grace, the manner of someone who could as easily be a danseur noble as a cocksure ganglord. And being a dancer, he worked much as a choreographer to music, using inflections of speech and body to *jazz* up the characters he played. "Jim Cagney worked with movement," appraised director Hawks. "He didn't work with lines. I don't remember him ever suggesting a line—it's the way he *does* the line, the stuff you feed him, that makes him so good." Even in *Ragtime*, with his movement so patently sluggish, it was the odd syncopation of his line-readings that gave Cagney's Police Chief Rheinlander Waldo such distinct flavor.

In the 1930s, Cagney told screenwriter Niven Busch that he had devised his own personal acting "stratagem." According to Busch, Cagney always tried to produce a topper for his scenes, a crowning bit of character detail. If he could not invent a topper, he would drop in some unexpected move—such as glancing at his hands before punching a guy—and that move would be worked into a three-fold cadence. Typically, Cagney would express the idea (of the scene), then move into the action and carry through with it, then *wait* for a reaction before continuing. "You could see this in all of his action, whether it is drastic action or detail," observed Busch. "It was almost a waltz-time, a three-beat rhythm. It was his own theory for how he worked."

Mimicry, too, was part of the Cagney arsenal. The actor once denounced "living-the-part mumbo jumbo" as "the purest bunk," adding, "All I try to do is to realize the man I'm playing fully, then put as much into my acting as I know how. To do it, I draw upon all I've ever known, heard, seen or remembered." His memory was keen going back to his earliest childhood; his powers of observation, eerily precise. When he first met Jack Lemmon, after having seen Lemmon on television's Kraft Theatre playing a soda-jerk in an adaptation of the play *The Man from Blankney's*, he startled him by asking, "By the way, you're not still pretending you're left-handed, are you?" Just for the challenge, the right-handed Lemmon had portrayed the soda-jerk as a southpaw.

Giving acting tips to brother William in 1933. (WCTR)

That is one reason why Cagney's acting rarely struck a false note: So much of what he did was borrowed from life, from incidents and people he vividly remembered. "New York's East Side was full of colorful people while I was growing up," he once explained.

Many had unusual mannerisms of body or speech. I studied them, and from time to time used them. Maybe these mannerisms I've collected and have used are one of the reasons that, along with Jimmy Stewart, Clark Gable and Cary Grant, I seem to be a target for mimics. Most impersonators think that they are taking me off when what they're really doing is imitating me imitating a character I knew back in the neighborhood where I grew up.

There are two primary background sources on Cagney's gallery of imitative characters: his autobiography and, equally, a rambling "oral autobiography" (as told to Pete Martin) published serially in *The Saturday Evening Post* in 1956.

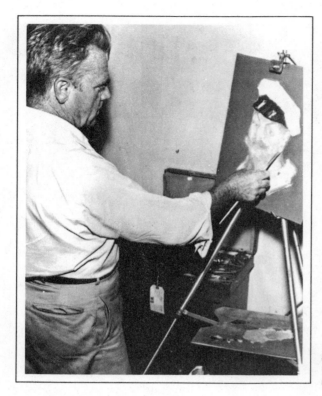

Self-portrait: A watercolor of himself as the Captain in MISTER ROBERTS. (UCLA Film Archives)

Together they indicate how extensive Cagney's use of mimicry was, how specific and organic his reflexes were in that regard. A partial listing of people and incidents that inspired memorable Cagney portrayals would have to include:

- His own father, James Francis Cagney, Sr., fondly evoked in *Taxi!* "Pop had an affectionate thing he did with his four sons; he'd put one hand behind the back of our necks, ball his other fist as if he were about to clout us, then say, 'If I thought you meant it'—It was always good for a laugh, for afterward, he'd put his arm around us. I used that gesture in a film I made with Loretta Young."
- The gorilla's "slow, amazed" death in a film by African explorer Frank Buck, which became the pattern for Cagney's own extended death throes in movies such as *The Roaring Twenties*.
- The pants-hitching, neck-jerking streetcorner pimp and hophead dredged out of his past for mannerisms in *Angels with Dirty Faces*.
- Blind pianist Alec Templeton, a model for Cagney's characterization in *City for Conquest*.
- George M. Cohan: "Most mimics inject a chronic hoarseness into my voice. The truth is, I'm not usually hoarse at all. That hoarseness they reproduce was

part of my George M. Cohan characterization in *Yankee Doodle Dandy*. As Cohan grew older, his voice grew husky and it had a kind of breathy quality it didn't have when he was younger. I didn't use that breathiness when I played the younger Cohan, but I did use it for the sequence when he was older. The whole thing was a trick of make-believe; nevertheless, the impersonators have latched on to the older Cohan's voice as being mine."

• A boyhood visit to the hospital for the insane on Ward's Island, which was remembered by Cagney and incorporated into the prison mess-hall scene in *White Heat* where Cody Jarrett (Cagney) goes uncontrollably berserk.

• Jim Richardson, a Los Angeles newspaper editor who was Cagney's friend and an ex-alcoholic. Richardson consulted on *Come Fill the Cup*.

• Martin "The Gimp" Snyder, subject of *Love Me or Leave Me*. The real Snyder walked with a limp, and Cagney conferred with his doctor–brothers, Harry and Ed, as well as other physicians, for advice about how to duplicate it. After conflicting recommendations, Cagney decided to make his limp "as unrepellant and usable as possible. I still don't know whether his real-life limp is worse than the one I used in the film or not. But I do know that when people who are so afflicted grow tired they limp more, and when they are rested, they limp less; so I figured that I could vary the limp as I saw it, and in that way keep it from being monotonous." After one sequence was filmed, Cagney apologized to director Charles Vidor for absent-mindedly neglecting to limp. But, Vidor informed the surprised actor, he had limped like a trouper. "By that time my limp had become so automatic with me that I did it without knowing it."

• An old friend, the president of a Massachusetts bank, whose characteristics were borrowed by Cagney for his part as the domineering skipper in *Mister Roberts*. "I asked myself, 'Who do I know who is like this skipper? How would he talk?' For a long time, I'd been aping one of my best friends, the president of a Massachusetts bank. I'd been telling stories about him featuring his New England accent, so I stole my bank president–pal's way of talking for my *Mister Roberts* role. This will probably come as news to him. . . . I don't mean that making one role different from another is altogether a matter of personal tricks, of copying mannerisms or imitating accents. As an actor, you have to find out what the fellow you're playing is all about. You must work him out in your mind. Just hitting upon an accent I could use wasn't understanding the Captain in *Mister Roberts*. Jack Ford [the codirector] saw him as the most pathetic man on the ship, entirely alone, and not knowing how to exert his authority. He was a lonely soul, removed from everybody and everything. I agreed."

• Lon Chaney, subject of *Man of a Thousand Faces*. Cagney studied Chaney's silent-era pictures and learned the deaf-mute language of Chaney's childhood. According to director Joseph Pevney, Cagney made "numerous suggestions in the areas of pantomime and dancing" during the filming.

Off-screen, Cagney was equally adept as an impersonator. Director–writer Peter Bogdanovich visited the retired actor in 1972 and reported in *Esquire*:

During the course of a small dinner party in Brentwood, he [Cagney] also proved to be an extraordinary raconteur. He doesn't just tell a story, he acts it out, playing all the parts, with remarkable precision and an economy of gesture that is as subtle and revealing as most of his professional performances. He gave us some memorable impressions that night of people he'd worked with—a gentle Hungarian-like Charles Vidor (Cagney had the accent down perfectly and thoughtfully pantomimed holding a cigarette from below, with thumb and forefinger, which immediately caught the flavor of the man), a not-so-gentle Hungarian director like Michael Curtiz (two hilariously unprintable stories here), and the absolute essence of John Ford (in this context, he gave a great one-word description of the Irish, of whom Cagney is one: "Malice").

Rhythm-and-dance, mimicry and . . . whatever. One cannot, should not, attempt to catalogue the secrets of a great performer, as if totting up so many ingredients in a recipe. Especially so in Cagney's case, where much remains locked inside "his dark Irish soul," in Elia Kazan's words, much that the man could not or chose not to articulate. As William Cagney put it, "All of the unhappiness of his childhood was inside him." How else to explain the cutting edge in his portrayal of the quintessential tough guy?

"Psychologically, it [the tough guy] is the other side of Cagney, that he is able to act out," observed screenwriter Ben Roberts.

Instead of acting it out in real life, he acted it out on the screen. He was born in Hell's Kitchen and, I think, when you learn to live in the gutter, when you really have to strike out, and when you're gentle by nature, this is a way of getting all those angry murderous hostilities out. A lot of the kids he grew up with wound up in prison or in the electric chair—because that was their outlook. Jim's outlook was he took whatever was in his unconscious and learned to use it, and used it.

He was a natural actor. He didn't have to learn to do anything. He instinctively knew where to go, and how to squeeze a scene until it was absolutely dry. He was daring. It took a lot of guts sometimes to do the things he did—because he exposed himself to the world every time he did. But he had no fear about that. He never said, "I can't do it." He always said, "I'll take a crack at it, fellas." He wasn't afraid to take a chance as an actor.

A method actor may not take as many chances as a natural actor because he is afraid of stepping beyond the range of what he thinks the part can take. Jimmy, as a natural actor, could sense instinctively that he could go higher than the part required and still get away with it—and not look foolish or broad. Very often, I think, method actors inhibit themselves. They're marvelous, but they limit their range because they think if they go beyond a certain point, they go beyond reality—and they don't want to

With James Stewart and Orson Welles on the set of MAN OF A THOUSAND FACES.
(Homer Dickens Still Collection)

take that chance of destroying the character. Jimmy doesn't do that. He says people exist as they exist. They live in highs and lows. He'll go as low as you want and as high as you want.

Certain words crop up again and again in interviews with people who admire Cagney: guts, daring, fearlessness, the courage "to do things that were outrageous" (in the words of Clint Eastwood). Peter Bogdanovich remembers the night he and Orson Welles watched *White Heat* together: "Afterward Orson got to musing about the absurdity of all the theoretical writings about the differences between movie acting and stage acting. 'Look at Cagney—everything he does is *big*—and yet it's never for a moment unbelievable, because it's *real*. It's true. He's a great movie actor and his performances are in no way modulated for the camera—he never scaled anything down."

This daring, this lack of any inhibition, this unwillingness to scale down life for the camera—this goes to the heart of Cagney's acting. And it harks back to

Four Cagneys: (left to right) William, James (in dark glasses), Jeanne, and
Doctor Harry Cagney on the set of KISS TOMORROW GOODBYE. (BFI)

his upbringing, his childhood, where people existed as they existed in lows and
highs; where the Cagney children were inculcated with survival instincts and
the work ethic. As much as he might wince at the term, it is certain that Cagney
was an artist, possibly an inadvertent one. But it may also be that only someone
who approached acting as "a job of work" (his words) could do it as reflexively,
as conscientiously, and with as much heave-ho as laying a brick. "My
philosophy," Cagney was fond of saying, "has always been to do anything that
comes my way seeking to be done. Back where I came from, if there was a buck
to be made, you didn't ask questions. You just went ahead and made it."

Remains: The Paradox

An inadvertent artist, maybe—a reluctant one, at times, without a doubt.
"Jimmy really never had steam for motion pictures," said William Cagney. "I can
say that he was never really happy in Hollywood." This is the paradox of any
actor-as-auteur theory that includes Cagney: He never embraced Hollywood. At
every stage of his career he had to be coaxed into persevering. Looking back, he
could cite only half-a-dozen films as his favorites and considered the rest a
monumental waste (his career, in Sarris' words, was "unusually spotty for a
performer of his magnitude").

Yet the history of Hollywood is writ long with stories of writers more proud of
their work in other arenas; of directors wounded in their battles with the

higher-ups; of stars who quit and turned their backs on careers that, from one standpoint or another, were compromises. Astaire could be as self-deprecating as Cagney, after all; Cary Grant was equally insecure about his "art" and just as adamantly withdrew from the scene; there was never a Garbo comeback. The disparagement is often an attitude that bespeaks profound disillusionment and the artist's strain of perfectionism.

In Cagney's career, he gave every outward indication of caring more, at one point, then he later preferred to let on. He fought the Warners' constrictions— winning contractually, losing again and again in his picture assignments; by the time he turned a corner with *Yankee Doodle Dandy* he had lost precious momentum because of concerted Hollywood resistance, World War II, and the ebb and flow of his own commitment. According to his brother William, Cagney had wanted to leave Hollywood after his first six weeks there; but he was lured to stay for half a century by the proverbial carrot on a stick: a pay-raise, a better role, a hope that sprang eternal. Grand National and Cagney Productions were part of that hope, part of the scheme of independence, and were the closest Cagney ever came to being the master of his destiny.

In his autobiography and in his other reminisces, Cagney played the it-was-just-a-job theme recurrently and convincingly. That was only part of his story. Cagney remained torn and regretful over aspects of his career, because he knew himself and the far-reaching possibilities best. He played Shakespeare only once. Later, he delighted in telling interviewers that he had no aspirations to perform high art or Shakespeare. Yet he did: He was a confirmed theater-goer and a student of his craft. He was struck by Laurette Taylor, the Barrymores, the greats of his profession. Not only did he openly yearn to play Shakespeare, O'Neill, Maxwell Anderson—and all the respected playwrights of the day—but he was galled by the straitjacket of his tough guy persona and in vain tried to vary it with musicals, projects such as the John Paul Jones saga, the Cagney Productions, Thorne Smith's *The Stray Lamb*.

In the 1930s he mused about the possibility of joining the Irish Players at the Abbey Theatre in Dublin or of performing Irish drama in repertory with Pat O'Brien and other Irish actor–pals. An article by John T. McManus in *The New York Times*, titled "James Cagney Dreams of O'Casey," whimsically posed the obstacles: "Like the white-collar worker who, just for the vicarious thrill of it, pores over heaps of world-tour pamphlets before sighing and going off on his two-week vacation in the Catskills, James Cagney toys frequently with the idea of playing Irish drama." Cagney envisioned a touring stock company consisting of Robert Montgomery, J. M. Kerrigan, William Gargan, Barry Fitzgerald, Edward McNamara, and Pat O'Brien. He talked of beginning with J. M. Synge's *Playboy of the Western World*.

Such plans, dreams, never materialized. They are perhaps just a footnote to the legend. Yet at the same time, the lost opportunities loomed tragically in the actor's own mind, so they are all-important to a complex understanding of the little giant who was James Cagney.

Dapper publicity pose from the mid-1930s. (WCTR)

Appendix

Filmography: Feature-Length Movies

SINNER'S HOLIDAY (1930). Lurid melodrama about the bad-seed son in a family that runs a carnival "penny arcade"; with Cagney as Harry Delano, the errant scion, who gets mixed up in bootlegging and murder. *Dir:* John G. Adolfi. *Sc:* Harvey Thew, George Rosener; based on the play *Penny Arcade* by Marie Baumer. *Ph:* Ira Morgan. *Ed:* James Gibbons. *Sound:* Clare A. Riggs. *Mus dir:* Leo F. Forbstein. *Makeup:* Perc Westmore. *Cast:* Grant Withers (Angel Harrigan), Evalyn Knapp (Jennie Delano), Joan Blondell (Myrtle), Lucille LaVerne (Ma Delano), Noel Madison (Buck), Otto Hoffman (George), Warren Hymer (Mitch McKane), Purnell B. Pratt (Sikes), Ray Gallagher (Joe Delano), and Hank Mann (Happy). *Prod:* Warner Bros. 55 min. The original title, *Penny Arcade*, was abandoned during postproduction.

DOORWAY TO HELL [GB: *A HANDFUL OF CLOUDS*] (1930). Somber drama about an underworld bootlegging czar who tries to quit the rackets; with Cagney as Steve Mileaway, the crime chieftain's sidekick. *Dir:* Archie Mayo. *Sc:* George Rosener; based on the story "A Handful of Clouds" by Rowland Brown. *Ph:* Barney "Chick" McGill. *Ed:* Robert Crandall. *Sound:* David Forrest. *Mus dir:* Leo F. Forbstein. *Makeup:* Perc Westmore. *Cast:* Lew Ayres (Louis Ricarno), Charles Judels (Sam Marconi), Dorothy Mathews (Doris), Leon Janney (Jackie Lamar), Robert Elliott (Captain O'Grady), Kenneth Thomson (captain of military academy), Jerry Mandy (Joe), Noel Madison (Rocco), Bernard "Bunny" Granville (man), Fred Argus (machine gunner), Ruth Hall (girl), and Dwight Frye, Tom Wilson, Al Hill, and Eddie Kane (gangsters). *Prod:* Warner Bros. 78 min. Brown's original story was nominated for an Academy Award.

OTHER MEN'S WOMEN (1931). Muddled but oft-intriguing melodrama involving a love triangle among railroad worker pals; with Cagney (as Ed) seen fleetingly as one of the gang of railmen. *Dir:* William A. Wellman. *Sc:* Maude Fulton, William K. Wells; based on a story by Fulton. *Ph:* Barney "Chick" McGill. *Ed:* Edward McDermott. *Mus dir:* Leo F. Forbstein. *Makeup:* Perc Westmore. *Cast:* Grant Withers (Bill), Mary Astor (Lily), Regis Toomey (Jack), Joan Blondell (Marie), Fred Kohler (Haley), J. Farrell MacDonald (Pegleg), Lillian Worth (waitress), Walter Long (Bixby), and Bob Perry, Lee Morgan, Kewpie Morgan, and Pat Hartigan (railroad workers). *Prod:* Warner Bros. 70 min. The original title was *The Steel Highway* (discarded after previews).

THE MILLIONAIRE (1931). Leisurely comedy about a retired millionaire who seeks escape from boredom; with Cagney as Schofield, a high-pressure insurance salesman. *Dir:* John G. Adolfi. *Sc:* Julian Josephson, Maude T. Powell. *Dialogue:* Booth Tarkington; based on "Idle Hands" by Earl Derr Biggers. *Ph:* James Van Trees. *Ed:* Owen Marks. *Mus dir:* Leo F. Forbstein. *Makeup:* Perc Westmore. *Cast:* George Arliss (James Alden), Evalyn Knapp (Barbara Alden), David Manners (Bill Merrick), Bramwell Fletcher (Carter Andrews), Florence Arliss (Mrs. Alden), Noah Beery (Peterson), Ivan Simpson (Dr. Harvey), Sam Hardy (McCoy), J. Farrell MacDonald (Dan Lewis), Tully Marshall (Briggs), J. C. Nugent (doctor), and Charles Grapewin, Charles E. Evans, Ethel Griffies, and Ben Hall. *Prod:* Warner Bros. 82 min. The film was remade by Warners in 1947 as *That Way with Women*, with Sydney Greenstreet, Dane Clark, and Martha Vickers.

THE PUBLIC ENEMY [GB: *ENEMIES OF THE PUBLIC*] (1931). Bleak parable of the rise and fall of two boyhood pals from the slums who graduate from petty crimes to full-scale racketeering; with Cagney as Tom Powers, the "public enemy." *Dir:* William A. Wellman. *Sc:* Kubec Glasmon, John Bright; adaptation and dialogue by: Harvey Thew; based on *BEER AND BLOOD* by Glasmon and Bright. *Ph:* Dev Jennings. *Art dir:* Max Parker. *Ed:* Ed McCormick. *Mus dir:* David Mendoza. *Cost:* Earl Luick. *Makeup:* Perc Westmore. *Cast:* Jean Harlow (Gwen Allen), Edward Woods (Matt Doyle), Joan Blondell (Mamie), Beryl Mercer (Ma Powers), Donald Cook (Mike Powers), Mae Clarke (Kitty), Mia Marvin (Jane), Leslie Fenton (Nails Nathan), Robert Emmett O'Connor (Paddy Ryan), Murray Kinnell (Putty Nose), Ben Hendricks, Jr. (Bugs Moran), Rita Flynn (Molly Doyle), Clark Burroughs (Dutch), Snitz Edwards '(Hack), Adele Watson (Mrs. Doyle), Frank Coghlan, Jr. (Tommy as a boy), Frankie Darro (Matt as a boy), Robert E. Homans (Officer Pat Burke), Dorothy Gee (Nails' Girl), Purnell Pratt (Officer Powers), Lee Phelps (Steve the bartender), Helen Parrish, Dorothy Gray, Nanci Price (little girls), Ben Hendricks, III (Bugs as a boy), George Daly (machine gunner), Eddie Kane (Joe the headwaiter), Charles Sullivan (Mug), Douglas Gerrard (assistant tailor), Sam McDaniel (black headwaiter), and William H. Strauss (pawnbroker). *Prod:* Warner Bros. 84 min. Glasmon and Bright's original story was nominated for an Academy Award. The film was re-released in 1953 on a double bill with *Little Caesar*.

With (l to r) Richard Purcell, Dorothy Mathews, and Lew Ayres in a scene from DOORWAY TO HELL. (WCTR)

With Eddie Woods: The death of his pal in PUBLIC ENEMY. (AMPAS)

SMART MONEY (1931). Appealing comedy–drama about a gambling country barber who travels to the big city in search of higher stakes; with Cagney as Jack, the barber's assistant and friend. *Dir:* Alfred E. Green. *Sc:* Kubec Glasmon, John Bright. *Add dialogue:* Lucien Hubbard, Joseph Jackson; based on an original story by Hubbard and Jackson. *Ph:* Robert Kurrle. *Ed:* Jack Killifer. *Mus dir:* Leo F. Forbstein. *Makeup:* Perc Westmore. *Cast:* Edward G. Robinson (Nick Venizelos), Evalyn Knapp (Irene Graham), Noel Francis (Marie), Morgan Wallace (district attorney), Paul Porcasi (Mr. Amenoppopolus), Maurice Black (Greek barber), Margaret Livingston (D.A.'s girl), Clark Burroughs (Schultz), Billy House (salesman), Edwin Argus (Two-Time Phil), Ralf Harolde (Sleepy Sam), Boris Karloff (Sport Williams), Mae Madison (small-town girl), Walter Percival (Dealer Barnes), John Larkin (Snake Eyes), Polly Walters (Lola), Ben Taggart (Hickory Short), Gladys Lloyd (cigar-stand clerk), Eulalie Jensen (matron), Charles Lane (desk clerk), Edward Hearn (reporter), Eddie Kane (Tom, a customer), Clinton Rosemond (George the porter), Charles O'Malley (machine gunner), Gus Leonard (Joe, barber customer), Wallace Mac-Donald (cigar-stand clerk), John George (dwarf on train), Harry Semels (gambler), Charlotte Merriam (girl at gaming table), with Larry McGrath, Spencer Bell, and Allen Lane. *Prod:* Warner Bros. 90 min. Hubbard and Jackson's original story was nominated for an Academy Award.

BLONDE CRAZY [GB: *LARCENY LANE*] (1931). Breezy, hardboiled comedy about a pair of scheming con artists on a romantic spree; with Cagney as Bert Harris, the "brains" of the duo. *Dir:* Roy Del Ruth. *Sc:* Kubec Glasmon, John Bright; based on an original story by Glasmon and Bright. *Ph:* Sid Hickox. *Ed:* Ralph Dawson. *Mus dir:* Leo F. Forbstein. *Makeup:* Perc Westmore. *Songs:* "When Your Lover Has Gone" by E. A. Swan; "I Can't Write the Words" by Gerald Marks, Buddy Fields; "Ain't That the Way It Goes?" by Roy Turk, Fred Ahlert; "I'm Just a Fool in Love with You" by Sidney Mitchell, Archie Gottlieb, George W. Meyer. *Cast:* Joan Blondell (Ann Roberts), Louis Calhern (Dapper Dan Barker), Noel Francis (Helen Wilson), Guy Kibbee (A. Rupert Johnson, Jr.), Raymond Milland (Joe Reynolds), Polly Walters (Peggy), Charles (Levinson) Lane (Four-Eyes the desk clerk), William Burress (Colonel Bellock), Peter Erkelenz (Dutch), Maude Eburne (Mrs. Snyder), Walter Percival (Lee), Nat Pendleton (Hank), Russell Hopton (Jerry), Dick Cramer (cabbie), Wade Boteler (detective), Ray Cooke, Edward Morgan (bellhops), and Phil Sleman (conman). *Prod:* Warner Bros. 73 min. The film retained its original title, *LARCENY LANE*, for British release.

TAXI! (1932) Engrossing comedy–drama about a metropolitan tax war; with Cagney as Matt Nolan, leader of the independent cabbies. *Dir:* Roy Del Ruth. *Sc:* Kubec Glasmon, John Bright; based on the play *The Blind Spot* by Kenyon Nicholson. *Ph:* James Van Trees. *Art dir:* Esdras Hartley. *Ed:* James Gibbons. *Mus dir:* Leo F. Forbstein. *Makeup:* Perc Westmore. *Assist dir:* William Cannon. *Cast:* Loretta Young (Sue Reilly), George E. Stone (Skeets), Guy Kibbee (Pop Reilly), David Landau (Buck Gerard), Ray Cooke (Danny Nolan), Leila Bennett (Ruby), Dorothy Burgess (Marie Costa), Matt McHugh (Joe Silva), George MacFarlane (Father Nulty), Polly Walters (Polly), Nat Pendleton (truckdriver), Berton Churchill (Mr. West), George Raft (William Kenny), Hector V. Sarno (monument salesman), Aggie Herring (cleaning lady), Lee Phelps (onlooker), Harry Tenbrook (cabbie), Robert Emmett O'Connor (cop with Jewish man), Eddie Fetherstone, Russ Powell (dance judges), Ben Taggart (cop), and The Cotton Club Orchestra. *Prod:* Warner Bros. 70 min. The working titles of the film were *THE BLIND SPOT* and *TAXI! PLEASE!* The movie-within-a-movie sequence is from *SIDE SHOW* (1931) with Donald Cook and Evalyn Knapp. *TAXI!* was re-released in 1936 on a double bill with *SMART MONEY*.

THE CROWD ROARS (1932). Effective melodrama about a champion racecar driver whose estrangement from his brother causes the speedway death of a friend and his own downfall on the circuit; with Cagney as Joe Greer, the self-destructive auto champ. *Dir:* Howard Hawks. *Sc:* Kubec Glasmon, John Bright, Niven Busch; based on a story by Hawks and Seton I. Miller. *Ph:* Sid Hickox, John Stumar. *Art dir:* Jack Okey. *Prod super:* Raymond Griffith. *Ed:* Thomas Pratt. *Mus dir:* Leo F. Forbstein. *Makeup:* Perc Westmore. *Assist dir:* Dick Rossen. *Cast:* Joan Blondell (Anne), Ann Dvorak (Lee), Eric Linden (Eddie Greer), Guy Kibbee (Dad Greer), Frank McHugh (Spud Connors), William Arnold (Bill Arnold), Leo Nomis (Jim), Charlotte Merriam (Mrs. Spud Connors), Regis Toomey (Dick Willshaw), Harry Hartz, Ralph Hepburn, Fred Guisso, Fred Frame, Phil Pardee, Spider Matlock, Jack Brisko, Lou Schneider, Bryan Salspaugh, Stubby Stubblefield, Shorty Cantlon, Mel Keneally, Wilbur Shaw (auto drivers), James Burtis (mechanic), Sam Hayes (Ascot announcer), Robert McWade (Tom the counterman), Ralph Dunn (official), John Conte (announcer), and John Harron (Red, Eddie's pitman). *Prod:* Warner Bros. 85 min. The film was originally titled *The Roar of the Crowd*, then *The Roaring Crowd*. Leftover racing footage was used for an unofficial remake called *Indianapolis Speedway* in 1939.

WINNER TAKE ALL (1932). Uneven but vivid programmer about a prizefighter who must choose between the affections of a rustic sweetheart and those of a flashy high society dame; with Cagney as Jim Kane, the broken-down pugilist who tries to recover his health at a Western ranch. *Dir:* Roy Del Ruth. *Sc:* Wilson Mizner, Robert Lord; based on the magazine story "133 at 3" by Gerald Beaumont. *Ph:* Robert Kurrle. *Art dir:* Robert Haas. *Ed:* Thomas Pratt. *Mus score:* W. Franke Harling. *Mus dir:* Leo F. Forbstein. *Cost:* Orry-Kelly. *Makeup:* Perc Westmore. *Cast:* Marian Nixon (Peggy Harmon), Virginia Bruce (Joan Gibson), Guy Kibbee (Pop Slavin), Clarence Muse (Rosebud the trainer), Dickie Moore (Dickie Harmon), Allan Lane (Monty), John Roche (Roger Elliott), Ralf Harolde (Legs Davis), Alan Mowbray (Forbes), Clarence Wilson (Ben Isaacs), Charles Coleman (Butler), Esther Howard (Ann), Renee Whitney (Lois), Harvey Perry (Al West), Julian Rivero (Pice), Selmer Jackson (ring announcer), Chris Pin Martin (manager), George Hayes (interne), Bob Perry (Tijuana referee), Billy West (second), Phil Tead (reporter), Rolfe Sedan (waiter), John Kelly (boxing spectator), Lee Phelps (ring announcer, championship), Jay Eaton (society man), and Charlotte Merriam (blonde). *Prod:* Warner Bros. 68 min. The movie-within-a-movie sequence is from *Queen of the Night Clubs* (1929) with Texas Guinan and George Raft.

HARD TO HANDLE (1933). Ingratiating cynical comedy about a fast-talking entrepreneur who stages a marathon dance contest and cannot come up with the prize money; with Cagney as Lefty Merrill, the irrepressible con artist. *Dir:* Mervyn LeRoy. *Sc:* Wilson Mizner, Robert Lord; based on a story by Houston Branch. *Ph:* Barney "Chick" McGill. *Art dir:* Robert Haas. *Ed:* William Holmes. *Mus cond:* Leo F. Forbstein. *Cost:* Orry-Kelly. *Makeup:* Perc Westmore. *Cast:* Mary Brian (Ruth Waters), Ruth Donnelly (Lil Waters), Allen Jenkins (radio announcer), Claire Dodd (Marlene Reeves), Gavin Gordon (John Hayden), Emma Dunn (Mrs. Hawks the landlady), Robert McWade (Charles Reeves), John Sheehan (Ed McGrath), Matt McHugh (Joe Goetz), Louis Mackintosh (Mrs. Weston Parks), William H. Strauss (antique dealer), Bess Flowers (Merrill's secretary), Lew Kelly (hash slinger), Berton Churchill (Colonel Wells), Harry Holman (Colonel's associates), Grace Hayle (fat lady with vanishing cream), George Pat Collins (dance judge), Douglass Dumbrille (district attorney), Sterling Holloway (Andy), Charles Wilson (jailer), and with Jack Crawford, Stanley Smith, Walter Walker, and Mary Doran. *Prod:* Warner Bros. 81 min. The working title of the film was originally *Bad Boy*, then *The Inside*.

PICTURE SNATCHER (1933). Snappy comedy–drama about an ex-racketeer turned "picture snatcher" for a disreputable tabloid; with Cagney as Danny Kean, the unscrupulous photographer. *Dir:* Lloyd Bacon. *Sc:* Allen Rivkin, P. J. Wolfson. *Add dialogue:* Ben

Markson; based on a story by Danny Ahern. *Dialogue dir:* William Keighley. *Ph:* Sol Polito. *Art dir:* Robert Haas. *Ed:* William Holmes. *Mus cond:* Leo F. Forbstein. *Cost:* Orry-Kelly. *Makeup:* Perc Westmore. *Assist dir:* Gordon Hollingshead. *Cast:* Ralph Bellamy (McLean), Patricia Ellis (Patricia Nolan), Alice White (Allison), Ralf Harolde (Jerry), Robert Emmett O'Connor (Casey Nolan), Robert Barrat (Grover), George Pat Collins (Hennessey the fireman), Tom Wilson (Leo), Barbara Rogers (Olive), Renee Whitney (Connie), Alice Jans (Colleen), Jill Dennett (speakeasy girl), Billy West (reporter), George Daly (machine gunner), Arthur Vinton (head keeper), Stanley Blystone (prison guard), Don Brodie (hood), George Chandler (reporter), Sterling Holloway (journalism student), Donald Kerr (Mike, Colleen's boyfriend), Hobart Cavanaugh (Pete, a drunken reporter), Phil Tead (strange reporter), Charles King (sick reporter), Milton Kibbee (reporter outside prison), Dick Elliott, Vaughn Taylor (editors), Bob Perry (bartender), Gino Corrado (barber), Maurice Black (speakeasy proprietor), Selmer Jackson (record editor), Jack Grey (police officer), John Ince (captain), and Cora Sue Collins (little girl). *Prod:* Warner Bros. 77 min.

THE MAYOR OF HELL (1933). Grim, but exciting melodrama about a hoodlum shocked into reform effort by conditions at a boys reformatory; with Cagney as Patsy Gargan, the gangster who moonlights as a reform school supervisor. *Dir:* Archie Mayo. *Sc:* Edward Chodorov; based on a story by Islin Auster. *Ph:* Barney "Chick" McGill. *Art dir:* Esdras Hartley. *Ed:* Jack Killifer. *Mus dir:* Leo F. Forbstein. *Cost:* Orry-Kelly. *Makeup:* Perc Westmore. *Assist dir:* Frank Shaw. *Cast:* Madge Evans (Dorothy Griffith), Allen Jenkins (Mike), Dudley Digges (Mr. Thompson), Frankie Darro (Jimmy Smith), Farina (Smoke), Dorothy Peterson (Mrs. Smith), John Marston (Hopkins), Charles Wilson (guard), Hobart Cavanaugh (Tommy's father), Raymond Borzage (Johnny Stone), Robert Barrat (Mr. Smith), George Pat Collins (Brandon), Mickey Bennett (Butch Kilgore), Arthur Byron (Judge Gilbert), Sheila Terry (the girl), Harold Huber (Joe), Edwin Maxwell (Louis Johnston), William V. Mong (Walters), Sidney Miller (Izzy Horowitz), George Humbert (Tony's father), George Offerman, Jr. (Charlie Burns), Charles Cane (Tommy Gorman), Wallace MacDonald (Johnson's assistant), Adrian Morris (car owner), Snowflake

With Joan Blondell in Glasmon and Bright's BLONDE CRAZY. (UCLA Film Archives)

With Ruth Donnelly in Mervyn LeRoy's HARD TO HANDLE. (WCTR)

(Hemingway), Wilfred Lucas (guard), Bob Perry, Charles Sullivan (collectors), and Ben Taggart (sheriff). *Prod:* Warner Bros. 90 min. The film was remade by Warners as *CRIME SCHOOL* in 1938 starring Humphrey Bogart.

FOOTLIGHT PARADE (1933). Glittering musical comedy about the multiple predicaments of a talented producer who stages theatrical prologues for movie theaters; with Cagney as Chester Kent, the beleaguered, resourceful impresario. *Dir:* Lloyd Bacon, Busby Berkeley. *Sc:* Manuel Seff, James Seymour. *Dialogue dir:* William Keighley. *Ph:* George Barnes. *Art dir:* Anton Grot, Jack Okey. *Ed:* George Amy. *Mus dir:* Leo F. Forbstein. *Cost:* Milo Anderson. *Makeup:* Perc Westmore. *Dir, mus numbers:* Busby Berkeley. *Songs:* "By A Waterfall," "Ah, the Moon Is Here," "Sittin' on a Backyard Fence" by Sammy Fain, Irving Kahal; "Shanghai Lil," "Honeymoon Hotel" by Harry Warren, Al Dubin. *Cast:* Joan Blondell (Nan Prescott), Ruby Keeler (Bea Thorn), Dick Powell (Scotty Blair), Guy Kibbee (Silas Gould), Ruth Donnelly (Harriet Bowers Gould), Claire Dodd (Vivian Rich), Hugh Herbert (Charlie Bowers), Frank McHugh (Francis), Arthur Hohl (Al Frazer), Gordon Westcott (Harry Thompson), Renee Whitney (Cynthia Kent), Philip Faversham (Joe Farrington), Juliet Ware (Miss Smythe), Herman Bing (Fralick the music director), Paul Porcasi (George Appolinaris), William Granger (doorman), Charles C. Wilson (cop), Barbara Rogers (Gracie), Billy Taft (specialty dancer), Marjean Rogers, Pat Wing, Donna Mae Roberts (chorus girls), Dave O'Brien (chorus boy), George Chandler (drugstore attendant), Hobart Cavanaugh (title thinker-upper), William V. Mong (auditor), Lee Moran (Mac the dance director), Billy Barty (mouse in "Sittin' on A Backyard Fence" number), Harry Seymour (desk clerk in "Honeymoon Hotel" number), Sam McDaniel (porter), Billy Barty (little boy), Fred Kelsey (house detective), Jimmy Conlin (uncle), Roger Gray (sailor–pal in "Shanghai Lil" number), John Garfield (sailor behind table), Duke York (sailor on table), Harry Seymour (Joe the assistant dance director), and Donna La Barr, Marlo Dwyer (chorus girls). *Prod:* Warner Bros. 104 min.

LADY KILLER (1933). Offbeat satire–drama about a lowly movie usher turned con artist turned Hollywood star; with Cagney as Dan Quigley, filmdom's ex-"finger man" who

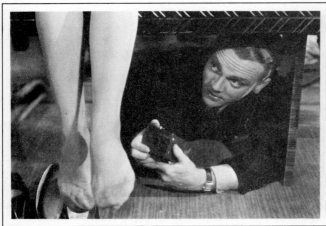

Cagney as the "picture snatcher." (WCTR)

With Ruby Keeler (at left), Joan Blondell, Frank McHugh, and Dick Powell in FOOTLIGHT PARADE. (WCTR)

cannot shake his shady past. *Dir:* Roy Del Ruth. *Sc:* Ben Markson, Lillie Hayward; based on *THE FINGER MAN* by Rosalind Keating Shaffer. *Ph:* Tony Gaudio. *Art dir:* Robert Haas. *Ed:* George Amy. *Mus cond:* Leo F. Forbstein. *Cost:* Orry-Kelly. *Makeup:* Perc Westmore. *Assist dir:* Chuck Hansen. *Cast:* Mae Clarke (Myra Gale), Leslie Fenton (Duke), Margaret Lindsay (Lois Underwood), Henry O'Neill (Ramick), Willard Robertson (Conroy), Douglas Cosgrove (Jones), Raymond Hatton (Pete), Russell Hopton (Smiley), William Davidson (Williams), Marjorie Gateson (Mrs. Wilbur Marley), Robert Elliott (Brannigan), John Marston (Kendall), Douglass Dumbrille (Spade Maddock), George Chandler (Thompson), George Blackwood (the escort), Jack Don Wong (oriental), Frank Sheridan (Los Angeles police chief), Edwin Maxwell (Jeffries the theater manager), Phil Tead (Usher Sargeant Seymour), Dewey Robinson (movie fan), H. C. Bradley (man with purse), Harry Holman (J. B. Roland), Harry Beresford (Dr. Crane), Olaf Hytten (butler), Harry Strong (ambulance attendant), Al Hill (casino cashier), Bud Flanagan/Dennis O'Keefe (man in casino), James Burke (Hand-Out), Robert Homans (jailer), Clarence Wilson (lawyer), Sam McDaniel (porter), Spencer Charters (Los Angeles cop), Herman Bing (Western director), Harold Waldridge (letter handler), Luis Alberni (director), Ray Cooke (property man), and Sam Ash (hood). *Prod:* Warner Bros. 76 min. The working title of the film was *The Finger Man*.

JIMMY THE GENT (1934). Breakneck-paced screwball comedy about the rivalry between two pseudo-respectable firms that specialize in tracing missing heirs to lost fortunes; with Cagney as Jimmy Corrigan, the more "ungentlemanly" of the two shysters. *Dir:* Michael Curtiz. *Sc:* Bertram Milhauser; based on an original story by Laird Doyle and Ray Nazarro. *Dialogue dir:* Daniel Reed. *Ph:* Ira Morgan. *Art dir:* Esdras Hartley. *Ed:* Thomas Richards. *Mus cond:* Leo F. Forbstein. *Cost:* Orry-Kelly. *Makeup:* Perc Westmore. *Cast:* Bette Davis (Joan Martin), Alice White (Mabel), Allen Jenkins (Louie), Arthur Hohl (Joe Rector/Monty Barton), Alan Dinehart (James J. Wallingham), Philip Reed (Ronnie Gatston), Hobart Cavanaugh (The Impostor), Mayo Methot (Gladys Farrell), Ralf Harolde (Hendrickson), Joseph Sawyer (Mike), Philip Faversham (Blair), Nora Lane (Posy Barton), Joseph Crehan (judge), Robert Warwick (civil judge), Merna Kennedy (Jitters), Renee Whitney (Bessie), Monica Bannister (tea assistant), Don Douglas (man drinking tea), Bud Flanagan/Dennis O'Keefe (Chester Coote), Leonard Mudie (man in flower shop), Harry Holman (justice of the peace), Camille Rovelle (file clerk), Stanley Mack (Pete), Tom Costello (Grant), Ben Hendricks (Ferris), Billy West (Halley), Eddie Shubert (Tim), Lee Moran (Stew), Harry Wallace (Eddie), Robert Homans (Irish cop), Milton Kibbee (ambulance driver), Howard Hickman (doctor), Eula Guy (nurse), Juliet Ware (Viola), Rickey Newell (blonde), Lorena Layson (brunette), Dick French (second young man), Jay Eaton (third young man), Harold Entwistle (Reverend Amiel Bottsford), Charles Hickman (bailiff), Leonard Mudie (ticket clerk, steamship), Olaf Hytten (steward), Vesey O'Davoren (second steward), Lester Dorr (Chalmers), and Pat Wing (secretary). *Prod:* Warner Bros. 67 min. The working title of the film was *The Heir Chaser*, then *Always a Gent*, then *Blondes and Bonds*.

HE WAS HER MAN (1934). Earnest melodrama about the precarious romance between a gangster on the lam from his rivals and an ex-prostitute en route to a mail-order marriage; with Cagney as Flicker Hayes, the doomed ex-safecracker. *Dir:* Lloyd Bacon. *Sc:* Tom Buckingham, Niven Busch; based on a story by Robert Lord. *Ph:* George Barnes. *Art dir:* Anton Grot. *Ed:* George Amy. *Mus dir:* Leo F. Forbstein. *Cost:* Orry-Kelly. *Makeup:* Perc Westmore. *Song:* "My Only Romance" by Sidney Mitchell, Lew Pollack. *Cast:* Joan Blondell (Rose Lawrence), Victor Jory (Nick Gardella), Frank Craven (Pop Sims), Harold Huber (J. C. Ward), Russell Hopton (Monk), Ralf Harolde (Red Deering), Sarah Padden (Mrs. Gardella), J. M. (John) Qualen (Dutch), Bradley Page (Dan Curly), Samuel S. Hinds

(Gassy), George Chandler (waiter), James Eagles (Whitey) Gino Corrado (fisherman), and with George Pat Collins. *Prod:* Warner Bros. 67 min. The working title of the film was *Without Honor*, then *Without Glory*.

HERE COMES THE NAVY (1934). Brisk comedy–drama about the hostility between a brash sailor and his superior officer; with Cagney as Seaman Chesty O'Connor, the misfit and latent hero. *Dir:* Lloyd Bacon. *Sc:* Ben Markson, Earl Baldwin; based on a story by Markson. *Ph:* Arthur Edeson. *Art dir:* Esdras Hartley. *Ed:* George Amy. *Mus dir:* Leo F. Forbstein. *Cost:* Orry-Kelly. *Makeup:* Perc Westmore. *Tech adv:* Commander Herbert A. Jones. *Song:* "Hey, Sailor!" by Irving Kahal, Sammy Fain. *Cast:* Pat O'Brien (Biff Martin), Gloria Stuart (Dorothy Martin), Frank McHugh (Droopy), Dorothy Tree (Gladys), Robert Barrat (Commander Denny), Willard Robertson (lieutenant commander), Guinn Williams (floor manager), Maude Eburne (Droopy's ma), Martha Merrill (first girl), Lorena Layson (second girl), Ida Darling (aunt), Henry Otho (riveter), Pauline True (hat check girl), Sam McDaniel (porter), Frank LaRue (foreman), Joseph Crehan (recruiting officer), James Burtis (chief petty officer), Edward Chandler (supply sergeant), Leo White (professor), Niles Welch (officer), Fred "Snowflake" Toone (sailor), Eddie Shubert (skipper), George Irving (admiral), Howard Hickman (captain), Edward Earle (Navy chaplain), Gordon (Bill) Elliott (Bit), Nick Copeland (workman), John Swor (attendant), Eddie Acuff (Marine orderly), Chuck Hamilton (hood at dance), and Eddie Fetherstone (sailor). *Prod:* Warner Bros. 86 min. The working title of the film was *Hey, Sailor!* First of eight Cagney–O'Brien pictures, the film was nominated for an Academy Award as Best Picture of 1934.

THE ST. LOUIS KID [GB: *A PERFECT WEEKEND*] (1934). Disappointing, topical comedy–drama about a truckdriver on the St. Louis to Chicago milk run who becomes embroiled in a dairymen's strike; with Cagney as Eddie Kennedy, the scab trucker. *Dir:* Ray Enright. *Sc:* Warren Duff, Seton I. Miller; based on a story by Frederick Hazlitt Brennan. *Ph:* Sid Hickox. *Dialogue dir:* Stanley Logan. *Art dir:* Jack Okey. *Ed:* Clarence Kolster. *Mus dir:* Leo F. Forbstein. *Cost:* Orry-Kelly. *Makeup:* Perc Westmore. *Cast:* Patricia Ellis (Ann Reid), Allen Jenkins (Buck Willetts), Robert Barrat (Farmer Benson), Hobart Cavanaugh (Richardson), Spencer Charters (Merseldopp), Addison Richards (Brown), Dorothy Dare (Gracie), Arthur Aylesworth (Judge Jones), Charles Wilson (Harris), William Davidson (Joe Hunter), Harry Woods (Louie), Gertrude Short (the girlfriend), Eddie Shubert (Pete), Russell Hicks (Gorman), Guy Usher (sergeant), Cliff Saum, Bruce Mitchell (cops), Wilfred Lucas (policeman), Rosalie Roy (girl), Mary Russell (office girl), Ben Hendricks (motor cop), Harry Tyler (Mike), Milton Kibbee (paymaster), Tom Wilson (cook), Alice Marr, Victoria Vinton (secretaries), Lee Phelps (farmer), Louise Seidel (girl in car), Mary Treen (giddy girl), Nan Grey (first girl), Virginia Grey (second girl), Martha Merrill (third girl), Charles B. Middleton (sheriff), Douglas Cosgrove (prosecutor), Monte Vandergrift (first deputy), Jack Cheatham (second deputy), Stanley Mack (driver), Grover Liggen (attendant), Frank Bull (broadcast officer), Wade Boteler (sergeant), Frank Fanning (policeman), Gene Strong (second policeman), Edna Bennett (Flora), Clay Clement (man), James Burtis (detective), and with Eddie Fetherstone, Joan Barclay. *Prod:* Warner Bros. 67 min.

DEVIL DOGS OF THE AIR (1935). Flimsy variation on *Here Comes the Navy*, emphasizing romantic rivalry between two boyhood chums, one a Marine Flying Corps lieutenant and the other a roughneck aviator; with Cagney as Tommy O'Toole, ace stunt flyer. *Dir:* Lloyd Bacon. *Sc:* Malcolm Stuart Boylan, Earl Baldwin; based on the story "Air Devils" by John Monk Saunders. *Ph:* Arthur Edeson. *Art dir:* Arthur J. Kooken. *Ed:* William Clemens. *Mus dir:* Leo F. Forbstein. *Cost:* Orry-Kelly. *Makeup:* Perc Westmore. *Tech adv:* Major Ralph J. Mitchell. *Assist dir:* Eric Stacey. *Cast:* Pat O'Brien (Lieutenant William Brannigan),

Margaret Lindsay (Betty Roberts), Frank McHugh (Crash Kelly), Helen Lowell (Ma Roberts), John Arledge (Mac), Robert Barrat (commandant), Russell Hicks (captain), William B. Davidson (adjutant), Ward Bond (senior instructor), Samuel S. Hinds (fleet commander), Harry Seymour (officer), Bill Beggs (second officer), Bob Spencer (mate), Newton House, Ralph Nye (officers), Selmer Jackson (medical officer), Bud Flanagan/ Dennis O'Keefe (student), Gordon (Bill) Elliott (instructor), Don Turner (first student), Dick French (second student), Charles Sherlock (third student), Carlyle Blackwell, Jr. (messenger), Martha Merrill (girl), David Newell (Lieutenant Brown), Olive Jones (Mrs. Brown), Helen Flint (Mrs. Johnson), and Joseph Crehan (communications officer). *Prod:* Cosmopolitan Productions for Warner Bros. 86 min. Working titles of the film included *Air Devils*, *All Good Soldiers Have Wings*, *Flying Leathernecks*, and *The Flying Marines*. The film was reissued nationally in 1941.

G-MEN (1935). Action-packed saga about the early exploits of the Federal Bureau of Investigation (FBI); with Cagney as James "Brick" Davis, an attorney who joins the FBI after a college buddy turned special agent is murdered by mobsters. *Dir:* William Keighley. *Sc:* Seton I. Miller; based on *Public Enemy No. 1* by Gregory Rogers. *Ph:* Sol Polito. *Art dir:* John J. Hughes. *Ed:* Jack Killifer. *Mus dir:* Leo F. Forbstein. *Cost:* Orry-Kelly. *Makeup:* Perc Westmore. *Assist dir:* William McGann. *Dance dir:* Bobby Connolly. *Tech adv:* Frank Gompert. *Song:* "You Bother Me an Awful Lot" by Sammy Fain, Irving Kahal. *Cast:* Ann Dvorak (Jean Morgan), Margaret Lindsay (Kay McCord), Robert Armstrong (Jeff McCord), Barton MacLane (Brad Collins), Lloyd Nolan (Hugh Farrell), William Harrigan (McKay), Edward Pawley (Danny Leggett), Russell Hopton (Gerard), Noel Madison (Durfee), Regis Toomey (Eddie Buchanan), Addison Richards (Bruce J. Gregory), Harold Huber (Venke), Raymond Hatton (the man), Monte Blue (analyst), Mary Treen (Gregory's secretary), Adrian Morris (accomplice), Edwin Maxwell (Joseph Kratz), Emmett Vogan (Bill the ballistics expert), James Flavin (agent), Stanley Blystone, Pat Flaherty (cops), James T. Mack (agent), Jonathan Hale (congressman), Ed Keane (bank cashier), Charles Sherlock (short man), Wheeler Oakman (henchman at lodge), Eddie Dunn (police broadcaster), Gordon (Bill) Elliott (interne), Perry Ivins (doctor at store), Frank Marlowe (hood shot at lodge), Gertrude Short (Collins' moll), Marie Astaire

...an Indian "extra" with Margaret Lindsay in LADY KILLER.   *With Allen Jenkins in Michael Curtiz's JIMMY THE GENT.*

(Gerard's moll), Florence Dudley (Durfee's moll), Frances Morris (moll), Al Hill (hood), Huey White (gangster), Glen Cavender (headwaiter), John Impolito (Tony), Bruce Mitchell (sergeant), Monte Vandergrift (deputy sheriff), Frank Shannon (chief), Frank Bull (announcer), Martha Merrill (nurse), Gene Morgan (lounger), Joseph DeStefani (J. E. Glattner the florist), George Daly, Ward Bond (machine gunners), Tom Wilson (prison guard), Henry Hall (police driver), Lee Phelps (McCord's aide), Marc Lawrence (hood at lodge), and Brooks Benedict (man). *Prod:* Warner Bros. 85 min. The working title of the film was *The Farrell Case.* The film was re-released in 1949 on the 25th anniversary of the founding of the FBI, with a special prologue featuring David Brian as the Chief and Douglas Kennedy as an FBI agent.

THE IRISH IN US (1935). Amiable hokum about three contrary sons in a close-knit Irish family; with Cagney as Danny O'Hara, the wayward son and manager of a long-shot prizefighter. *Dir:* Lloyd Bacon. *Sc:* Earl Baldwin; based on a story by Frank Orsatti. *Ph:* George Barnes. *Art dir:* Esdras Hartley. *Ed:* James Gibbons. *Mus dir:* Leo F. Forbstein. *Cost:* Orry-Kelly. *Makeup:* Perc Westmore. *Assist dir:* Jack Sullivan. *Unit mgr:* Bob Fellows. *Cast:* Pat O'Brien (Pat O'Hara), Olivia De Havilland (Lucille Jackson), Frank McHugh (Mike O'Hara), Allen Jenkins (Car-Barn McCarthy), Mary Gordon (Ma O'Hara), J. Farrell MacDonald (Captain Jackson), Thomas Jackson (Doc Mullins), Harvey Perry (Joe Delancy), Bess Flowers (lady in ring), Mabel Colcord (neighbor), Edward Keane (doctor), Herb Haywood (cook), Lucille Collins (girl), Harry Seymour (announcer), Sailor Vincent (Chick), Mushy Callahan (referee), Jack McHugh (messenger boy), and Edward Gargan, Huntly Gordon, Emmett Vogan, Will Stanton (men). *Prod:* Warner Bros. 84 min.

A MIDSUMMER NIGHT'S DREAM (1935). Lavish adaptation of William Shakespeare's classic comedy; with Cagney as Bottom. *Dir:* Max Reinhardt, William Dieterle. *Prod sup:* Henry Blanke. *Sc:* Charles Kenyon, Mary McCall, Jr.; based on the play by William Shakespeare. *Ph:* Hal Mohr. *Art dir:* Anton Grot. *Ed:* Ralph Dawson. *Dialogue dir:* Stanley Logan. *Sound:* Major Nathan Levison. *Mus score:* Felix Mendelssohn. *Mus dir:* Leo F. Forbstein. *Mus arr:* Erich Wolfgang Korngold. *Cost:* Max Ree. *Choreog:* Bronislava Nijinska, Nini Theilade. *Makeup:* Perc Westmore. *Spec ph eff:* Fred Jackman, Byron Haskin, H. F. Koenekamp. *Assist dir:* Sherry Shourds. *Cast:* Dick Powell (Lysander), Joe E. Brown (Flute), Jean Muir (Helena), Hugh Herbert (Snout), Ian Hunter (Theseus), Frank McHugh (Quince), Victor Jory (Oberon), Olivia De Havilland (Hermia), Ross Alexander (Demetrius), Grant Mitchell (Egeus), Nini Theilade (first fairy/prima ballerina), Verree Teasdale (Hippolyta, Queen of Amazons), Anita Louise (Titania), Mickey Rooney (Puck), Dewey Robinson (Snug), Hobart Cavanaugh (Philostrate), Otis Harlan (Starveling), Arthur Treacher (Ninny's tomb), Katherine Frey (Pease-Blossom, a fairy), Helen Westcott (Cobweb), Fred Sale (Moth) and Billy Barty (Mustard-Seed). *Prod:* Warner Bros. 132 min. The film's Academy Award nominations included Best Editing (Ralph Dawson), Best Cinematography (Hal Mohr), and Best Picture of 1935.

FRISCO KID (1935). Fanciful but uninspired rags-to-riches melodrama about a rowdy sailor who rises to power among the coarse citizenry of San Francisco's Barbary Coast during the Gay Nineties; with Cagney as Bat Morgan, the tough seaman. *Dir:* Lloyd Bacon. *Sc:* Warren Duff, Seton I. Miller; based on an original story by Duff and Miller. *Ph:* Sol Polito. *Art dir:* John Hughes. *Ed:* Owen Marks. *Mus dir:* Leo F. Forbstein. *Cost:* Orry-Kelly. *Makeup:* Perc Westmore. *Sound:* James Thompson. *Cast:* Margaret Lindsay (Jean Barrat), Ricardo Cortez (Paul Morra), Lily Damita (Bella Morra), Donald Woods (Charles Ford), Barton MacLane (Spider Burke), George E. Stone (Solly), Addison Richards (William T. Coleman), Joseph King (James Daley), Robert McWade (Judge Crawford), Joseph Crehan (McClanahan), Robert Strange (Graber), Joseph Sawyer (Slugs

Crippen), Fred Kohler (Shanghai Duck), Edward McWade (Tupper), Claudia Coleman (Jumping Whale), John Wray (The Weasel), Ivar McFadden (first lookout), Lee Phelps (second lookout), William Wagner (evangelist), Don Barclay (drunk), Jack Curtis (captain), Walter Long (miner), James Farley (man), Milton Kibbee (shop man), Harry Seymour (salesman), Claire Sinclair (madame), Alan Davis (young drunk), Karl Hackett (dealer), Wilfred Lucas (first policeman), John T. (Jack) Dillon (second policeman), Edward Mortimer (first man), William Holmes (second man), Don Downen (usher), Mrs. Wilfred North (Mrs. Crawford), Charles Middleton (speaker), Joe Smith Marba (man), Landers Stevens (doctor), Frank Sheridan (Mulligan), J. C. Morton, Harry Tenbrook (man), Lew Harvey (dealer), Eddie Sturgis (Rat Face), William Desmond (captain/vigilante), Jessie Perry (maid), Edward Keane, Edward Le Saint (contractors), Robert Dudley, Dick Rush (vigilante leaders), John Elliott (doctor), and with Helene Chadwick, Bill Dale, Dick Kerr, Alice Lake, Vera Stedman, and Jane Tallent. *Prod:* Warner Bros. 77 min.

CEILING ZERO (1935). Taut aviation drama about civilian flyers who risk dangerous "ceiling-zero" weather on their assignments; with Cagney as Dizzy Davis, the woman-chasing pilot whose amorous entanglements lead to the death of a fellow aviator. *Dir:* Howard Hawks. *Prod:* Harry Joe Brown. *Sc:* Frank Wead; based on the play *Ceiling Zero* by Wead. *Ph:* Arthur Edeson. *Art dir:* John Hughes. *Ed:* William Holmes. *Mus dir:* Leo F. Forbstein. *Cost:* Orry-Kelly. *Makeup:* Perc Westmore. *Assist dir:* Lee Selander. *Unit mgr:* Bob Fellows. *Cast:* Pat O'Brien (Jack Lee), June Travis (Tommy Thomas), Stuart Erwin (Texas Clark), Henry Wadsworth (Tay Lawson), Isabel Jewell (Lou Clark), Barton Mac-Lane (Al Stone), Martha Tibbetts (Mary Lee), Craig Reynolds (Joe Allen), James H. Bush (Buzz Gordon), Robert Light (Les Bogan), Addison Richards (Fred Adams), Carlyle Moore, Jr. (Eddie Payson), Richard Purcell (Smiley Johnson), Gordon (Bill) Elliott (transportation agent), Pat West (Baldy Wright), Edward Gargan (Doc Wilson), Garry Owen (Mike Owens), Mathilde Comont (Mama Gini), Carol Hughes (Birdie), Frank Tomick, Paul Mantz (stunt fliers), Jimmy Aye, Howard Allen, Mike Lally, Harold Miller (pilots), Jerry Jerome (mechanic), Helene McAdoo, Gay Sheridan, Mary Lou Dix, Louise Seidel, Helen Erickson (hostesses), Don Wayson, Dick Cherney, Jimmie Barnes, Frank McDonald (office workers), J. K. Kane (teletype operator), Jayne Manners (tall girl), and Maryon Curtiz and Margaret Perry (girls). *Prod:* Cosmopolitan Productions for Warner Bros. 95 min.

GREAT GUY [GB: *PLUCK OF THE IRISH*] (1936) Nifty comedy–drama about a deputy's crusade to combat fraudulent market practices in a metropolitan bureau of weights and measures; with Cagney as Johnny Cave, the intrepid reformer. *Dir:* John G. Blystone. *Prod:* Douglas MacLean. *Sc:* Henry McCarty, Henry Johnson, James Edward Grant, Harry Ruskin. *Add dialogue:* Horace McCoy; based on "The Johnny Cave Stories" by James Edward Grant. *Ph:* Jack McKenzie. *Art dir:* Ben Carre. *Ed:* Russell Schoengarth. *Sound:* Harold Bumbaugh. *Mus dir:* Merlin Skiles. *Cost:* Dorothy Beal. *Assist dir:* John Sherwood. *Presented by:* Edward L. Alperson. *Cast:* Mae Clarke (Janet Henry), James Burke (Pat Haley), Edward Brophy (Pete Reilly), Henry Kolker (Conning), Bernadene Hayes (Hazel Scott), Edward J. McNamara (Captain Pat Hanlon), Robert Gleckler (Cavanaugh), Joe Sawyer (Joe Burton), Ed Gargan (Al), Matty Fain (Tim), Mary Gordon (Mrs. Ogilvie), Wallis Clark (Joel Green), Douglas Wood (the mayor), Jeffrey Sayre (clerk), Eddy Chandler (meat clerk), Henry Roquemore (store manager), Murdock MacQuarrie (client), Kate Price (woman at accident), Frank O'Connor (detective), Arthur Hoyt (furniture salesman), Jack Pennick (truck driver), Lynton Brent (reporter), John Dilson (city editor), Bud Geary, Dennis O'Keefe (guests), Robert Lowery (Parker), Bobby Barber (grocery clerk), Gertrude Green (nurse), Ethelreda Leopold (Burton's girl friend), Bruce Mitchell (cop at accident), James Ford, Frank Mills, Ben Hendricks, Jr. (party guests), Kernan Cripps (deputy), Bill O'Brien (second meat clerk), Lester Dorr (chauffeur), Harry Tenbrook (receiving clerk), Lee Shumway (Mike the cop), and with Gertrude Astor, Vera Steadman, Mildred Harris, Bert Kalmar, Jr., and Walter D. Clarke, Jr. *Prod:* Grand National. 75 min.

SOMETHING TO SING ABOUT (1937). Likeable if threadbare musical comedy about a Manhattan bandleader who becomes a Hollywood movie star; with Cagney as Terry Rooney, the singing–dancing bandleader. *Dir:* Victor Schertzinger. *Prod:* Zion Myers. *Sc:* Austin Parker; based on a story by Schertzinger. *Ph:* John Stumar. *Art dir:* Robert Lee, Paul Murphy. *Ed:* Gene Milford. *Mus dir:* C. Bakaleinkoff. *Dance dir:* Harland Dixon. *Arrangements:* Myrl Alderman. *Assist dir:* John Sherwood. *Prod mgr:* Harold Lewis. *Unit mgr:* Gaston Glass. *Still ph:* Tad A. Gillum. *Songs:* "Right or Wrong," "Any Old Love," "Something to Sing About," "Loving You," "Out of the Blue" by Schertzinger. *Cast:* Evelyn Daw (Rita Wyatt), William Frawley (Hank Meyers), Mona Barrie (Stephanie Hajos), Gene Lockhart (Bennett O. Regan), James Newill (orchestra soloist), Harry Barris (Pinky), Candy Candido (Candy), Cully Richards (soloist), William B. Davidson (cafe manager), Richard Tucker (Blaine), Marek Windheim (Farney), Dwight Frye (Easton), John Arthur (Daviani), Philip Ahn (Ito), Kathleen Lockhart (Miss Robbins), Kenneth Harlan (transportation manager), Herbert Rawlinson (studio attorney), Ernest Wood (Edward Burns), Chuck Collins (man Terry fights), Duke Green (other man), Harland Dixon, Johnny Boyle, Johnny (Skins) Miller, Pat Moran, Joe Bennett, Buck Mack, Eddie Allen (dancers), Bill Carey (singer), The Vagabonds (specialty), Elinore Welz, Eleanor Prentiss (girls), Pinkie and Pal (Arthur Nelson's Fighting Cats), Frank Mills (cabby), Duke Green (stuntman), Larry Steers (studio official), John (Skins) Miller (sailor in drag), Eddie Kane (San Francisco theater manager), Edward Hearn (studio guard), Dottie Messmer, Virginia Lee Irwin, Dolly Waldorf (Three Shades of Blue), Robert McKenzie (ship's captain), Alphonse Martel (waiter), and with Bo Peep Karlin and Paul McLarand. *Prod:* Grand National. 84 min. The film was reissued in 1947 as *Battling Hoofer* by Screencraft Pictures.

Cagney with actor Chester Morris and screenwriter Charles Bracket in the 1930s.

With temptress Mona Barrie in SOMETHING TO SING ABOUT. (WCTR)

BOY MEETS GIRL (1938). Raucous satire about two Hollywood scenarists who scheme to make a star of a baby named "Happy"; with Cagney as Robert Law, one half of the zany screenwriting team. *Dir:* Lloyd Bacon. *Prod:* George Abbott. *Sc:* Bella Spewack, Sam Spewack; based on a play by the Spewacks. *Ph:* Sol Polito. *Art dir:* Esdras Hartley. *Ed:* William Holmes. *Sound:* Dolph Thomas. *Mus dir:* Leo F. Forbstein. *Cost:* Milo Anderson. *Makeup:* Perc Westmore. *Song:* "With A Pain in My Heart" by Jack Scholl, M. K. Jerome. *Cast:* Pat O'Brien (J. C. Benson), Marie Wilson (Susie), Ralph Bellamy (C. Elliott Friday), Frank McHugh (Rossetti), Dick Foran (Larry Toms), Bruce Lester (Rodney Bevan), Ronald Reagan (announcer), Paul Clark (Happy), Penny Singleton (Peggy), Dennie Moore (Miss Crews), Harry Seymour, Bert Hanlon (songwriters), James Stephenson (Major Thompson), Pierre Watkin (B. K.), John Ridgely (cutter), George Hickman (office boy), Cliff Saum (Smitty), Carole Landis (commissary cashier), Curt Bois (dance director), Otto Fries (Olaf), John Harron (extra), Hal K. Dawson (wardrobe attendant), Dorothy Vaughan (nurse), Bert Howard (director), James Nolan (young man), Bill Telaak (Bruiser), Vera Lewis (cleaning woman), Jan Holm, Rosella Towne, Loi Cheaney (nurses), Janet Shaw (Los Angeles operator), Nanette Lafayette (Paris operator), Peggy Moran (New York operator), Eddy Conrad (Jascha), and with Sidney Bracy, William Haade, Clem Bevans. *Prod:* Warner Bros. 80 min.

ANGELS WITH DIRTY FACES (1938). Rousing vintage drama about the return of a notorious gangster to his childhood neighborhood; with Cagney as Rocky Sullivan, a hoodlum who is the idol of a local youth gang and pals with the parish priest. *Dir:* Michael Curtiz. *Prod:* Sam Bischoff. *Sc:* John Wexley, Warren Duff; based on an original story by Rowland Brown. *Ph:* Sol Polito. *Art dir:* Robert Haas. *Ed:* Owen Marks. *Sound:* Everett A. Brown. *Mus score:* Max Steiner. *Orchestrator:* Hugo Friedhofer. *Cost:* Orry-Kelly. *Dialogue dir:* Jo Graham. *Makeup:* Perc Westmore. *Assist dir:* Sherry Shourds. *Tech adv:* Father J. J. Devlin. *Song:* "Angels with Dirty Faces" by Fred Fisher, Maurice Spitalny. *Cast:* Pat O'Brien (Jerry Connelly), Humphrey Bogart (James Frazier), Ann Sheridan (Laury Martin), George Bancroft (MacKeefer), Billy Halop (Soapy), Bobby Jordan (Swing), Leo Gorcey (Bim), Bernard Punsley (Hunky), Gabriel Dell (Pasty), Huntz Hall (Crab), Frankie Burke (Rockie as a boy), William Tracy (Jerry as a boy), Marilyn Knowlden (Laury as a girl), Joe Downing (Steve), Adrian Morris (Blackie), Oscar O'Shea (Guard Kennedy), Edward Pawley (Guard Edwards), William Pawley (Bugs the gunman), John Hamilton (police captain), Earl Dwire (priest), Jack Perrin (death row guard), Mary Gordon (Mrs. Patrick), Vera Lewis (Soapy's mother), William Worthington (warden), James Farley (railroad yard watchman), Chuck Stubbs (Red), Eddie Syracuse (Maggione Boy), Robert Homans (policeman), Harris Berger (basketball captain), Harry Hayden (pharmacist), Dick Rich, Steven Darrell, Joe A. Devlin (gangsters), William Edmunds (Italian storekeeper), Charles Wilson (Buckley), Frank Cochlan, Jr., David Durant (boys in poolroom), Bill Cohee, Lavel Lund, Norman Wallace, Gary Carthew, Bibby Mayer (church basketball team), Belle Mitchell (Mrs. Maggione), Eddie Brian (newsboy), Billy McLain (janitor), Wilbur Mack (croupier), Poppy Wilde (girl at gaming table), George Offerman, Jr. (adult boy), Charles Trowbridge (Norton J. White), Ralph Sanford (city editor, press), Wilfred Lucas (police officer), Lane Chandler (guard), Elliott Sullivan (cop), and with Lottie Williams, George Mori, Dick Wessell, John Harron, Vince Lombardi, Al Hill, Thomas Jackson, and Jeffrey Sayre. *Prod:* Warner Bros. 97 min. The working title of the film was *Battle of City Hall*. The film was nominated for Academy Awards for Best Actor (Cagney) and Best Director (Curtiz). Cagney won the Best Actor award from the New York Film Critics for 1938.

THE OKLAHOMA KID (1939). Frivolous Western shoot-'em-up concerning outlaw rule in newly settled Oklahoma; with Cagney as Jim Kincaid, the "Oklahoma Kid," who fights to rid the territory of desperadoes and to clear his own name. *Dir:* Lloyd Bacon. *Assoc prod:* Samuel Bischoff. *Sc:* Warren Duff, Robert Buckner, Edward E. Paramore; based on an original story by Paramore and Wally Klein. *Ph:* James Wong Howe. *Art dir:* Esdras Hartley. *Ed:* Owen Marks. *Sound:* Stanley Jones. *Mus score:* Max Steiner. *Orchestrators:* Hugo Friedhofer, Adolph Deutsch, George Parrish, Murray Cutter. *Cost:* Orry-Kelly. *Makeup:* Perc Westmore. *Assist dir:* Dick Mayberry. *Tech adv:* Al Jennings. *Cast:* Humphrey Bogart (Whip McCord), Rosemary Lane (Jane Hardwick), Donald Crisp (Judge Hardwick), Harvey Stephens (Ned Kincaid), Hugh Sothern (John Kincaid), Charles Middleton (Alec Martin), Edward Pawley (Doolin), Ward Bond (Wes Handley), Lew Harvey (Curley), Trevor Bardette (Indian Jack Pasco), John Miljan (Ringo), Arthur Aylesworth (Judge Morgan), Irving Bacon (hotel clerk), Joe Devlin (Keely), Wade Boteler (Sheriff Abe Collins), Whizzer (Kincaid's horse), Ray Mayer (professor), Dan Wolheim (deputy), Bob Kortman (juryman), Tex Cooper (old man in bar), John Harron (secretary), Stuart Holmes (President Cleveland), Jeffrey Sayre (*Times* reporter), Frank Mayo (land agent), Jack Mower (mail clerk), Al Bridge (settler), Don Barclay (drunk), Horace Murphy, Robert Homans, George Lloyd (bartenders), Rosina Galli (Manuelita), George Regas (Pedro), Clem Bevans (postman), Soledad Jiminez (Indian woman), Ed Brady (foreman), Tom Chatterton (homesteader), Elliott Sullivan (henchman), and with Joe Kirkson, William Worthington, and Spencer Charters. *Prod:* Warner Bros. 85 min.

EACH DAWN I DIE (1939). Crackling drama about a falsely imprisoned newsman's fight to prove his innocence; with Cagney as Frank Ross, the journalist who becomes embittered by his jailhouse experience and allies himself with a "lifer." *Dir:* William Keighley. *Assoc prod:* David Lewis. *Sc:* Norman Reilly Raine, Warren Duff, Charles Perry; based on the novel by Jerome Odlum. *Ph:* Arthur Edeson. *Art dir:* Max Parker. *Ed:* Thomas Richards. *Sound:* E. A. Brown. *Mus score:* Max Steiner. *Mus dir:* Leo F. Forbstein. *Cost:* Howard Shoup. *Makeup:* Perc Westmore. *Assist dir:* Frank Heath. *Tech adv:* William Buckley. *Narrator:* John Conte. *Cast:* George Raft (Hood Stacey), Jane Bryan (Joyce Conover), George Bancroft (Warden John Armstrong), Maxie Rosenbloom (Fargo Red), Stanley Ridges (Mueller), Alan Baxter (Pole Cat Carlisle), Victor Jory (W. J. Grayce), John Wray (Pete Kassock), Edward Pawley (Dale), Willard Robertson (Lang), Emma Dunn (Mrs. Ross), Paul Hurst (Garsky), Louis Jean Heydt (Joe Lassiter), Joe Downing (Limpy Julien), Thurston Hall (D.A. Jesse Hanley), William Davidson (Bill Mason), Clay Clement (Stacey's attorney), Charles Trowbridge (judge), Harry Cording (Temple), John Harron (Lew Keller), John Ridgely (Jerry Poague), Selmer Jackson (Patterson), Robert Homans (Mac), Abner Biberman (Snake Edwards), Napoleon Simpson (Mose), Stuart Holmes (accident witness), Maris Wrixon (girl in car), Garland Smith, Arthur Gardner (men in car), James Flavin (policeman), Max Hoffman, Jr. (gate guard), Walter Miller (turnkey), Fred Graham (guard in cell), Wilfred Lucas (bailiff), Vera Lewis (jury woman), Emmett Vogan (prosecutor), Earl Dwire (Judge Crowder), Bob Perry (Bud), Al Hill (Johnny, a hood), Elliot Sullivan (convict), Chuch Hamilton (court officer), and with Nat Carr, Wedgewood Nowell, Frank Mayo, Dick Rich, Lee Phelps, Jack Wise, and Granville Bates. *Prod:* Warner Bros. 92 min.

THE ROARING TWENTIES (1939). Ambitious and compelling melodrama about the rise and fall of a bootlegging napoleon; with Cagney as Eddie Bartlett, a former garage mechanic whose Achilles' heel is a woman. *Dir:* Raoul Walsh. *Prod:* Hal B. Wallis. *Assoc prod:* Samuel Bischoff. *Sc:* Jerry Wald, Richard Macaulay, Robert Rossen; based on an original story by Mark Hellinger. *Dial dir:* Hugh Cummings. *Ph:* Ernie Haller. *Art dir:* Max Parker. *Ed:* Jack Killifer. *Sound:* Everett A. Brown. *Mus score:* Heinz Roemheld, Ray Heindorf. *Mus dir:* Leo F. Forbstein. *Orchestrator:* Ray Heindorf. *Cost:* Milo Anderson. *Makeup:* Perc Westmore. *Spec eff:* Byron Haskin, Edwin A. Dupar. *Assist dir:* Dick

Mayberry. *Script girl:* Virginia Moore. *Montages:* Don Siegel. *Songs:* "My Melancholy Baby" by Ernie Burnett, George A. Norton; "I'm Just Wild About Harry" by Eubie Blake, Nobel Sissle; "It Had To Be You" by Isham Jones, Gus Kahn; "In a Shanty in Old Shanty Town" by Jack Little, Joseph Young, John Siras. *Cast:* Priscilla Lane (Jean Sherman), Humphrey Bogart (George Hally), Jeffrey Lynn (Lloyd Hart), Gladys George (Panama Smith), Frank McHugh (Danny Green), Paul Kelly (Nick Brown), Elisabeth Risdon (Mrs. Sherman), Ed Keane (Pete Henderson), Joseph Sawyer (Sergeant Pete Jones), Abner Biberman (Lefty), George Humbert (Luigi the proprietor), Clay Clement (Bramfield the broker), Don Thaddeus Kerr (Bobby Hart), Ray Cooke (orderly), Vera Lewis (Mrs. Gray), Murray Alper (first mechanic), Dick Wessel (second mechanic), Joseph Crehan (Fletcher the foreman), Norman Willis (bootlegger), Robert Elliott (first officer), Eddy Chandler (second officer), John Hamilton (judge), Elliott Sullivan (man in jail), Pat O'Malley (jailer), Arthur Loft (proprietor of still), Al Hill, Raymond Bailey, Lew Harvey (ex-cons), Joe Devlin, Jeffrey Sayre (order-takers), Paul Phillips (Mike), George Meeker (Masters), Bert Hanlon (piano player), Jack Norton (drunk), Alan Bridge (captain), Fred Graham (henchman), James Blaine (doorman), Henry C. Bradley, Lottie Williams (couple in restaurant), John Deering (commentator), John Harron (soldier), Lee Phelps (bailiff), Nat Carr (waiter), Wade Boteler (policeman), Creighton Hale (customer), Ann Codee (saleswoman), Eddie Acuff, Milton Kibbee, John Ridgely (cab drivers), and with James Flavin, Oscar O'Shea, Frank Wilcox, The Jane Jones Trio, Harry Hollingsworth, Frank Mayo, Emory Parnell, Billy Wayne, Philip Morris, Maurice Costello, John St. Clair, and Max Wagner. *Prod:* Warner Bros. 104 min. The film was originally titled *THE WORLD MOVES ON*.

THE FIGHTING 69th (1940). Predictable comedy–drama about a coward in the ranks of the "Fighting Irish," New York's celebrated Irish regiment of the First World War; with Cagney as Jerry Plunkett, the "yellow" soldier. *Dir:* William Keighley. *Prod:* Jack L. Warner. *Exec prod:* Hal B. Wallis. *Assoc prod:* Louis I. Edelman. *Sc:* Norman Reilly Raine, Fred Niblo, Jr., Dean Franklin. *Ph:* Tony Gaudio. *Art dir:* Ted Smith. *Ed:* Owen Marks. *Sound:* Charles Lang. *Mus score:* Adolph Deutsch. *Orchestrator:* Hugo Friedhofer. *Mus dir:* Leo F. Forbstein. *Makeup:* Perc Westmore. *Spec eff:* Byron Haskin, Rex Wimpy. *Assist dir:* Frank Heath. *Tech advs:* Captain John T. Prout, Mark White. *Cast:* Pat O'Brien (Father Duffy), George Brent (Wild Bill Donovan), Jeffrey Lynn (Joyce Kilmer), Alan Hale (Sergeant Big Mike Wynn), Frank McHugh ("Crepe Hanger" Burke), Dennis Morgan (Lieutenant Ames), Dick Foran (Lieutenant Long John Wynn), William Lundigan (Timmy Wynn), Guinn "Big Boy" Williams (Paddy Dolan), Henry O'Neill (the colonel), John Litel (Captain Mangan), Sammy Cohen (Mike Murphy), Harvey Stephens (Major Anderson), DeWolfe (William) Hopper (Private Turner), Tom Dugan (Private McManus), George Reeves (Jack O'Keefe), John Ridgely (Moran), Charles Trowbridge (Chaplain Holmes), Frank Wilcox (Lieutenant Norman), Herbert Anderson (Casey), J. Anthony Hughes (Healey), Frank Mayo (Captain Bootz), John Harron (Carroll), George Kilgen (Ryan), Richard Clayton (Tierney), Edward Dew (Regan), Wilfred Lucas, Emmett Vogan (doctors), Frank Sully (sergeant), Joseph Crehan (doctor), James Flavin (supply sergeant), Frank Coghlan, Jr. (Jimmy), George O'Hanlon (Eddie), Jack Perrin (major), Trevor Bardette, John Arledge, Frank Melton, Edmund Glover (Alabama men), Edgar Edwards (engineer officer), Frank Faylen (engineer sergeant), Ralph Dunn (medical captain), Arno Frey, Roland Varno (German officers), Robert Layne Ireland (Hefferman), Elmo Murray (O'Brien), Jacques Lory (waiter), Jack Boyle, Jr. (Chuck), and with Creighton Hale, Benny Rubin, Eddie Acuff, Jack Mower, Nat Carr, and Jack Wise. *Prod:* Warner Bros. 90 min.

TORRID ZONE (1940). Delightfully absurd comedy–drama of romantic intrigue and pseudo-revolutionary banditry set on a Central American banana plantation; with Cagney as Nick Butler, the banana plantation trouble-shooter, who vies with his friend, the estate manager, for the affections of a footloose torch singer. *Dir:* William Keighley. *Prod:* Mark Hellinger. *Sc:* Richard Macaulay, Jerry Wald. *Ph:* James Wong Howe. *Art dir:* Ted Smith. *Set dec:* Edward Thorne. *Ed:* Jack Killifer. *Sound:* Oliver S. Garretson. *Mus score:* Adolph Deutsch. *Mus dir:* Leo F. Forbstein. *Cost:* Howard Shoup. *Makeup:* Perc Westmore. *Spec eff:* Byron Haskin, H. F. Koenekamp. *Tech adv:* John Mari. *Song:* "Mi Caballero" by M. K. Jerome, Jack Scholl. *Cast:* Pat O'Brien (Steve Case), Ann Sheridan (Lee Donley), Andy Devine (Wally Davis), Helen Vinson (Gloria Anderson), Jerome Cowan (Bob Anderson), George Tobias (Rosario), George Reeves (Sancho), Victor Kilian (Carlos), Frank Puglia (Rodriquez), John Ridgely (Gardner), Grady Sutton (Sam), Paul Porcasi (Garcia), Frank Yaconelli (Lopez), Dick Boteler (Hernandez), Frank Mayo (Shaffer), Jack Mower (McNama), Paul Hurst (Daniels), George Regas (sergeant of police), Elvira Sanchez (Rita), George Humbert (hotel manager), Trevor Bardette (first policeman), Ernesto Piedra (second policeman), Manuel Lopez (Chico), Tony Paton (Charley), and with Max Blum, Betty Sanko, Don Orlando, Victor Sabuni, Paul Renay, and Joe Molina. *Prod:* Warner Bros. 88 min.

CITY FOR CONQUEST (1941). Poignant, poetical boxing melodrama about a likeable salt-of-the-earth prizefighter who is blinded in the ring; with Cagney as Danny Kenny, the sweet-natured one-time trucker who is urged on by his sweetheart's ambitions and who flirts with tragedy in the ring so his musical kid brother can compose a "symphony of a city." *Dir:* Anatole Litvak. *Assoc prod:* William Cagney. *Sc:* John Wexley; based on the novel *City for Conquest* by Aben Kandel. *Phs:* Sol Polito, James Wong Howe. *Dialogue dir:* Irving Rapper. *Art dir:* Robert Haas. *Ed:* William Holmes. *Sound:* E. A. Brown. *Mus score:* Max Steiner. *Orchestrator:* Hugo Friedhofer. *Musical dir:* Leo F. Forbstein. *Dance dir:* Robert Vreeland. *Cost:* Howard Shoup. *Makeup:* Perc Westmore. *Spec eff:* Byron Haskin, Rex Wimpy. *Assist dir:* Chuch Hansen. *Cast:* Ann Sheridan (Peggy Nash), Frank Craven (Old Timer), Donald Crisp (Scotty McPherson), Arthur Kennedy (Eddie Kenny), Frank McHugh (Mutt), George Tobias (Pinky), Elia Kazan (Googi), Jerome Cowan (Dutch), Anthony Quinn (Murray Burns), Lee Patrick (Gladys), Blanche Yurka (Mrs. Nash), George Lloyd (Goldie), Joyce Compton (Lilly), Thurston Hall (Max Leonard), Ben Welden (Cobb), John Arledge (salesman), Ed Keane (Gaul), Selmer Jackson, Joseph Crehan (doctors), Bob Steele (Callahan), Billy Wayne (henchman), Pat Flaherty (floor guard), Sidney Miller (M.C.), Ethelreda Leopold (dressing-room blonde), and with Lee Phelps, Charles Wilson, Ed Gargan, Howard Hickman, Murray Alper, Dick Wessell, Bernice Pilot, Charles Lane, Dana Dale (Margaret Hayes), Ed Pawley, William Newell, and Lucia Carroll. *Prod:* Warner Bros. 101 min.

THE STRAWBERRY BLONDE (1941). Blithe, sentimental, turn-of-the-century semimusical comedy about a correspondence school dentist who never quite overcomes his youthful crush on a "strawberry blonde"—until a stretch in prison opens his eyes; with Cagney as Biff Grimes, the pugnacious self-taught dentist. *Dir:* Raoul Walsh. *Prod:* Jack L. Warner, Hal B. Wallis. *Assoc prod:* William Cagney. *Sc:* Julius J. Epstein, Philip G. Epstein; based on the play *One Sunday Afternoon* by James Hagan. *Dialogue dir:* Hugh Cummings. *Ph:* James Wong Howe. *Art dir:* Robert Haas. *Ed:* William Holmes. *Sound:* Robert E. Lee. *Mus score:* Heinz Roemheld. *Orchestrator:* Ray Heindorf. *Cost:* Orry-Kelly. *Makeup:* Perc Westmore. *Assist dir:* Russ Saunders. *Cast:* Olivia De Havilland (Amy Lind), Rita Hayworth (Virginia Brush), Alan Hale (Old Man Grimes), George Tobias (Nick Pappalas), Jack Carson (Hugo Barnstead), Una O'Connor (Mrs. Mulcahey), George Reeves (Harold), Lucile Fairbanks (Harold's girlfriend), Edward McNamara (Big Joe), Herbert Heywood (Toby), Helen Lynd (Josephine), Roy Gordon (bank president), Tim Ryan (street cleaner foreman), Addison Richards (official), Frank Mayo (policeman), Jack Daley (bartender), Suzanne Carnahan/Susan Peters (girl), Herbert Anderson (boy), Frank Orth (Baxter), James Flavin (inspector), George Campeau (sailor), Abe Dinovitch (singer), George Humbert (Guiseppi), Creighton Hale (secretary), Russell Hicks (Treadway), Wade Boteler (warden), Peter Ashley (young man), Max Hoffman, Jr., Pat Flaherty (policemen), Peggy Diggins (girl), Bob Perry (hanger-on), Dorothy Vaughan (woman), Richard Clayton (dandy), Ann Edmonds (girl), Lucia Carroll (nurse), and with Harrison Green, Eddie Chandler, Carl Harbaugh, Frank Melton, Dick Wessell, Paul Barrett, and Nora Gale. *Prod:* Warner Bros. 97 min. The film is the second of at least three Hollywood versions of *ONE SUNDAY AFTERNOON*. Besides the original with Gary Cooper (Paramount, 1933), Warners remade the property as a musical in 1948 with Dennis Morgan, Janis Paige, and Dorothy Malone.

THE BRIDE CAME C.O.D. (1941). Shrill screwball comedy about an oil heiress abducted by an aviator who is promised ten dollars per pound freight rate provided he delivers her, unmarried, into her tycoon daddy's arms; with Cagney as Steve Collins, the flyer. *Dir:* William Keighley. *Exec prod:* Hal B. Wallis. *Assoc prod:* William Cagney. *Sc:* Julius J. Epstein, Philip G. Epstein; based on a story by Kenneth Earl, M. M. Musselman. *Ph:* Ernest Haller. *Art dir:* Ted Smith. *Ed:* Thomas Richards. *Sound:* Robert E. Lee. *Mus score:* Max Steiner. *Mus dir:* Leo F. Forbstein. *Orchestrator:* Hugo Friedhofer. *Cost:* Orry-Kelly. *Makeup:* Perc Westmore. *Spec eff:* Byron Haskin, Rex Wimpy. *Assist dir:* Frank Heath. *Cast:* Bette Davis (Joan Winfield), Stuart Erwin (Tommy Keenan), Jack Carson (Allen Brice), George Tobias (Peewee), Eugene Pallette (Lucius K. Winfield), Harry Davenport (Pop Tolliver), William Frawley (Sheriff McGee), Edward Brophy (Hinkle), Harry Holman (Judge Sobler), Chick Chandler, Keith Douglas, Douglas Kennedy, Herbert Anderson (reporters), DeWolfe/William Hopper (Keenan's pilot), William Newell (McGee's pilot), Charles Sullivan (ambulance driver), Eddy Chandler, Tony Hughes, Lee Phelps (policemen), Jean Ames (Mabel), Alphonse Martell (headwaiter), The Rogers Dancers (dance trio), Peggy Diggins (first operator), Mary Brodel (second operator), Olaf Hytten (valet), James Flavin (detective), Sam Hayes (announcer), William Justice/Richard Travis (airline dispatcher), Lester Towne, Richard Clayton, Garland Smith, Claude Wisberg (news-

With Alan Hale, who plays his father in THE STRAWBERRY BLONDE.
(WCTR)

Cagney on set in 13 RUE MADELEINE.

boys), and with Lucia Carroll, Peter Ashley, John Ridgely, Saul Gorss, Jack Mower, Creighton Hale, and Garrett Craig. *Prod:* Warner Bros. 92 min.

CAPTAINS OF THE CLOUDS (1942). Formulaic potboiler about a cocky American bush pilot who joins the Royal Canadian Air Force (RCAF); with Cagney as Brian MacLean, the flyer who eventually dies a hero's death overseas in a skyfight with Nazi raiders. *Dir:* Michael Curtiz. *Prod:* Hal B. Wallis. *Assoc prod:* William Cagney. *Sc:* Arthur T. Horman, Richard Macaulay, Norman Reilly Raine; based on a story by Horman and Toland Gillett. *Ph:* Sol Polito, Wilfred M. Cline. *Aerial ph:* Elmer Dyer, Charles Marshall, Winton C. Hoch. *Art dir:* Ted Smith. *Ed:* George Amy. *Dialogue dir:* Hugh MacMullan. *Sound:* C. A. Riggs. *Mus score:* Max Steiner. *Mus dir:* Leo F. Forbstein. *Cost:* Howard Shoup. *Makeup:* Perc Westmore. *Spec eff:* Byron Haskin, Rex Wimpy. *Technicolor consult:* Natalie Kalmus. *Technicolor assoc:* Henri Jaffa. *Warner's Chief Pilot:* Frank Clarke. *Tech advisor:* RCAF Squadron Leader O. Cathcart-Jones. *Song:* "Captains of the Clouds" by Harold Arlen and Johnny Mercer. *Cast:* Dennis Morgan (Johnny Dutton), Brenda Marshall (Emily Foster), Alan Hale (Tiny Murphy), George Tobias (Blimp Lebec), Reginald Gardiner (Scrounger Harris), RCAF Air Marshal W. A. Bishop (himself), Reginald Denny (commanding officer), Russell Arms (Prentiss), Paul Cavanagh (Group Captain), Clem Bevans (Store-Teeth Morrison), J. M. Kerrigan (Foster), J. Farrell MacDonald (Doctor Neville), Patrick O'Moore (Fyffo), Morton Lowry (Carmichael), O. Cathcart-Jones (chief instructor), Frederic Worlock (president of courts-martial), Roland Drew (officer), Lucia Carroll (blonde), George Meeker (playboy), Benny Baker (Popcorn Kearns), Hardie Albright (Kingsley), Roy Walker (Mason), Charles Halton (Nolan), Louis Jean Heydt (provost marshall), Byron Barr/Gig Young, Michael Ames/Tod Andrews (student pilots), Willie Fung (Willie), Carl Harbord (Blake), James Stevens, Bill Wilkerson, Frank Lackteen (Indians), Edward McNamara (dog man), Charles Smith (bellboy), Emmett Vogan (clerk), Winifred Harris (woman), Miles Mander (Churchill's voice), Pat Flaherty (drill sergeant), Tom Dugan (bartender), George Offerman, Jr. (mechanic), Gavin Muir (orderly), Larry Williams (duty officer), and with John Hartley, John Kellogg, Charles Irwin, Billy Wayne, Rafael Storm, John Gallaudet, Barry Bernard, George Ovey, Walter Brooks, Ray Montgomery, Herbert Gunn, Donald Dillaway, and James Bush. *Prod:* Warner Bros. 113 min. Technicolor. Polito was nominated for an Academy Award for his Technicolor cinematography for *Clouds*, Cagney's first color feature.

YANKEE DOODLE DANDY (1942). Tour-de-force musical biography of Broadway showman George M. Cohan; with Cagney as Cohan. *Dir:* Michael Curtiz. *Prod:* Jack L. Warner. *Exec prod:* Hal B. Wallis. *Assoc prod:* William Cagney. *Sc:* Robert Buckner, Edmund Joseph; based on an original story by Buckner. *Dialogue dir:* Hugh MacMullan. *Ph:* James Wong Howe. *Art dir:* Carl Jules Weyl. *Montages:* Don Siegel. *Ed:* George Amy. *Sound:* Everett A. Brown. *Mus adapt:* Heinz Roemheld. *Mus dir:* Leo F. Forbstein. *Orchestrator:* Ray Heindorf. *Choreog:* LeRoy Prinz, Seymour Felix. *Cost:* Milo Anderson. *Makeup:* Perc Westmore. *Mr. Cagney's dances staged by:* John Boyle. *Tech adv:* William Collier, Sr. *Songs:* "I Was Born in Virginia," "The Warmest Baby in the Bunch," "Give My Regards to Broadway," "Mary's a Grand Old Name," "So Long Mary," "Yankee Doodle Boy," "Over There," "Harrigan," "Forty-five Minutes from Broadway," "You're a Grand Old Flag" by George M. Cohan; "All Aboard for Old Broadway" by Jack Scholl, M. K. Jerome. *Cast:* Joan Leslie (Mary), Walter Huston (Jerry Cohan), Richard Whorf (Sam Harris), George Tobias (Dietz), Fay Templeton (Irene Manning), Rosemary De Camp (Nellie Cohan), Jeanne Cagney (Josie Cohan), S. Z. "Cuddles" Sakall (Schwab), George Barbier (Erlanger), Walter Catlett (manager), Frances Langford (Nora Bayes), Minor Watson (Ed Albee), Eddie Foy, Jr. (Eddie Foy), Chester Clute (Harold Goff), Douglas Croft (George M. Cohan, age 13), Patsy Lee Parsons (Josie, age 12), Captain Jack Young (Franklin D.

Roosevelt), Audrey Long (receptionist), Odette Myrtil (Madame Bartholdi), Clinton Rosemond (White House butler), Spencer Charters (stage manager in Providence), Dorothy Kelly, Marijo James (sister act), Henry Blair (George M. Cohan, age 7), Jo Ann Marlow (Josie Cohan, age 6), Thomas Jackson (stage manager), Phyllis Kennedy (Fanny), Pat Flaherty (White House guard), Leon Belasco (magician), Syd Saylor (star boarder), William B. Davidson (stage manager, New York), Harry Hayden (Dr. Lewellyn), Francis Pierlot (Dr. Anderson), Charles Smith, Joyce Reynolds, Dick Chandlee, Joyce Horne (teenagers), Frank Faylen (sergeant), Wallis Clark (Theodore Roosevelt), Georgia Carroll (Betsy Ross), Joan Winfield (Sally), Dick Wessel, James Flavin (Union Army veterans), Sailor Vincent (Schultz in "Peck's Bad Boy"), Fred Kelsey (Irish cop in "Peck's Bad Boy"), George Meeker, Frank Mayo (hotel clerks), Tom Dugan (actor, railroad station), Creighton Hale (telegraph operator), Murray Alper (wise guy), Garry Owen (army clerk), Ruth Robinson (nurse), Eddie Acuff, Walter Brooke, Bill Edwards, William Hopper (reporters), William Forrest (first critic), Ed Keane (second critic), Dolores Moran (girl), and Poppy Wilde and Lorraine Gettman/Leslie Brooks (Chorus Girls in "Little Johnny Jones"). *Cut from final print:* Vera Lewis, Jim Toney, Charles Drake (actors), Ann Doran (receptionist), Napoleon Simpson (porter), Buddy (Lon) McCallister (call boy) and Leah Baird (housekeeper). *Prod:* Warner Bros. 126 min. The film's Academy Award nominations included Best Sound Recording (Nathan Levinson), Best Score (Ray Heindorf, Heinz Roemheld), Best Original Story (Buckner), Best Supporting Actor (Huston), Best Actor (Cagney), Best Director (Curtiz), and Best Picture of 1942. Levinson, Heindorf and Roemheld, and Cagney won Oscars. Cagney also won the Best Actor prize from the New York Film Critics for his performance.

JOHNNY COME LATELY (1943). Whimsical turn-of-the-century comedy–drama about an elderly lady newspaper publisher who enlists the help of a vagabond journalist in her crusade against corrupt small town politicians; with Cagney as Tom Richards, the vagrant newspaperman. *Dir:* William K. Howard. *Prod:* William Cagney. *Sc:* John Van Druten; based on the novel *McLeod's Folly* by Louis Bromfield. *Ph:* Theodore Sparkuhl. *Art dir:* Jack Okey. *Set dec:* Julia Heron. *Ed:* George Arthur. *Sound rec:* Benjamin Winkler. *Mus dir:* Leigh Harline. *Assist dir:* Lowell Farrell. *Cast:* Grace George (Vinnie McLeod), Marjorie Main (Gashouse Mary), Marjorie Lord (Jane), Hattie McDaniel (Aida), Edward McNamara (W. W. Dougherty), Bill Henry (Pete Dougherty), Robert Barrat (Bill Swain), George Cleveland (Willie Ferguson), Margaret Hamilton (Myrtle Ferguson), Norman Willis (Dudley Hirsh), Lucien Littlefield (Blaker), Edwin Stanley (Winterbottom), Irving Bacon (chief of police), Tom Dugan (first cop), Charles Irwin (second cop), John Sheehan (third cop), Clarence Muse (butler), John Miller (first tramp), Arthur Hunnicutt (second tramp), Victor Kilian (tramp in boxcar), Wee Willie Davis (bouncer), and Henry Hall (old timer). *Prod:* William Cagney Production for United Artists. 97 min.

BLOOD ON THE SUN (1945). Routine action drama set in Tokyo in the 1920s; with Cagney as Nick Condon, an American reporter who learns of Japan's militarist plans for world conquest and tries to smuggle the incriminating documents out of the country. *Dir:* Frank Lloyd. *Prod:* William Cagney. *Assist to prod:* George Arthur. *Sc:* Lester Cole. *Add scenes:* Nathaniel Curtis; based on a story by Garrett Fort. *Ph:* Theodore Sparkuhl. *Art dir:* Wiard Ihnen. *Set dir:* A. Roland Fields. *Prod mgr:* Daniel Keefe. *Ed:* Truman K. Wood, Walter Hanneman. *Sound rec:* Richard De Wesse. *Mus score:* Miklos Rozsa. *Cost:* Robert Martien. *Makeup:* Ern Westmore, Josef Norin. *Assist dir:* Harvey Dwight. *Tech adv:* Alice Barlow. *Cast:* Sylvia Sidney (Iris Hilliard), Wallace Ford (Ollie Miller), Rosemary De Camp (Edith Miller), Robert Armstrong (Colonel Tojo), John Emery (Premiere Tanaka), Leonard Strong (Hijikata), Frank Puglia (Prince Tatsugi), Jack Halloran (Captain Oshima), Hugh Ho (Kajioka), Philip Ahn (Yamamoto), Joseph Kim (Hayoshi), Marvin Miller (Yamada),

Rhys Williams (Joseph Cassell), Porter Hall (Arthur Bickett), James Bell (Charley Sprague), Grace Lem (amah), Oy Chan (Chinese servant), George Paris (hotel manager), Hugh Beaumont (Johnny Clarke), and Gregory Gay, Arthur Loft, Emmett Vogan, and Charlie Wayne (American newspapermen in Tokyo). *Prod:* William Cagney Production for United Artists. 98 min.

13 RUE MADELEINE (1946). Crisp documentary-style drama about the overseas espionage missions of American agents during World War II; with Cagney as Bob Sharkey, heroic leader of the American spy group, one member of which is a German operative. *Dir:* Henry Hathaway. *Prod:* Louis De Rochemont. *Sc:* John Monks, Jr., Sy Bartlett. *Ph:* Norbert Brodine. *Art dir:* James Basevi, Maurice Ransford. *Set dec:* Thomas Little. *Ed:* Harmon Jones. *Sound:* W. D. Flick, Harry M. Leonard. *Mus score:* Alfred Newman. *Mus dir:* David Buttolph. *Orch arrangements:* Edward Powell, Sidney Cutner, Leo Shuken. *Cost:* Rene Hubert. *Makeup:* Ben Nye. *Spec ph eff:* Fred Sersen. *Assist dir:* Abe Steinberg. *Cast:* Annabella (Suzanne de Bouchard), Richard Conte (Bill O'Connell), Frank Latimore (Jeff Lassiter), Walter Abel (Charles Gibson), Melville Cooper (Pappy Simpson), Sam Jaffe (Mayor Galimard), Marcel Rousseau (Duclois), Richard Gordon (psychiatrist), Everett C. Marshall (Emile), Blanche Yurka (Madame Thillot), Peter Von Zerneck (Karl), Alfred Linder (Hans Feinkl), Ben Low (hotel clerk), James Craven (RAF officer), Roland Belanger (Joseph), Horace MacMahon (burglary instructor), Alexander Kirkland (briefing officer), Donald Randolph (La Roche), Judith Lowry (peasant lady), Red Buttons (dispatcher), Otto Simanek (German staff officer), Walter Greaza (psychiatrist), Roland Winters (Van Duyval), Harold Young (tailor), Sally McMarrow (chief operator), Coby Neal, Karl Malden (flyers), Jean Del Val (French peasant), and Reed Hadley (narrator). *Prod:* 20th Century-Fox. 95 min.

THE TIME OF YOUR LIFE (1948). Loving adaptation of novelist–playwright William Saroyan's cockeyed comedy–drama of passing life in a San Francisco waterfront saloon; with Cagney as Joe, the barroom philosopher. *Dir:* H. C. Potter. *Prod:* William Cagney. *Sc:* Nathaniel Curtis; based on the play by William Saroyan. *Ph:* James Wong Howe. *Art dir:* Wiard Ihnen. *Prod mgr:* Kan Keefe. *Assist prod mgr:* Edward Cagney. *Unit prod mgr:* John W. Kirsten. *Set dec:* A. Roland Fields. *Ed:* Walter Hannemann, Truman K. Wood. *Sound:* Earl Sitar. *Mus score:* Carmen Dragon. *Piano comp:* Reginald Beane. *Cost:* Courtney Haslam. *Talent:* Irving Kumin. *Makeup:* Otis Malcolm. *Hair stylist:* Scotty Rackin. *Still ph:* Madison S. Lacy. *Assist dir:* Harvey Dwight. *Cast:* William Bendix (Nick), Wayne Morris (Tom), Jeanne Cagney (Kitty Duval), Broderick Crawford (policeman), Ward Bond (McCarthy), James Barton (Kit Carson), Paul Draper (Harry), Gale Page (Mary L.), James Lydon (Dudley), Richard Erdman (Willie), Pedro De Cordoba (Arab), Reginald Beane (Wesley), Tom Powers (Blick), John "Skins" Miller (a drunk), Natalie Schafer (society lady), Howard Freeman (society gentleman), Renie Riano (blind date), Lanny Rees (newsboy), Nanette Parks (girl in love), Grazia Marciso (Nick's mother), Claire Carleton ("Killer"), Gladys Blake (sidekick), Marlene Aames (Nick's daughter), Moy Ming (cook), Donald Kerr (bookie), Ann Cameron (B girl), Floyd Walters (sailor), Eddie Borden (Salvation Army man), and Rena Case (Salvation Army woman). *Prod:* William Cagney Production for United Artists. 109 min.

WHITE HEAT (1949). Chilling melodrama about the violent criminal exploits of a homicidal, paranoiac "mama's boy" outlaw; with Cagney as Cody Jarrett, the bestial thug afflicted with recurrent, brutal headaches. *Dir:* Raoul Walsh. *Prod:* Louis F. Edelman. *Sc:* Ivan Goff, Ben Roberts; based on a story by Virginia Kellogg. *Script super:* Irva Mae Ross. *Ph:* Sid Hickox. *Oper cameraman:* Mike Joyce. *Art dir:* Edward Carrere. *Ed:* Owen Marks. *Sound:* Leslie Hewitt. *Mus score:* Max Steiner. *Orchestrator:* Murray Cutner. *Hair stylist:*

Gertrude Wheeler. *Cost:* Leah Rhodes. *Makeup:* Perc Westmore, Eddie Allen. *Spec eff:* Roy Davidson, H. F. Koenekamp. *Assist dir:* Russell Saunders. *Grip:* Rudy Mashmeyer. *Gaffer:* Paul Burnett. *Still man:* Frank Bjeering. *Cast:* Virginia Mayo (Verna Jarrett), Edmond O'Brien (Hank Fallon), Margaret Wycherly (Ma Jarrett), Steve Cochran ("Big Ed" Somers), John Archer (Philip Evans), Wally Cassell (Cotton Valetti), Mickey Knox (Het Kohler), Fred Clark (The Trader), G. Pat Collins (the reader), Paul Guilfoyle (Roy Parker), Fred Coby (Happy Taylor), Ford Rainey (Zuckie Hommell), Robert Osterloh (Tommy Ryley), Ian MacDonald (Bo Creel), Marshall Bradford (chief of police), Ray Montgomery (Ernie Trent), George Taylor (police surgeon), Milton Parsons (Willie Rolf), Claudia Barrett (cashier), Buddy Gorman (popcorn vendor), DeForrest Lawrence (Jim Donovan), Garrett Craig (Ted Clark), George Spaulding (judge), Sherry Hall (clerk), Harry Strang, Jack Worth (guards), Sid Melton (Russell Hughes), Fern Eggen (Margaret Baxter), Eddie Foster (Nat Lefeld), and Lee Phelps (tower guard). *Prod:* Warner Bros. 114 min. Kellogg's original story was nominated for an Academy Award.

WEST POINT STORY (1950). Bombastic musical comedy about a brash Broadway musical director's assignment to mount the annual West Point cadet variety show; with Cagney as Elwin Bixby, the theatrical impresario. *Dir:* Roy Del Ruth. *Prod:* Louis F. Edelman. *Sc:* John Monks, Jr., Charles Hoffman, Irving Wallace; based on a story by Wallace. *Prod mgr:* Al Alleborn. *Script super:* Jean Baker. *Ph:* Sid Hickox. *Oper cameraman:* Mike Joyce. *Art dir:* Charles H. Clarke. *Hair stylist:* Gertrude Wheeler. *Set dec:* Armor E. Marlowe. *Ed:* Owen Marks. *Gaffer:* Paul Burnett. *Sound:* Francis J. Scheid. *Mus dir:* Ray Heindorf. *Dance dir:* LeRoy Prinz. *Staged by:* Eddie Prinz, Al White. *Mr. Cagney's dances created by:* Johnny Boyle, Jr. *Vocal arrang:* Hugh Martin. *Orchestrator:* Frank Perkins. *Makeup:* Otis Malcolm. *Cost:* Milo Anderson, Marjorie Best. *Spec eff:* Edwin DuPar. *Assist dir:* Mel Deller. *Grip:* Dude Naschmeyer. *Still man:* Mac Julian. *Songs:* "Ten Thousand Sheep," "By the Kissing Rock," "You Love Me," "Military Polka," "Long before I Knew You," "It Could Only Happen in Brooklyn," "Brooklyn" by Julie Styne, Sammy Cahn; musical number "The Corps" ensembled, vocaled by Gordon MacRae. *Cast:* Virginia Mayo (Eve Dillon), Doris Day (Jan Wilson), Gordon MacRae (Tom Fletcher), Gene Nelson (Hal Courtland), Alan Hale, Jr. (Bull Gilbert), Roland Winters (Harry Eberhart), Raymond Roe (Bixby's "wife"), Wilton Graff (Lieutenant Colonel Martin), Jerome Cowan (Jocelyn), Frank Ferguson (Commandant), Russ Saunders (acrobat), Jack Kelly (officer-in-charge), Glen Turnbull (hoofer), Walter Ruick (piano player), Lute Crockett (senator), and James Dobson, Joel Marston, Bob Hayden, and DeWit Bishop (cadets). *Prod:* Warner Bros. 107 min.

KISS TOMORROW GOODBYE (1950). Sordid crime melodrama about a vicious crook involved in a bribery–blackmail scheme with the police of a big city; with Cagney as Ralph Cotter, the brutal villain. *Dir:* Gordon Douglas. *Prod:* William Cagney. *Sc:* Harry Brown; based on the novel *Kiss Tomorrow Goodbye* by Horace McCoy. *Ph:* Peverell Marley. *Art dir:* Wiard Ihnen. *Set dec:* Joe Kish. *Ed:* Truman K. Wood, Walter Hannemann. *Sound:* William Lynch. *Mus score:* Carmen Dragon. *Makeup:* Otis Malcolm. *Spec eff:* Paul Eagler. *Assist dir:* William Kissell. *Cast:* Barbara Payton (Holiday), Ward Bond (Inspector Weber), Luther Adler (Mandon), Helena Carter (Margaret Dobson), Steve Brodie (Jinx), Rhys Williams (Vic Mason), Barton MacLane (Reece), Herbert Heyes (Ezra Dobson), Frank Reicher (Doc Green), John Litel (Tolgate), Dan Riss (district attorney), John Halloran (Cobbett), William Frawley (Byers), Robert Karnes (Detective Gray), Kenneth Tobey (Detective Fowler), Neville Brand (Carleton), William Cagney (Ralph's brother), George Spaulding (judge), Mark Strong (bailiff), Matt McHugh (Satterfield), Georgia Caine (Julia), King Donovan (driver), Frank Wilcox (doctor), and Gordon Richards (butler). *Prod:* William Cagney Production for Warner Bros. 102 min.

COME FILL THE CUP (1951). Sincere, gripping melodrama about a city newspaperman's struggle against alcoholism and the local underworld; with Cagney as Lew Marsh, the sodden journalist. *Dir:* Gordon Douglas. *Prod:* Henry Blanke. *Sc:* Ivan Goff, Ben Roberts; based on a novel by Harlan Ware. *Ph:* Robert Burks. *Oper cameraman:* William Scheerr. *Art dir:* Leo F. Kuter. *Set dec:* William L. Kuehl. *Hair stylist:* Tillie Starrett. *Ed:* Alan Crosland, Jr. *Sound:* Stanley Jones. *Mus dir:* Ray Heindorf. *Cost:* Leah Rhodes. *Makeup:* Gordon Bau. *Stills:* Mac Julian. *Assist dir:* Frank Mattison. *Cast:* Phyllis Thaxter (Paula Copeland), Raymond Massey (John Ives), James Gleason (Charley Dolan), Gig Young (Boyd Copeland), Selena Royle (Dolly Copeland), Larry Keating (Julian Cuscaden), Charlita (Maria Diego), Sheldon Leonard (Lennie Carr), Douglas Spencer (Ike Bashaw), John Kellogg (Don Bell), William Bakewell (Hal Ortman), John Alvin (Travis Ashbourne II), King Donovan (Kip Zunches), James Flavin (homicide captain), Torben Meyer (welder), Norma Jean Macias (Ora), Elizabeth Flournoy (Lila), and Henry Blair (Bobby). *Prod:* Warner Bros. 113 min. Young was nominated for an Academy Award for Best Supporting Actor of 1951.

STARLIFT (1951). Forgettable musical comedy about Hollywood film stars who visit Travis Air Force Base near San Francisco to boost the Korean War effort; with Cagney as himself. *Dir:* Roy Del Ruth. *Prod:* Robert Arthur. *Sc:* John Klorer, Karl Kamb; based on a story by Klorer. *Ph:* Ted McCord. *Art dir:* Charles H. Clarke. *Set dec:* G. W. Berntsen. *Ed:* William Ziegler. *Sound:* Francis J. Scheid. *Mus dir:* Ray Heindorf. *Cost:* Leah Rhodes. *Makeup:* Gordon Bau. *Hair stylist:* Gertrude Wheeler. *Choreog:* LeRoy Prinz. *Assist dir:* Mel Dellar. *Tech adv:* Major James G. Smith, USAF, MATS, Major George E. Andrews, USAF, SAC. *Songs:* "S'wonderful" by Ira Gershwin; "Liza" by George Gershwin; "You Do Something to Me," "What Is This Thing Called Love?" by Cole Porter; "You're Gonna Lose Your Gal" by Joe Young, Jimmy Monaco; "You Ought To Be in Pictures" by Edward Heyman, David Suesse; "It's Magic" by Sammy Cahn, Julie Styne; "Good Green Acres of Home" by Irving Kahal, Sammy Fain; "I May Be Wrong, But I Think You're Wonderful" by Harry Ruskin, Henry Sullivan; "Look Out, Stranger, I'm a Texas Ranger" by Ruby Ralesin, Phil Harris; "Noche Carib" by Percy Faith. *Cast:* Doris Day, Gordon MacRae, Virginia Mayo, Gene Nelson, Ruth Roman (themselves), Janice Rule (Nell Wayne), Dick Wesson (Sergeant Mike Nolan), Ron Hagerthy (Corporal Rick Williams), Richard Webb (Colonel Callan), Hayden Rorke (Chaplain), Howard St. John (Steve Rogers), Ann Doran (Mrs. Callan), Tommy Farrell (Turner), John Maxwell (George Norris), Don Beddoe (Bob Wayne), Mary Adams (Sue Wayne), Bigelowe Sayre (Dr. Williams), Eleanor Audley (Mrs. Williams), Pat Henry (theater manager), Gordon Polk (chief usher), Robert Hammack (piano player), Ray Montgomery (Captain Nelson), Bill Neff (copilot), Stan Holbrook (ground officer), Jill Richards (flight nurse), Joe Turkel (litter case), Rush Williams (Virginia boy), Brian McKay (Pete), Jack Larson (Will), Lyle Clark (Nebraska boy), Dorothy Kennedy, Jean Dean, Dolores Castle (nurses), William Hunt (boy with cane), Elizabeth Flournoy (Army nurse), Walter Brennan, Jr. (driver), Robert Karnes, John Hedloe (lieutenants), Steve Gregory (boy with camera), Richard Monohan (Morgan), Joe Recht, Herb Latimer (soldiers in bed), Dick Ryan (doctor), Bill Hudson (crew chief), Sarah Spencer (Miss Parson's assistant), James Brown (noncom), Ezelle Poule (waitress), and with the following guest stars: James Cagney, Gary Cooper, Virginia Gibson, Phil Harris, Frank Lovejoy, Lucille Norman, Louella Parsons, Randolph Scott, Jane Wyman, and Patrice Wymore. *Prod:* Warner Bros. 103 min. Cagney makes a cameo appearance only.

WHAT PRICE GLORY? (1952). Ill-conceived, farcical semimusical remake of the stage classic about two American military officers in France during World War I who must bulwark the front-line trenches with area villagers; with Cagney as Captain Flagg. *Dir:* John Ford. *Prod:* Sol C. Siegel. *Sc:* Phoebe Ephron, Henry Ephron; based on the play by

Maxwell Anderson and Laurence Stallings. *Ph:* Joseph MacDonald. *Art dir:* Lyle R. Wheeler, George W. Davis. *Set dec:* Thomas Little, Stuart A. Reiss. *Ed:* Dorothy Spencer. *Sound:* Winston Leverett, Roger Heman. *Mus score:* Alfred Newman. *Orchestrator:* Edward Powell. *Technicolor consult:* Leonard Doss. *Songs:* "My Love, My Life" by Jay Livingston, Ray Evans; "Oui, Oui, Marie" sung by Corinne Calvet. *Cast:* Corinne Calvet (Charmaine), Dan Dailey (Sergeant Quirt), William DeMarest (Corporal Kiper), Craig Hill (Lieutenant Aldrich), Robert Wagner (Llewisohn), Marisa Pavan (Nicole Bouchard), Casey Adams (Lieutenant Moore), James Gleason (General Cokely), Wally Vernon (Lipinsky), Henry Letondal (Cognac Pete), Fred Libby (Lieutenant Schmidt), Ray Hyke (Mulcahy), Paul Fix (Gowdy), James Lilburn (young soldier), Henry Morgan (Morgan), Dan Borzage (Gilbert), Bill Henry (Holsen), Henry "Bomber" Kulkovich (company cook), Jack Pennick (Ferguson), Ann Codee (nun), Stanley Johnson (Lieutenant Cunningham), Tom Tyler (Captain Davis), Olga Andre (Sister Clotilde), Barry Norton (priest), Luis Alberni (the great-uncle), Torben Meyer (mayor), Alfred Ziesler (English colonel), George Bruggeman (English lieutenant), Scott Forbes (Lieutenant Bennett), Sean McClory (Lieutenant Austin), Charles Fitzsimmons (Captain Wickham), Louis Mercier (Bouchard) and Mickey Simpson (MP). *Prod:* 20th Century-Fox; Technicolor. 111 min.

A LION IS IN THE STREETS (1953). Flawed drama about the political ascent of a Huey Long-type Southern demagogue; with Cagney as Hank Martin, the personable, self-taught swamp peddler who mounts a populist campaign for governor. *Dir:* Raoul Walsh. *Prod:* William Cagney. *Sc:* Luther Davis; based on the novel by Adria Locke Langley. *Ph:* Harry Stradling. *Prod des:* Wiard Ihnen. *Set dec:* Fred M. MacLean. *Ed:* George Amy. *Sound:* John Kean. *Mus score:* Franz Waxman. *Makeup:* Otis Malcolm. *Spec eff:* Roscoe Cline. *Assist dir:* William Kissel. *Technicolor consult:* Monroe W. Burbank. *Story ed:* Edward Cagney. *Cast:* Barbara Hale (Verity Wade), Anne Francis (Flamingo), Warner Anderson (Jules Bolduc), John McIntyre (Jeb Brown), Jeanne Cagney (Jennie Brown), Lon Chaney, Jr. (Spurge), Frank McHugh (Rector), Larry Keating (Robert J. Castelberry), Onslow Stevens (Guy Polli), James Millican (Mr. Beach), Mickey Simpson (Tim Beck), Sara Haden (Lula May), Ellen Corby (singing woman), Roland Winters (prosecutor), Burt Mustin

On the WHITE HEAT set with children James (Jimmy) Cagney, Jr. and Kathleen Cagney.

On the set of RUN FOR COVER with wife Billie Cagney.

(Smith), Irene Tedrow (Sophy), and Sarah Selby (townswoman). *Prod:* William Cagney Production for Warner Bros; Technicolor. 88 min.

RUN FOR COVER (1955). Provocative Western drama about a wronged ex-con who becomes a small-town sheriff; with Cagney as Matt Dow, the gun-handy lawman who befriends a treacherous youth. *Dir:* Nicholas Ray. *Prod:* William H. Pine. *Sc:* William C. Thomas; based on a story by Harriet Frank, Jr., and Irving Ravetch. *Ph:* Daniel Fapp. *Art dir:* Hal Pereira, Henry Bumstead. *Set dec:* Sam Comer, Frank McKelvy. *Ed:* Howard Smith. *Sound:* Gene Merritt, John Cope. *Mus dir:* Howard Jackson. *Cost:* Edith Head. *Makeup:* Wally Westmore. *Spec eff:* John P. Fulton. *Spec ph eff:* Farciot Edouart. *Assist dir:* Francisco Day. *Technicolor consult:* Richard Mueller. *Song:* "Run for Cover" by Howard Jackson, Jack Brooks. *Cast:* Viveca Lindfors (Helga Swenson), John Derek (Davey Bishop), Jean Hersholt (Mr. Swenson), Grant Withers (Gentry), Jack Lambert (Larsen), Ernest Borgnine (Morgan), Ray Teal (sheriff), Irving Bacon (Scotty), Trevor Bardette (Paulsen), John Miljan (Mayor Walsh), Gus Schilling (Doc Ridgeway), Emerson Tracy (bank manager), Denver Pyle (Harvey), and Henry Wills (townsman). *Prod:* Pine-Thomas/Paramount; Technicolor and VistaVision. 92 min.

LOVE ME OR LEAVE ME (1955). Authentic, hard-boiled musical biography of singer Ruth Etting and her stormy relationship with her patron, racketeer Martin "The Gimp" Snyder; with Cagney as Snyder. *Dir:* Charles Vidor. *Prod:* Joe Pasternak. *Sc:* Daniel Fuchs, Isobel Lennart; based on an original story by Fuchs. *Ph:* Arthur E. Arling. *Art dir:* Cedric Gibbons, Urie McCleary. *Ed:* Ralph E. Winters. *Mus dir:* George Stoll. *Miss Day's mus:* Percy Faith. *Sound:* Wesley C. Miller. *Choreog:* Alex Romero. *Cost:* Helen Rose. *Mus adv:* Irving Aaronson. *Spec eff:* Warren Newcombe. *Songs:* "Stay on the Right Side, Sister" by Ted Koehler, Rube Bloom; "You Made Me Love You" by Joe McCarthy, James Monaco; "Everybody Loves My Baby" by Jack Palmer, Spencer Williams; "Sam, the Old Accordian Man" by Walter Donaldson; "At Sundown" by Walter Donaldson; "It All Depends on You" by B. G. DeSylva, Lew Brown, Ray Henderson; "Love Me or Leave Me" by Gus Kahn, Walter Donaldson; "Mean to Me" by Roy Turk, Fred Ahlert; "Ten Cents a Dance" by Richard Rodgers, Lorenz Hart; "Shaking the Blues Away" by Irving Berlin; "Never Look Back" by Chilton Price; "I'll Never Stop Loving You" by Nicholas Brodzky, Sammy Cahn. *Cast:* Doris Day (Ruth Etting), Cameron Mitchell (Johnny Alderman), Robert Keith (Bernard V. Loomis), Tom Tully (Frobisher), Harry Bellaver (Georgie), Richard Gaines (Paul Hunter), Peter Leeds (Fred Taylor), Claude Stroud (Eddie Fulton), Audrey Young (jingle girl), John Harding (Greg Trent), Dorothy Abbott (dancer), Phil Schumacher (bouncer), Otto Reichow (second bouncer), Henry Kulky (bouncer), Jay Adler (Orry), Mauritz Hugo (irate customer), Veda Ann Borg (hostess), Claire Carleton (Claire), Benny Burt (stage manager), Robert B. Carson (Mr. Brelston, radio station manager), James Drury (assistant director), Richard Simmons (dance director), Michael Kostrick (assistant director), Roy Engel (first reporter), John Damler (second reporter), Genevieve Aumont (woman), Roy Engel (propman), Dale Van Sickel, Johnny Day (stagehands), Larri Thomas, Patti Nestor, Winona Smith, Shirley Wilson (chorus girls), Robert Malcolm (doorman), Robert Stephenson (waiter), Paul McGuire (drapery man), Barry Regan (guard), Jimmy Cross, Henry Randolph (photographers), and Chet Brandenberg (chauffeur). *Prod:* MGM; Cinemascope and Eastman color. 122 min. The film's Academy Award nominations included Best Sound (Wesley C. Miller), Best Song ("I'll Never Stop Loving You" by Brodszky and Cahn), Best Scoring of a Musical (Percy Faith and George Stoll), Best Story (Daniel Fuchs), Best Screenplay (Fuchs and Isobel Lennart) and Best Actor (Cagney). Fuchs won for Best Story.

MISTER ROBERTS (1955). Engaging adaptation of long-running comedy–drama stage classic about near-mutinous conditions aboard a Naval vessel in the Pacific; with Cagney as the bull-headed captain. *Dir:* John Ford, Mervyn LeRoy. *Prod:* Leland Hayward. *Sc:* Frank Nugent, Joshua Logan; from the play by Logan and Thomas Heggen; based on the novel by Heggen. *Ph:* Winton C. Hoch. *Art dir:* Art Loel. *Set dec:* William L. Kuehl. *Ed:* Jack Murray. *Prod mgr:* Norman Cook. *Sound:* Earl N. Crain. *Mus score:* Franz Waxman. *Orchestrator:* Leonid Raab. *Makeup:* Gordon Bau. *Assist dir:* Wingate Smith. *Tech adv:* Admiral John Dale Price, USN, Commander Merle MacBain, USN. *Cast:* Henry Fonda (Lieutenant [Junior Grade] Roberts), Jack Lemmon (Ensign Frank Thurlowe Pulver), William Powell (Doc), Ward Bond (Chief Petty Officer Dowdy), Betsy Palmer (Lieutenant Ann Girard), Phil Carey (Mannion), Nick Adams (Reber), Harry Carey, Jr. (Stefanowski), Ken Curtis (Dolan), Frank Aletter (Gerhart), Fritz Ford (Lidstrom), Buck Kartalian (Mason), William Henry (Lieutenant Billings), William Hudson (Olson), Stubby Kruger (Schlemmer), Harry Tenbrook (Cookie), Perry Lopez (Rodrigues), Robert Roark (Insignia), Pat Wayne (Bookser), Tige Andrews (Wiley), Jim Moloney (Kennedy), Denny Niles (Gilbert), Francis Conner (Johnson), Shug Fisher (Cochran), Danny Borzage (Jonesy), Jim Murphy (Taylor), Kathleen O'Malley, Maura Murphy, Mimi Doyle, Jeanne Murray-Vanderbilt, Lonnie Pierce (nurses), Martin Milner (shore patrol officer), Gregory Walcott (shore patrolman), James Flavin (J.P.), Jack Pennick (Marine sergeant), Duke Kahanamoko (native chief), Carolyn Tong (Chinese girl who kisses Bookser), George Brangier (French colonial officer), and Clarence E. Frank (Naval officer). *Prod:* Orange Production for Warner Bros; CinemaScope and Warner–Color. 123 min. The film's Academy Award nominations included Best Sound Recording (Earl N. Crain), Best Supporting Actor (Lemmon) and Best Picture. Lemmon won the Oscar for Best Supporting Actor.

THE SEVEN LITTLE FOYS (1955). Overly cute semimusical biography of vaudevillian Eddie Foy; with Cagney as his pal George M. Cohan, who stops by a Friars Club dinner to honor Foy with an impromptu dancing challenge. *Dir:* Melville Shavelson. *Prod:* Jack Rose. *Sc:* Shavelson, Jack Rose. *Ph:* John F. Warren. *Art dir:* Hal Pereira, John Goodman. *Ed:* Ellsworth Hoagland. *Mus dir:* Joseph J. Lilley. *Narrator:* Eddie Foy, Jr. *Choreog:* Nick Castle. *Tech adv:* Charley Foy. *Cast:* Bob Hope (Eddie Foy), Milly Vitale (Madeleine Morando), George Tobias (Barney Green), Angela Clarke (Clara), Herbert Heyes (Judge), Richard Shannon (stage manager), Billy Gray (Brynie), Lee Erickson (Charley), Paul De Rolf (Richard Foy), Lydia Reed (Mary Foy), Linda Bennett (Madeleine Foy), Jimmy Baird (Eddie, Jr.), Tommy Duran (Irving), Lester Matthews (Father O'Casey), Joe Evans, George Boyce (elephant act), Oliver Blake (Santa Claus), Milton Frome (Driscoll), King Donovan (Harrison), Jimmy Conlin (stage doorman), Marian Carr (soubrette), Harry Cheshire (stage doorman at Iroquois), Renata Vanni (Italian ballerina mistress), Betty Uitti (dance specialty double), Noel Drayton (priest), Jack Pepper (theater manager), Dabbs Greer (tutor), Billy Nelson (customs inspector), Joe Flynn (second priest), Jerry Mathers (Brynie, age 5), and Lewis Martin (Presbyterian minister). *Prod:* Paramount; VistaVision and Technicolor. 93 min. The film was nominated for an Academy Award for Best Screenplay (Shavelson and Rose). Cagney recreated his George M. Cohan role in a cameo appearance.

TRIBUTE TO A BAD MAN (1956). Routine Western drama about a crusty Colorado horse rancher who is fiercely protective of his holdings and resorts to lynching thieves and rustlers; with Cagney as Jeremy Rodock, the aging rancher. *Dir:* Robert Wise. *Prod:* Sam Zimbalist. *Sc:* Michael Blankfort; based on a short story by Jack Schaefer. *Ph:* Robert Surtees. *Art dir:* Cedric Gibbons, Paul Broesse. *Set dir:* Edwin B. Willis, Fred MacLean. *Ed:* Ralph E. Winters. *Sound:* Dr. Wesley C. Miller. *Mus score:* Miklos Rozsa. *Cost:* Walter Plunkett. *Hair stylist:* Sydney Guilaroff. *Makeup:* William Tuttle. *Assist dir:* Arvid Griffen. *Color consult:* Charles K. Hagedon. *Cast:* Don Dubbins (Steve Miller), Stephen McNally (McNulty), Irene Papas (Jocasta Constantine), Vic Morrow (Lars Peterson), James Griffith (Barjak), Onslow Stevens (Hearn), James Bell (L. A. Peterson), Jeanette Nolan (Mrs. L. A.

Peterson), Chubby Johnson (Baldy), Royal Dano (Abe), Lee Van Cleef (Fat Jones), Peter Chong (Cooky), James McCallion (Shorty), Clint Sharp (Red), Carl Pitti (Tom), Tony Hughes (first buyer), Roy Engel (second buyer), and Bud Osborne, John Halloran, Tom London, Dennis Moore, Buddy Roosevelt, and Billy Dix (cowboys). *Prod:* MGM; Cinemascope and Eastman Color. 95 min.

THESE WILDER YEARS (1956). Emotional but snail-paced soap opera about a middle-aged multimillionaire who searches adoption centers for the son he illegitimately fathered in his reckless youth; with Cagney as Steve Bradford, the penitent tycoon. *Dir:* Roy Rowland. *Prod:* Jules Schermer. *Sc:* Frank Fenton; based on a story by Ralph Wheelwright. *Ph:* George J. Folsey. *Art dir:* Cedric Gibbons, Preston Ames. *Set dec:* Edwin B. Willis, Edward G. Boyle. *Ed:* Ben Lewis. *Sound:* Dr. Wesley C. Miller. *Mus score:* Jeff Alexander. *Miss Stanwyck's costumes:* Helen Rose. *Makeup:* William Tuttle. *Hair stylist:* Sydney Guilaroff. *Assist dir:* Al Jennings. *Cast:* Barbara Stanwyck (Ann Dempster), Walter Pidgeon (James Rayburn), Betty Lou Keim (Suzie Keller), Don Dubbins (Mark), Edward Andrews (Mr. Spottsford), Basil Ruysdael (Judge), Grandon Rhodes (Roy Oliphant), Will Wright (old cab driver), Lewis Martin (Dr. Miller), Dorothy Adams (Aunt Martha), Dean Jones (hardware clerk), Herb Vigran (traffic cop), Ruth Lee (Miss Finch), Matt Moore (gateman), Jack Kenny (chauffeur), Harry Tyler (doorman), Luana Lee (stenographer), William Forrest, John Jaxwell, Emmett Vogan, Charles Evans (board of directors), Tom Laughlin (football player), Bob Alden (bellhop), Michael Landon (boy in pool room), Jimmy Ogg (ad-lib boy), Elizabeth Flournoy (Spottsford's secretary), Russell Simpson (farmer), Kathleen Mulqueen (prim lady), Russ Whitney (hotel clerk) and Lillian Powell (proprietress). *Prod:* MGM. 91 min.

MAN OF A THOUSAND FACES (1957). Fascinating biography–drama of silent screen star Lon Chaney; with Cagney as Chaney. *Dir:* Joseph Pevney. *Prod:* Robert Arthur. *Sc:* R. Wright Campbell, Ivan Goff, Ben Roberts; based on a story by Ralph Wheelwright. *Ph:* Russell Metty. *Art dir:* Alexander Golitzen, Eric Orbom. *Sound:* Leslie I. Carey, Robert Pritchard. *Ed:* Ted J. Kent. *Mus score:* Frank Skinner. *Orchestrator:* Joseph Gershenson. *Cost:* Bill Thomas. *Makeup:* Bud Westmore, Jack Kevan. *Spec eff:* Clifford Stine. *Assist dir:* Phil Bowles. *Cast:* Dorothy Malone (Cleva Creighton Chaney), Jane Greer (Hazel Bennett), Marjorie Rambeau (Gert), Jim Backus (Clarence Locan), Robert J. Evans (Irving Thalberg), Celia Lovsky (Mrs. Chaney), Jeanne Cagney (Carrie Chaney), Jack Albertson (Dr. J. Wilson Shields), Nolan Leary (Pa Chaney), Roger Smith (Creighton Chaney, age 21), Robert Lyden (Creighton Chaney, age 13), Rickie Sorensen (Creighton Chaney, age 8), Dennis Rush (Creighton Chaney, age 4), Simon Scott (Carl Hastings), Clarence Kolb (himself), Danny Beck (Max Dill), Phil Van Zandt (George Loane Tucker), and Hank Mann and Snub Pollard (comedy waiters). *Prod:* Universal–International; Cinemascope. 122 min. Wheelwright, Campbell, Goff, and Roberts shared an Academy Award nomination for Best Story and Screenplay (written directly for the screen).

SHORT CUT TO HELL (1957). Conventional low-budget remake of *This Gun for Hire*; Cagney directed. *Dir:* James Cagney. *Prod:* A. C. Lyles. *Sc:* Ted Berkman, Raphael Blau; based on a screenplay by W. R. Burnett. From the novel *A Gun for Sale* by Graham Greene. *Ph:* Haskell Boggs. *Art dir:* Hal Pereira, Roland Anderson. *Set dec:* Sam Comer, Frank McKelvy. *Ed:* Tom McAdoo. *Sound rec:* Lyle Figland, Winston Leverett. *Mus score:* Irvin Talbot. *Cost:* Edith Head. *Makeup:* Wally Westmore. *Spec ph eff:* John P. Fulton. *Hair stylist:* Nellie Manley. *Assist dir:* Richard Caffey. *Cast:* Robert Ivers (Kyle), Georgann Johnson (Glory Hamilton), William Bishop (Stan), Jacques Aubuchon (Bahrwell), Peter Baldwin (Adams), Yvette Vickers (Daisy), Murvyn Vye (Nichols), Milton Frome (Los Angeles police captain), Jacqueline Beer (waitress), Gail Land (girl), Dennis McMullen (Los Angeles policeman), William Newell (hotel manager), Sarah Selby (Adam's secretary), Mike Ross (Inspector Ross), Douglas Spencer (conductor), Danny Lewis (piano player), Richard Hale (A.T.), Douglas Evans (Mr. Henry), Hugh Lawrence (patrolman), Joe Bassett (patrolman), William Pullen (used car lot manager), Russell Trent (trainman), Joe Forte (ticket seller), Roscoe Ates (ext. road driver) and John Halloran (guard). *Prod:* Paramount; 87 min. The actor-turned-director appeared in a brief prologue to the film.

NEVER STEAL ANYTHING SMALL (1958). Belabored semimusical comedy–drama about a crooked stevedore who muscles his way to power in the longshoremen's union; with Cagney as Jake MacIllaney, the waterfront hoodlum. *Dir:* Charles Lederer. *Prod:* Aaron Rosenberg. *Sc:* Charles Lederer; based on the play *Devil's Hornpipe* by Maxwell Anderson and Rouben Mamoulian. *Ph:* Harold Lipstein. *Unit prod mgr:* Lew Leary. *Art dir:* Alexander Golitzen. *Set dec:* Russell A. Gausman, Ollie Emert. *Ed:* Russ Schoengarth. *Sound:* Leslie I. Carey, Robert Pritchard. *Mus score:* Allie Wrubel. *Mus super:* Joseph Gershenson. *Choreog:* Hermes Pan. *Cost:* Bill Thomas. *Makeup:* Bud Westmore. *Assist dir:* Dave Silver, Ray De Camp. *Songs:* "Never Steal Anything Small," "I'm Sorry, I Want a Ferrari," "I Haven't Got a Thing to Wear," "It Takes Love to Make a Home," "Helping Our Friends" by Allie Wrubel, Maxwell Anderson. *Cast:* Shirley Jones (Linda Cabot), Roger Smith (Dan Cabot), Cara Williams (Winnipeg), Nehemiah Persoff (Pinelli), Royal Dano (Words Cannon), Anthony Caruso (Lieutenant Tevis), Horace MacMahon (O. K. Merritt), Virginia Vincent (Ginger), Jack Albertson (Sleep-Out Charlie), Robert J. Wilke (Lennie), Herbie Faye (Hymie), Billy M. Greene (Ed), John Duke (Ward), Jack Orrison (Osborne), Roland Winters (Doctor), Ingrid Goude (model), Sanford Seegar (Fats Ranney), Ed (Skipper) McNally (Thomas), Gregg Barton (deputy warden), Edwin Parker (policeman), Jay Jostyn (judge), John Halloran (first detective), Harvey Perry (second detective), Phyllis Kennedy (waitress), and Rebecca Sand (coffee vendor). *Prod:* Universal–International; CinemaScope and Eastman color. 94 min.

SHAKE HANDS WITH THE DEVIL (1959). Tightly knit drama about a skilled surgeon who aids the clandestine independence movement in Ireland, set during the Irish "home rule" struggle of the 1920s; with Cagney as Sean Lenihan, the rebel doctor. *Dir:* Michael Anderson. *Prod:* Michael Anderson. *Exec prod:* George Glass, Walter Seltzer. *Sc:* Ivan Goff, Ben Roberts. *Adap:* Marian Thompson; based on the novel by Reardon Conner. *Ph:* Erwin Hillier. *Prod des:* Tom Morahan. *Prod super:* William J. Kirby. *Set dec:* Josie Macavin. *Ed:* Gordon Pilkington. *Sound:* William Buckley. *Mus score:* William Alwyn. *Mus played by:* Sinfonia of London. *Mus dir:* Muir Mathieson. *Wardrobe Super:* Tony Sforzini. *Ladies' Cost:* Irene Gilbert. *Assist dir:* Chris Sutton. *Spec military adv:* Lieutenant Colonel William O'Kelly. *Cast:* Don Murray (Kerry O'Shea), Dana Wynter (Jennifer Curtis), Glynis Johns (Kitty), Michael Redgrave (General), Sybil Thorndike (Lady Fitzhugh), Cyril Cusack (Chris), John Breslin (McGrath), Harry Brogan (Cassidy), Robert Brown (sergeant), Marianne Benet (Mary Madigan), Lewis Carson (the judge), John Cairney (Mike O'Callaghan), Harry Corbett (Clancy), Eileen Crowe (Mrs. Madigan), Alan Cuthbertson (captain, Black and Tans), Donal Donnelly (Willie Cafferty), Wilfred Dawning (Tommy Connor), Eithne Dunne (Eileen O'Leary), Paul Farrell (Doyle), Richard Harris (Terence O'Brien), William Hartnell (Sergeant Jenkins), John Le Mesurier (British general), Niall MacGinnis (Michael O'Leary), Patrick McAlinney (Donovan), Ray McAnally (Paddy Nolan), Clive Morton (Sir Arnold Fielding), Noel Purcell (Liam O'Sullivan), Peter Reynolds (captain, Black and Tans), Christopher Rhodes (Colonel Smithson), Ronald Walsh (sergeant, Black and Tans) and Alan White (Captain Fleming). *Prod:* Pennebaker for United Artists. 110 min.

THE GALLANT HOURS (1960). Dignified documentary-style drama covering a five-week period in 1942 during a critical Pacific battle between American and Japanese forces; with Cagney as Admiral William F. "Bull" Halsey, who played an instrumental role in the

Allied victory. *Dir:* Robert Montgomery. *Prod:* Robert Montgomery. *Sc:* Beirne Lay, Jr., Frank Gilroy. *Ph:* Joe MacDonald. *Prod mgr:* Gene Bryant. *Art dir:* Wiard Ihman. *Set dec:* Frank McKelvey. *Ed:* Frederick Y. Smith. *Mus score:* Roger Wagner. *Sung by:* Roger Wagner Chorale. *Mus ed:* Alfred Perry. *Cost:* Jack Martell. *Makeup:* Lorand Cosand. *Spec eff:* Finn Ulback. *Assist dir:* Joseph C. Behm. *Narrator of Japanese sequences:* Art Gilmore. *Casting dir:* Leonard Murray. *Tech super:* Captain Idris B. Monahan, USN (Ret.). *Tech consult:* Captain Joseph U. Lademan, USN (Ret.) *Japanese Naval tech adv:* James T. Goto. *Cast:* Dennis Weaver (Lieutenant Commander Andy Lowe), Ward Costello (Captain Harry Black), Richard Jaeckel (Lieutenant Commander Roy Webb), Les Tremayne (Captain Frank Enright), Robert Burton (Major General Roy Geiger), Raymond Bailey (Major General Archie Vandergrift), Carl Benton Reid (Vice Admiral Robert Ghormley), Walter Sande (Captain Horace Keys), Karl Swenson (Captain Bill Bailey), Vaughan Taylor (Commander Mike Pulaski), Harry Landers (Captain Joe Foss), Richard Carlyle (Father Gehring), Leon Lontoc (Manuel), James T. Goto (Admiral Isoroku Hamamoto), James Yagi (Rear Admiral Jiro Kobe), John McKee (Lieutenant Harrison Ludlum), John Zaremba (Major General Harmon), Carleton Young (Colonel Evans Carlson), William Schallert (Captain Tom Lamphier), Nelson Leigh (Admiral Callaghan), Sydney Smith (Admiral Scott), Herbert Lytton (Admiral Murray), Selmer Jackson (Admiral Chester Nimitz), Tyler McVey (Admiral Ernest J. King), Maggie Magennio (Red Cross girl), and with James Cagney, Jr., and Robert Montgomery, Jr. *Prod:* Cagney–Montgomery Production for United Artists. 115 min.

ONE, TWO, THREE (1961). Rapid-fire Cold War comedy about an ambitious Coca-Cola sales executive stranded in West Berlin; with Cagney as C. P. MacNamara, the soft drink boss. *Dir:* Billy Wilder. *Prod:* Billy Wilder. *Assoc prod:* I.A.L. Diamond, Doane Harrison. *Sc:* Wilder, Diamond; based on a one-act play by Ferenc Molnar. *Ph:* Daniel Fapp. *Art dir:* Alexander Trauner. *Ed:* Daniel Mandell. *Sound:* Basil Fenton-Smith. *Mus score:* Andre Previn. *Prod mgr:* William Calihan, Werner Fischer. *Second Unit dir:* Andre Smagghe. *Spec eff:* Milton Rice. *Assist dir:* Tom Pevsner. *Cast:* Horst Buchholz (Otto Ludwig Piffl), Pamela Tiffin (Scarlett), Arlene Francis (Mrs. MacNamara), Lilo Pulver (Ingeborg), Howard St.

A scene from SHORT CUT TO HELL, the only film Cagney directed, with Georgann Johnson and Robert Ivers. (Copyright © 1957 by Paramount Pictures. All Rights Reserved.)

Off camera with Glynnis Johns on location at Bram, Ireland filming SHAKE HANDS WITH THE DEVIL. (UPI)

John (Hazeltine), Hanns Lothar (Schlemmer), Leon Askin (Peripetchikoff), Peter Capell (Mishkin), Ralf Wolter (Borodenko), Karl Lieffen (Fritz), Henning Schluter (Dr. Bauer), Hubert Von Meyerinck (Count Von Droste-Schattenburg), Lois Bolton (Mrs. Hazeltine), Tile Kiwe (newspaperman), Karl Ludwig Lindt (Zeidlitz), Red Buttons (military police sergeant), John Allen (Tommy MacNamara), Christine Allen (Cindy MacNamara), Rose Renee Roth (Bertha), Ivan Arnold (military police corporal), Helmud Schmid (East German police corporal), Otto Friebel (East German interrogator), Werner Butler (East German police sergeant), Klaus Becker (second policeman), Siegfried Dornbusch (third policeman), Paul Bos (Krause), Max Buschbaum (tailor), Jaspar Von Oertzen (haberdasher), Inga De Toro (stewardess), Jacques Chevalier (Pierre), and Werner Hassenland (shoeman). *Prod:* Mirisch/Pyramid for United Artists; Panavision. 108 min. Fapp was nominated for an Academy Award for his (black-and-white) photography.

ARIZONA BUSHWHACKERS (1968). Undistinguished Western drama about Confederate prisoners assigned to patrol the frontier as members of federal forces; Cagney narrated. *Dir:* Lesley Selander. *Prod:* A. C. Lyles. *Sc:* Steve Fisher; based on a story by Fisher and Andrew Craddock. *Ph:* Lester Shorr. *Art dir:* Hal Pereira, Al Roelofs. *Ed:* John F. Schreyer. *Mus score:* Jimmie Haskell. *Set dec:* Robert Benton, Jerry Welch. *Makeup:* Wally Westmore. *Spec camera eff:* Paul K. Lerpae. *Assist dir:* Dale Hutchinson. *Cast:* Howard Keel (Lee Travis), Yvonne De Carlo (Jill Wyler), John Ireland (Dan Shelby), Marilyn Maxwell (Molly), Scott Brady (Tom Rile), Brian Donlevy (Mayor Joe Smith), Barton MacLane (Sheriff Lloyd Grover), James Craig (Ike Clanton), Roy Rogers, Jr. (Roy), Reg Parton (Curly), Montie Montana (stage driver), Eric Cody (bushwhacker). *Prod:* A. C. Lyles for Paramount. 87 min. Techniscope and color. Cagney narrated the opening of the film.

RAGTIME (1981). Richly mounted pseudohistorical turn-of-the-century tapestry of an America in transition; with Cagney as New York Police Chief Rheinlander Waldo. *Dir:* Milos Forman. *Prod:* Dino De Laurentiis. *Sc:* Michael Weller; based on the novel by E. L. Doctorow. *Mus by:* Randy Newman. *Exec prod:* Michael Hausman, Bernard Williams. *Assoc prod:* Fredric M. Sidewater. *Ph:* Miroslav Ondricek. *Prod des:* John Graysmark. *Film ed:* Anne V. Coates (UK), Antony Gibbs, Stanley Warnow. *Cost des:* Anna Hill Johnstone. *Choreog:* Twyla Tharp. *Prod mgr:* Pat Churchill (USA), Malcolm Christopher (UK). *First assist dir:* Michael Hausman. *Second assist dir:* Joel Tuber (USA), Michael Stevenson (UK), Andy Armstrong (UK), Ken Touhy (UK). *Art dir:* Patrizia Von Brandenstein (USA), Anthony Reading (UK). *Set dec:* George De Titta, Sr. (USA), George De Titta, Jr. (USA), Peter Howitt (UK). *Assist art dir:* John Dapper (USA), May Callas (USA), Steve Spence (UK), Ted Clements (UK). *Casting:* Mary Goldberg (USA), Maggie Cartier (UK). *Hair by:* Leonard of London. *Prop master:* Joe Caracciolo, Jr. *Gaffer elec:* Richard Quinlan (USA), Maurice Gillette (UK). *Key grip:* Ed Quinn. *Spec eff super:* Ed Drohan (USA), George Gibbs (UK). *Makeup:* Max Henriquez (USA), Joe Cuervo (USA), Paul Engelen (UK), Peter Frampton (UK). *Hairdressers:* Robert Grimaldi (USA), Frank Bianco (USA), Colin Jamison (UK), Stephanie Hall (UK). *Assoc cost des:* Peggy Farrell (USA), John Boyt (USA). *Wardrobe super:* Marilyn Putnam (USA), Ron Beck (UK). *Wardrobe assist:* Janet Tebrooke (USA), Bill Christians (UK), Ian Hickinbotton (UK). *Camera oper:* Thomas A. Priestley, Jr. *Camera assist:* Vinnie Gerardo (USA), Douglas Milsome (UK). *Second camera oper:* Ronald M. Lautore (USA), Peter MacDonald (UK). *Script super:* Martha Pinson. *Sound mixer:* Chris Newman. *Boom oper:* Dennis Maitland II (USA), Ken Weston (UK), Roland Rowles (UK). *Dubbing Mixer:* Gerry Humphreys. *Sound ed:* Les Wiggins, Archie Ludski. *Assist sound ed:* Terry Busby, Nigel Galt. *Postprod coord:* Roberta Friedman (USA). *Assoc ed:* Nena Danevic (USA). *Assist ed:* Leslie Gaulin (USA), Patrick Mullins (USA), Peter Honess (UK), Chris Kelly (UK), Patrick Moore (UK). *Location mgr:* Richard Brick (USA), Terry Needham. *Prod coord:* Golda Offenheim. *Prod office coord:* Adeline Leonard-Seakwood (USA). *Prod sec:*

Marilyse Morgan (UK). *Location coord (USA):* David Ticotin, Shawn Huasman, Carol Cuddy, Lee Mayes, Regge Life, Christopher Goode. *Assist to Mr. Cagney:* Marge Zimmerman. *Assist to Mr. Forman:* Amy Ness. *Consult to Mr. Forman:* Miroslav Hajek. *Spec ph:* Mary Ellen Mark. *Super accountant:* Len Barnard. *Prod accountant:* Mary Breen-Farrelly. *Assist accountant (NY):* Martha Schumacher. *Assist choreog:* Terry Gilbert. *Researcher:* Charles Musser. *Mus coach to Mr. Rollins:* Stanley Cowell. *Casting assoc:* Patricia Golden (USA). *Unit pub:* Gordon Arnell. *Pub assist:* June Broom. *Still cameramen:* Bob Penn, Muky Munkacsi (USA). *Process ph:* Charles D. Staffell, B.S.C. *Construc mgr:* Vic Simpson (UK), Carlos Quiles, Sr. (USA). *Prop master:* Bert Hearn (UK). *Prop buyer:* John Lanzer (UK). *Scenic artists:* Edward Garzero (USA), Ted Michell (UK). *Head const grip:* Joe Williams, Sr. (USA). *Camera grip:* Tony Cridlin (UK). *Stunt coord:* Vic Magnotta (USA). *Trans capt:* James J. Fanning (USA), Gerald Makein (UK). *Mus ed:* John Strauss. *Mus consult:* Gilbert Marouani. *Orchestrations:* Jack Hayes. *Song:* "One More Hour" by Randy Newman, sung by Jennifer Warnes. *Cast:* Brad Dourif (younger brother), Moses Gunn (Booker T. Washington), Elizabeth McGovern (Evelyn Nesbit), Kenneth McMillan (Willie Conklin), Pat O'Brien (Delmas), Donald O'Connor (Evelyn's dance instructor), James Olson (father), Mandy Patinkin (Tateh), Howard E. Rollins (Coalhouse Walker, Jr.), Mary Steenburgen (mother), Debbie Allen (Sarah), Jeff DeMunn (Houdini), Robert Joy (Harry K. Thaw), Norman Mailer (Stanford White), Bruce Boa (Jerome), Hoolihan Burke (Brigit), Norman Chancer (Gent No. 1—agent), Edwin Cooper (grandfather), Jeff Daniels (P. C. O'Donnell), Fran Drescher (Mameh), Frankie Faison (Gang Member No. 1), Hal Galili (Police Captain No. 1), Alan Gifford (judge), Richard Griffiths (Delmas Assistant No. 1), Samuel L. Jackson (Gang Member No. 2), Michael Jeter (special reporter), Calvin Levels (Gang Member No. 3), Bessie Love (Old Lady, T.O.C.), Christopher Malcolm (Police Captain No. 2), Herman Meckler (Vernon Elliott), Billy J. Mitchell (Delmas Assistant No. 2), Jenny Nichols (little girl), Max Nichols (little boy), Zack Norman (Gent No. 2—Manager), Eloise O'Brien (Mrs. Thaw), Don Plumley (Inspector McNeil), Ted Ross (black lawyer), Dorsey Wright (Gang Member No. 4), Robert Arden (foreman of the jury), Robert Boyd (Teddy Roosevelt), Thomas A. Carlin (Vice President Fairbanks), John Clarkson (Plainclothes Detective No. 1), Brian E. Dean (Fireman No. 1), Harry Ditson (county clerk), Robert Dorning (gent with Stanford White), Geoffrey Greenhill (police guard, T.O.C.), Ray Hassett (Policeman No. 12), Robert Hitt (Plainclothes Detective No. 2), Rodney James (sleek male dancer), George Harris (band leader, Clef Club), George J. Manos (novelty shop storeman), Val Pringle (Clef Club manager), Ron Weyand (Doctor Muller), Sonny Abagnale (Evelyn's driver), John Alderson (Waldo's Aide No. 1), Nesbitt Blaisdell (Policeman No. 5), Chaim Blatter (rabbi), Donald Bissett (J. P. Morgan), Joe Cirillo (stunt fireman), Josh Clark (Fireman No. 3), Robert Coffin (desk clerk), Patrick Connor (Waldo's Aide No. 3), Joel Cutrara (Policeman No. 11), Jake Dengel (Fireman No. 2), Barry Dennen (stage manager), Natalia Dobrer (Woman No. 1), Frank Ferrara (stunt fireman), Daniel Foley (stock reporter), Gretchen Franklin (elderly woman), Nick Giangiulio (stunt fireman), Pat Gorman (Thug No. 2), Guy Gregory (Black Butler No. 2), Dave Griffiths (Thug No. 1), Jeff Harding (Policeman No. 13), Robert Henderson (elderly man), Collette Hiller (Lawyer's Female Companion No. 1), Patrick M. Hughes (Policeman No. 7), Elaine Ives-Cameron (Lawyer's Female Companion No. 2), Andreas Katsulas (Policeman No. 3), Douglas Lambert (police sergeant), Pavel Landovsky (Solomon Peretz), Norris Mailer (lady with Stanford White), Derek Martin (Waldo's Aide No. 2), Al Matthews (maitre d'), Stuart Milligan (marksman), Richard Oldfield (stock reporter), Nelly Polissky (woman in window), Mike Potter (Thug No. 4), Anthony Powell (Policeman No. 9), Ethan Phillips (guard at family house), Joe Praml (Policeman No. 8), John Ratzenberger (fireman), Bill Reimbold (Gent No. 3—Lawyer), Bob Sherman (Policeman No. 10), Tony Sibbald (stock reporter), Stan Simmons (Thug No. 3), John Sterland (library guard), Jan Triska (special reporter), Burnell Tucker (reporter), Britt Walker (Black Butler No. 1), Peter Witman (stock reporter), and Edward Wiley (conductor). A Sunley Production for Paramount; Todd–Ao and Technicolor. The film was nominated for eight Academy Awards but lost in every category.

Short Subjects

His short subjects (incomplete listing) include: *Intimate Interview* (Talking Picture Epics, 1930, directed by Grace Elliott); *Practice Shots* (No. 11 of Bobby Jones' *How I Play Golf* series, directed by George Marshall, with Cagney as a learner who asks golf questions of pro Bobby Jones; 1931); *Hollywood on Parade #8* (Cagney promotional short, also with Frankie Darro and Joe E. Brown, on the Warners lot); *Screen Snapshots #11* (Columbia, 1934, with Cagney as one of many Hollywood stars at a charity event); *The Hollywood Gad-About* (Skibo Productions, Inc., an Educational Films Corporation of America Treasure Chest short, with Cagney and an all-star cast in a skit about a missing necklace; 1934); *A Trip Through a Hollywood Studio* (Warner Bros., with Cagney in cameo as one of many Warners stars on the sets busy filming; 1935); *Hollywood Star Hobbies* (MGM, with Cagney playing in all-star baseball game between Hollywood comedians and leading men at Wrigley Field, Los Angeles); *For Auld Lang Syne* (Warner Bros., directed by George Bilson, with Cagney as one of many stars giving tribute to Will Rogers; 1938); *Show Business at War* (Vol. 9, No. 10 of *The March of Time*, 20th Century-Fox, including Cagney as one of many film stars doing troop shows for servicemen; 1943); *You, John Jones* (MGM, directed by Mervyn LeRoy, with Cagney as an air-raid warden who demonstrates the procedure in America in case of attack; 1943); and *Battle Stations* (20th Century-Fox, a U.S. Coast Guard documentary short, narrated by Cagney and Ginger Rogers; 1944).

Stage

James Cagney's New York stage appearances (excepting vaudeville and summer stock) include: *Pitter Patter* (Longacre Theatre, book by Will M. Hough, lyrics and music by William B. Friedlander, staged by David Bennett; 1920); *Outside Looking In* (Greenwich Village Playhouse, Inc., moving to 39th Street Theatre, written by Maxwell Anderson, directed by Augustin Duncan; 1925; 113 performances); *Broadway* (Broadhurst Theatre, staged by authors Philip Dunning and George Abbott; 1926–1927); *Women Go On Forever* (Forrest Theatre, written by Daniel N. Rubin, staged by John Cromwell; 1927; 117 performances); *Grand Street Follies of 1928* (Booth Theatre, directed by Agnes Morgan, dances by Cagney and Michel Fokine, 1928; 144 performances); *The Grand Street Follies of 1929* (Booth Theatre, book and lyrics by Agnes Morgan, staged by Agnes Morgan, 1929; 53 performances); *Maggie the Magnificent* (Cort Theatre, written by George Kelly, staged by the author; 1929; 32 performances); and *Penny Arcade* (Fulton Theatre, written by Marie Baumer, directed by William Keighley; 1930; 24 performances).

Radio

His radio work includes national radio broadcasts of *Is Zat So?* (with sister-in-law Boots Mallory for Lux Radio Theater in 1936), *Winterset* (in 1936), *Ceiling Zero* (with Ralph Bellamy and Stuart Erwin for Lux in 1939), *Angels with Dirty Faces* (with Pat O'Brien and Gloria Dickson for Lux in 1939), *Revlon Revue* (with Gertrude Lawrence for the NBC Blue Network, later ABC), *Johnny Got His Gun* (1940), *Captains of the Clouds* (Cavalcade of America program on NBC in 1942) and *Yankee Doodle Dandy* (Screen Guild Players in 1942).

Rare television appearance in the 1950s with, among others, John Wayne and Fred MacMurray (back row) on a THIS IS YOUR LIFE tribute to director William Wellman (in front row, seated).

Television

Cagney's dramatic television appearances have been rare. They include appearances on *The Ed Sullivan Show* ("live" dramatic scene from *Mister Roberts*, with Henry Fonda and Jack Lemmon, on June 20, 1955) and Robert Montgomery Presents (dramatic play, *Soldier from the War Returning*, with Cagney as a cynical Army sergeant assigned to escort home the body of a soldier killed in the Korean war; directed by Peter Lafferty, September 10, 1956, NBC).

Apart from acting appearances, Cagney has made a number of guest appearances on TV, including a *This Is Your Life* tribute to director William Wellman in the 1950s. After his return to public fore with the broadcast of the American Film Institute's Life Achievement Award banquet in 1974, Cagney showed up with increasing frequency on television, ranging from the occasional talk show interview to tossing out the ball for photographers at the second game of the World Series in New York in 1981. He was one of five illustrious artists (Agnes De Mille, Leontyne Price, Leonard Bernstein, and Lynn Fontanne were the others) honored for their "lifetime achievement in the performing arts" at a Washington, D.C., Kennedy Center telecast in 1980. He attended a subsequent AFI tribute to another aging song-and-dance man, Fred Astaire, in 1981 and was one of many Hollywood veterans on stage in New York for the so-called *Night of One Hundred Stars* in 1982, a telecast to benefit the Actor's Fund Home.

Documentaries

Cagney narrated at least two extended-length documentaries on patriotic and agricultural themes late in his career, including *Road to the Wall* (produced by CBS for the Department of Defense, with Cagney narrating; 1962), and *Ballad of Smokey the Bear* (produced by General Electric Theatre in cooperation with the U.S. Department of Agriculture, with Cagney as the voice of Big Brother Bear in this animated feature; 1966). Cagney is the Depression's symbolic Everyman in the 1975 compilation documentary, *Brother, Can You Spare a Dime?*, directed by Philippe Mora. Additionally, on the occasion of Cagney's comeback in *Ragtime*, the documentary *The Return of Cagney* was broadcast on public television in 1981 and hosted by Richard Schickel.

The Cagney Family and Cagney Productions

William Cagney's screen appearances include: *Ace of Aces* (1933), *Lost in the Stratosphere* (1933), *Palooka* (1934), *Flirting with Danger* (1934), *Stolen Harmony* (1935), and *Kiss Tomorrow Goodbye* (1950).

Jeanne Cagney's screen appearances include: *All Women Have Secrets* (1939), *Golden Gloves* (1940), *Queen of the Mob* (1940), *Yankee Doodle Dandy* (1942), *The Time of Your Life* (1948), *Don't Bother to Knock* (1952), *Quicksand* (1950), *A Lion Is in the Streets* (1953), *Kentucky Rifle* (1955), *Man of a Thousand Faces* (1957), *Town Tamer* (1965).

Cagney Productions in which James Cagney did not appear include: *Only the Valiant* (directed by Gordon Douglas, starring Gregory Peck; 1951) and *Bugles in the Afternoon* (directed by Roy Rowland, starring Ray Milland; 1952), both coproduced with Warner Bros.

Sources and Bibliography

Only the principal, available sources are listed. The author has relied on extensive, undated clippings from *The Boston Globe*, *The New York Times*, *The Hollywood Reporter*, and *Variety*, as well as fan magazines, studio contractual and publicity files, and scripts from the archives of the Wisconsin Center for Film and Theatre Research at the University of Wisconsin, and the Warners' repository at the University of Southern California in Los Angeles.

In addition, the author conducted interviews, in-person or through correspondence, with the following persons associated with Cagney's career: John Bright, Harry Brown, Robert Buckner, Niven Busch, James Cagney, William Cagney, Bette Davis, Luther Davis, Gordon Douglas, Julius J. Epstein, Ivan Goff, Howard Hawks, Elia Kazan, William Keighley, Pat O'Brien, Joseph Pevney, George Raft, Allen Rivkin, Ben Roberts, Sylvia Sidney, Raoul Walsh, William Wellman, Billy Wilder, and Robert Wise.

Books

Agee, James. *Agee on Film*. Boston: Beacon Press, 1966.

Arliss, George. *My Ten Years in the Studios*. Boston: Little, Brown and Company, 1940.

Balio, Tino. *United Artists: The Company Built by the Stars*. Madison: University of Wisconsin Press, 1976.

Bellamy, Ralph. *When the Smoke Hit the Fan*. Garden City, NY: Doubleday & Co., 1979.

Bergman, Andrew. *We're in the Money*. New York: New York University Press, 1971.

——. *James Cagney*. New York: Pyramid, 1973.

Bluen, A. William, ed. *The Movie Business: American Film Industry Practice*. New York: Hastings House, 1972.

Bogdanovich, Peter. *Pieces of Time*. New York: Delta, 1974.

Bromfield, Louis. *It Takes All Kinds*. London: Harper and Bros., 1931.

Brown, Joe E., as told to Ralph Hancock. *Laughter Is a Wonderful Thing*, New York: A. S. Barnes & Co., 1956.

Cagney, James. *Cagney by Cagney*. New York: Doubleday & Co., 1976.

Cohen, Henry, ed. *The Public Enemy*. Madison: University of Wisconsin Press, 1981.

Cole, Lester. *Hollywood Red*. Palo Alto, Calif.: Ramparts Press, 1981.

Davis, Bette. *The Lonely Life*. New York: G. P. Putnam's Sons, 1962.

Dickens, Homer. *The Films of James Cagney*. Secaucus, NJ: Lyle Stuart, 1972.

Ephron, Henry. *We Thought We Could Do Anything: The Life of Screenwriters Phoebe and Henry Ephron*. New York: W. W. Norton, 1972.

Farber, Manny. *Negative Space*. New York: Praeger, 1971.

Gussow, Mel. *Don't Say Yes until I Finish Talking: The Biography of Darryl F. Zanuck*. New York: Doubleday & Co., 1971.

Hotchner, A. E. *Doris Day: Her Own Story*. New York: William Morrow, 1975.

Kanin, Garson. *Tracy and Hepburn: An Intimate Memoir*. New York: Viking, 1971.

Kauffmann, Stanley, ed. with Bruce Henstell. *American Film Criticism*. New York: Liveright, 1972.

Lacy, Madison S. and Don Morgan. *Leg Art*. Secaucus, NJ: Lyle Stuart, 1981. (foreword by James Cagney)

Lahr, John. *Notes on a Cowardly Lion: The Biography of Bert Lahr*. New York: Alfred A. Knopf, 1969.

Lawson, John Howard. *Film in the Battle of Ideas*. New York: Masses and Mainstream, 1953.

LeRoy, Mervyn. *Take One: Mervyn LeRoy*. New York: Hawthorn, 1974.

Levin, Martin, ed. *Hollywood and the Great Fan Magazines*. New York: Arbor House, 1970.

Logan, Joshua. *Movie Stars, Real People and Me*. New York: Delacorte, 1978.

Madsen, Axel. *Billy Wilder*. London: Secker and Warburg, 1968.

McBride, Joseph. *Focus on Howard Hawks*. Englewood Cliffs, NJ: Prentice-Hall, 1972.

————. *Hawks on Hawks*. Los Angeles: University of California Press, 1981.

McCoy, Horace. *Kiss Tomorrow Goodbye*. New York: Random House, 1948.

McGilligan, Patrick, ed. *Yankee Doodle Dandy*. Madison: University of Wisconsin Press, 1981.

Miller, Don. *B Movies*. New York: Curtis, 1973.

Meyer, William R. *Warner Brothers Directors*. New Rochelle, NY: Arlington House, 1978.

Moley, Raymond. *The Hays Office*. New York: Bobbs-Merrill, 1945.

Navasky, Victor. *Naming Names*. New York: Viking, 1980.

O'Brien, Pat. *The Wind at My Back*. New York: Doubleday & Co., 1964.

Offen, Ron. *Cagney*. Chicago: Henry Regnery, 1972.

Parish, James Robert. *Tough Guys*. Carlstadt, NJ: Rainbow Books, 1977.

Peary, Danny, ed. *Close-Ups: The Movie Star Book*. New York: Galahad Books, 1978.

Rainsberger, Todd. *James Wong Howe: Cinematographer*. San Diego: A. S. Barnes & Co., 1981.

Reagan, Ronald (with Richard G. Hubler). *Where's the Rest of Me?* New York: Duell, Sloan and Pearce, 1965.

Rivkin, Allen. *Hello Hollywood*. New York: Doubleday & Co., 1962.

Robson, E. W. and M. M. Robson. *The Film Answers Back: An Historical Appreciation of the Cinema*. London: John Lane/The Brodley Head, 1934.

Rosten, Leo C. *Hollywood*. New York: Harcourt, Brace & Co., 1941.

Sarris, Andrew. *The American Cinema*. New York: E. P. Dutton, 1968.

Schwartz, Nancy Lynn. *The Hollywood Writers' Wars*. New York: Alfred A. Knopf, 1982.

Sennett, Ted. *Warner Brothers Presents*. New Rochelle, NY: Arlington House, 1971.

Shipman, David. *The Great Movie Stars: The Golden Years*. New York: Crown, 1970.

Sinclair, Andrew. *John Ford*. New York: Dial Press, 1979.

Taylor, John Russell, ed. *Grahame Greene on Film*. New York: Simon & Schuster, 1972.

Thomson, David. *A Biographical Dictionary of Film*. New York: William Morrow, 1981.

Tynan, Kenneth. *Curtains*. New York: Atheneum, 1961.

Walsh, Raoul. *Each Man in His Time: The Life Story of a Director*. New York: Farrar, Strauss & Giroux, 1974.

Warner, Jack L. (with Dean Jennings). *My First Hundred Years in Hollywood*. New York: Random House, 1964.

Wallis, Hal, and Charles Higham. *Starmaker: The Autobiography of Hal Wallis*. New York: Macmillan, 1980.

Warshow, Robert. *The Immediate Experience: Movies, Comics, Theatre and Other Aspects of Popular Culture*. New York: Doubleday & Co., 1964.

Wellman, William. *A Short Time for Insanity*. New York: Hawthorn, 1974.

Wilson, Robert, ed. *The Film Criticism of Otis Ferguson*. Philadelphia: Temple University Press, 1971.

Wood, Tom. *The Bright Side of Billy Wilder, Primarily*. New York: Doubleday & Co., 1970.

Zierold, Norman. *The Moguls*. New York: Coward-McCann, 1969.

Periodicals

Benz, H. "Gentle Tough of Martha's Vineyard." *Coronet*, November 1955.

Bergquist, Laura. "The New Craze for Cagney." *Look*, 20 September 1955.

Cagney, James (as told to Pete Martin). "How I Got This Way." *Saturday Evening Post*, 7 January 1956.

———. 14 January 1956.

———. 21 January 1956.

Champlin, Charles. "Cagney Is Alive and Well and Living in Retirement." *Los Angeles Times*, 20 May 1973.

Chase, Chris. "Cagney, 82, Is Embarrassed Anew at Being a Star." *New York Times*, 17 November 1981.

Childs, James. "Can You Ride the Horse: An Interview with Raoul Walsh." *Sight and Sound*, Winter 1972–1973.

Clark, Forrest. "James Cagney." *New Theater and Film*, December 1935.

Cole, Lester. "Unhappy Ending." *Hollywood Quarterly*, October 1945.

"The Conversation: James Cagney and Studs Terkel." *Esquire*, October 1981.

"A Cutter at Heart: Anatole Litvak." *Films and Filming*, February 1969.

Delahanty, Thornton. "James Cagney Lives Down on Two Farms." *New York Herald Tribune*, 24 April 1955.

Durant, John. "Tough, on and Off." *Colliers*, 31 August 1940.

Harmetz, Aljean. "Cagney: The Man Who Got Away." *New York Times*, 3 March 1974.

Haskell, Molly. "Partners in Crime and Conversation." *Village Voice*, 7 December 1972.

"Interview with Clint Eastwood." *Focus on Film* No. 7.

"Interview with Henry Hathaway." *Focus on Film* No. 7.

"Interview with Nicholas Ray." *Movie*, May 1963.

"Interview with Virginia Mayo." *Focus on Film* No. 37.

"James Cagney, Actor." *New York Times*, 28 June 1931.

"James Cagney Talking." *Films and Filming*, March 1959.

Jamison, Barbara Beach. "That's Cagney All Over." *New York Times*, 6 March 1955.

Johnston, Alva. "They Toughened Him Up." *Women's Home Companion*, November 1959.

Joseph, Robert. "Unions in Hollywood." *Films*, Summer 1940.

McManus, John T. "James Cagney Dreams of O'Casey." *New York Times*, 27 December 1936.

Miller, Don. "James Cagney." *Films in Review*, August–September 1958.

Nichols, Bill. "The American Photo League." *Screen*, Winter 1972–1973.

Oakes, Philip. "James Cagney." *Sight and Sound*, Winter 1959.

"On the Current Screen." *Literary Digest*, 7 April 1934.

Parsons, Louella O. "Cagney's Year." June 1955.

Potamkin, H. A. "The Personality of the Player: A Phase of Unity." *Closeup*, April 1930.

———. "The Year of the Eclipse." *Closeup*, March 1933.

Pringle, Henry F. "Tough, by Request." *Colliers*, 3 September 1932.

Schrader, Paul. "Notes on Film Noir." Delivered at the First Los Angeles International Film Exposition (Filmex), 1976.

Screen Actor, Summer 1979.

Shipp, Cameron. "Cagney." *Colliers*, 28 October 1955.

Smith, H. Allen. "The Cantankerous Cagneys." *Saturday Evening Post*, 2 October 1943.

Strauss, Theodore. "The Firm of Cagney Brothers, Inc." *New York Times*, 5 September 1943.

Tuck, J. Nelson. "America's Most Lovable Bad Boy." *Read*, February 1944.

"Warner Brothers." *Fortune*, December 1937.

White, Timothy. "James Cagney: Looking Backward." *Rolling Stone*, 18 February 1982.

"Yankee Doodle Dandy." *Newsweek*, 22 April 1968.

INDEX OF NAMES

Index of Films, Plays and Television Productions